"At such a young age, Josh's aptitude for producing compelling works that clearly consist of endless hours of effort, make him one of the most exciting easels to watch."

–ROBERT LANGE, Established Artist and Gallery Owner of Robert Lange Studios

"I first met Josh when he was about 17... I couldn't believe that a 17-year-old could create such beautiful, elaborate and detailed art. It's been a pleasure to learn more about Josh over the last few years, including his remarkable path to prodigy, his stunning artwork and his charitable work in the community."

–MIKE PEARSON, Editor, Stoney Creek News

"Josh Tiessen is an exciting new talent in wildlife art. He has all the tools for becoming a master wildlife painter: strong grasp of technical precision, bold innovative sense of composition, and – most importantly – a vibrant imagination. These characteristics make Josh a rare gift to wildlife art."

–JOEL IRWIN, General Manager, Algonquin Art Centre

"What impresses me about Josh Tiessen runs the gamut from A to Z beginning with the ambition he possessed at a young age to establish himself as a *bona fide* artist... to his zest and zeal to express himself through the creative process of art."

–DAVID J. WAGNER, PhD, Author of *American Wildlife Art*, Curator and Tour Director

"His art speaks for itself, but spend time with him, and you realize what an amazing human being he is. I'm honored to call him my friend."

–STEVE MILLS, Established Photorealist Oil Painter

"Josh Tiessen is a young brilliant artist and his work is very mature. This kid has so much potential and room to grow as a realist painter."

–BRIAN LASAGA, Newfoundland's Foremost Realist Painter

"I was introduced to Josh's amazing talent early on. I'm not surprised to see him now recognized as one of the top prodigy artists in the world."

–BOB COWAN, TV Host of CHCH Morning Live

"Josh Tiessen's work is lyrical, dramatic and speaks to the viewer as a great musical composition speaks to the listener. We have two paintings and enjoy them greatly. He is continuing to evolve as an artist and we look forward to each new work."

–BORIS BROTT, Internationally Acclaimed Opera and Symphony Conductor

"Josh Tiessen has achieved a level of artistic maturity and technical mastery far beyond his years. Few people are so fortunate to find their calling so early in life. But we are all fortunate that this young and passionate artist is using his talent to enunciate the beauty of nature and the importance of our spiritual, cultural and existential relationship with it. I am already looking forward to the second volume in Josh's creative career."

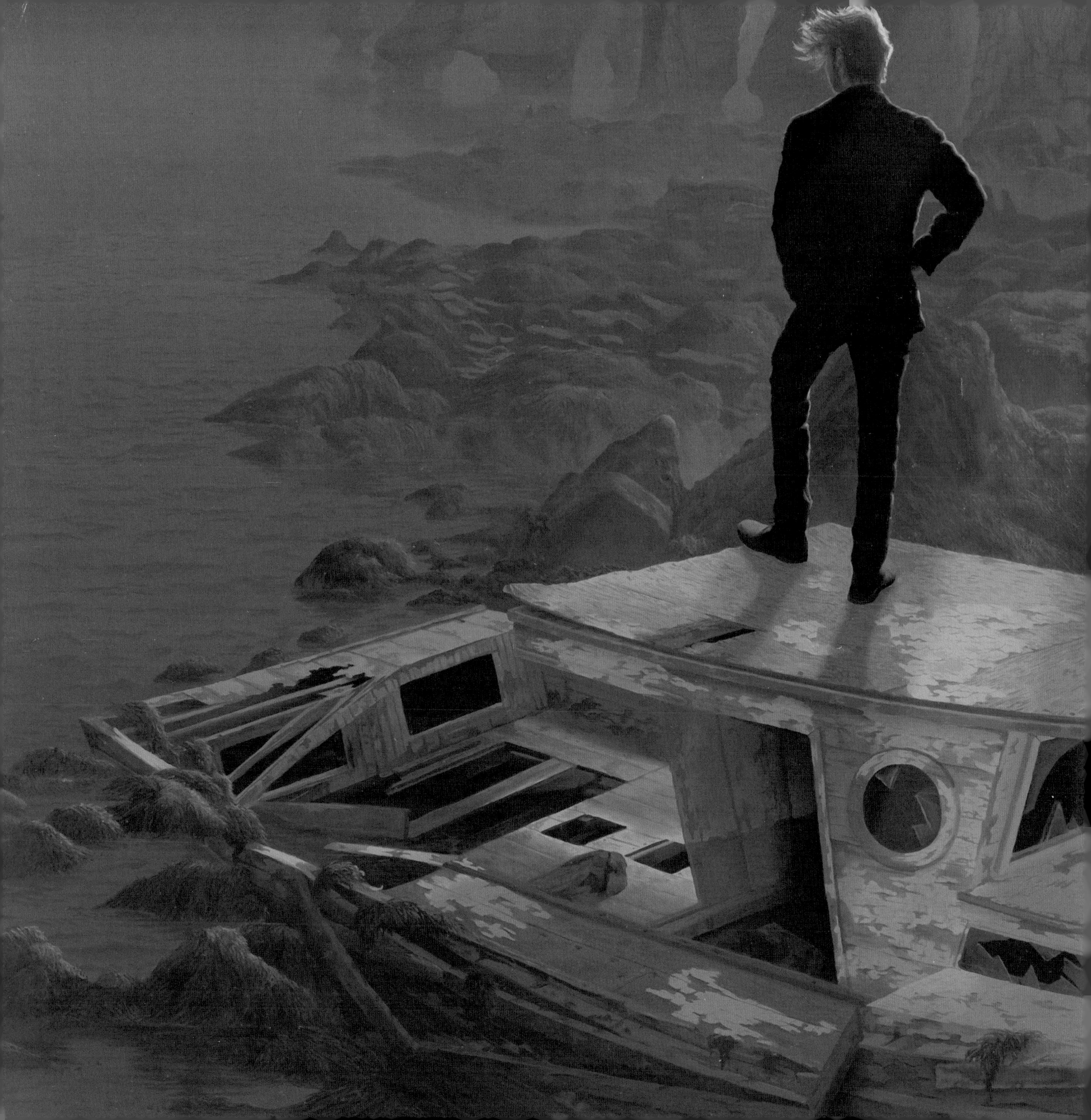

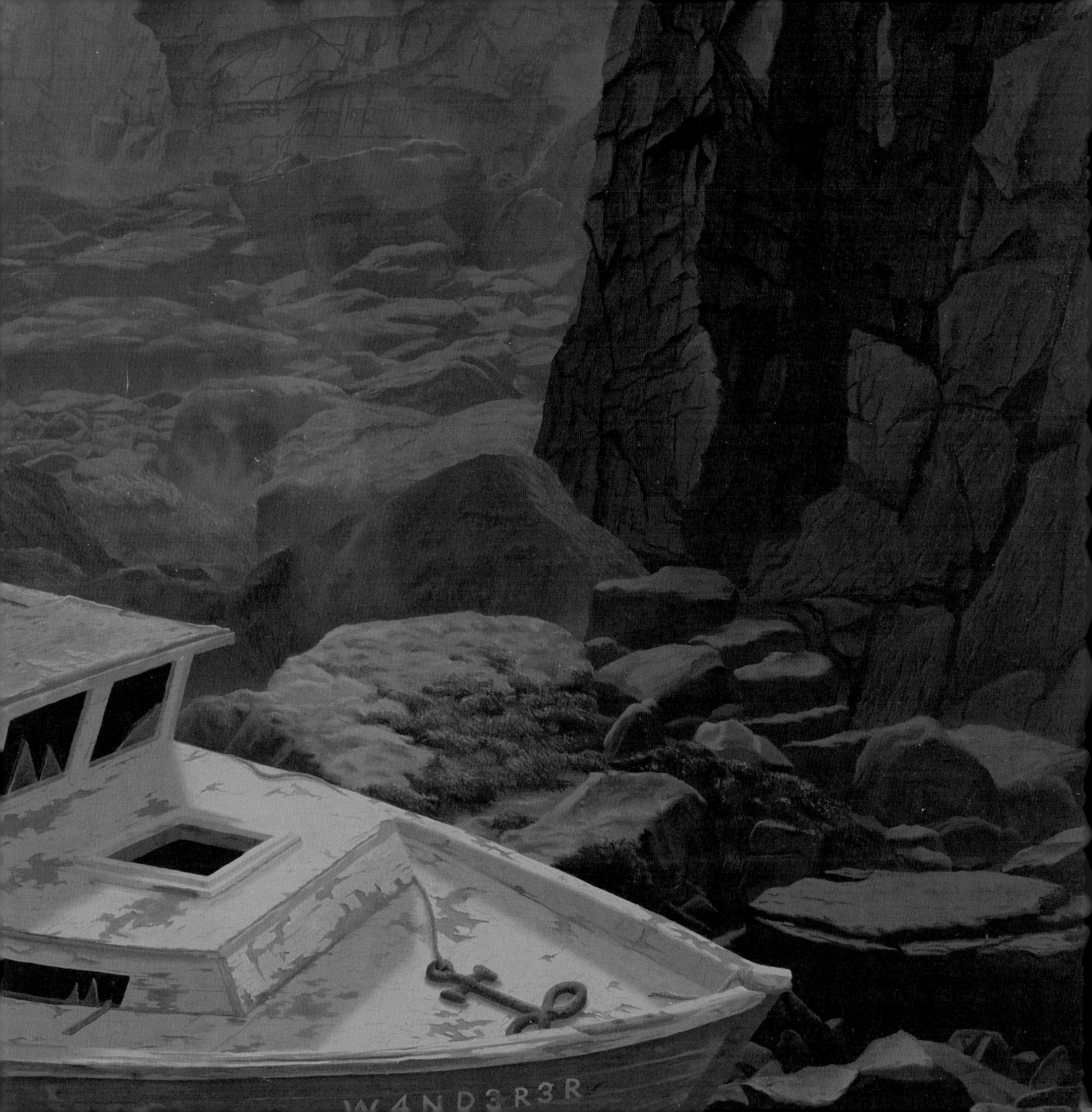
W4ND3R3R

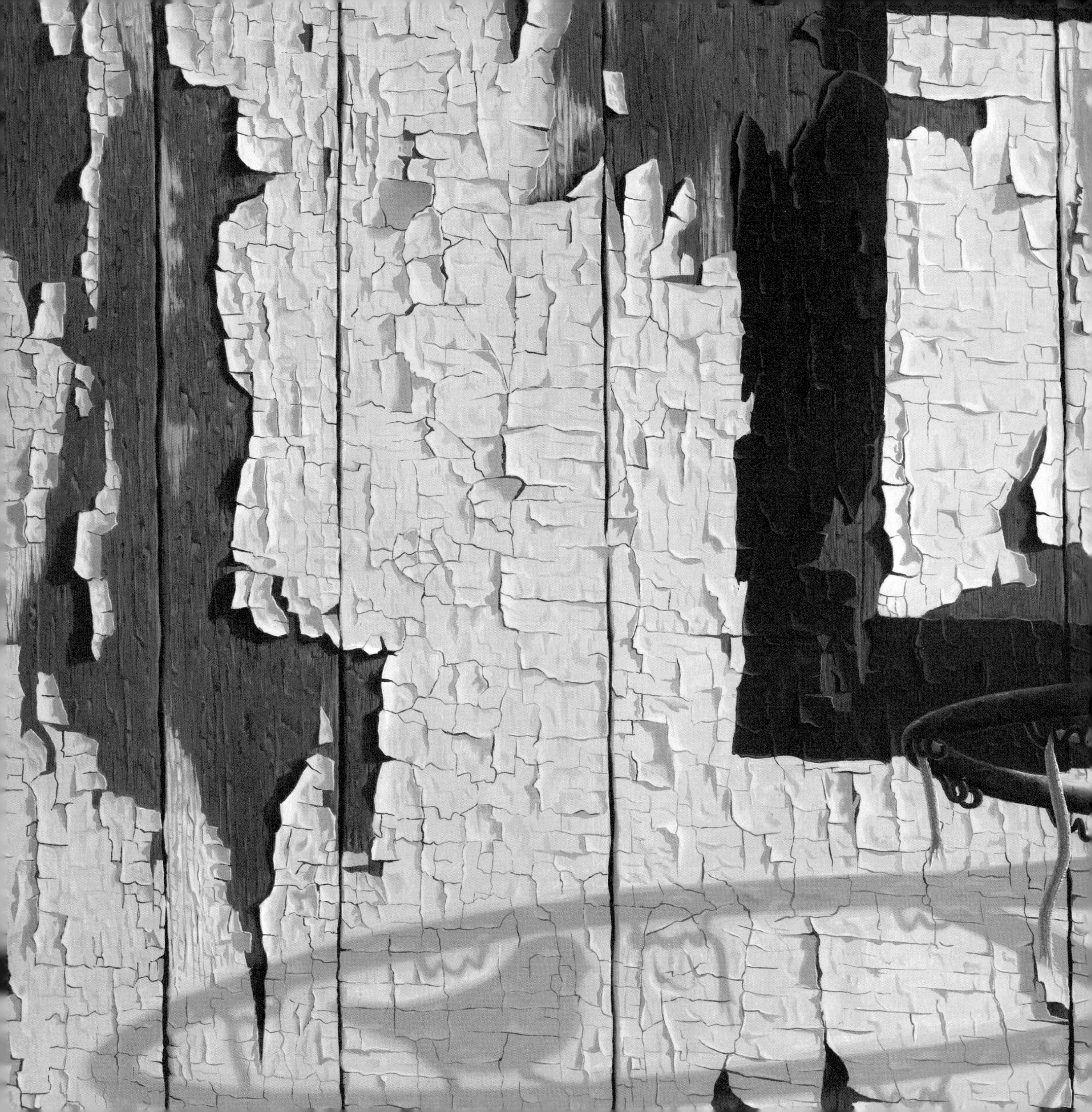

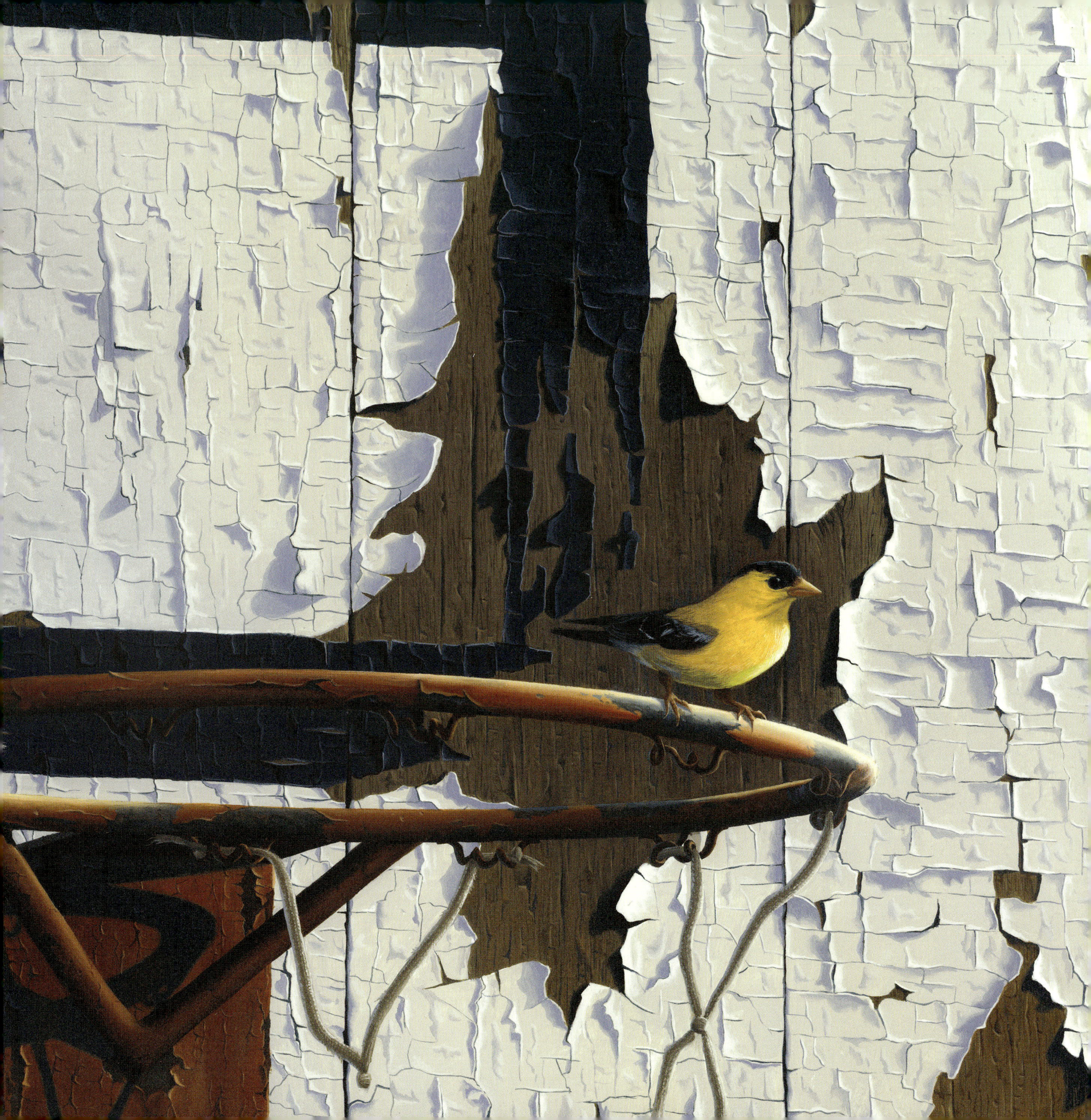

Donna,

Thank you for all the support for my art and our family!

Josh

JOSH TIESSEN

A DECADE OF INSPIRATION

foreward by
DR. JOANNE RUTHSATZ

story compiled and edited by DR. JULIE A. TIESSEN
book design and text for art by JOSH TIESSEN

JOSH TIESSEN STUDIO GALLERY Est. 2010
JTSG
PUBLISHING

JTSG Publishing
148 King St. E. Stoney Creek, Ontario, Canada L8G 1L5
info@joshtiessen.com | www.joshtiessen.com

Cataloguing Data available from Library and Archives Canada

ISBN 978-0-9953337-0-3

Josh Tiessen: A Decade of Inspiration

1. Tiessen, Josh, 1995- 2. Realism in art. 3. Art, contemporary-21st century.
3. Architecture in art. 4. Animals in art. 5. Nature in art.
I. Tiessen, Josh, 1995- II. Josh Tiessen Studio Gallery

Story compiled and edited by Dr. Julie A. Tiessen
Book design and text for art by Josh Tiessen
Copy edited by Marjorie Cairns and Tricia Maughan

Printed and bound in South Korea

This book has been printed on 150gsm Korean Matt Art paper stock, from an FSC-certified source using sustainable forestry practices.

FSC www.fsc.org MIX Paper from responsible sources FSC® C005413

Dates of artworks indicate the year in which the work was completed.

With special thanks to Princeton Artist Brush Co., Abundance Canada, and Kiwanis Hamilton Inc. 1916, for their generous sponsorship of this project.

PRINCETON ARTIST BRUSH CO.™ Abundance CANADA Kiwanis®

To my Creator, for providing an endless amount of inspiration through your Being and creation

To my family, I would not be where I am without you

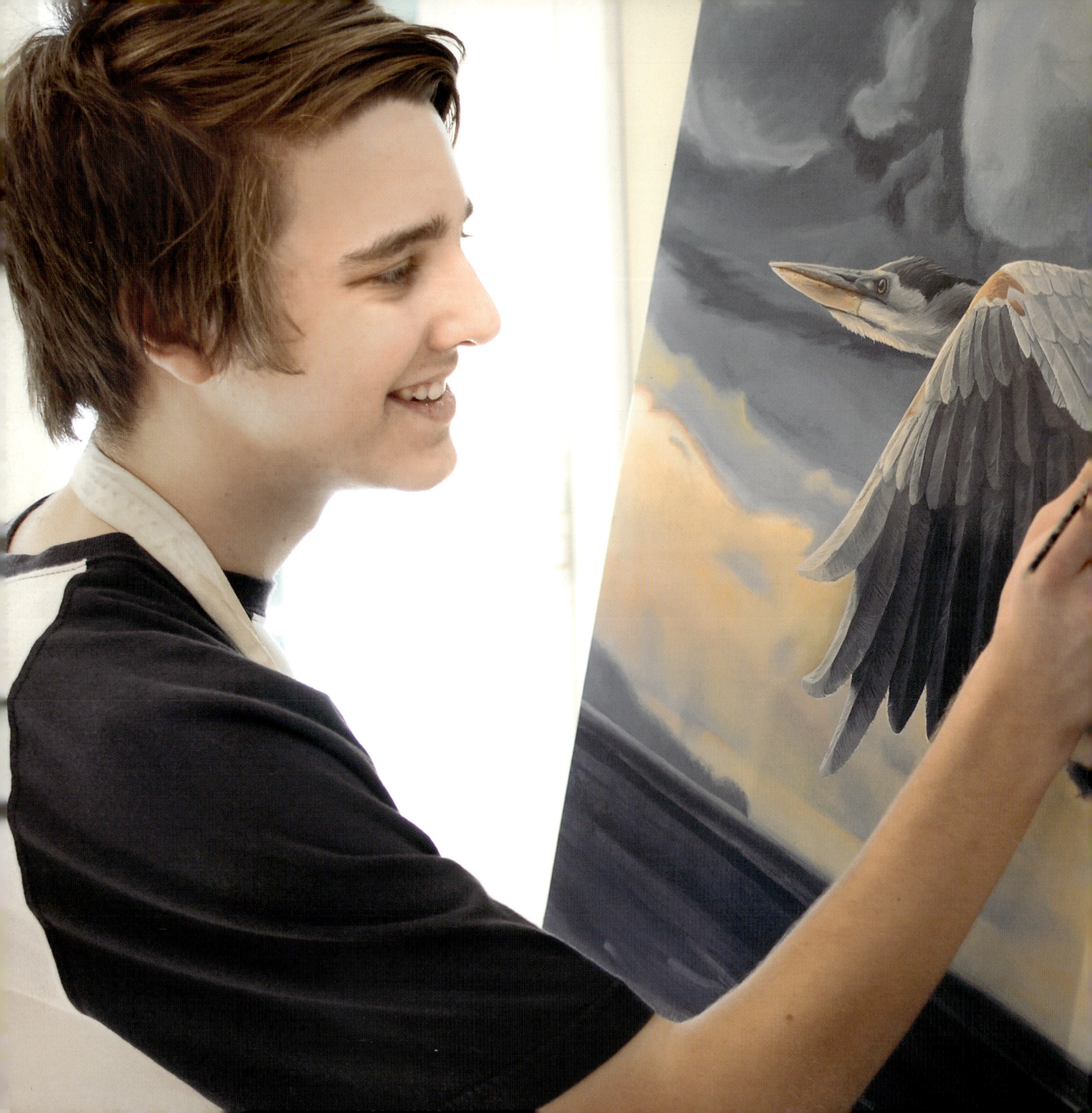

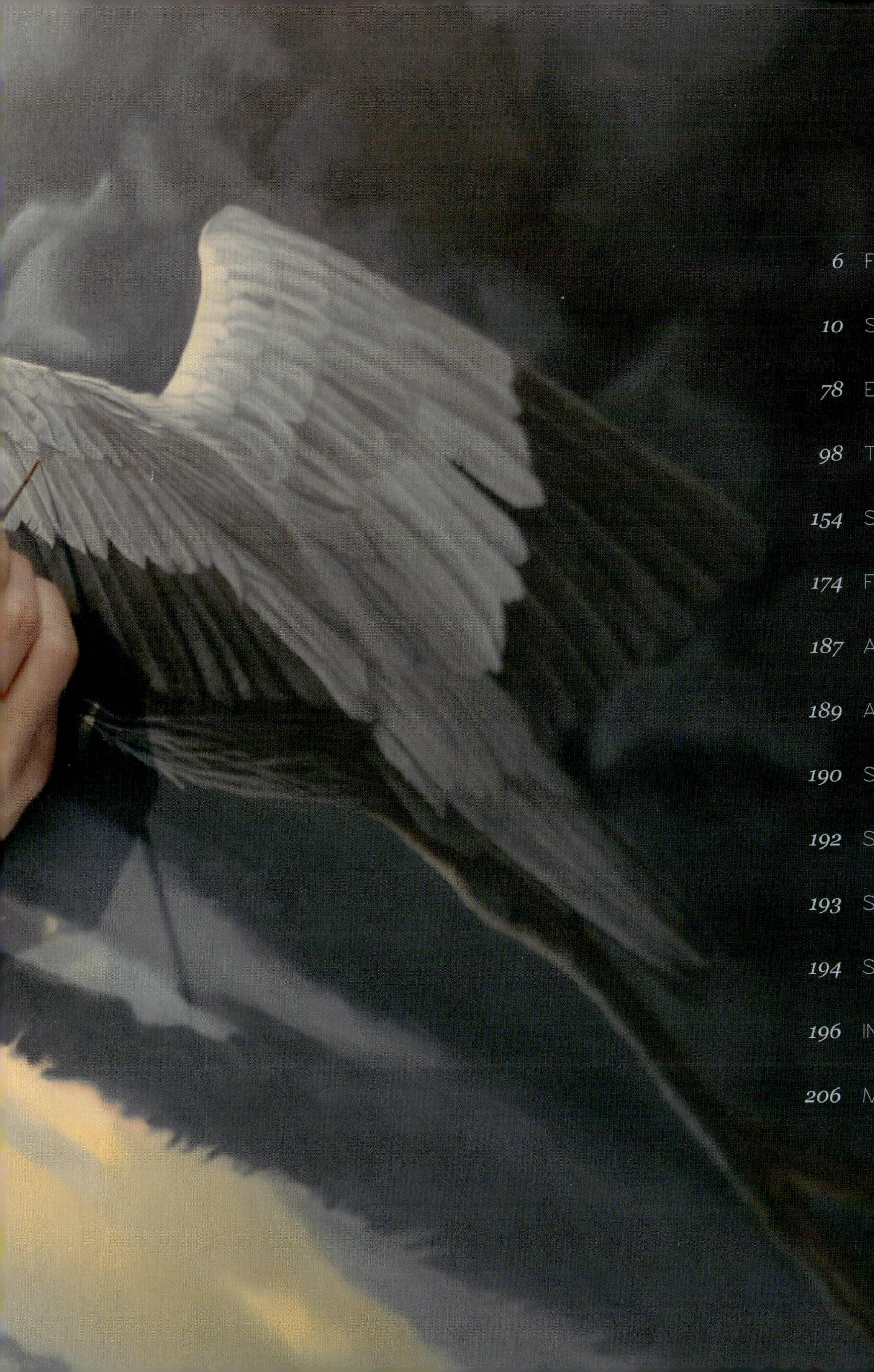

CONTENTS

FOREWARD

Child prodigies have fascinated the world for centuries, yet an explanation of their early talent and a definition of who qualifies has only recently been explored. Feldman in 1986 gave us the first and most accepted definition of what constitutes a child prodigy. He stated, "A prodigy is a child that reaches professional status before the age of ten in a culturally relevant domain." Others have expanded the age limit to adolescence, citing those who reach *advanced* professional status, shown in a mature body of work before adulthood. But these definitions leave key questions unanswered: How do they do it? Are these children and teens cognitively distinctive from others their age? The answer is *yes*.

Recent research by Ruthsatz and Stephens has found that all child prodigies have exceptional memories, strong attention to detail, a rage to master their domain, and a possible genetic link to autism. The observable behavior couples strongly with autistic savants and falls within the same domains: Art, music, math and chess. A new book entitled, *The Prodigy's Cousin: The Family Link Between Autism and Extraordinary Talent*, expands upon this theory. Chapter 8, "Another Path to Prodigy," outlines the remarkable stories of Josh and Zac Tiessen, two prodigies in one family, which is extremely rare. The Tiessen brothers are examples of prodigies who, although they appear to have no family link to autism, share in common environmental risk factors that may be the source of their savant-like talents.

While child prodigies are difficult to recruit because of their scarcity (1 in 5-10 million of the population), art prodigies are the most difficult, especially males. It was while I was specifically researching art prodigies that Josh Tiessen came up as one of the top ten art prodigies in the world. I had not come across any male art prodigies in

North America, so I was very interested in meeting and testing Josh, and he only lived six hours away.

The encounter was an eye opener for my research. Within the first five minutes of meeting Josh, my suspicions were confirmed about his prodigiousness. His articulate speech showed maturity well beyond his years, his body of work was astounding for its attention to detail and technical excellence, and his writings that accompanied his paintings were shocking for their depth and perception. Administering the Stanford-Binet Intelligence Scale, Josh scored in the high range and, like the other art prodigies I had tested, had a specific visual-spatial profile. He also scored high on the Autistic Spectrum Quotient measuring autistic tendencies, and so did his brother and parents.

As you will read, the Tiessens have an extraordinary story to tell about Josh's difficult pregnancy and his mother's fall shortly before his birth during an attempted break-in while they were serving as missionaries in Russia. Josh's talent displayed itself at a young age. His parents were skeptical that they had a great artist on their hands, believing the artwork had been enhanced by Josh's Russian nanny. Yet as he continued to develop and the family moved back to Canada, it became clear that Josh had a gift.

Josh also had a normally developing younger brother Zac, but that was about to change. After suffering a massive concussion at thirteen when he banged his head on a church floor, Zac became a musical prodigy. Within three months he was a performing guitarist at a professional level, and within a year he was composing complex pieces, totalling sixteen by the time of his sixteenth birthday. Although this is rare, other cases have validated that left hemisphere damage can evolve into right hemisphere enhancement in a very small percentage of patients.

My theory of child prodigies being genetically related to autism happened by a chance meeting. I was testing my first prodigy in the South when he got tired of me and asked go to a local restaurant. His mother agreed and we set out on a whim for McDonalds. While we were there his only maternal male cousin came in with his mother. As the two sisters chatted, the young teenager stood behind flapping his arms and grunting. When they left, the prodigy's mother told me her nephew was autistic. On my way home I began to think of ways to explore this unlikely connection. I started to ask the child prodigies and their parents if anyone in their family had autism. Over 50% of the families said *yes*. I began to collect data using the Autistic Spectrum Quotient on all of my next 30 prodigies, including Josh and Zac Tiessen. After confirming that they had the talent that is evident in autistic savants, without the deficits, I began to collect DNA. A preliminary finding established a genetic link between child prodigies and their autistic relatives on chromosome one. Both Josh and Zac's DNA shared this distinction. Further work in this field may identify why the child prodigies display the talent that is sometimes linked to autism, such as autistic savants, without the deficits.

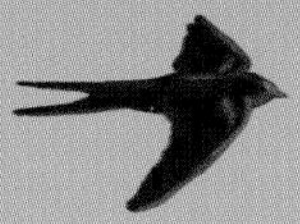

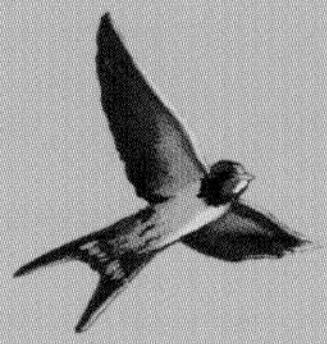

I have been closely associated with the Tiessen family for the past five years and have visited on three occasions. It has been a pleasure to observe Josh through to adulthood and see his extraordinary talent mature and refine. Reading his biography and viewing his art from the past decade, you too will experience this rare gift.

—DR. JOANNE RUTHSATZ
Ohio, September 25, 2016

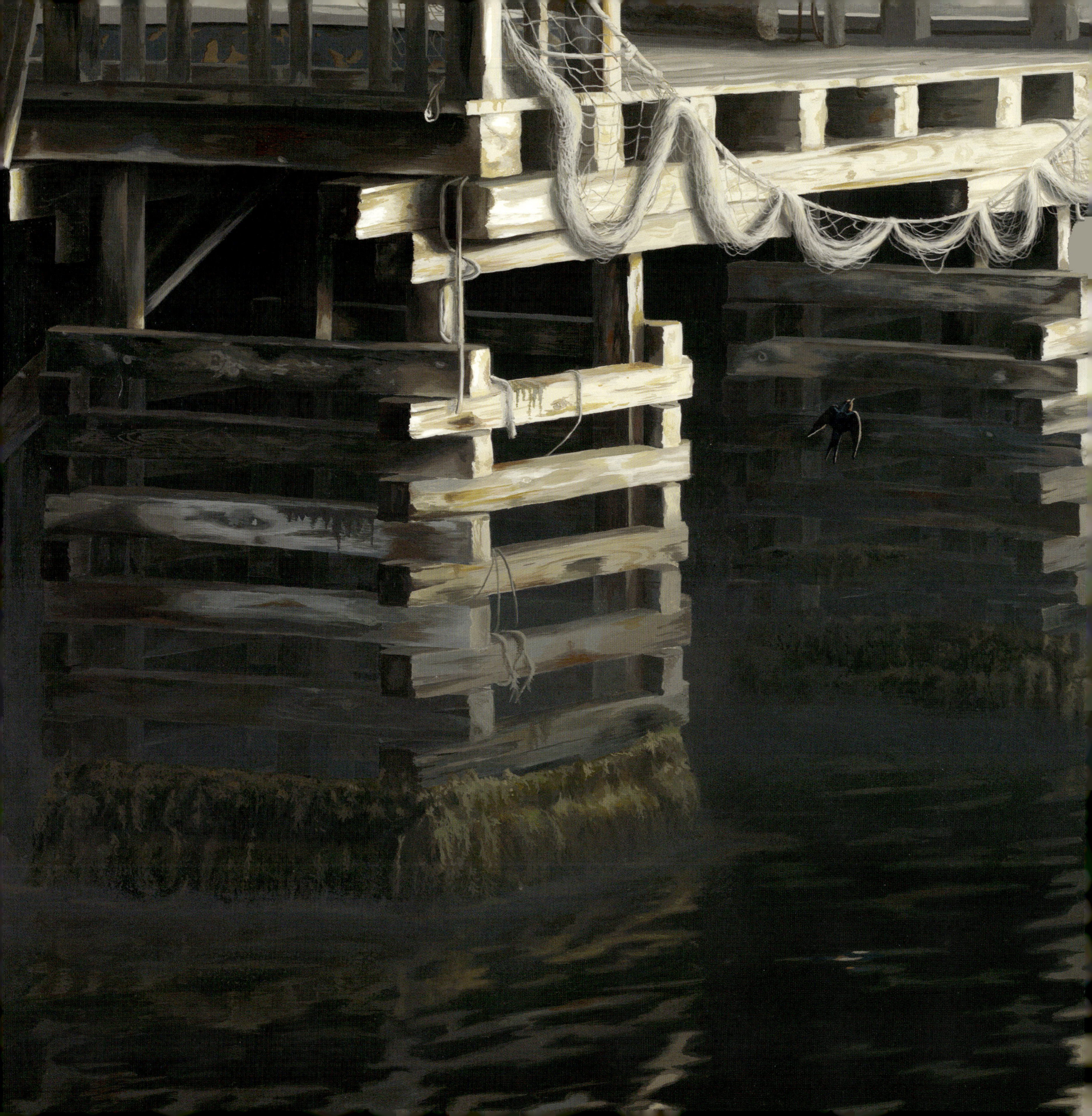

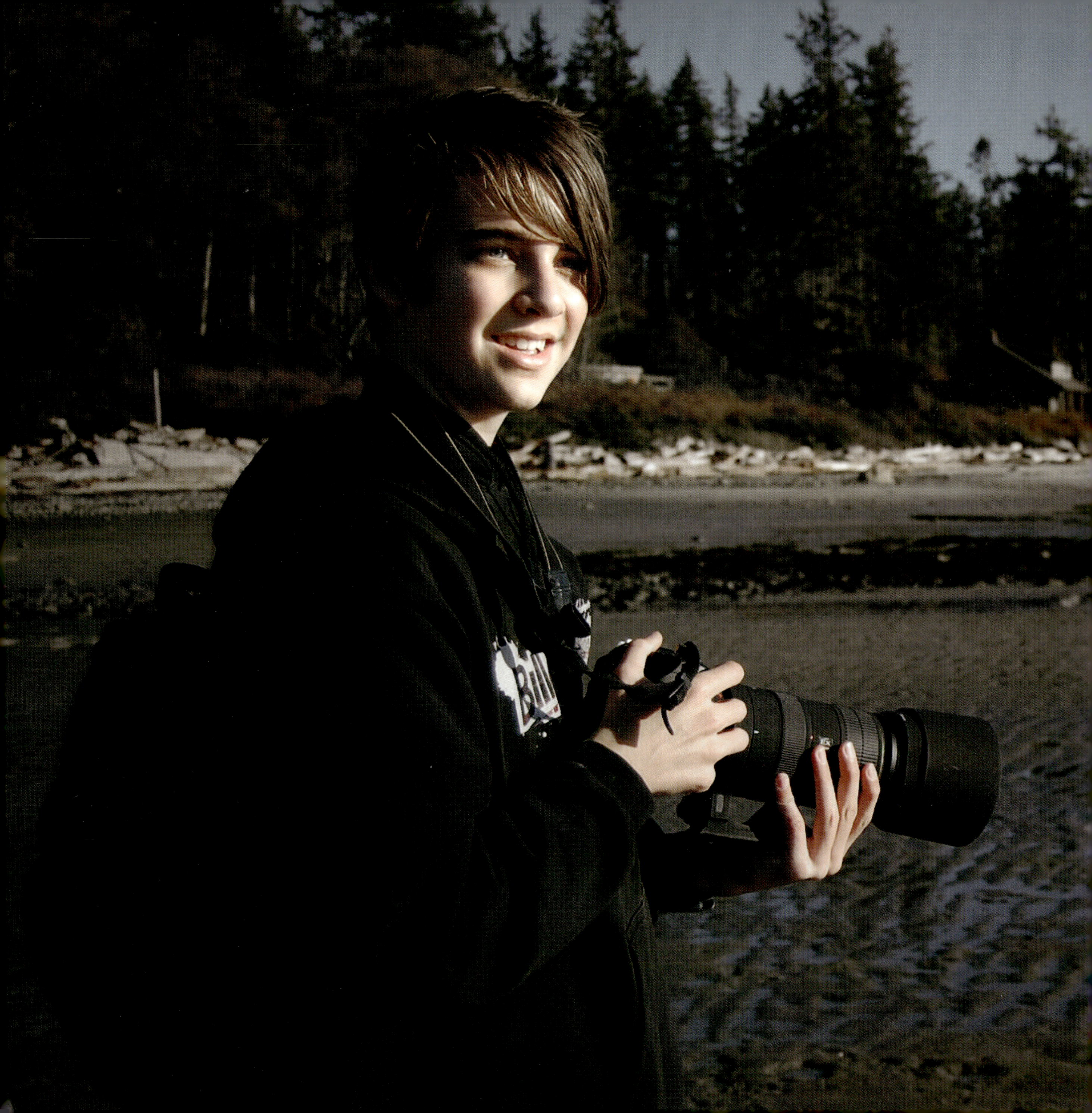

STORY

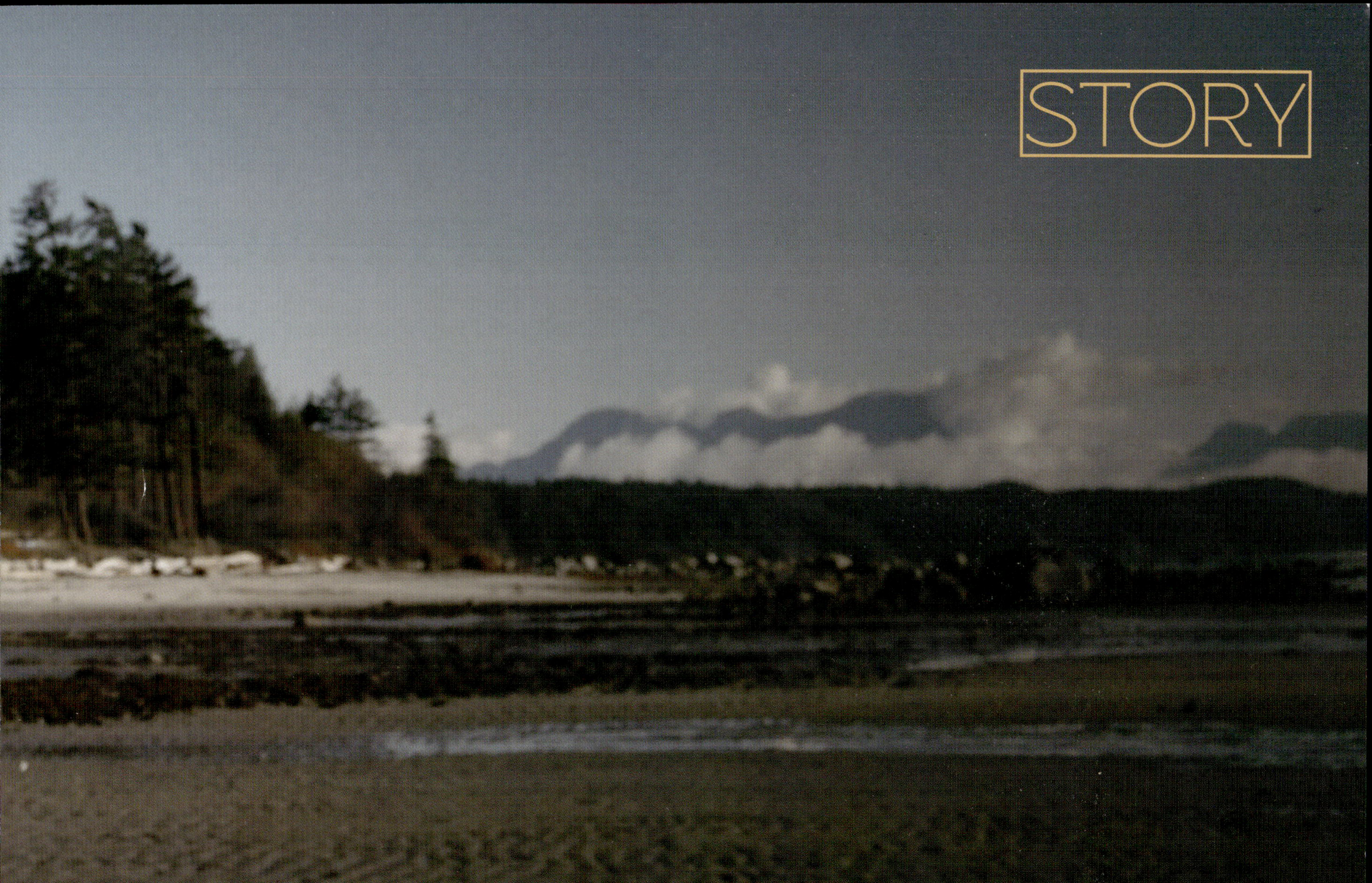

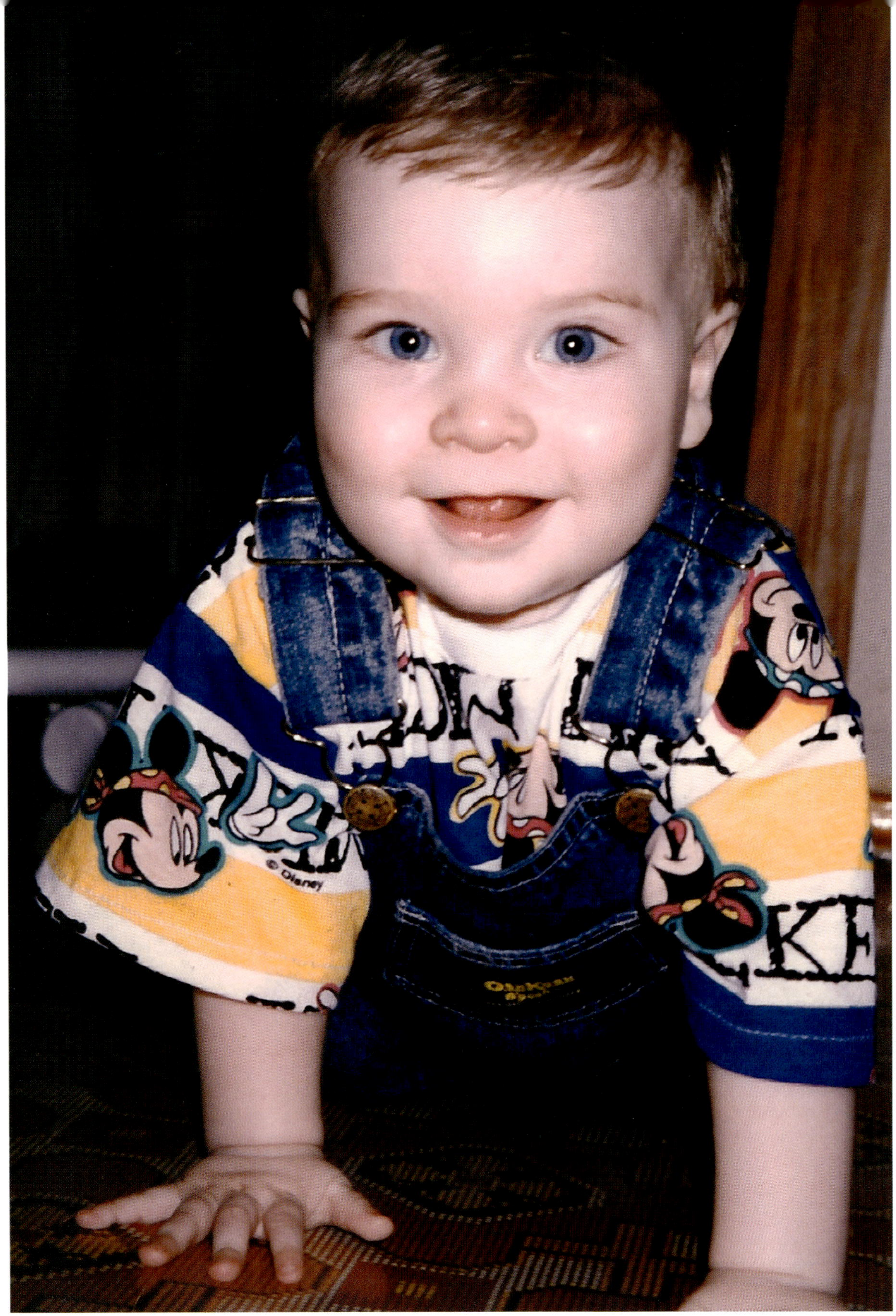

An Unusual Beginning

Eleven days before his birth, Joshua lay snug inside his mother's womb, while a gruff Russian detective sat across the table lecturing his parents, Doug and Julie, in spitfire rhetoric. Sternly and repeatedly he pointed to Julie's pregnant belly exclaiming, "Danger to baby!" and making what could only be understood as a slicing action across her body.

The Canadian couple had studied the Russian language full-time at Kuban State University for over a year, and could easily carry on a conversation. However, sitting opposite the verbose detective in their shocked state, police jargon like "crime" lay beyond their grasp. They were able to pick up the man's frequent use of the word "ring" and deduced that he must be speaking of the crime rings they had heard about in Moscow.

Months later, their worst suspicions were confirmed when they read about an attacker cutting a baby out of a woman's full-term tummy, leaving her to bleed to death and abducting the infant. Babies up for adoption to Westerners could fetch $20,000 on the orphan black market in Russia. Doug and Julie were stunned, chilled to the bone by the thought that their healthy baby boy, who was now just beginning to crawl, had narrowly escaped a prenatal abduction!

The pregnancy had been tumultuous from the start, necessitating several emergency three-hour flights to Moscow. Having checked out medical facilities in the large city of Krasnodar, where they were stationed in southwestern Russia, they knew Julie could not get the necessary prenatal care locally. During their emergency trips, twice Doug had to smuggle her out of airport medical offices, where she was being interrogated and threatened with internal exams by medical personnel of dubious intentions. The final middle-of-the-night flight to Moscow landed Julie for a one week stay in the Kremlin hospital. Once admitted, she had no choice but to be pumped full of unknown drugs to stop the bleeding, drugs to stop the contractions, drugs to make her sleep, and drugs to quiet all her questioning (unacceptable in the Russian culture). After the baby was stabilized and Julie was released, her Canadian doctor at the International Medical Clinic in Moscow insisted she stay close by until the baby was born. Julie would be the first foreigner to give birth in a new Turkish-Russian joint venture birth hospital.

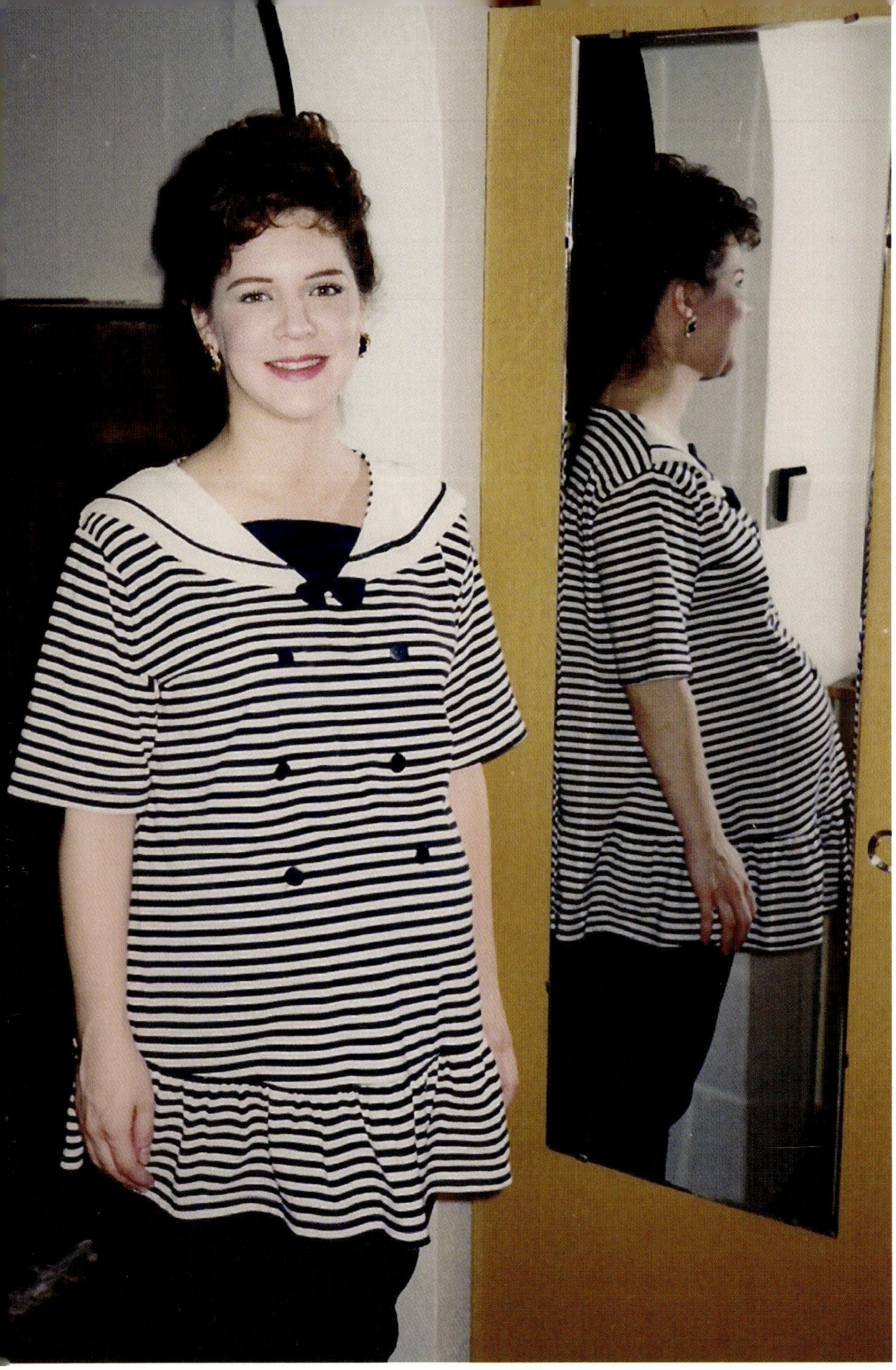

That's when the suspicious activity began. Doug and Julie had settled into a third floor Soviet-style apartment, the "guest flat" as it was called, owned and maintained by the Christian mission organization they were working under. Unbeknownst to the Tiessens, shortly before their arrival a short-term mission team had stayed at the apartment and unwittingly given out the address to some con artists on Red Square. A Russian couple had come to visit the team at the guest flat one evening, but they soon realized the shady pair only had intentions on their money and possessions, so a few of the men had to promptly usher them out.

The team left, the Tiessens arrived, and the disturbing phone calls started. It was usually a Russian-speaking male who, employing various ruses, attempted to confirm that the phone number matched the address of the apartment. It was also becoming apparent to the Tiessens that they were being watched as they passed through the little outdoor market across the street from the guest flat. In her third trimester, it had gradually dawned on them that no other largely pregnant women were out and about, so they chalked it up to curiosity. Julie left the flat only when necessary for doctor's appointments, since she had been placed on strict bed rest. The only time she went to the market with Doug was when they were dropped off by taxi coming home from the doctor, and they had to pass through it on the way to the guest flat since their street was one-way traffic going the other direction.

As usual and as expected, Doug often bartered and bantered with the market vendors. However, on one occasion after he had purchased some peaches, another seller grabbed him and held a knife to his throat, demanding to know why he hadn't purchased *his peaches*! The Tiessens were well aware of the pecking order and the mafia that ran the markets, since they'd had previous encounters in Krasnodar. After that incident, they decided to avoid this local market for the remainder of their stay in Moscow. But had the information about Westerners living in the neighbourhood already fallen into the wrong hands?

The disturbing phone calls continued. Julie received them while Doug was out doing errands, accompanied by his mother who had come from Canada to help. There were many trips to the Canadian Embassy and other offices to prepare paperwork for the baby's arrival. Doug and his mom tried to go out in the mornings when Julie was still sleeping, so they could be back in time to make her lunch.

It was one such morning that Julie was awakened by the doorbell. As she struggled to her feet and donned her housecoat, the ringing became frantic. She looked through the peephole and no one was in sight. So she opened her apartment door and went out to the locked French doors that serviced the corridor of four apartments. The doorbell, located outside those doors, was still being rung repeatedly, and through the frosted panes Julie could see the figure of a large man. When he realized she was there he began trying the handle and insisting she let him in, mumbling something Julie could not make out, but it seemed rather urgent. Her first inclination was to help him, but although she would not usually hesitate to do so a streak of fear rushed through Julie in that moment. She apologized that she did not know him and would not open the door, as she scurried back into the apartment and bolted the door shut. Peering through the peephole, none of the other apartments seemed to have been rung. A *babushka* came out to sweep the hallway with her short cornbroom and seemed oblivious.

Within minutes the phone rang and there was heavy breathing before the line went dead. The phone soon rang again and it was a man asking why she hadn't opened the door, saying he was a friend from Krasnodar with gifts and souvenirs to give her. Julie did not recognize the name he gave, so hung up the phone and was still sitting by it trying to settle her racing heart when the doorbell rang again. It took all the courage she could muster to go out to the corridor and let in a Canadian colleague, a tall slender man who was due to arrive that morning and whose voice she was relieved to hear. She had just finished relaying the incident to him when Doug and his mother arrived home.

Two days later, on the morning of Julie's 29th birthday, Doug and his mom were preparing to head out for more errands. At the last minute their plans were changed as a Peruvian missionary colleague had lost his passport, and a new one was being delivered by courier to the guest flat within the hour. While they waited, Doug's mom washed the breakfast dishes. Julie lay on the padded corner bench behind the kitchen table, propped up on a pillow.

Soon the doorbell rang. Julie could see down the long narrow hallway from the kitchen to where Doug would open the apartment door without looking through the peephole. When he heard the doorbell, Doug assumed it was the courier, ringing from outside the locked French doors in the corridor. Since they were expecting him with the passport, Doug did not give it a second thought.

Julie watched in horror, as the instant Doug opened the apartment door a large black-gloved hand thrust in and grabbed him by the throat! From her vantage point, Julie could see a tall imposing figure trying to force his way in. Doug struggled to free the grip around his neck and push back against the door, clearly on the losing side of a surprise attack.

Instinctively, Julie sprang into action, shimmying down the bench, pushing against the table to get up, and rushing down the long hallway to the door. Amidst a scuffle and

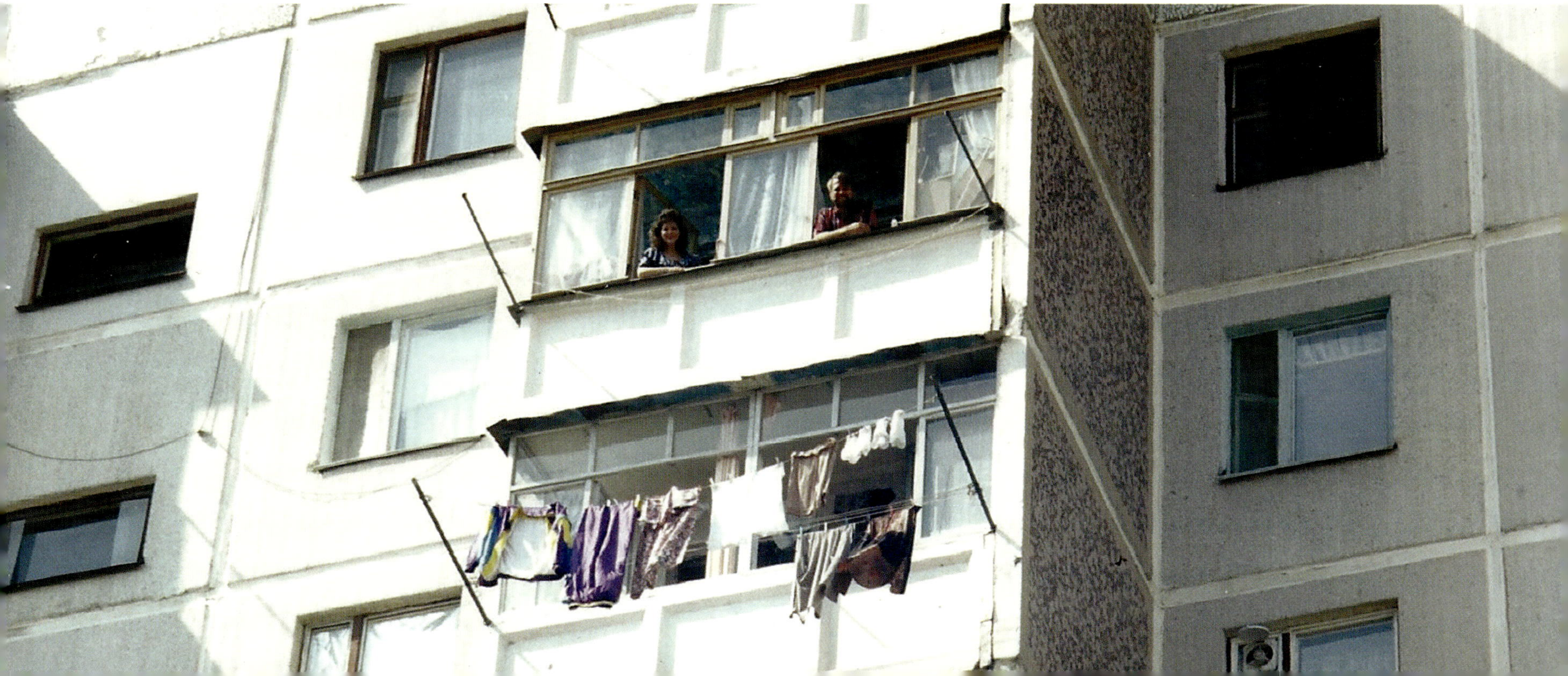

loud grunts she caught view of the man's head, wrapped like a mummy in white cloth with holes cut out for his eyes. This sight, coupled with the adrenaline rush to assist her husband in the fight, caused Julie to trip on the long hallway carpet and fall headlong onto her pregnant belly. As she struggled to her feet, the sound of an inhuman shriek filled the air. Scrambling to the door, she found Doug by some supernatural power had shut and bolted it. They both watched as three fingers of the large black rubber glove fell to the floor inside the apartment.

Julie consoled her hyperventilating husband and prayed aloud, "Thank you God for making Doug strong!" Assuming the man had fled, she quickly gathered her senses and ran back up the long hall past Doug's bewildered mother, to the kitchen where she looked down from a large open screenless window to the front door of the building. Almost immediately, she saw the figure of a large man dart from the building with a white bundle in his hand and get into the passenger side of a waiting red Lada. The car sped off and around to the back of the building. Still disregarding her awkward size, Julie bolted back down the hallway, dodging furniture through the rear bedroom where she and Doug struggled to open the door to a closed-in balcony. They caught a glimpse of the car driving away but could not make out the license plate.

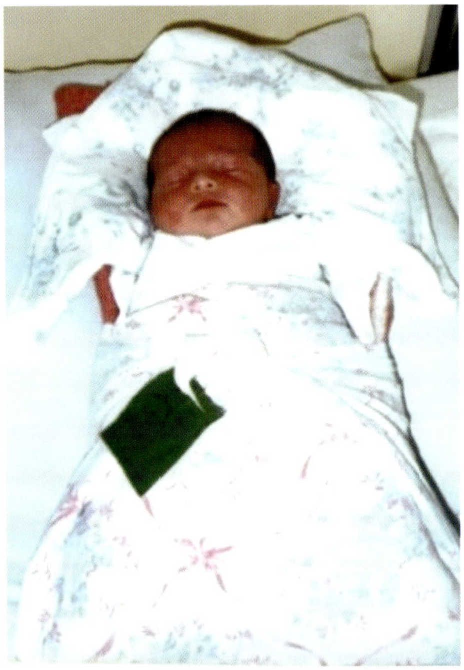

A call to the nearby police station brought a S.W.A.T. team in full army fatigues with sub machine guns. The deeply shaken couple breathlessly and in broken Russian tried to describe the horrific incident and the attacker. Their American colleague who ran the guest flat arrived in the midst of it carrying a baseball bat, having inched up the stairwell not knowing what to expect after their frantic phone call.

A couple hours later, still reeling from the events of the morning, Doug cautiously opened the door to the burly Russian detective who had called ahead. The Tiessens' American colleagues and their young children arrived later with dinner from Moscow's first Pizza Hut, in an attempt to celebrate Julie's birthday. She sat quietly holding her tummy, wondering if the baby was okay and whether she was going into *real labour* this time. It would be eleven more days of nervous waiting for the baby's arrival, feeling traumatized every time the doorbell rang. The disturbing phone calls persisted; one time a man posed as a police officer. The detective insisted it was no longer safe at that apartment since it was now 'marked' by the crime ring. But the Tiessens had nowhere else to go.

On June 25, 1995 the day of their firstborn's birth finally arrived. Julie's water broke and they called the birth hospital, which sent its shiny new Ford ambulance, a much gentler ride than all the rickety Russian ambulances she and the baby had survived in the previous months. She was marched up to the sterile glass-walled birthing theatres, where the stern attendants and other expectant mothers were not accustomed to admitting men. They begrudgingly allowed Doug to join his wife, on account of him being a foreigner with a document showing he had prepaid for this right. Disregarding the birth plan Julie had submitted to the head doctor weeks before, she was immediately put on an IV drip to hasten the contractions, in what seemed like a birthing assembly line. A few hours later, after the head doctor presiding over the midwives climbed onto Julie's stomach to help push from the outside, the baby popped out, lethargic but seemingly no worse for the wear. However, as global child prodigy expert Dr. Joanne Ruthsatz posits in her book, *The Prodigy's Cousin*, could this newborn have been "*different* for the wear?"

At the time of his birth, Doug and Julie were just relieved to have a healthy baby boy, after all the challenges they had overcome to bring him safely into this world. The baby was immediately whisked away from Julie, vigourously rubbed down with oil and tightly swaddled. Doug would not let his son out of his sight until he had memorized his face and ensured the correct nametag had been pinned onto his swaddling. The nurses insisted on keeping him in the nursery the first night, since Julie was still woozy after being anaesthetized to quiet her hollering during the delivery. The next morning the nurse wheeled in something like a metal grocery cart, with the babies in their tight swaddling stacked side-by-side and upright like bowling pins.

Upon release from the birth home a few days later, the new parents cautiously took their baby back to the guest flat, intent on getting little Joshua stable enough for the return to their apartment in Krasnodar, where a brightly coloured nursery awaited him. Two weeks later, he was finally waking up long enough to catch onto nursing. With his jaundice disappearing, the Tiessens were only too happy to leave Moscow and fly back down to their home in Krasnodar, to begin their new life as a family of three.

Their mission colleagues and Russian friends were delighted to welcome them home, especially their Russian language teachers. These meddling women had repeatedly badgered Doug and Julie as to why, after six years of marriage, they still did not have children, as this was unheard of in their society. One day in class, when Julie finally learned some new Russian vocabulary to explain it, she said that they were "not able" to have children, intending to mean not physically able. She did not yet realize there were two verbs for "to be able," and she had used the one that meant they were not able to have children because they hadn't *learned how*. After that, the teachers brought in diagrams and shared old wives' tales in attempts to help Julie conceive. They were elated with the news of her pregnancy and enthusiastically claimed full responsibility for the birth of this child.

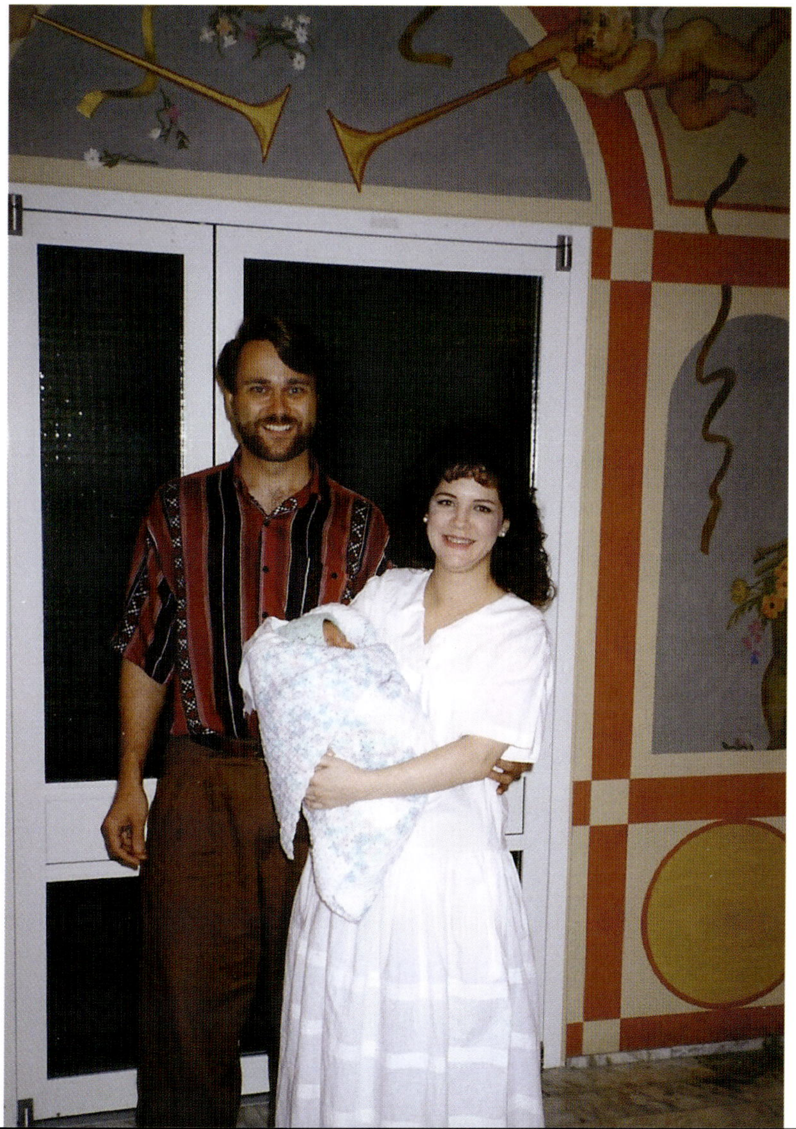

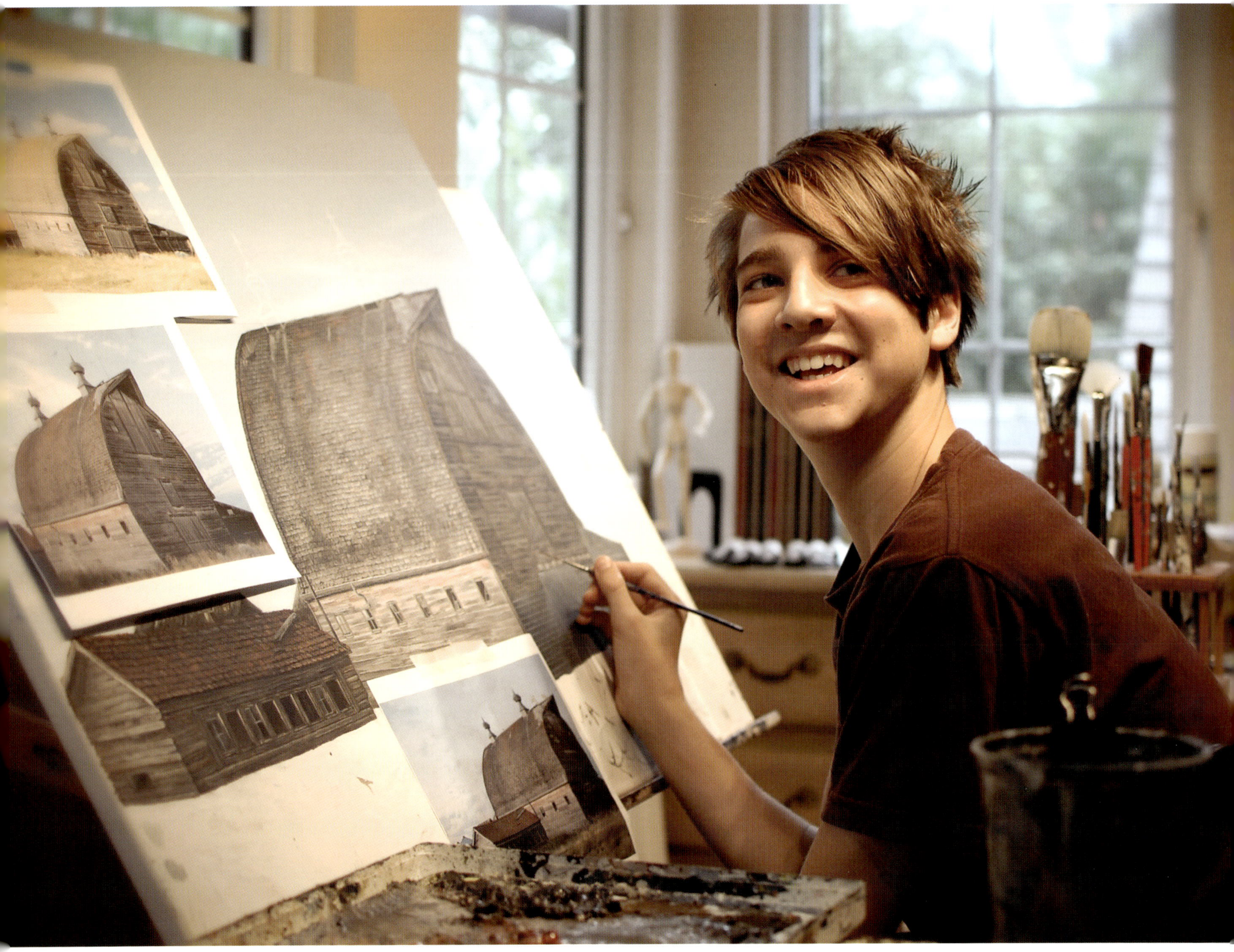

Family Heritage

Almost prophetically, long before he was born, the Tiessens chose for their firstborn son the name Joshua, after the biblical character associated with strength and courage. They never imagined the extent to which those virtues would first be demanded of them as expectant parents, before they would be able to welcome him as their son. His middle name, Paul, was given in honour of Julie's father, and it also happened to be Doug's middle name, after the Apostle Paul in the Bible.

Early in the child's life, he came to be known by everyone simply as Josh, or *Dzhosh* as the Russians called him since they have no 'J' sound. In the Russian language, Joshua from the Bible is the same word as Jesus (from a common Hebrew root) with a second name used to distinguish Joshua. To avoid this complication, the Russians used a phonetic pronunciation from the English.

Initially Josh liked his name, but later when the family returned to Canada and there were three boys by the name of Josh in his first-grade classroom, he began to think it was too common. When he started signing his name on canvasses around ten, one day it occurred to him that perhaps it was so common he would never stand out as an artist. This concern dissolved by the time he was a teenager – with all the press and media attention he was receiving, his name soon became a household word in the community and people started recognizing him when he was out in public. The local newspaper wrote numerous articles about him and eventually tagged him as "Stoney Creek's Fine Artist."

Josh came from a godly heritage of Dutch-German Mennonites who were chased around Europe and ended up emigrating from the Ukraine to Mountain Lake, Minnesota over a century before the artist was born. From there they moved north to farm in the prairie province of Saskatchewan, Canada. Josh's Uncle Daryl and cousin Kyle farm large sections of land located south of the cities of Moose Jaw and Regina. Several of Josh's early paintings were inspired by visits to the farm, where the big prairie skies meet endless fields of grain, and where time has taken its toll on old abandoned homesteads.

Over many centuries of Josh's predecessors, the Tiessen family consisted of farmers, ministers and missionaries, so it was no coincidence that Doug became an ordained minister like his father. Having spent the first part of his life in India, he would also follow in the footsteps of his missionary parents. After marriage, pastoral ministry and masters degrees, in 1993 Doug and Julie went as missionaries to Russia. They worked under the Christian and Missionary Alliance, a mission organization that had been invited by the Russians in the wake of new religious freedom after the fall of Communism. Gaining early proficiency in the Russian language, the pair were invited to teach at a new Christian university in the large city of Krasnodar, located between the Black and Caspian Seas.

Later, the Tiessens became the Field Director couple for their mission's large international team scattered throughout post-Soviet Russia. They travelled all over the country (eventually with two young sons in tow) visiting their missionary colleagues and Russian co-workers, who were starting contemporary evangelical churches, providing humanitarian aid, opening drug and alcohol rehab centres, camps for children and teens, etc. It was not an easy life living in a developing nation far away from their family in Canada, especially once Julie became pregnant, but they felt called to it and loved the challenge and adventure it provided.

In the midst of this busy life, Joshua had come into the picture. He seemed just like any other Russian baby, as he loved the tight swaddling customary for calming newborns. In fact, he preferred the calm so much that they had to swaddle him for the first three months of his life.

Leaving the birth hospital in Moscow, Doug joked to the doctor that they'd be back the next summer. Exactly thirteen months later to the day, Joshua's brother Zachary was born in the same Moscow hospital, having undergone none of the prenatal complications his older brother had endured. Josh spent the first six years of his life happily living with his parents, younger brother and a Boxer named Jessica in mild Southern Russia, across the Black Sea from where his Mennonite ancestors had once lived in Odessa, Ukraine.

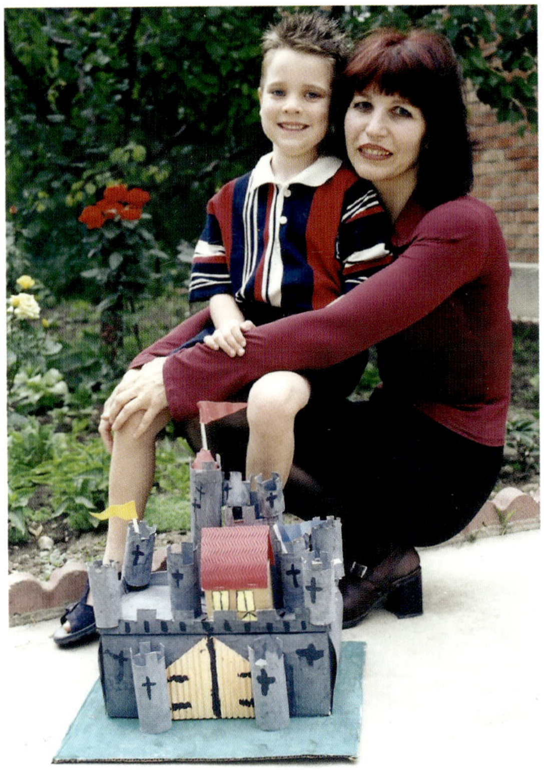

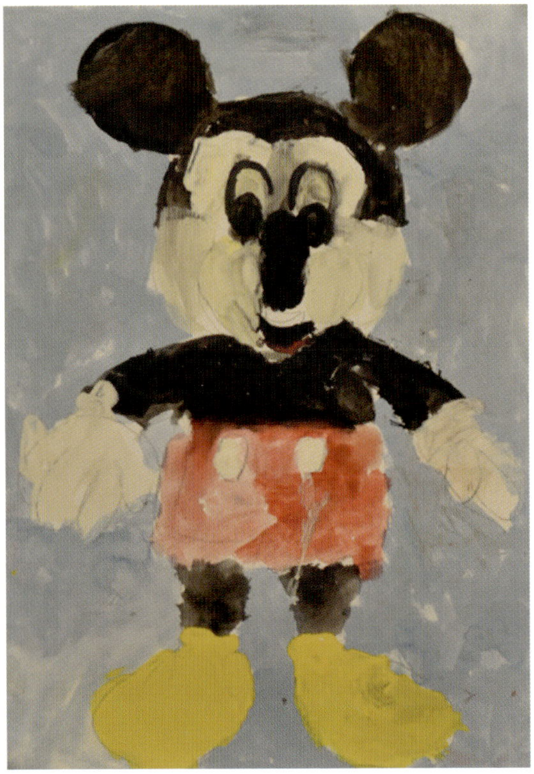

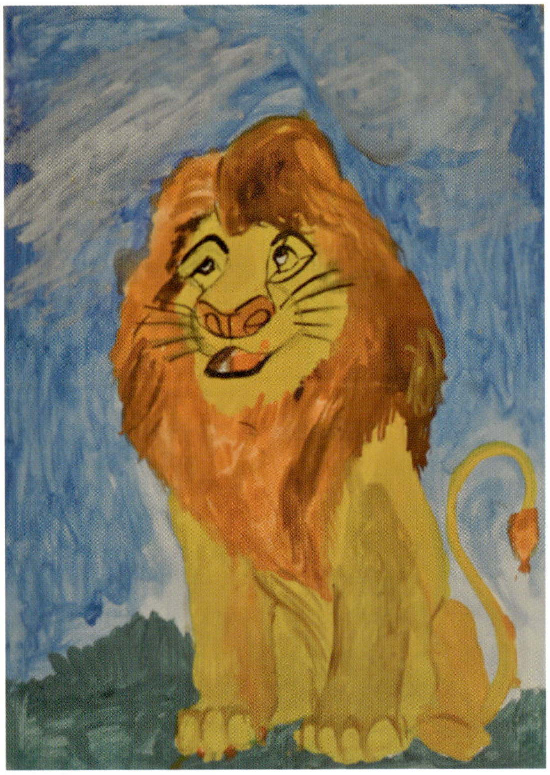

Tempera Paintings at Age 4 and 5

A Preschooler's Art

As a toddler, from the time he could hold fat crayons in his little hands, Josh preferred to draw his own pictures, and the stacks of colouring books sent to Russia by well-meaning grandmothers were given away to other children. He enjoyed painting with bright-coloured tempera paints, always under the watchful eye and helping hand of his artistic Russian nanny Lena Zhuk. She would correct things and make it look so good, that nobody believed Josh had done any of it. But it gave him the confidence to believe he could make something great.

His parents would chuckle at how "Tyotya Lena" (Auntie) held up stuffed animals trying to teach a four-year-old how to paint 3D with shading and perspective. As a trained kindergarten teacher, she was amazed by Josh's fine motor skills. With his tongue sticking out of the side of his mouth, he would cut fine details with preschool scissors, soon requesting his mother's sharper pair. He ditched the fat crayons for thin ones, and thick paintbrushes for finer fare. The young artist focused on realistic painting, selecting objects from his playroom and the world around him. He seemed disinterested in drawing people or faces. These artistic preferences would be seen throughout his childhood and beyond.

Julie, who also had a bit of artistic flare, would do arts and crafts with the boys when she took breaks from her mission work. She demonstrated western pedagogy to Lena, which emphasized giving the child freedom to create, without excessive correction. Both women were surprised that, while his younger brother Zac buzzed around the playroom making little boy noises with toy trucks and cars, Josh could concentrate on a project for hours. His mother and nanny began to quietly believe he may have a special gift for art.

The Tiessens' colleagues who came to visit and saw Josh's creations assumed, like Doug and Julie did, that Lena had a hand in all his artwork. But increasingly Lena insisted that she was no longer touching his projects, and that these were Josh's own masterpieces. Nobody believed her, except his mom who observed it happening. Julie started calling his works of art "Joshy originals" and made sure he signed his pieces on the back, thinking maybe someday something might come of it.

When Josh was five, she and Lena took the boys to a professional photographer in Krasnodar to get portraits done. Julie took props that represented each boy's interests at the time, not realizing how iconic Josh's portrait would become.

Josh relished the peace and quiet. The last year they lived in Russia was difficult for him, as Julie took on a few other colleagues' children in their home. She was advised by educators that she would need to homescool Josh using kindergarten curriculum to prepare him for Grade One in Canada the next year. Since a couple other families also had children that age, but the parents were busy in full-time language study, Julie decided it would not take much more work to add their kids to the kindergarten. She thought it would be helpful 'Socialization 101' for all of them. With those children came younger siblings, so there were three in kindergarten and three in preschool. What began as a foray into home education, morphed into a one-room schoolhouse. Julie did not understand the difference until Josh started acting out, as he now had to share his mother, brother, nanny and playroom.

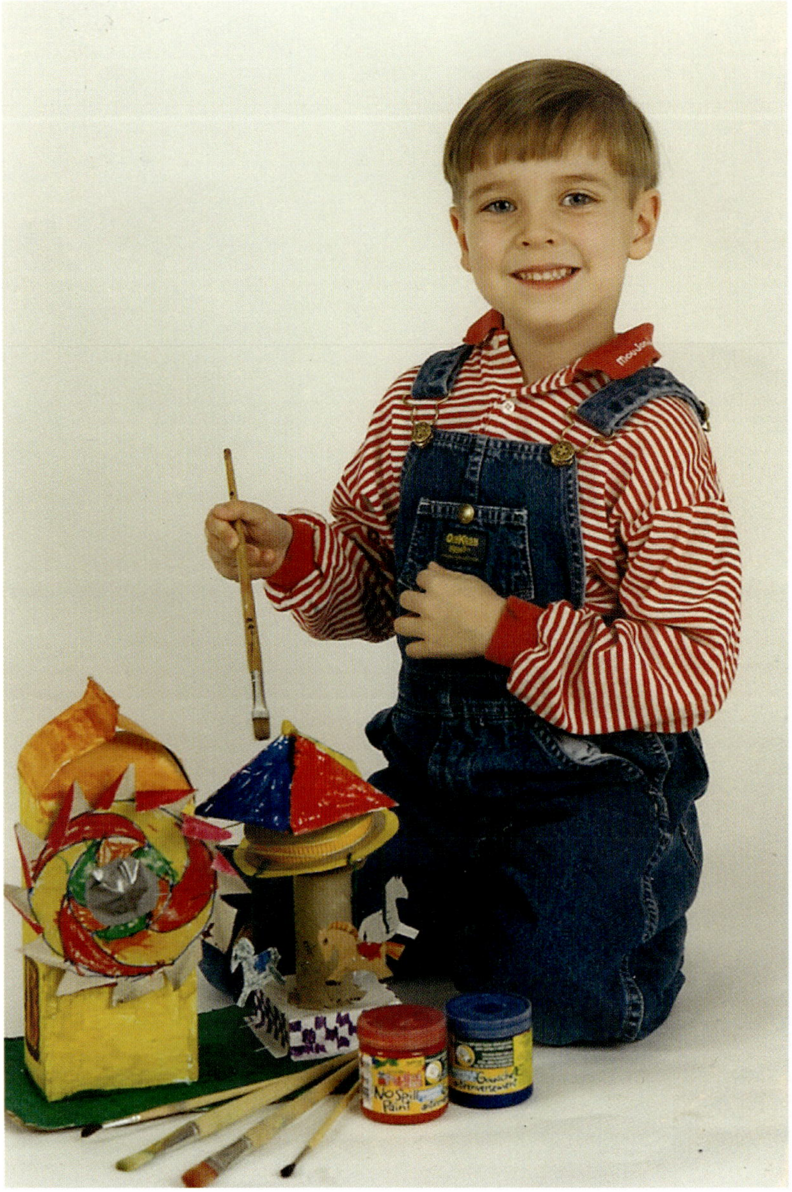

The serious young artist was not amused by having a houseful of noisy, messy children in his home every morning. He got upset when they messed up the playroom and would chide them if they did not put every toy back in its alloted place on the shelf. Later, in Canada, he would similarly obsess about the Lego city he and his brother Zac built the size of their playroom, equipped with the most advanced sets including a real working train and station that they had requested for Christmas and birthdays. Josh was very concerned about kids dismantling it when they came over for play dates, and this created some tensions. For years he had recurring dreams of his Lego city being destroyed by careless children.

Back in the one-room schoolhouse that had taken over his playroom in Russia, Josh became agitated when the other kids would not listen, or disobeyed his mother and nanny. He would sometimes take discipline into his own hands. Worse still, when conflicts arose between another child and his brother, the usually mild-mannered Josh would intervene and 'wallop' the other kid. Once Julie figured out what was happening, she worked with Josh and saw some improvement. It was a challenging and busy year, during which she repeatedly begged the mission to send out a teacher, to no avail. At least Josh picked up math and reading concepts quickly, so he was easy to teach. Once the children left each day, he breathed a sigh of relief and happily settled in for the long, quiet afternoons working on his art.

Transition to Canada

When the family returned to Canada for an extended study leave, with financial help from anonymous friends the Tiessen boys attended Burlington Christian Academy – Josh from grades one to three. It was a welcome soft landing to Canada, but Josh's artistic talent stagnated due to the system where everyone was required to do the same assignment. He got straight A's in art and won some awards, but it was as if his creativity had been stifled. He was so busy with school and other activities like swimming lessons and sports that he rarely created his own art at home anymore.

When he did produce work independently during those years, it was influenced by what was popular with school friends and the media: hockey and basketball logos, running shoes and concept cars – mostly illustrative designs, but with an innovative twist. He also loved playing outdoors. He commandeered his brother to build an elaborate fort in the ravine next to the home they rented on a large property on the edge of Burlington, Ontario. Even when Zac soon lost interest, as he often did with his brother's ambitious pursuits, Josh would persevere to completion then roll his eyes as Zac claimed joint credit. Surprisingly for all his seriousness, Josh was also the source behind much of the humour that Zac would parrot and get credit for. Josh resigned himself to this pattern, which persists to this day. People are still caught off guard when they discover Josh's sense of humour, even more so when they see him cut loose and have fun.

In spite of creating few pieces of art, those early elementary years saw development in other areas that made Josh stand out from his peers. His teachers loved him, as he was a well-behaved and conscientious student who got excellent grades and could be paired as a mentor with 'bad boys'. This became a common theme that would follow Josh into his teens and leave him longing for his own mentors. His parents had always quipped that he was "born an adult" on account of his highly developed moral sensibilities, and his theological and philosophical musings, which were shocking for their level of articulation and maturity beginning at the age of five.

Starting in Grade One, the quiet boy astounded everyone when he came alive on stage for speeches, delivered with intelligence, charm and wit, winning school and regional competitions. This launched him into speaking engagements after each of the three mission trips he went on by the time he was eleven. He created Powerpoint slide presentations from his own photos, with assistance from his dad.

Later, Josh would emerge as a seasoned public speaker, captivating audiences with the story of how he became a professional artist by sixteen. He spoke to hundreds of people at over twenty venues in the first two years, becoming a sought-after speaker for various age groups in a wide variety of venues. This developed into speaking at schools and teaching as Guest Artist for elementary, high school and community college by the time he was eighteen. Parents started requesting that he teach their children privately, but the emerging professional artist opted to volunteer his time instructing art at a yearly March Break Camp at his church. Josh enjoys having artistic children and teens visit his studio gallery and exhibitions, often inviting them to bring their art portfolios to him for a "gentle critique." He spends time with them carefully going through their art, encouraging and inspiring young artists like himself.

When Josh and Zac were eight and nine, their parents took them for interviews at the Burlington Post, where the newspaper delivery manager seemed particularly impressed by these two polite and well-spoken brothers. With a strong work ethic characteristic of their family heritage, the boys took on one paper route then gradually worked up to three. Since they lived on the edge of the city, Doug and Julie took turns driving them to their routes, where they trudged through rain, wind and Canadian winter snowstorms.

Doug and Julie coached their boys along in this first job, exhorting them to be friendly to customers and go the second mile. Josh and Zac learned to compliment people's gardens and never cut across lawns. They added some personal touches by creating Christmas and Easter greetings on their computer, and tucking them in with the newspapers. During the holiday season they received generous tips, and cards with notes of appreciation for their faithful service. One that Josh received started with "Dear Papergirl," for by then his hair was almost shoulder length, but the inference did not phase him.

From the time Josh had gotten into the scissors and cut both his own and his brother's hair when they were preschoolers (resulting in brush-cuts, then spiky do's) Josh had become very particular about his hair. He would ask his mom to spike it up with gel each morning. When he discovered coloured gels he was hooked, and wore them proudly to sporting events even though few other children did. Josh's artistic flare increasingly expressed itself in his hair and clothing. Regardless of what other people thought, he wore them how he liked. Years later, walking to and from high school repeatedly being called a "fagot" never caused him to change the way he wore his hair or clothes, or the way he walked, which may have accounted for part of the teasing (his family jests, "he walks like a duck" with large feet on a tall lanky body).

After the first year delivering newspapers, the brothers noticed that an award was given to the Carrier of the Year. With the positive feedback they were receiving from their customers, when it came time for voting the second year they were delighted to discover that they had been selected as runners-up to the Carrier of the Year. The manager told them that the child who won had mounted a campaign to get his customers to vote for him, and suggested they do the same. The following year they made and passed out flyers encouraging their people to vote. Sure enough, out of hundreds of children they were chosen together as Carriers of the Year. The speech that their manager made about them at the award dinner reflected the glowing comments that their customers had written and phoned into the newspaper.

Shortly afterwards, they had to say good-bye to their paper routes and customers as the family was moving to the town of Stoney Creek, twenty minutes by highway from where they had been living in Burlington. Everyone was sad to see them go. Their boss offered to write them letters of recommendation. Unfortunately, their new community did not have a well-developed newspaper carrier program, so the boys decided it was not worth their time and effort. Instead, at Josh's initiative, they made flyers on the computer and started their own "J & Z Services," weeding and cutting lawns. This lasted for several years until they each had the *real* jobs they desired. The brothers still returned to their old newspaper route on occasion to visit a few customers they had become close to, especially a widow who used to have a grocery bag of cookies and chips waiting for them every Friday evening.

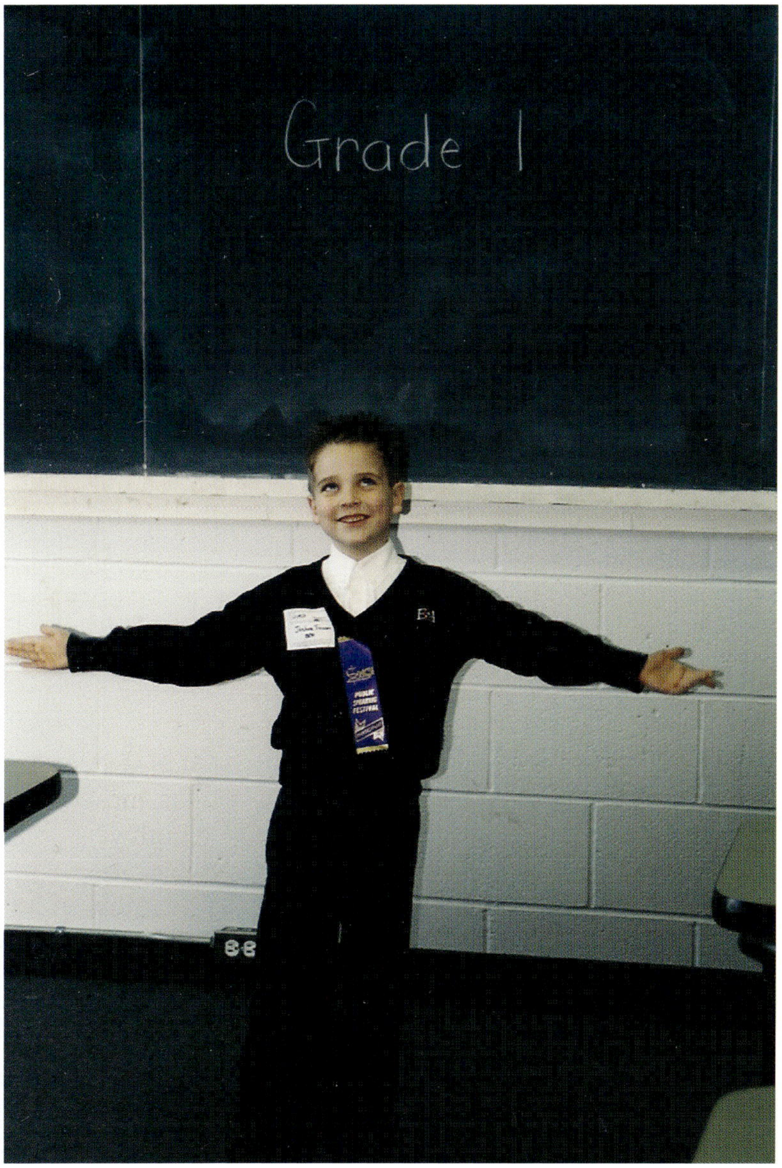

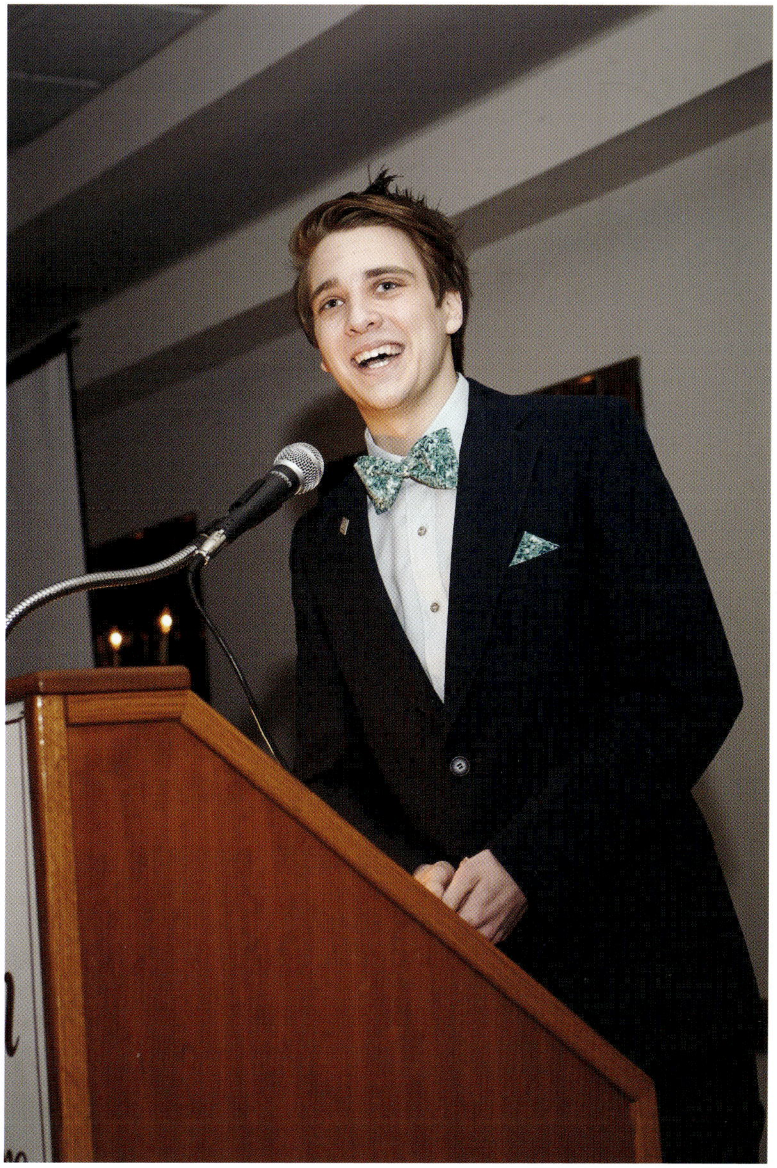

Photo by The Stoney Creek Chamber of Commerce

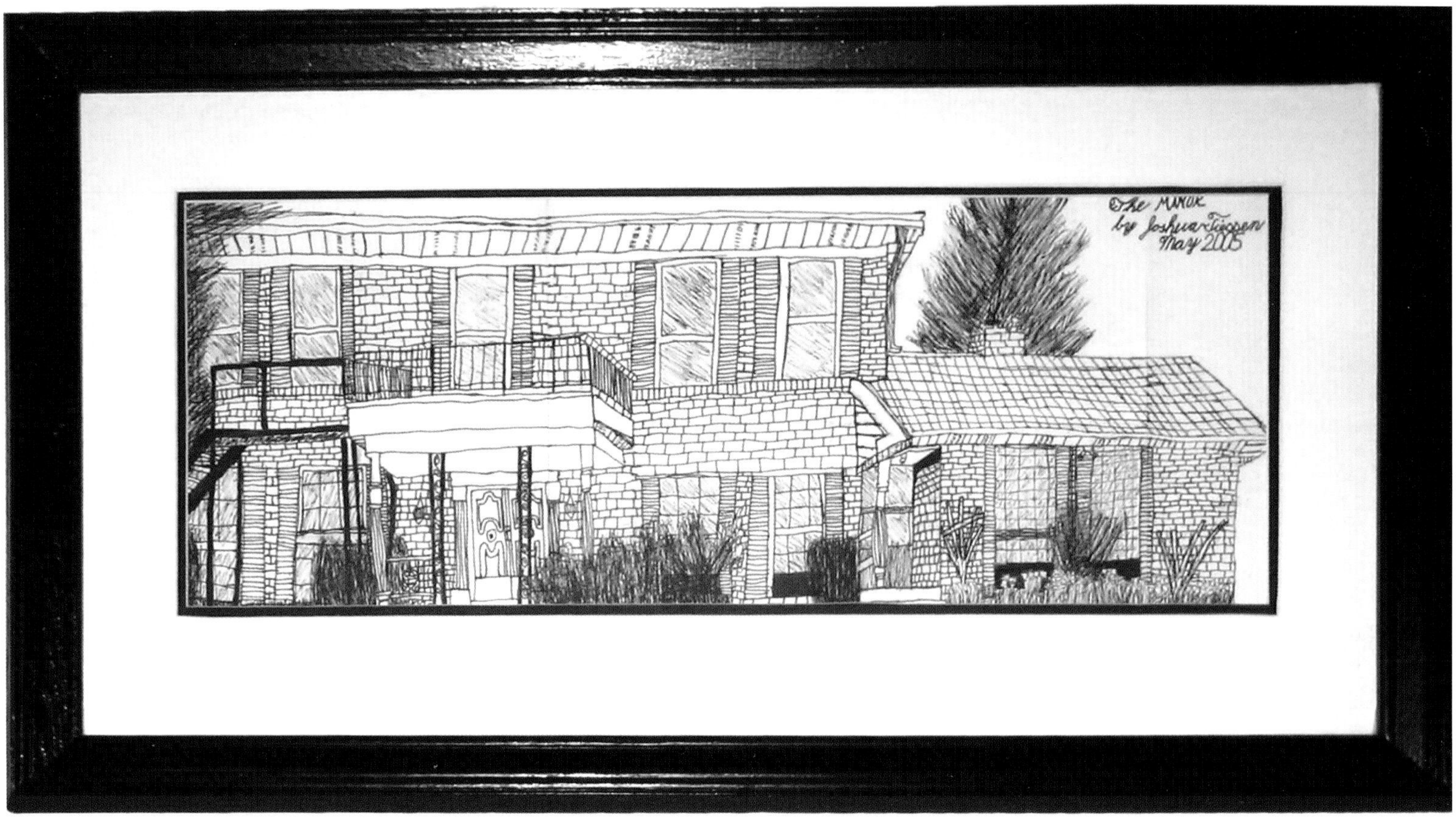

Pen Sketch of Josh's House at Age 9

Educational Shift

Doug had completed a PhD and Julie was working on a doctoral degree when they resumed travelling the world, now with Doug based out of an office in Toronto. Josh and Zac started pressuring Julie to homeschool them again, so they would have the freedom to travel like they did as a family in Russia and surrounding countries. Still recalling how, after that final difficult year in Krasnodar she never wanted to home educate again, it took six months for the boys to convince their mom. She only relented when, shortly before the next school year began, they were informed that the funding would no longer be provided since they were no longer technically missionaries. They couldn't afford the tuition on one ministry-income, so Julie finally agreed to try homeschooling for one year.

This time around, with only her own two bright students who had already been given a good foundation, Julie was soon a homeschool enthusiast. She crafted subjects around their travels and permitted the boys to learn at their own speed. The Tiessens did not have much money for curriculum, but were blessed with boxes of textbooks and empty workbooks handed down from a family who owned an organic farm. Loading the boxes into her car, this family gleefully declared that they had become "unschoolers." Julie was bewildered, but gratefully received their valuable resources.

Being a perfectionist, Julie sought to teach all of the subjects they had at the Christian private school. They went from morning until late afternoon each day. Doug enjoyed helping the boys with hands-on creative building projects in the evenings and on weekends. Josh cherished the quiet, relaxed atmosphere, and finally had time to work on his art again.

The family could not afford art lessons. For Art Class Julie dug out an old cartooning book from her early teens and started showing the boys how to draw cartoon figures of animals and people. Although Josh was extremely good at it, he was not particularly interested as he could soon master any of the drawings. Besides, he said it was just copying someone else's art.

Julie thought perhaps nature drawing might provide a greater challenge. After lunch one day, she sent the boys out to do sketching while she was busy with her own studies. Josh chose to draw the large house they were renting at that time, called "The Manor" (p. 26). He perched himself halfway down the sprawling front lawn and worked at it all afternoon. They had to coax him in for supper as he was still meticulously drawing every brick, having carefully taped two more sheets of paper to allow for the width of the home. After dinner, he hastily finished the roof shingles and a tree, but was never happy with the final product. Still, his mom thought it was good enough to have Josh's grandfather frame it in a repurposed frame he had painted. The family proudly hung it for many years, even at the house they later purchased in Stoney Creek, as a reminder of their years in Burlington. Seeing from his sketch that Josh had a natural eye for depth and perspective, Julie found a little book called *The Seven Laws of Perspective* at the cooperative homeschool library she had joined with other keen moms. She led the boys through the lessons, and Josh completed every drawing impeccably, assimilating the concepts quickly and applying them to his own drawings. Years later, with the book out of print, Josh would use it to teach children and teens, whose parents often express disdain for the lack of formal art instruction in schools.

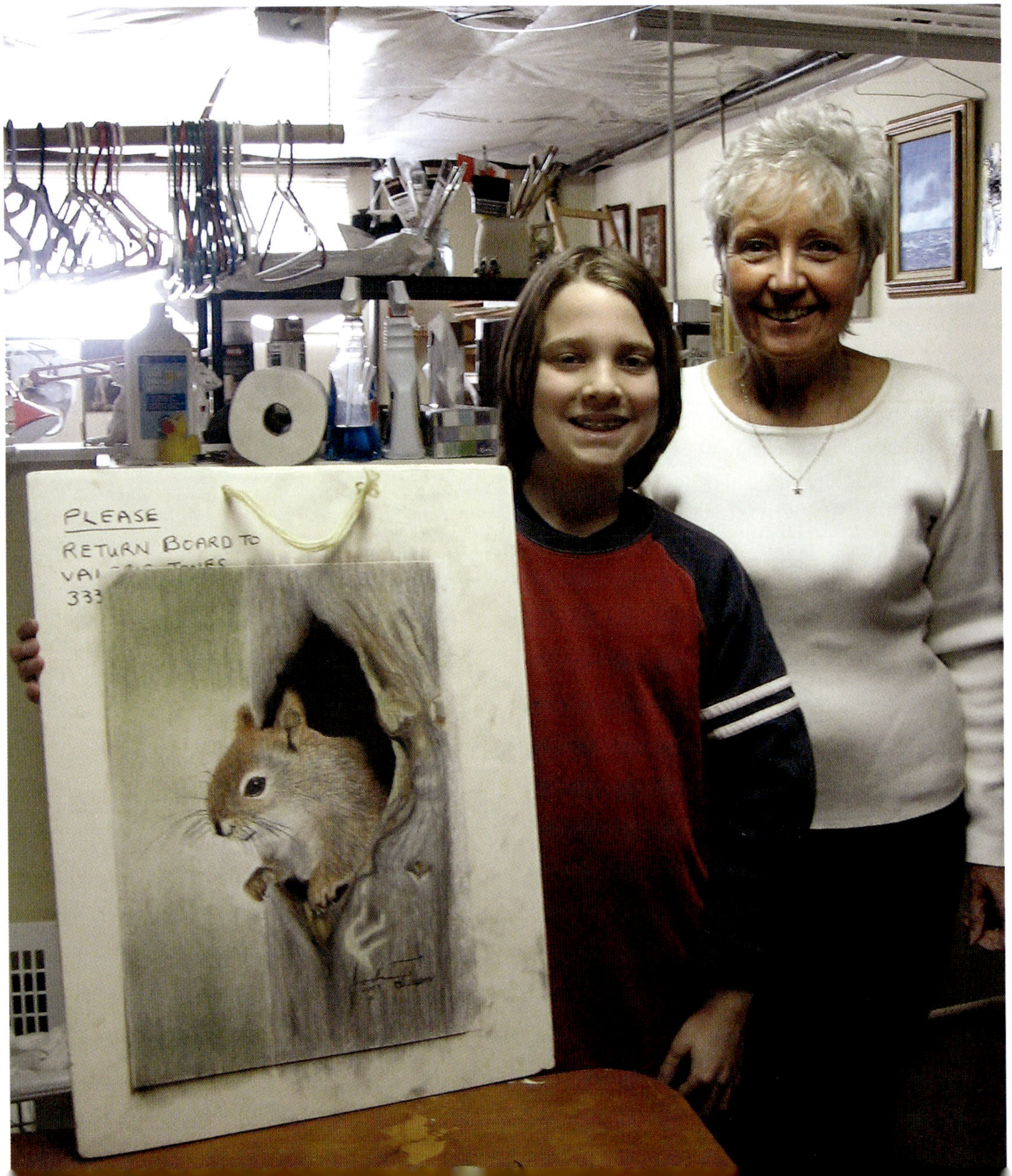

THE WOMAN WHO CHANGED HIS LIFE

Shortly thereafter, local wildlife and pet portrait artist Valerie Jones discovered Josh as a nine-year-old budding artist at a church children's club. On the first night, among fifty children Val noticed immediately that Josh's artwork stood out... and he was only making his nametag. She kept peering over his shoulder as he spent the whole evening on an intricate geometric design, yet appeared to have not yet signed his name. When she approached him suggesting he make sure to put his name on his picture, Josh responded shyly, "That *is* my name," and then Val saw that indeed it was. Over the following weeks, his skill and extreme focus astonished her and she thought to herself, "This is no ordinary child artist."

Val and her husband Rob had moved to Canada from England many years before with no children of their own and were now retired. She had never done anything like this before, but after observing Josh for about a month she looked up his parents and phoned them. The Tiessens were fairly new to the church and did not know Val, so it took Julie by surprise when this British woman proceeded to 'gush' about her talented son for over forty-five minutes. Val invited him to her studio. Since Josh now had a flexible schedule due to homeschooling, for a couple of years he spent Wednesday afternoons with Val, as she passed on her skills in chalk pastel and painting.

Josh had not wanted to draw animals when his mother suggested it earlier, although he always loved the animals in the travelling Russian circuses and zoos. He thrilled at seeing big cats from six feet away, while simultaneously felt sorry for them in their cramped cages. Val's forte was animals. Since Josh had fallen in love with the Chronicles of Narnia series, he decided to try his hand at the lion Aslan from *The Lion, The Witch and the Wardrobe*. Val was impressed that Josh would choose such an ambitious subject for a ten-year-old, but she did not know him very well yet. It would not be long before she discovered that this was Josh's *modus operandi*, as he took pleasure in challenging himself with the most difficult subjects, and he still does.

One day when Julie came to pick him up at Val's, they took her downstairs to the laundry room where Josh worked adjacent to her studio. Julie stood in disbelief at his completed *Aslan* (see p. 31). Suddenly, she sensed a *déjà vu*, recalling how they suspected Lena had enhanced Josh's art. She queried Val, who insisted she had not touched his piece, pulling out the small studies she had done with him demonstrating how to draw eyes and fur.

His grandpa had by that time framed a few of Josh's creations in used painted frames and matting. *Aslan* was the first piece of Josh's art to be professionally framed. Josh paid for it himself and asked Doug to hang it above his bed. Over the years he's had many requests to buy it, in fact one of his collectors asks for it every time she visits his studio gallery. It was the first piece he was truly proud of, and his first exhibition piece, so he says he'll never part with it. Almost ten years later, at an estate sale he finally found the antique frame he had long envisioned for it. He had it reframed and hung in the family's living room above their mantle, where it remains to this day (see pp. 80-81).

With that piece, Josh's interest in animals and metaphorical meanings had its genesis. Around that time he started sharing conceptual ideas about his art, which did not surprise his parents since Josh had expounded theological and philosophical concepts from early childhood. After a few years Julie convinced him to start writing down his ideas. He began composing story descriptions for each of his paintings and was soon waxing eloquent, as they expected. When he created his own website he began posting the stories with his painting images. Later, he would include the stories with sales of his original paintings and limited edition giclée prints, and hang the stories in his own gallery beside each piece.

Some people assumed that Doug or Julie were drafting Josh's stories, but apart from some proofreading the compositions have all been his own. Just like his paintings, the stories gradually matured and refined over the years through his teens. However, he mostly kept each story how he had originally written it, usually right after the painting was completed. While he painted for long hours he would pray and listen to music and audio books (later art lectures and podcasts from around the world), and ideas for the stories would come to him.

Val was not a professionally-trained artist and would not permit Josh to call her his teacher, so they referred to her as his art mentor. At her request, from the beginning he called her Val, but gradually she became like another grandmother to both Josh and Zac (into whose hands she would later place an old guitar and inspire a prodigy musician). Because of Val, who changed both their lives forever, when Josh speaks to audiences of adults and older teens he always encourages them to consider taking a child under their wing to pass on whatever special knowledge or skill they may have. Conversely, when he speaks to children and younger teens he urges them to find a mentor, explaining how helpful older mentors have been to him, even seniors like grandparents.

Once Val put the first canvas and acrylic paint into Josh's hands he had found his passion, as he could cover larger areas, like the paintings he had done as a preschooler in Russia. Val and Josh did a couple of paintings working side-by-side. When his parents returned from a work-related trip to China, Josh chose photos they had taken as the sun set on a Nestorian Monastery outside the city of X'ian, where the first missionaries had attempted to bring Christianity to China. It was fascinating to see how the two artists' interpretations of the same photos produced different paintings – Josh's pagoda was thicker, his colours were more saturated, and the sunset light was more pronounced (see p. 32).

The second painting they worked on together was in Val's backyard, where they spread out flower and animal photos they had each taken in their gardens, and painted in the sunshine like Claude Monet. It was just meant to be a practice piece with no particular attention to composition or perspective. They never had an opportunity to finish, so it was put aside until after the family moved to Stoney Creek. A year later, in the dead of winter, Josh pulled it out in his laundry room studio and finished it, much to the delight of his mother and several people who wanted to purchase this painting, which he entitled *His* (meaning God's) *Garden* (see p. 33).

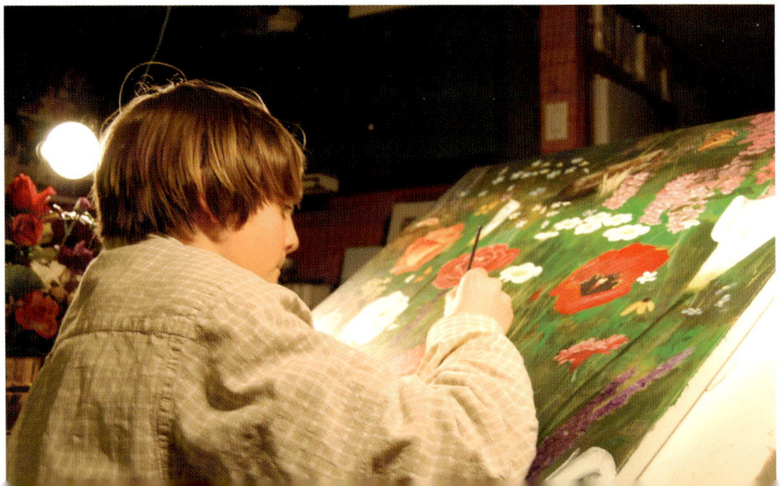

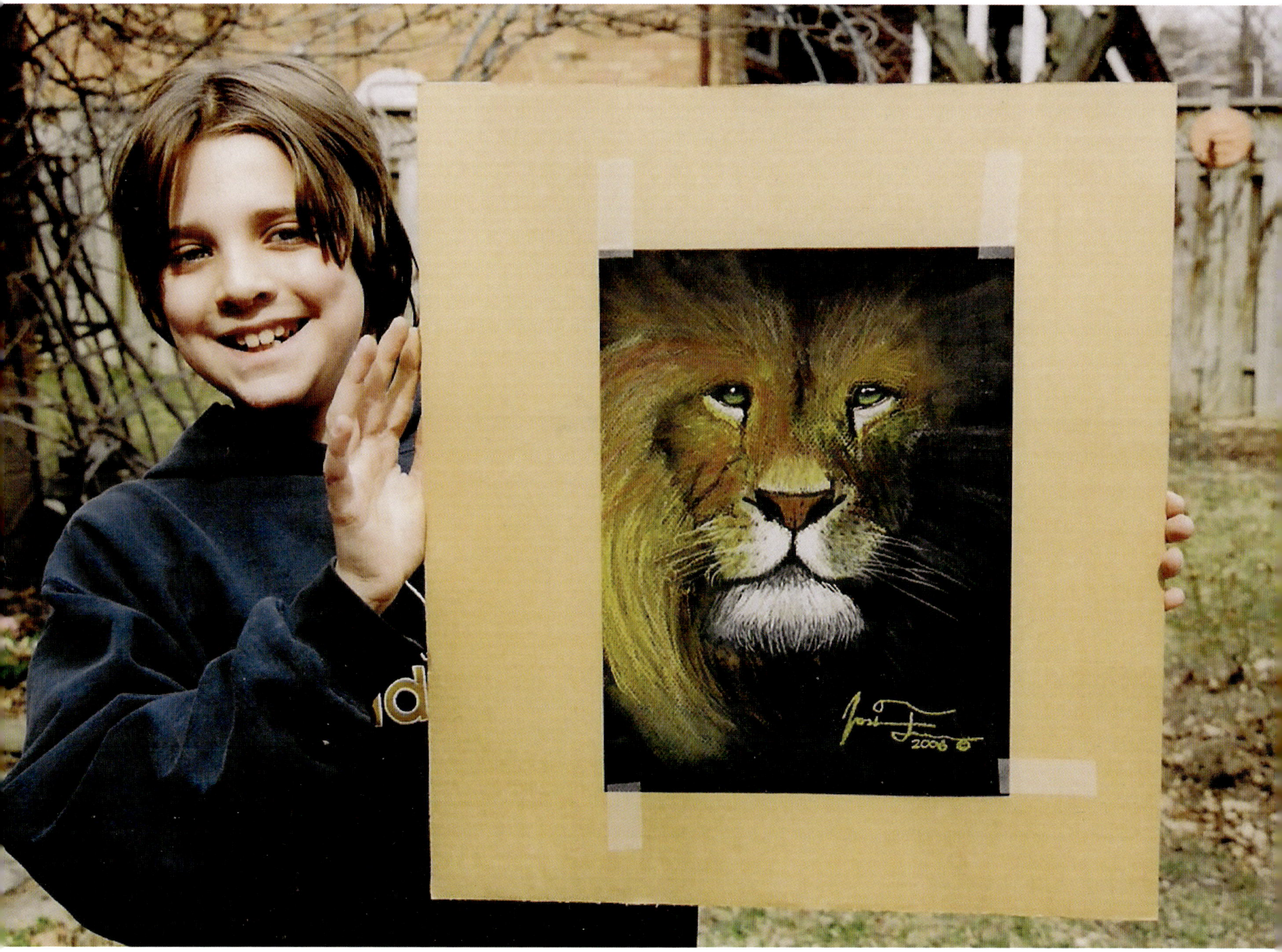

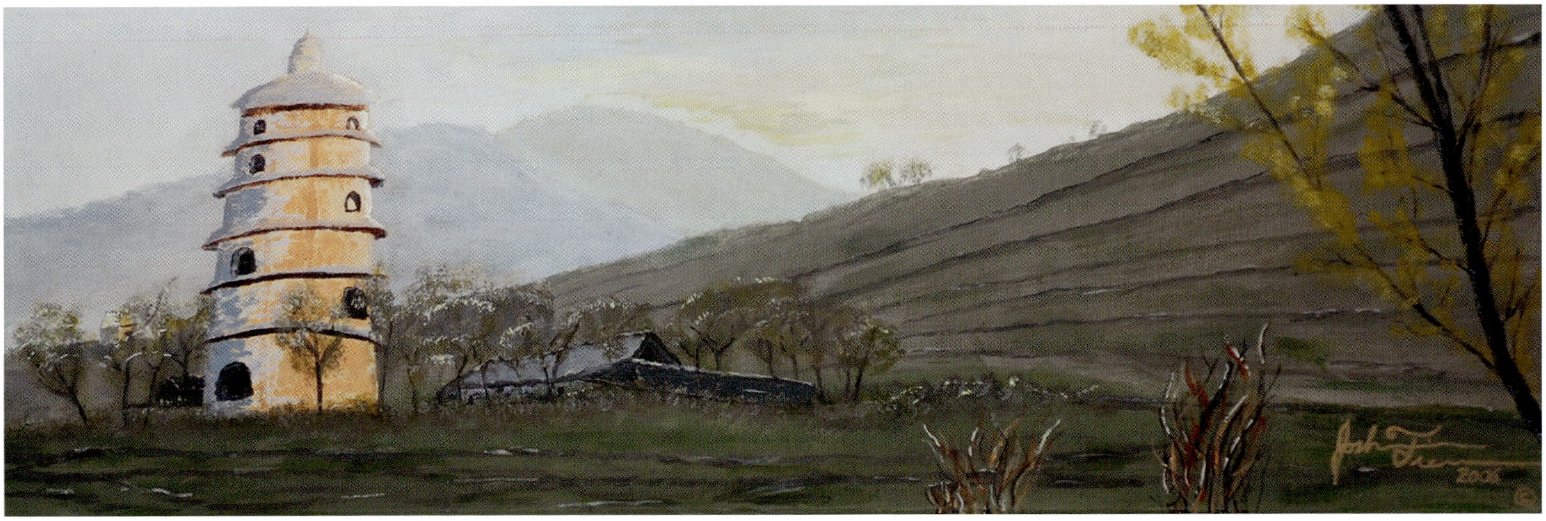

LOST MONASTERY IN CHINA
Acrylic on Canvas 12" x 30" 2006 (Age 11)

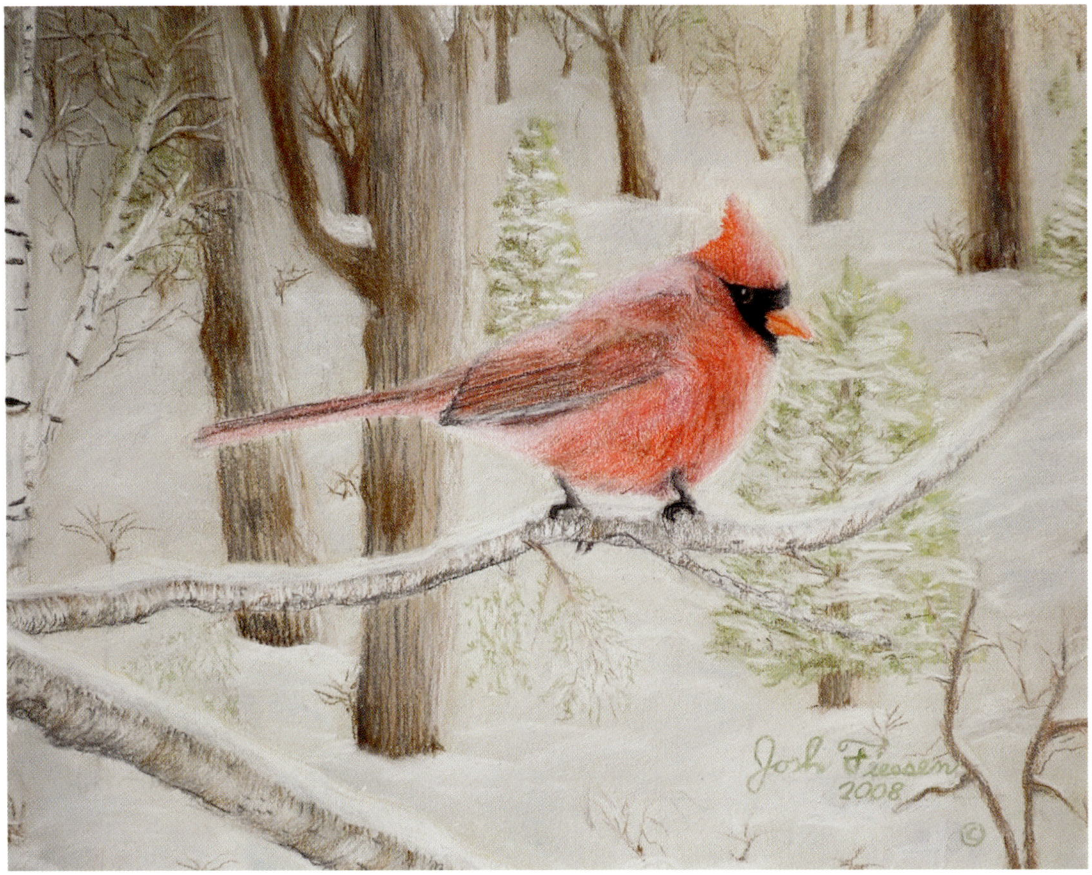

CARL THE CARDINAL
Chalk Pastel 9" x 11" 2008 (Age 11-12)

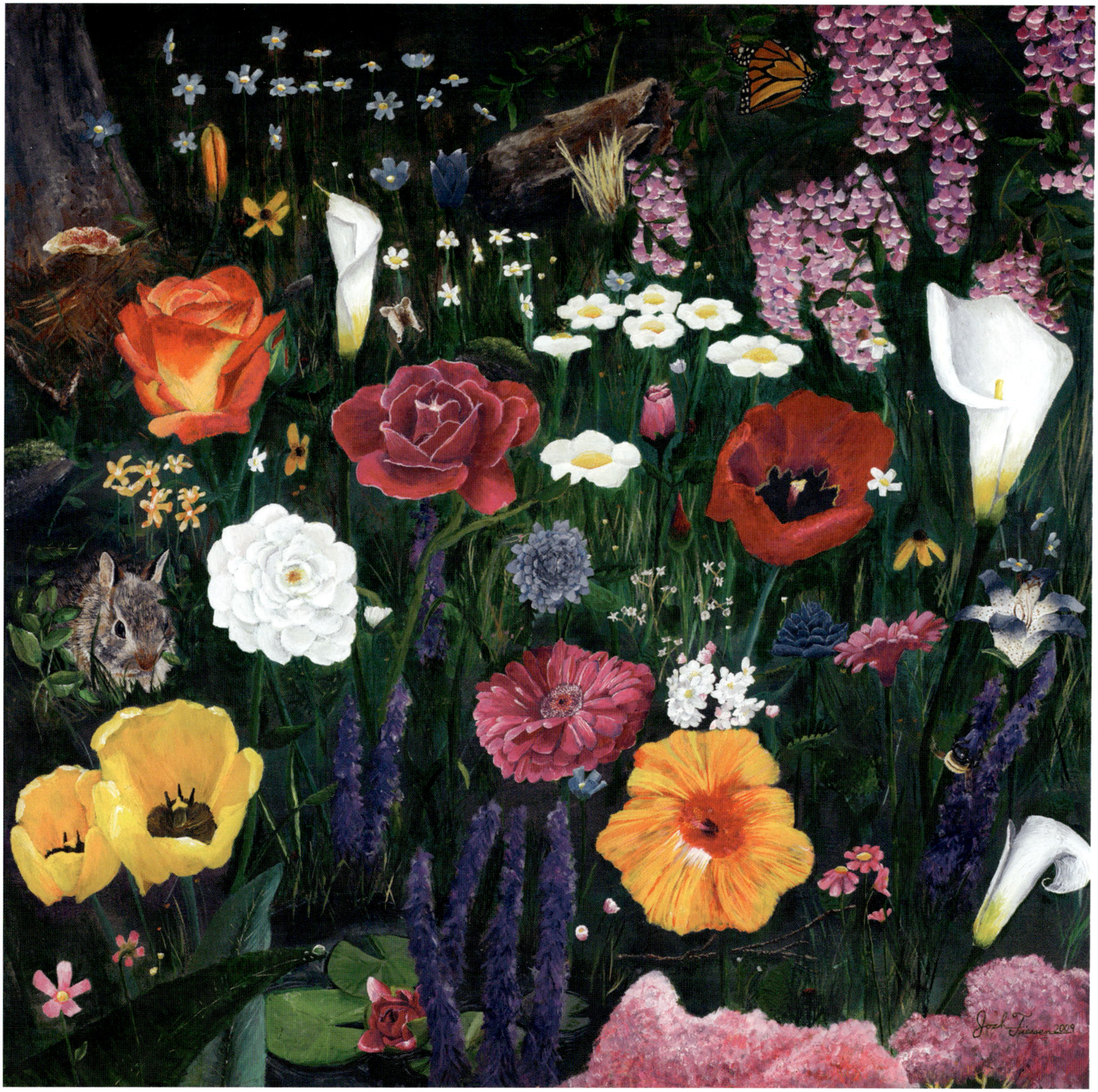

HIS GARDEN
Acrylic 30" x 30" 2009 (Age 12-13)

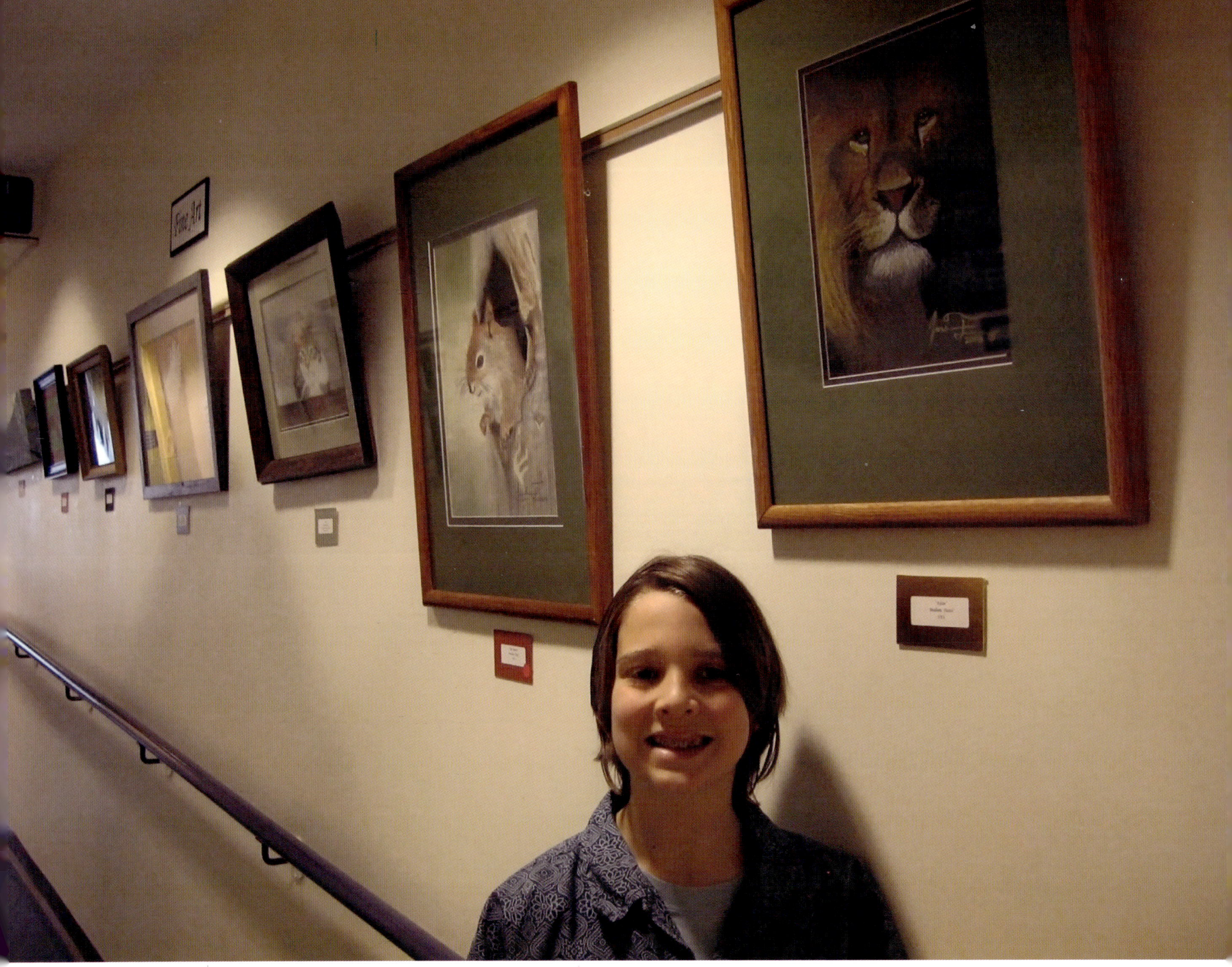
Fine Art

First Public Exhibitions

Alongside his painting, with newspaper delivery earnings Josh purchased his first camera and Adobe Photoshop computer program. He started into photography and graphic design with a little help from his dad, who had been a hobby photographer and was adept at learning computer programs. Josh caught on quickly as usual, and the student soon outgrew his teacher.

Josh was self-motivated and sensitive to capturing the beauty of the natural world in his photography. He challenged himself by finding unique angles on still life subjects. He started using compositional concepts like the 'rule of thirds' and off-centre subjects, which he then began applying to his paintings. At the age of ten Josh got his first assignment as 'official photographer' for his grandparents' anniversary tea. He bypassed most of the guests as he was mesmerized by the cake, china teacups and décor. Some of his photography became geometric and even abstract in nature, different than most of his paintings but a glimpse into another stylistic side of the creative artist.

After a few months of Josh being mentored under Valerie Jones, she asked Julie if she could book him for his first public art exhibition the next year. Julie retorted, "Val, he's ten!" With feigned indignation in her British accent Val snapped back, "So what! The public needs to see this child's work!" The following year at age eleven Josh held his first month-long solo exhibition in the Artway on Two at Joseph Brant Hospital in Burlington.

Right from the start, Josh used all his own money and designed his own posters and invitations on Photoshop, finding this to be a handy skill as an artist to save money. He also developed his first website, logo and business card, all of which would soon be replaced by new versions. Josh was always aiming for a higher level of professionalism, comparing his work to that of professional adults and wanting to reach that bar. His parents attributed it to inherited perfectionist tendencies, which carried over to every area of his art, and later his studio gallery business.

For his first exhibition Val showed the Tiessens how to hang and label Josh's art, encouraging him to make some of his pieces available for sale. This was a new concept to a child who had been giving his art as gifts to family members. Josh exhibited seven fine art pieces, six photos and six graphic designs. He hosted four weekly 'Meet the

Artist' noon-hours. His display stirred up a lot of interest at the hospital, where they had never exhibited such a young artist and were amazed by his talent. Someone phoned the local newspaper and they did a big article about him.

People started asking to purchase Josh's art, in addition to relatives and friends who were his first collectors. Josh was especially excited when the first stranger, a nurse, purchased one of his pieces. This was also around the same time that he did his first art commission. He was thrilled to see how the lady had it professionally matted and framed, and hung it in a prominent place in her home. Josh is still tickled to see his original paintings and limited edition giclée prints hanging in people's homes. His collectors have been very gracious, even eager, to loan their pieces back to him for exhibitions, and appear delighted to see them hung in fine art shows and galleries.

Val bought a small wooden drafting table for Josh at a second-hand sale when he turned twelve, and he soon set out on his own doing acrylic paintings on larger and larger canvases that he purchased himself. The first painting that he did from start to finish at home, which Val only saw after it was finished and hanging in the Tiessens' front hallway, was the *South African Cheetah*. He had chosen a more controlled, muted colour palette, which he increasingly preferred over bright colours as the young artist began to develop his own style.

When Val saw his painting she was flabbergasted by his advancement. Her only suggestion was that he 'push back' the background by fading the colours, so he made the revision. As with other artistic concepts, he caught onto an idea immediately and applied it in future paintings. Val liked the painting so much, that Josh decided he wanted to give it to her as a gift. But she insisted on purchasing it, so he gave her the 'family discount' and they were both happy.

Val introduced Josh to Curry's Art Store in nearby Hamilton, and he was like a kid in a candy shop! The cashiers smirked as this ambitious young boy would come up with such large canvases that they could hardly see him behind the counter. After a while they got to know Josh and realized he was doing more than just finger-painting on those canvases.

Acrylic paint was Josh's preferred medium because of its fast drying time, allowing him to put many layers over each other. Because of the paint's water-based consistency, he found it suitable for using with small-bristled brushes to achieve fine detail. Later, he would experiment with adding layers of oil paint on top of an acrylic underpainting, and come to prefer the slow drying time and richness of colour. Josh also discovered higher quality paintbrushes, like the ones he loves from Princeton Artist Brush Company, which eventually offered to endorse him. He receives boxes of high-end brushes and new product lines to try out and review, and they feature Josh and his art on their website.

Val observed that Josh had an eye for mixing paint accurately. He would establish a colour scheme, carefully prepare his paints and store them in aluminum tubes before beginning each new work. Although she would usually give some input and critique when she came to his house and saw his paintings in progress, Val started admitting that he had gone beyond her. In any case, by that point she had become more of a surrogate grandmother than an art mentor, so she was thrilled by it. Eventually she stopped critiquing his paintings altogether. Although they stayed in touch, the boy grew into a man and their relationship changed, but he will forever be indebted to her early influence on his art and career.

An expressionist artist challenged Josh to move beyond realism to what she viewed as a more mature expression in art. As a young teen Josh tried his hand at cubism and abstract-expressionism (see pp. 38-39). But he soon returned to the representational, realistic style that suited his meticulous personality, and which he felt captured his subjects the best.

Although Josh appeared quiet and perhaps even submissive back then, he had strong opinions and would come to trust his own intuition as an artist. Val and his parents gradually came to trust him too. Although they would throw in their 'two cents' here and there, they were well aware that Josh had his own mind. When choosing titles for his paintings, although he sometimes accepted their creative suggestions, he would always have the final say – and even if the family disliked it and teased him, in certain instances he was unmoved.

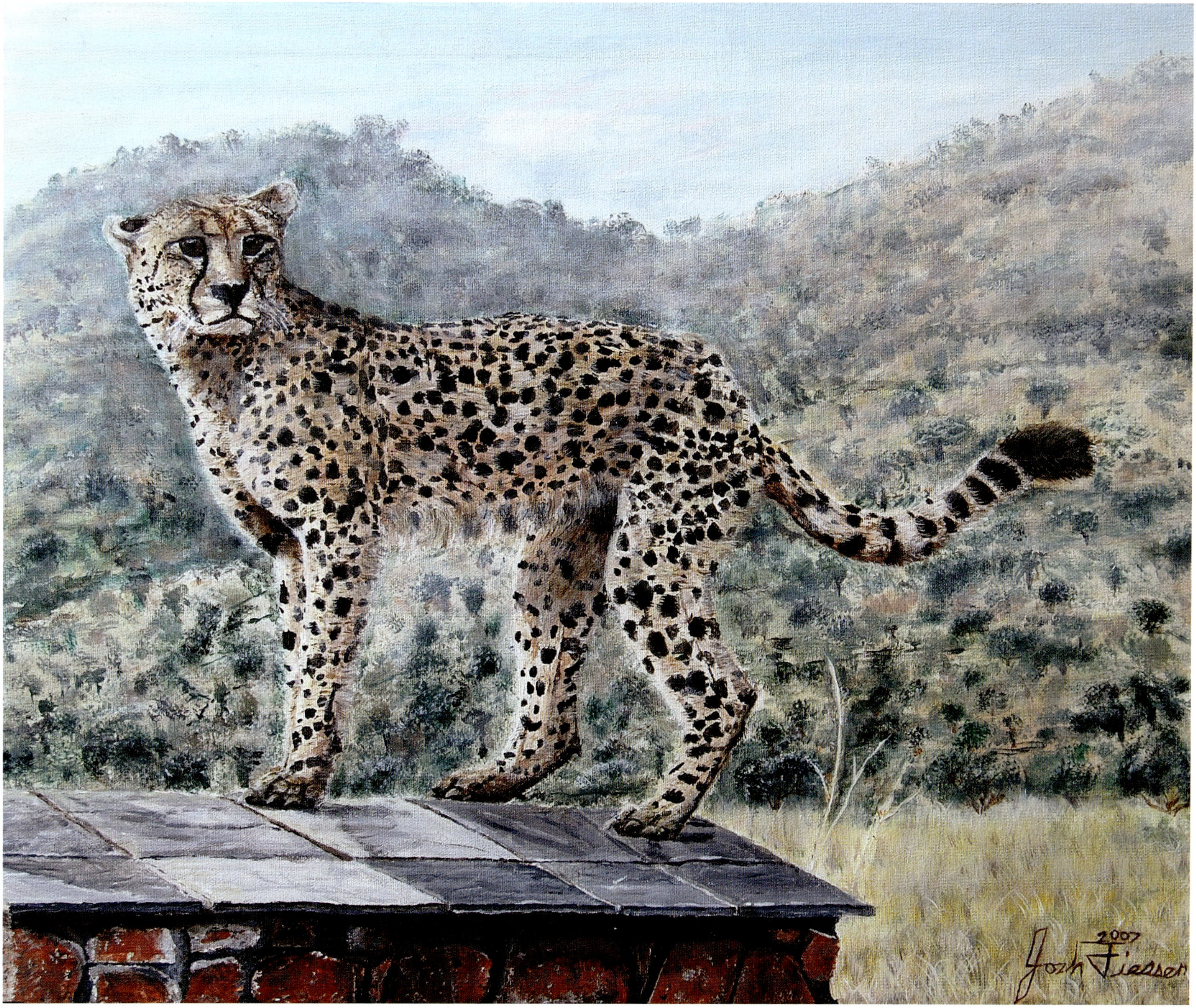

SOUTH AFRICAN CHEETAH
Acrylic on Canvas 20" x 24" 2007 (Age 12)

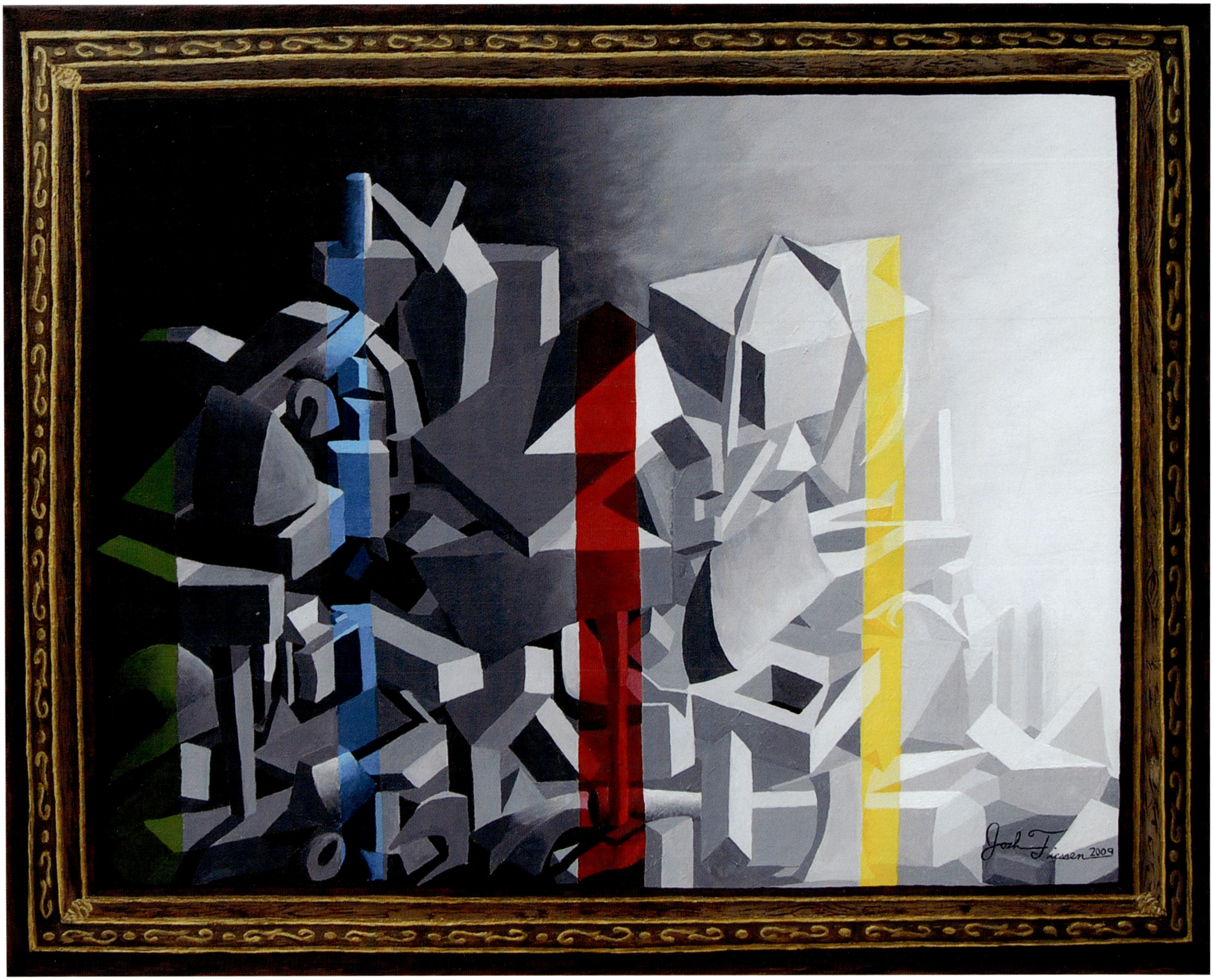

PERSPECTIVE ON LIFE

Acrylic on Canvas 24" x 30" 2009 (Age 13)

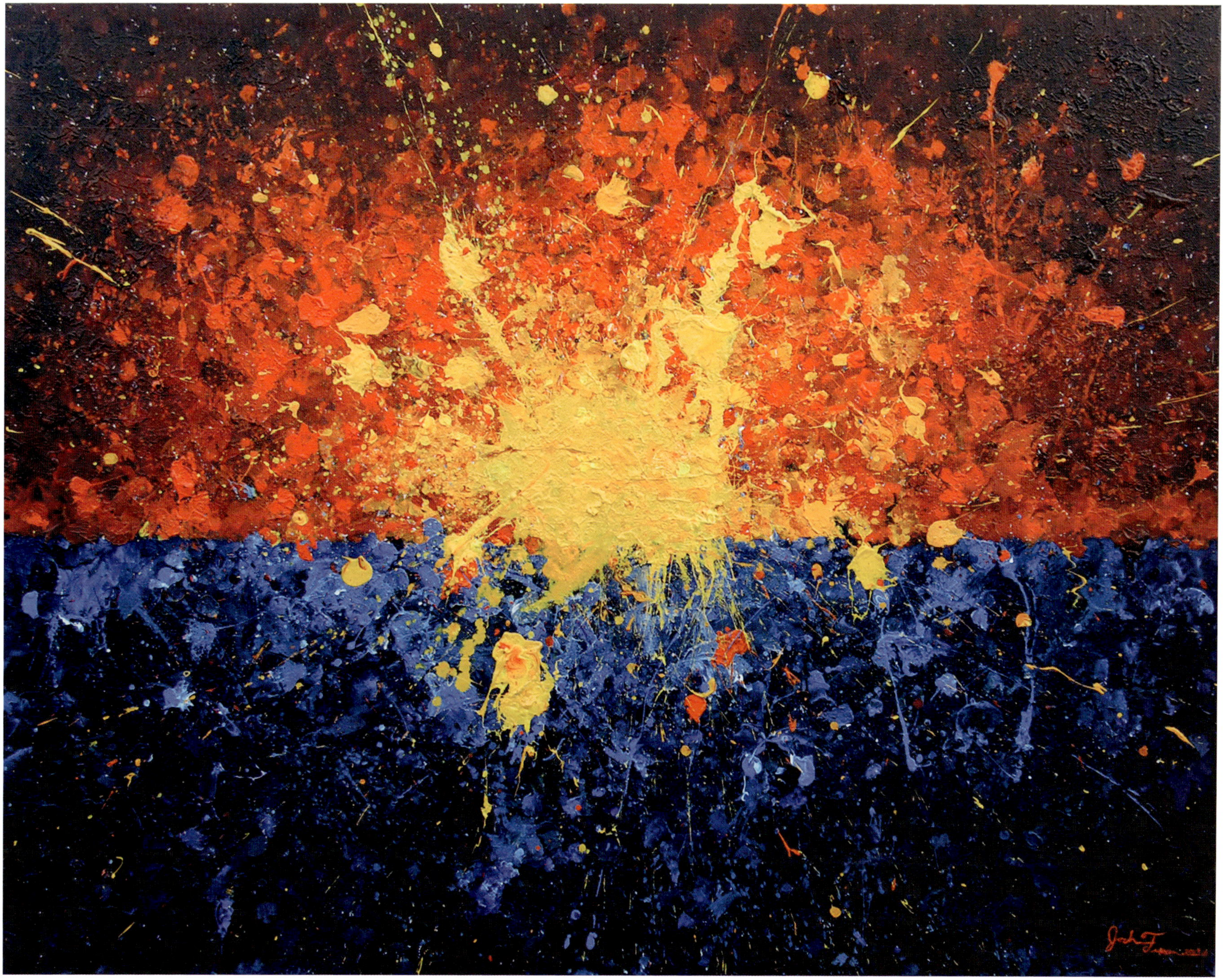

SUN SPLASH

Acrylic on Canvas 30" x 40" 2009 (Age 13)

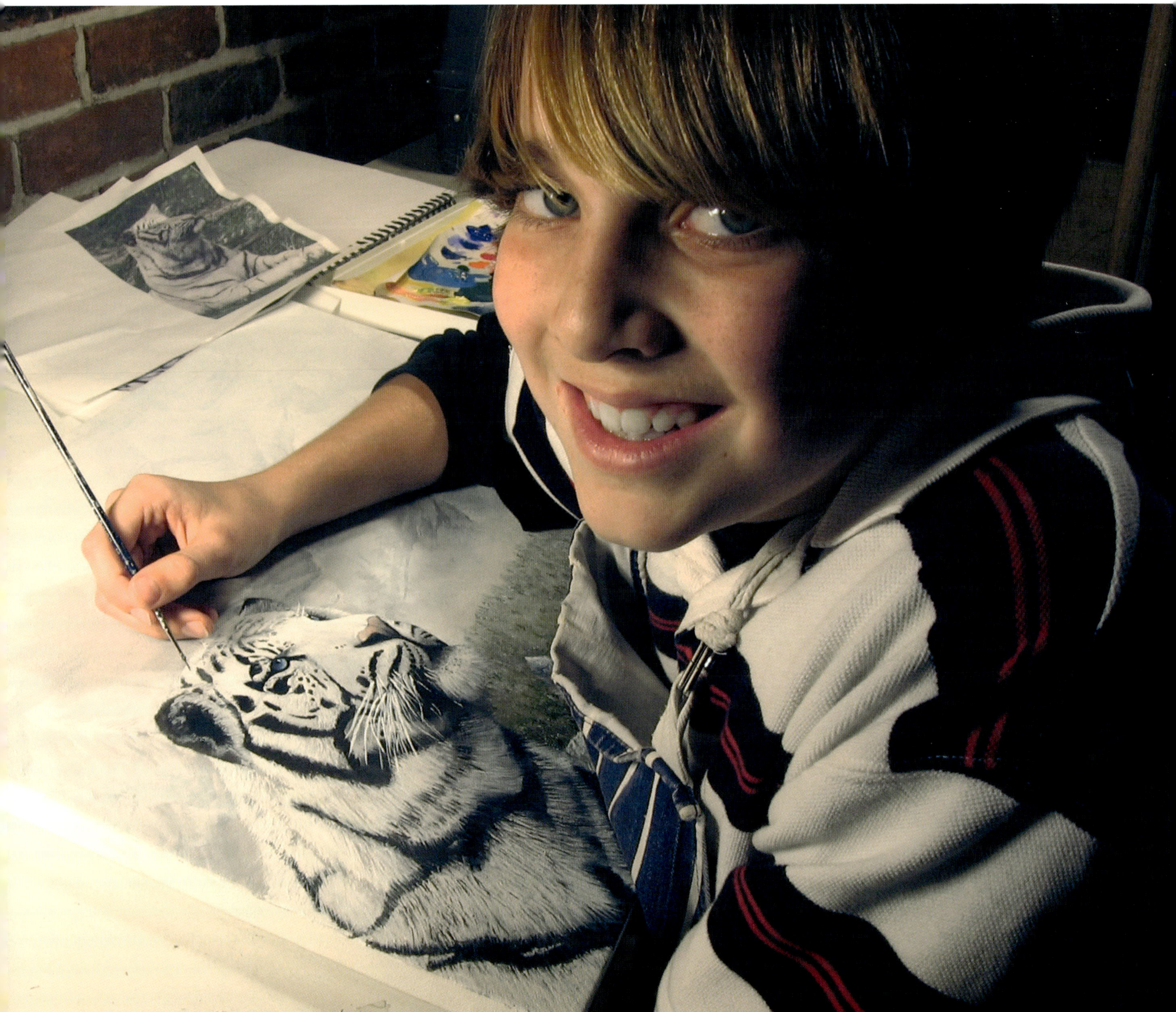

Not-So-Typical Teen

After his first exhibition at eleven Josh kept painting on his own, and displayed his art at a couple more local venues like Anastasia Art Gallery in Hamilton, Ontario. Shortly after turning thirteen, his grandmother saw an ad in the local newspaper for artists to submit their work to a small festival at The Wine Village in Stoney Creek. Josh sent in photos of his paintings and was selected as one of five artists from dozens of adults who applied. He was the only kid there. His parents sat back and chuckled as people came up to look at the art and saw Josh sitting beside it, but didn't think he could be the artist.

His display caught the attention of the local television reporter covering the event. He came later to Josh's studio, which was then located in the garage of the house they had moved to in Stoney Creek. They filmed Josh for a short segment, which was aired on the *Urban Cut* TV show. Little did the Tiessens know, this would be the start of a media frenzy over Josh that would happen in the years to come.

At the end of the television clip they included a glimpse of Josh shooting hoops at his basketball net, as they had asked about his other interests. Josh was one of those kids who seemed to be good at almost anything he tried. When the family started homeschooling, Julie enrolled the boys in an afternoon phys-ed program at the YMCA. With their membership, the boys could continue swimming lessons, plus choose one other sport.

The brothers had tried house-league soccer earlier on. Josh seemed to have a natural ability for it, but the family joked about him 'out picking daisies' since he would become focused on some wildflower or mushroom and forget to watch for the ball (foreshadowing a roadtrip in Nova Scotia, where they would leave on a ferry while he was photographing driftwood).

At the YMCA the boys chose basketball, as they had become interested in the sport from Julie's dad who used to play it himself, and now followed the NBA and collected cards. Josh loved to draw basketball shoe designs. Both boys wanted specific models of name brand shoes right from the start of playing – inevitably ones that couldn't be found in Canada. Every year it was a challenge for Doug to secure very specific pairs from the United States. The brothers were required to provide the additional funds beyond what their parents would normally spend.

At Josh's urging, for the boys' birthdays their parents replaced the Little Tikes basketball stand with a *real* regulation-sized model. Doug and the boys planned and painted a half-court on the parking lot beside their home in Burlington (formerly a group home for seniors). Josh would be out practicing for hours, rain or shine, just like his hero Steve Nash, with similar tenacity and determination. Both Josh and Zac excelled at YMCA basketball, quickly moving up levels to where they were limited only by their physical stature, playing with boys a few years older who had reached puberty.

One of the coaches recommended they try out for a rep-level city league, and they played at that level until they entered high school. Josh led his team to a win at the regional championships. In high school, once again they came up against a size barrier since they were younger than the other high school students. By this point, Josh was a year and a half ahead in school, which Julie presumed was due to homeschooling. Although the coaches seemed impressed with the Tiessen brothers' skills, and the other boys trying out said they would get on the team for sure, neither Josh nor Zac made the cut. In Zac's words, it was all "politics and popularity!" They later consoled themselves that their chances as two short white guys from Canada getting into the NBA were next to nil, so they busied themselves with other activities.

Josh had been longing for more time to spend on his art, so he decided from that point to make it a serious pursuit. Zac took up skateboarding. Still, both Josh and Zac would always enjoy shooting hoops together on their backyard patio in Stoney Creek – almost a half-court like they'd had in Burlington, only Julie wouldn't allow them to paint lines on the patio stones.

The brothers continued to follow the NBA and kept their beloved collectible jerseys hanging on their bedroom walls for several years. They gradually transitioned their room décor to art and music. By the end of high school, which they each finished before turning sixteen, they had sold the repainted basketball-theme furniture their mom had embossed with NBA logos. Zac purchased his own contemporary black and white furniture from Ikea to go with his music theme. Josh settled for old colonial wooden furniture from elsewhere in the house instead of his Ikea dream room, since by then his money was going into his studio gallery furnishings (from Ikea, of course).

As Josh spent more time on his art he spent less time watching television, and no time on gaming like other teenage boys did. But one extra-curricular activity Josh started as a preteen and continued through to the end of high school was Bible Quizzing. It was a highly organized program that fit his highly disciplined personality – a cross between the National Spelling Bee and Jeopardy. Each year the kids studied a different book of the Bible (about 800 verses) memorizing as much as they could to quote verses and answer questions about the content.

Since he was home educated and a grade ahead when he wanted to start quizzing, they let him into the program one year early. Josh faithfully studied ½ hour each day and memorized everything including chapter and verse numbers, soon becoming his team's *quote guy*. His coaches told him shortly after the start of the first year that, in the rare chance at regional competition he qualified for the international level, due to him being a year younger he would not be eligible. They didn't know Josh very well yet, but by the end of the year they were not surprised when he qualified. He was crestfallen when his coaches had to pull him from the final round of competition, and he sat holding back tears as he watched to the end.

The next year in Bible Quizzing Josh was even more determined. At the end of the year he received the "Most Improved Award" out of hundreds of teens in the region. That was the first of five years he qualified for the international competition, spending an hour studying each day in the months leading up to it. In his final year at internationals his team finished a close second. Everyone agreed that Josh, their team captain, had gotten them that far with his quick mind and uncanny ability to retrieve verses in a millisecond from his cranial computer. He quoted them verbatim, at lightning speed and seemingly in one breath, such that it made everyone nervous he might pass out.

By the end of each quizzing year Josh's study books were dog-eared and marked up like a rainbow, as he found highlighting aided his photographic memorization of the pages. When he finished high school two years early Josh was no longer eligible to stay in quizzing. In spite of his age, they asked him to be a regional official. He felt young and unqualified, but he really wanted to do it. Much to his consternation, art festivals and exhibitions would now prevent him from going to the weekend tournaments.

It still bothers Josh that he no longer has time to be involved in this program that he so loved and believed in. It left him with much of the New Testament committed to memory, a solid moral and ethical foundation for life. Josh still begins each day with systematic reading of the Scriptures. He also studies through distance education classes from a Bible College. It is, therefore, no surprise that Bible verses sometimes find their way into the stories he writes for his paintings.

When Josh was thirteen, along with his mother and brother, he went with a group from their church to the International House of Prayer in Ottawa, Canada's capital. The leader of the team was trying to think of a local artisan's work that the team could take as a gift for their Member of Parliament, Dean Allison, whom she had arranged to meet with and pray for at his office in parliament. Then she thought of the young artist who was going with the group... Josh!

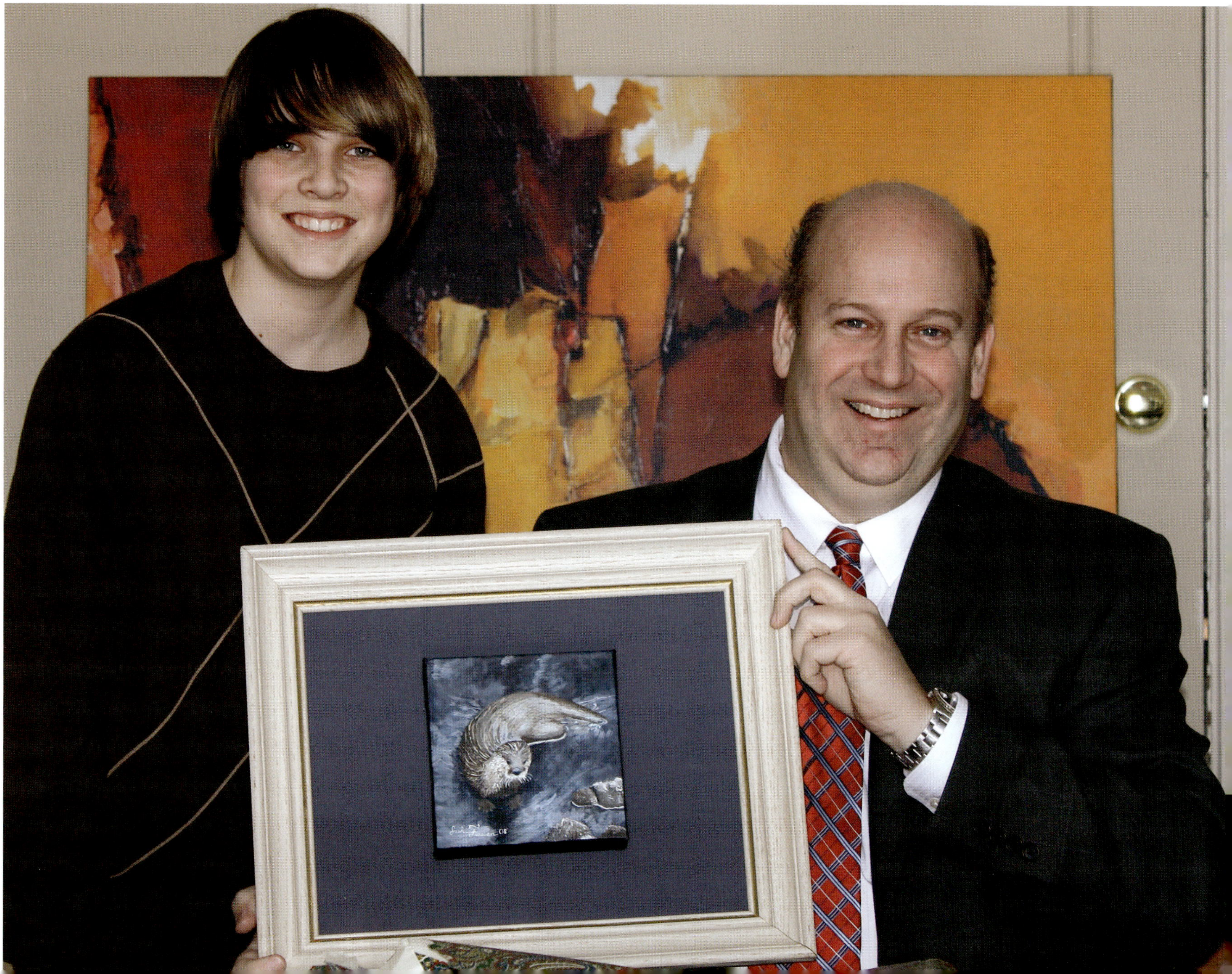

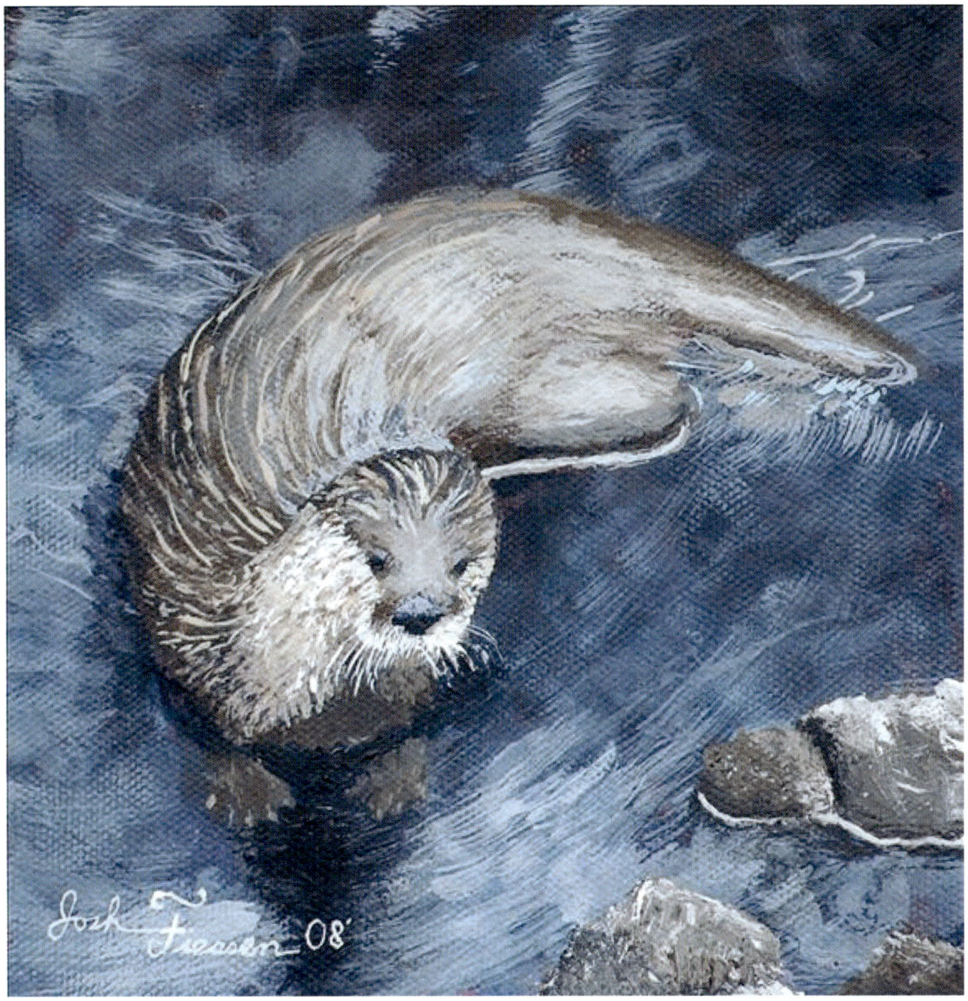

OSCILLATING OTTER
Acrylic on Canvas 5" x 5" 2008 (Age 12)

The team all agreed to ask Josh to donate a piece of his art, in exchange for help with his trip expenses. Josh was so shocked that they would consider his work worthy, and felt honoured to personally present this gift on behalf of the team. Dean was very gracious in receiving it from the young artist. He later sent Josh a photo of him with it hanging in his office and a personal note written on official parliamentary stationery. Five years later, Dean came to one of the yearly open houses at Josh Tiessen Studio Gallery, and the two re-connected.

At thirteen, Josh was also asked to be involved in a "Celebration of the Arts" at Paramount Drive Alliance Church in Stoney Creek, where he attended at the time. He started working on his painting *A Winter's Reward* as a visual expression of worship (see p. 87). He had become interested in penguins from watching the documentary, *March of the Penguins*. By the end of the service people could tell it would be a little penguin couple with their newly hatched fluffy chick. This depiction was a powerful metaphor that touched several people who were there and saw Josh paint it. A few of them requested to purchase it when it was completed, but of course only one could have the original. At people's request, Josh made his first reproductions, and many others have since purchased his signed limited edition giclée prints of this painting. People began requesting more and more prints. To date, Josh has over fifty print series, which in addition to his original paintings have been shipped to private and corporate collections worldwide.

Although artists had told him he'd never get into the Art Gallery of Burlington (formerly Burlington Art Centre), at fourteen Josh applied and was accepted for a month-long solo exhibition on the Community Wall. He hosted three 'Meet the Artist' Saturdays and crowds of people came. Even though he put "not for sale" on all the pieces, people requested them and Josh ended up deciding to sell more original paintings. He figured that after he had looked at them for a few months he would be happy to release them to those who wanted to enjoy them in their homes. Besides that, after a while he would begin seeing his mistakes and it would bother him. If he kept all of them the family would soon run out of space on their walls.

It was at that exhibition where Josh sold his first limited edition giclée prints, as well as the first artist notecards someone had suggested he design. This whole *art thing* was a steep learning curve for Josh and his parents, who were neither artists nor art entrepreneurs. They mostly acted on people's suggestions and were delighted by the results. When he chose the title "Launching into Fine Art" for that first gallery exhibition, Josh had no idea how much the experience would in fact *launch him* from what was initially just a hobby, into something that seemed like it could become a future career. But the future wasn't as far off as he imagined.

At the exhibition, people were advising that he enter art competitions. Josh didn't know where to begin, until someone emailed him about a provincial fine arts festival. At fourteen, he won the highest awards in painting and media arts for grades 9-12. The organizers of the event were so taken with Josh that they hauled him and his painting *Snow Leopards* up to the front and interviewed him in front of everyone (see p. 97). It was a welcome opportunity for him to speak about the meaning behind this painting, and to be an inspiration and encouragement to other teenagers at the competition.

By the next year, at the same competition, Josh's paintings had taken a huge leap forward in refinement. They had gone from realism to *high realism* as he relentlessly forged ahead, for nothing else but the sheer joy he experienced in the process. Adding to wildlife subjects, he had become enamoured with the interaction between the natural world and the man-made world. He was especially fascinated by the weathering effects of nature on architectural structures.

His *Behold The Door* painting, which he had completed while still fifteen, won "Best 2D Work in Show" and sold almost immediately afterwards (see p. 109). The buyers, who happened to be Josh's uncle and aunt from the farm in Saskatchewan, let him keep it for almost a year to exhibit. The *trompe l'oeil* (trick of the eye) effect of the peeling paint on the door looked so real that even in art galleries, where people usually know not to touch the art, patrons were spotted attempting to chip off flakes of paint with their fingernails. The painting could have sold many times over, to numerous collectors who requested it. After it was finally shipped off to its new owners, a giclée print series was initiated due to the demand. It quickly became Josh's most popular print, and remains so to this day.

That year at the same provincial festival Josh also won "Best Photography in Show" for his landscape of Scott

Island at Killbear Provincial Park in Northern Ontario, where he had enjoyed yearly vacations with his family. Josh loved photography almost as much as painting. However, he was already finding that once people saw his paintings they usually bypassed his fine art photography. His talent for intricate photo-like brushwork stood out as exceptional for his age. Still, he took his camera everywhere, using his skills as a photographer to take his own reference shots. He purchased better and better equipment with earnings from painting sales. After creating an original composition through small rough concept sketches, Josh would typically select up to thirty of his own photographs as references for each painting.

Initially Josh would print off his photos and tape them all around his easel. But when his parents started charging him for all the coloured ink cartridges he was blasting through, he soon purchased a Mac laptop and began arranging his photos in collages on his computer so he wouldn't have to print them. Using Photoshop he would move the photos around and refine the composition that he had already established in his sketches.

Doug built a computer stand out of old parts and mounted it on Josh's easel. Now Josh could easily refer at the click of a button to any of his reference photos, as he often zooms in on small details as he paints. He could also switch to answering emails and doing social media posts from his easel. He views these as a 'necessary evil' for promoting his art on the contemporary market. Of course Josh would rather just paint all day.

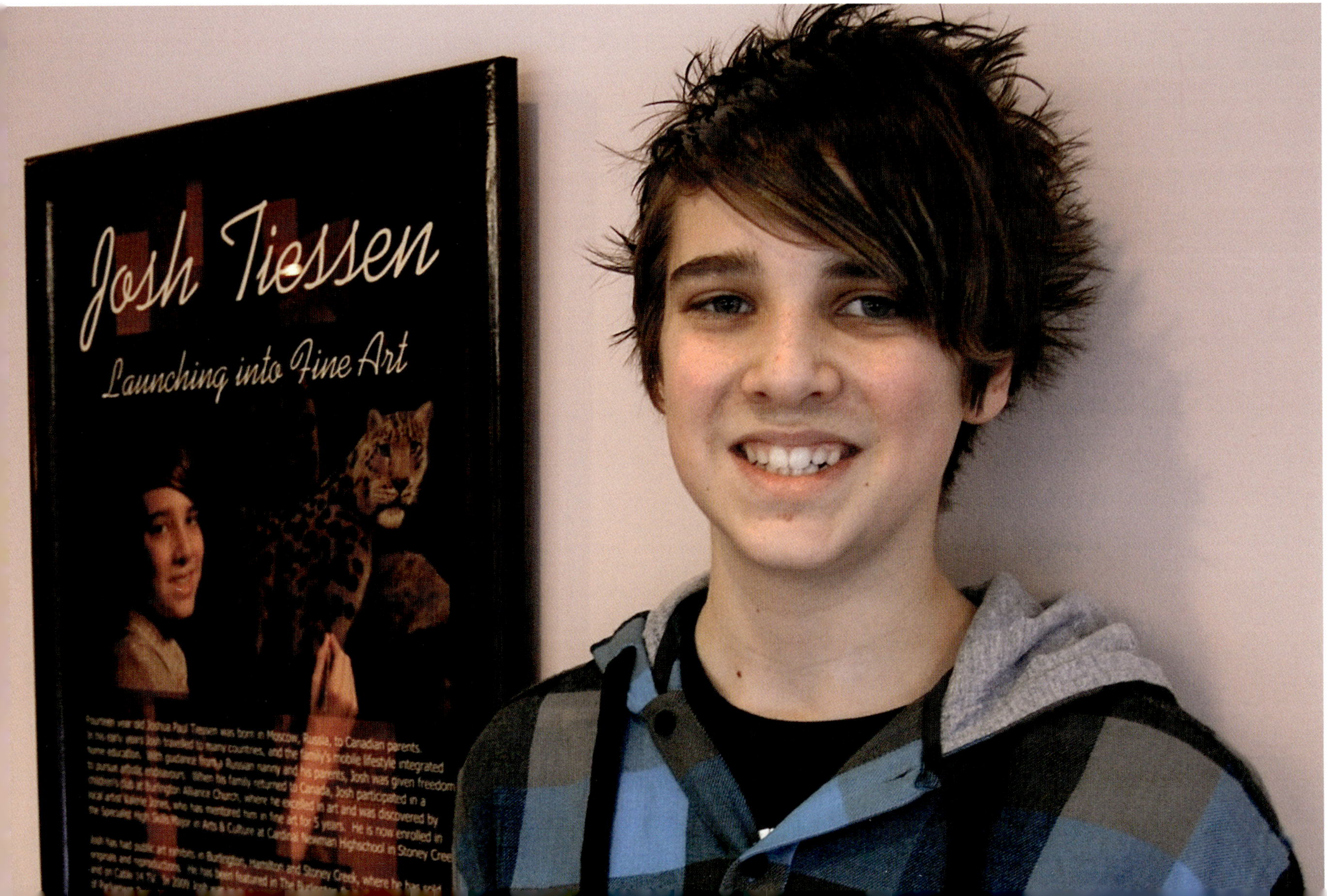

Mentored by a Master

A number of admirers had suggested that Josh's work reminded them of foremost Canadian wildlife artist Robert Bateman. Since Bateman got his start in Burlington, it was suggested that Josh write him and let him know about his exhibition at the Art Gallery of Burlington. Although Bateman lives on Salt Spring Island in British Columbia, he still supports this gallery. So Josh wrote him a letter and sent some photos of his wildlife paintings a few months before the exhibition.

The day after they took down Josh's paintings from the gallery exhibition, he received a personal email from Bateman answering his questions and giving him advice about post-secondary education. He wrote, "You are indeed very good," and invited Josh to a Master Artist Seminar that he was holding in British Columbia for a select group of artists. He said Josh would likely be the youngest person there, but judging by his talent he could benefit from it.

Josh's relatives, who happened to be visiting and were sitting at the family's dining room table when the email came in, immediately offered airmiles. But Doug and Julie were still doubtful that he could go. There would be other expenses they probably couldn't afford. Doug had fallen ill with Chronic Lyme Disease and was without an income for two years, while he fought to get on Long Term Disability.

About a month later, when they finally got around to phoning Hollyhock Educational Retreat Centre where the seminar was to be held, it happened to be the *one day of the year* that their board met to decide scholarships for the whole year. They looked at Josh's website and emailed saying he was "quite the protégé!" That same day Josh received a letter in the mail from an older artist he barely knew, with a cheque for $500. A few days later he got an email from the Hollyhock board granting him a scholarship that would cover his accommodation and meals. Later, the local Kiwanis Club also gave him a $500 donation in exchange for one of his original paintings. Josh had been praying about all these details with his parents, and it seemed obvious that he was meant to go.

Josh had turned fifteen by the time he flew across the country to the Robert Bateman Master Artist Seminar, which was held on Cortes Island. He was the youngest participant among professional artists from across North America and even Europe, who were mostly double to triple his age. Robert Bateman taught from morning to night for five days. At that time he was a little over eighty years old, but looked and acted like sixty-five. He told stories from his long career and painted in front of them, showing how he worked on a painting from start to finish. Josh learned some helpful techniques and began assimilating them into his own paintings.

Bateman's influence on Josh can be seen most in the painting he completed right after returning from being mentored under him, entitled *Solitude* (see p. 103). From there Josh would go on to develop his own style, increasingly characterized by deep saturated colours, a limited and often dark palette, and strong *chiaroscuro* (dynamic shift of light to dark values).

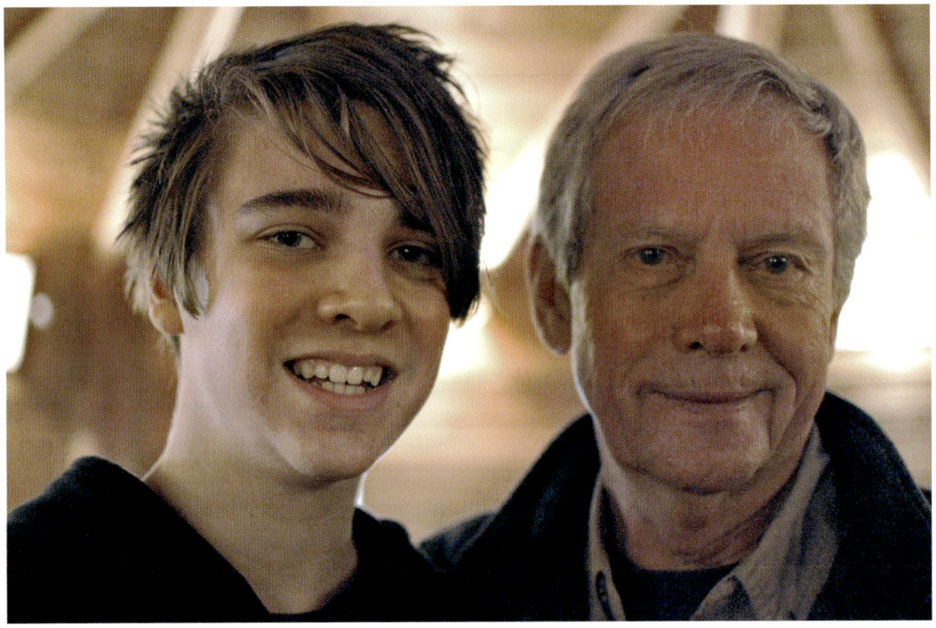

Bateman and the other artists at the seminar were gracious in answering Josh and his mom's questions. Bateman was fine with Josh attending the seminar on his own, but Hollyhock required him to have a chaperone to stay there. Julie made the sacrifice and spent a week on a beautiful island. Apart from being chased down by a growling cougar late one evening going up a dark path to meet Josh after the session, she had a great time and tried her best to get some photos of Josh. He was also able to take photos of wildlife and landscape as references for future paintings.

Josh and his mom learned so much from the generous artists, who gave them advice about sending out press releases, applying to artist guilds, doing limited edition prints, and submissions for jury into art festivals and galleries. Amazingly, these professional artists accepted Josh as a colleague and he made some new long-distance friends that he still has today. They tried to help him understand that he was no longer an amateur artist, since he already had several exhibitions under his belt and was consistently selling his art, making a decent part-time income for a teenager.

Along with Bateman, they also taught him how to price his art properly, as Josh was underselling his fine detailed work. Even though Josh has since raised his prices several times, many contemporary realist artists of his caliber are selling for more. Each large painting takes up to 500 hours, so it's not like abstract or expressionist art, which is done much faster. Less than one year later, by his sixteenth birthday Josh was making an adult's full-time income, which he viewed as a blessing, enabling him to do what he loved and share it with others.

The highlight of Josh's week with Bateman was when he critiqued a piece of his art. Josh was nervous, since "Bob" as he insisted they call him (out of respect Josh still can't) decided to do the critiques anonymously. That meant Josh's painting would be critiqued alongside the work of the established professional artists who were there. When Bateman did the critiques, Josh was surprised at how critical he was toward some of the pieces that Josh initially thought were very good, so he was even more nervous. But Bateman gave Josh's *Nesting Trumpeter Swan* a positive critique, and the young artist breathed a sigh of relief (see p. 50).

After the session that day, Josh finally got a chance to ask Mr. Bateman if he would sit with him for dinner. Bateman said to save him a seat. When he joined Josh and Julie, and figured out that it was his *mom* and not his *sister* accompanying him, the three of them had a special visit together. Josh and Julie were able to ask him many questions, and he shared very openly with them. They learned so much in one meal that would literally set the course for Josh's future.

When Bateman heard about Josh's exhibitions and sales, he pronounced him "precocious," giving the analogy of a precocious bird that learns to fly quickly. He also told Julie that an artist could not do it alone, so she and her husband would have to step up and help Josh in his career. The other professional artists also urged her to become more proactive, so from then on she did. Due to the demand on Julie's time the following year, to be fair Josh decided to start paying her a percentage of his sales, but she would only take a small amount. The mother was now officialy working for her teenage son.

After dinner with the Tiessens, Bateman must have found on his computer which piece had been Josh's in the critiques. The next day during his outdoor painting session he announced to the whole group that the *Nesting Trumpeter Swan*, "that amazing piece" as he called it, was done by Josh the precocious fifteen-year-old. Josh was a little embarrassed to be centred out, but said that Mr. Bateman's compliment made him feel as if his heart would leap out of his chest!

A few weeks later, when a relative in Calgary read about this on Josh's website, he purchased the painting sight-unseen. That was the first time they shipped a painting away, so it was a bittersweet experience for Josh. But it was the first piece that sold at his *new prices*. So it was another big sigh of relief for Josh, as he thought no one would ever pay that much for one of his paintings. The man told him on the phone that he knew this kind of fine detailed art, and Josh should not be apologetic since his work was worth the price.

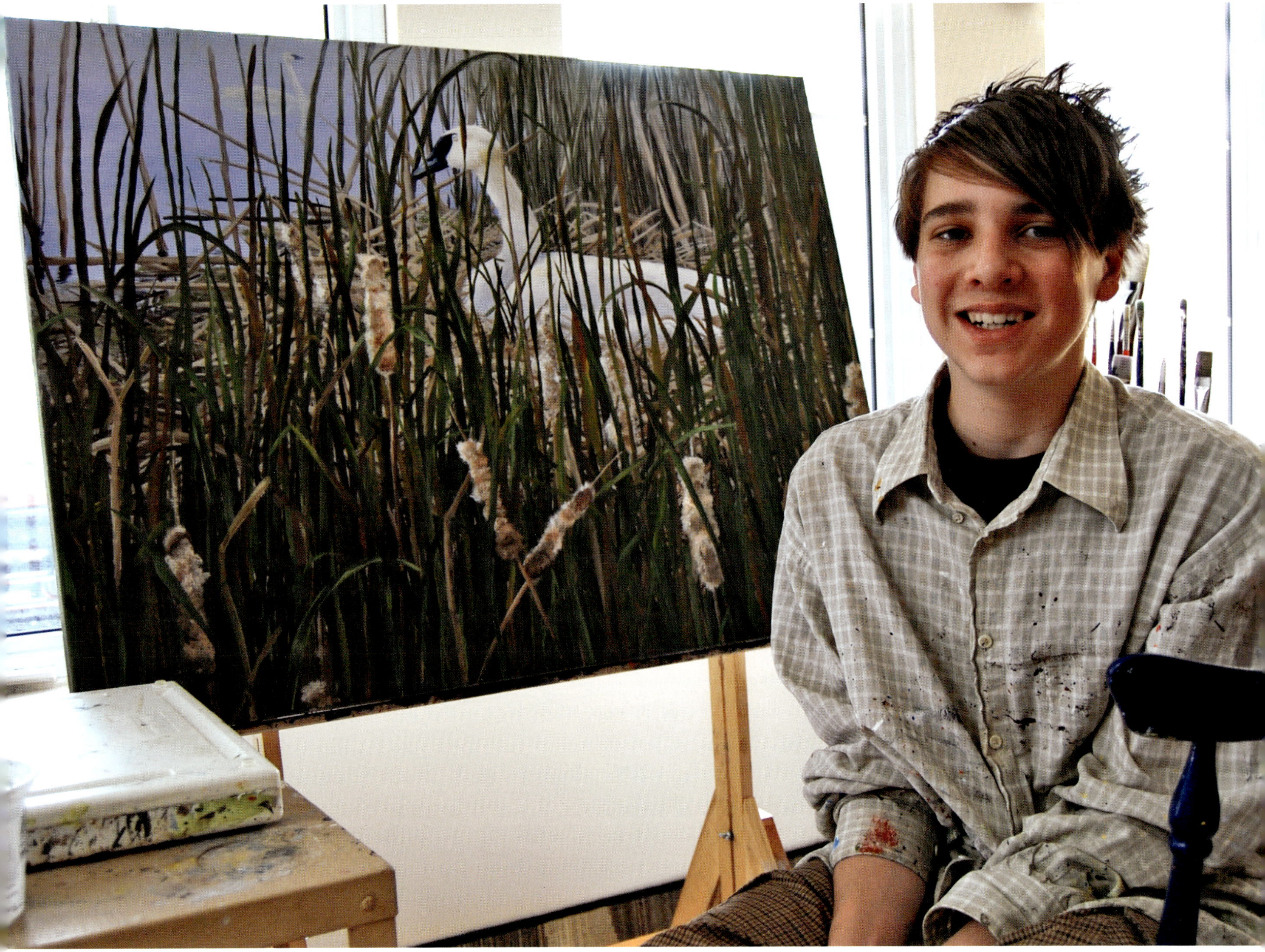

The Snowball Effect

After being with Bateman, Josh and his mom got to work following up on all the advice he and the other artists had offered. As a result of the Press Release they were told to send out with a photo of Bateman and Josh, he started to be featured in numerous newspapers, magazines and on a video documentary. He was also interviewed on a Christian television show that was aired across Canada, and later around the world. As she had noticed on other artists' CVs, Julie started keeping a record of press and media on Josh's CV, which was prudent as there are now over 140 entries to date.

The computer-savvy artist began posting the articles and videos on the website he had created. Josh continued re-designing his site, always frustrated that his was never as good as the most accomplished professional artists' sites. His parents reminded him that theirs were probably done by professional web designers... but neither did Josh want to pay thousands of dollars to have someone else do it. As his mom and dad teased, from a young age Josh was a '*me do it*' type of kid. He continued improving his website by reading and watching tutorials to enhance his skills, and taking community college graphic design courses.

Through the media and his website, Josh felt that God was increasing his opportunity to use his art as a way to draw people's attention back to the Creator. Josh's work has been greatly influenced by his faith in God, whom he believes designed and created the amazing world we live in. He also views God as the Source from which people get their capacity to create, since we're made in His image. Although Josh's art is not necessarily *religious* in subject matter, he tries to illustrate the beauty and diversity of creation and the image of God in human creativity. He sees his artistic ability as a gift from God. As a contemporary artist in the 21st century, he would like to be a positive and uplifting presence in the art world. Josh says that he hopes people looking at his art will feel the sense of "wonder and awesomeness" that is in the natural world all around us.

As he begins each painting Josh prays, asking God to work through the process. As a result, just like the little penguin family, metaphorical and spiritual meaning seem to be infused into his paintings and people often comment on the analogies they draw from them. Many people who have purchased Josh's art have done so not just because they like it, but because of the deeper meaning behind it.

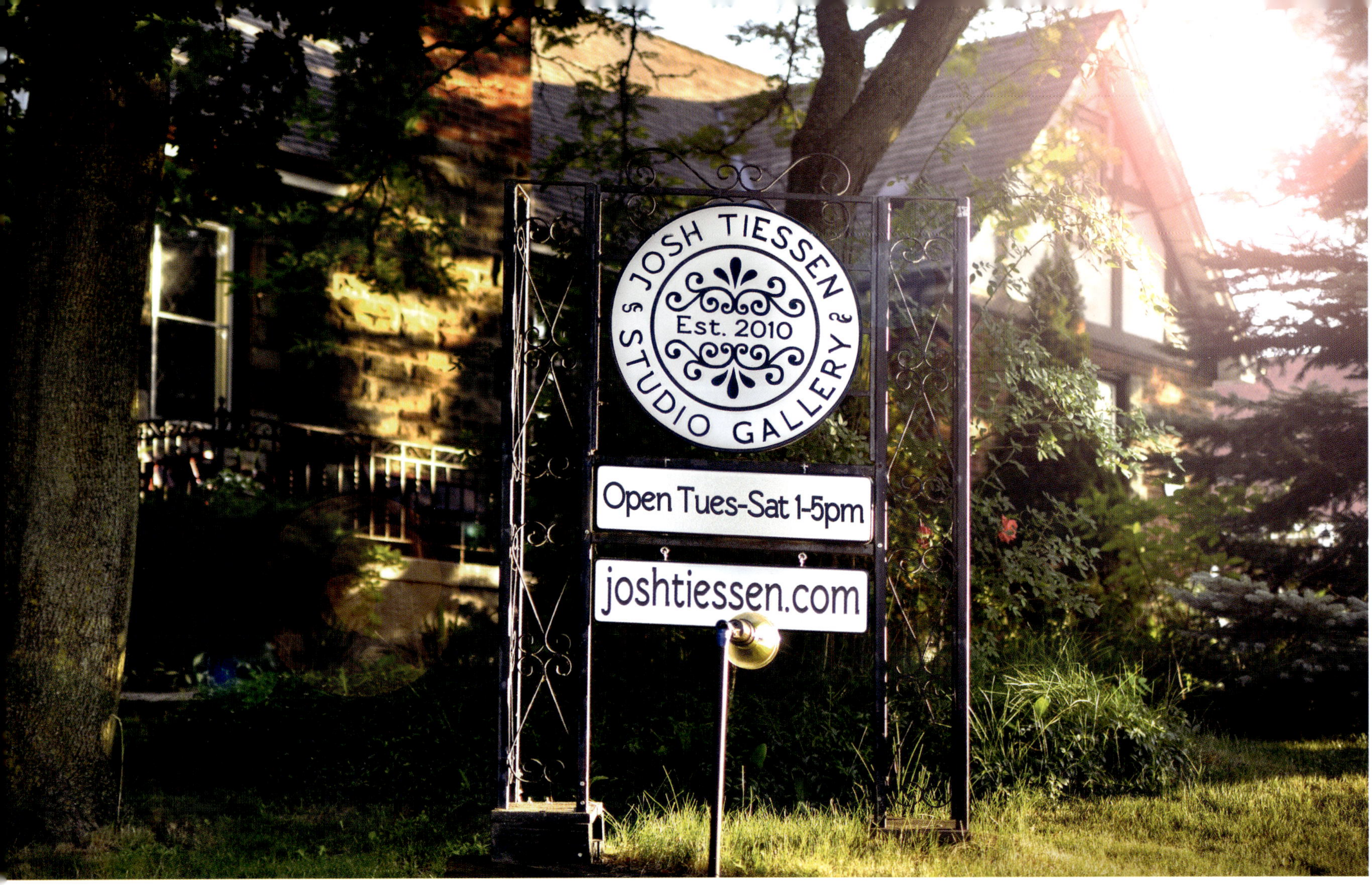

While Josh posts the story descriptions for each of his paintings on his website and social media, he does not intend them to be didactic. He is always open to people making their own interpretations and sharing their discoveries from his art. To date, Josh has sold upwards to ninety original works in fine art, photography and graphic design. It always amazes him how God speaks to people's hearts even through seemingly non-religious art. He asserts that, "it shows how God's work through visual art is not limited to religious symbols; it is a reflection of common grace and general revelation."

In 2010, when Josh was fifteen he designed signs and opened his own Josh Tiessen Studio Gallery, at the back of his family's home on a busy corner in the historic town of Olde Stoney Creek. The garage had gotten too cold, and it was embarrassing taking collectors down to the laundry room, where Josh had splattered paint all over the new washer and dryer. So Doug and Julie offered to move their large library out of the sunroom at the back of the house, in order for Josh to set up his studio gallery with its own entrance. In the natural light from skylights, and windows spanning the width of the house, Josh paints for many hours each day, to the sights and sounds of a deep yard full of chirping birds, squirrels and rabbits, with a south-facing view of the Niagara Escarpment. He enjoys walking from his house to the Bruce Trail of the escarpment, and in the opposite direction he can bike a couple kilometers north to the Waterfront Trail on the shores of Lake Ontario.

Someone suggested Josh have an open house for his new studio gallery, so he designed posters and invitations. He was delighted by all the businesses in Stoney Creek that were happy to meet him as their neighbour and willing to hang his posters (seven years later, they still do this for him every year). Over 250 people and press from the community came that weekend, and more people and politicians came subsequent years. Word got around that there was this talented young artist on the corner of King and Gray. The Tiessens were glad they took the risk a couple years earlier, purchasing a home on a major corner not far from the historic downtown and the Queen Elizabeth Way (QEW) highway.

Josh, a natural introvert, grew in his social skills and confidence through interactions in the community and having visitors to his studio gallery on a call-ahead basis. Recently, he established regular business hours after being approved for Ontario Attraction Signs on the QEW highway, which is only a few kilometers away. People travelling between Toronto and New York State are finding their way to Josh Tiessen Studio Gallery in greater numbers. For the past two consecutive years, he has been voted #1 (Diamond) in the Reader's Choice Awards for "Best Local Artist" *and* "Best Art Gallery," unseating the larger more established galleries that held the position in years past. Always softhearted, Josh's first response upon winning was concern for how the others might feel.

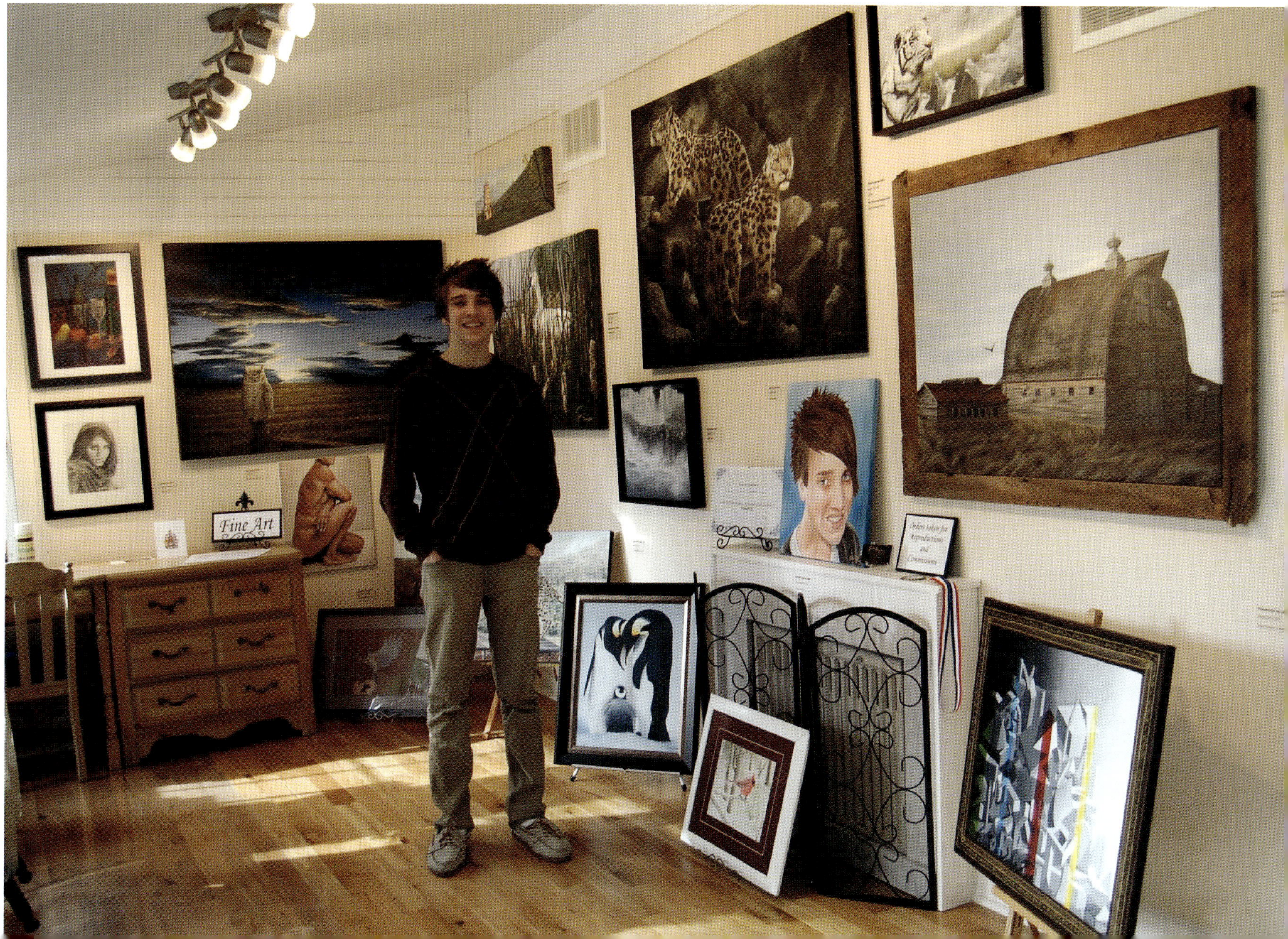

In addition to the open house he holds at his studio gallery every December, Josh later initiated a Spring artist studio tour in his town, which he called the Stoney Creek Studio Stroll. He recruited other professional artists, designed the brochure, and found local advertisers to help sponsor the cost. He coordinated it with the biggest local tourist event of the year, the Re-Enactment of the Battle of Stoney Creek (a pivotal battle during the War of 1812). It is held every year at the historic Battlefield Park, located just down the street from Josh Tiessen Studio Gallery. After a successful first year, the other professional artists on the tour, all adults, remarked that it took a sixteen-year-old to finally get something off the ground in Stoney Creek.

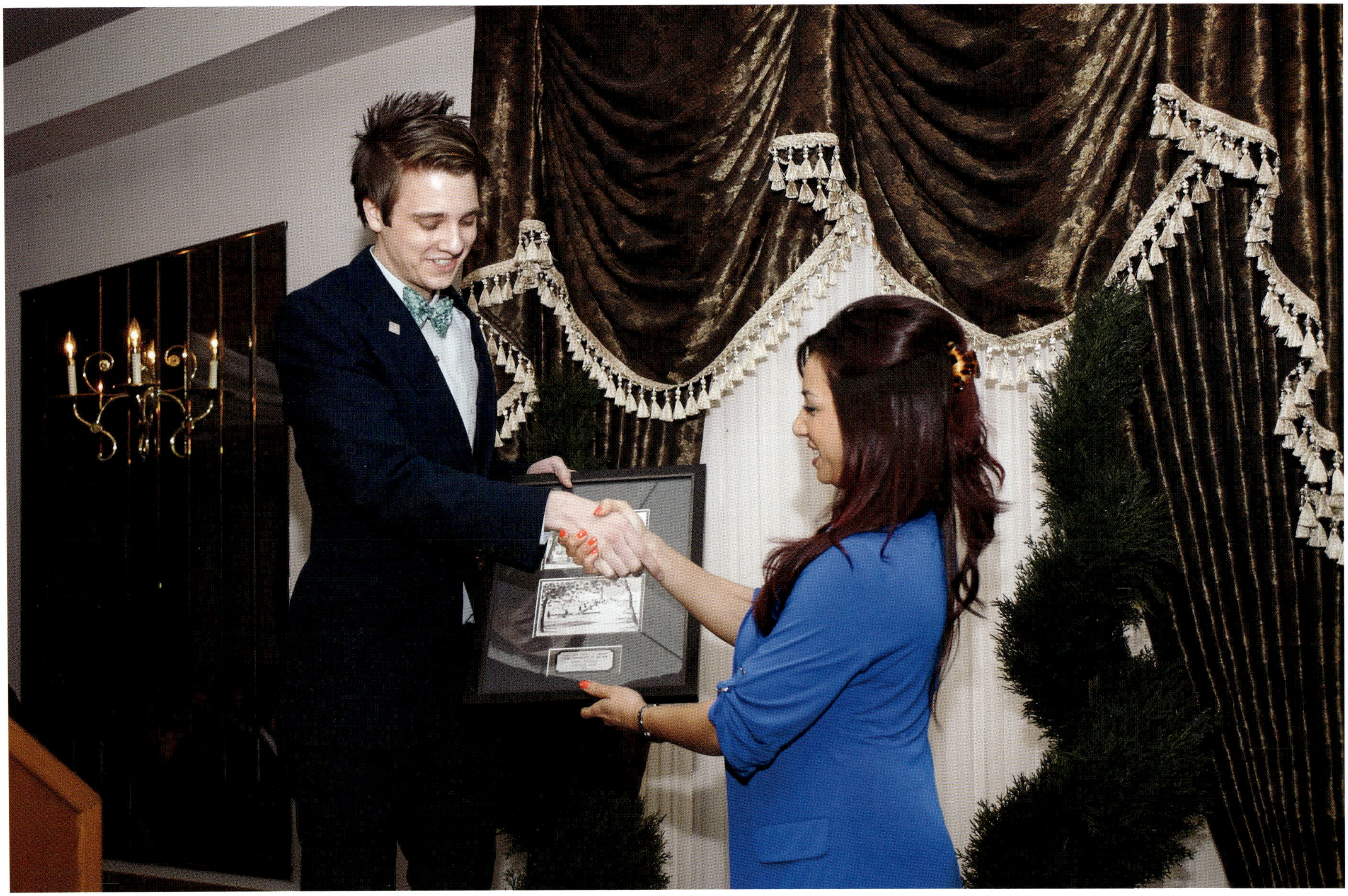

Photo by The Stoney Creek Chamber of Commerce

Entrepreneur and Philanthropist

From the start, Josh wanted to make this studio tour "art with a purpose." He ensured that the other artists each chose a charity and promoted it with a display in their studio, committing to donate a portion of their sales afterwards. As Josh does during his open house, they also collected items at each studio for the local food bank in exchange for a draw ballot for a free piece of art. The artists dropped off several loads of food afterwards. Josh inspired other artists to make a difference in the community by giving back, instead of having the typical 'starving artist' mentality.

With every year Josh sought to make the studio tour bigger and better, encouraging the community to *buy local* when it comes to art, rather than at the big box stores. With funding from the city granted to hold a festival, eventually the studio tour was merged into a new event called Saturdays in the Creek. As an associate member of the Stoney Creek BIA, Josh serves on the planning team for this larger event. Although his studio gallery is located a couple blocks east of the downtown, Josh takes every opportunity to connect and participate with the business community.

As a teenager Josh was already becoming a respected entrepreneur and leader in the local art and business community. He grew comfortable with being the youngest person by far at many community events attended by businesspeople and politicians. At seventeen, Josh was awarded "Young Entrepreneur of the Year" by the Stoney Creek Chamber of Commerce.

Josh appreciated how the whole community, and even the region, got behind him. After his first open house galleries began to express interest, but Josh soon realized they take 50% of sales. The entrepreneur in him did not like the sound of that. He was selling enough from his own studio gallery and juried art festivals. In fact, Josh was selling his paintings almost as fast as he could paint them, with pre-solds and commissions piling up. Eventually Josh began exhibiting in galleries other than his own for greater exposure, as in the case of international exhibitions in the United States, where there is a much larger market for contemporary realist art.

Josh submitted a painting for the first time at age sixteen to the Art Gallery of Burlington's yearly auction. He was the youngest artist (as usual by far) to be juried in. His painting *Unabandoned* (see p. 101) sold in the top ten highest priced pieces out of 101 entries, alongside the works of his mentor Bateman and other well-known Canadian artists. Josh and his parents have always prayed together for God's guidance with each new opportunity that has come up. He often publicly acknowledges them and expresses gratitude for how they have helped him.

In addition to selling his art, from the time that he was an early teenager Josh had started contributing his photography and graphic designs to be used in his school, church and youth group. He also began donating his prints to more and more charitable organizations that came asking, and he has been the featured artist at many fundraising banquets. When he started selling his first artist notecards, Josh donated part of the proceeds to The Canadian Lyme Disease Foundation (CanLyme) since his dad had been diagnosed with the disease.

Josh delights in supporting worthy causes and being generous in sharing his work with people who enjoy this style of contemporary realist art. As he says, "God has blessed me with this gift and I want my art to be a blessing to others." Through raffles and auctions Josh's art donations have multiplied, generating over fifty thousand dollars for 75 charities. Since the time he was a young boy, coached by his father when he got his first allowance, Josh has given 15-20% of his income to his church and other charities. At seventeen he started sponsoring basketball teams for a league he used to play in. He established his own charitable foundation to better coordinate his philanthropic efforts. He called it the "Arts for a Change Foundation" and it is administered by Abundance Canada (formerly Mennonite Foundation of Canada).

Throughout his life Josh has also donated his *time* to volunteer. In addition to teaching art at the March Break Camps, as a teenager he served in the church café, Easter and Christmas hamper deliveries, soup kitchens, shoebox warehouse, mission trips, and tree-planting for a conservation area (of which he is now a board member). He still has a humanitarian missionary heart, and is as much a philanthropist as a successful professional artist and entrepreneur. He was awarded Canada's Top 20 Under 20 at seventeen, from over 500 nominees. He attended the award breakfast with his parents in Toronto, and participated in a week-long Leadership Summit with the other outstanding teenagers from across the country.

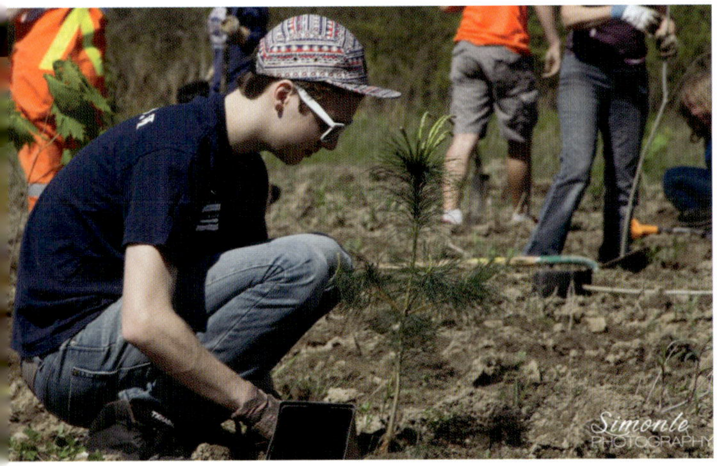

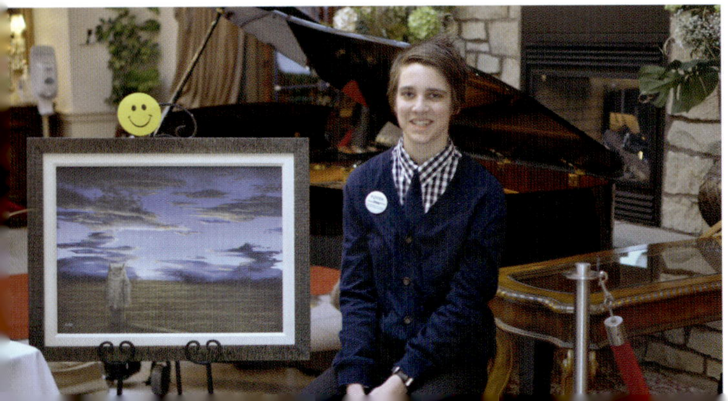

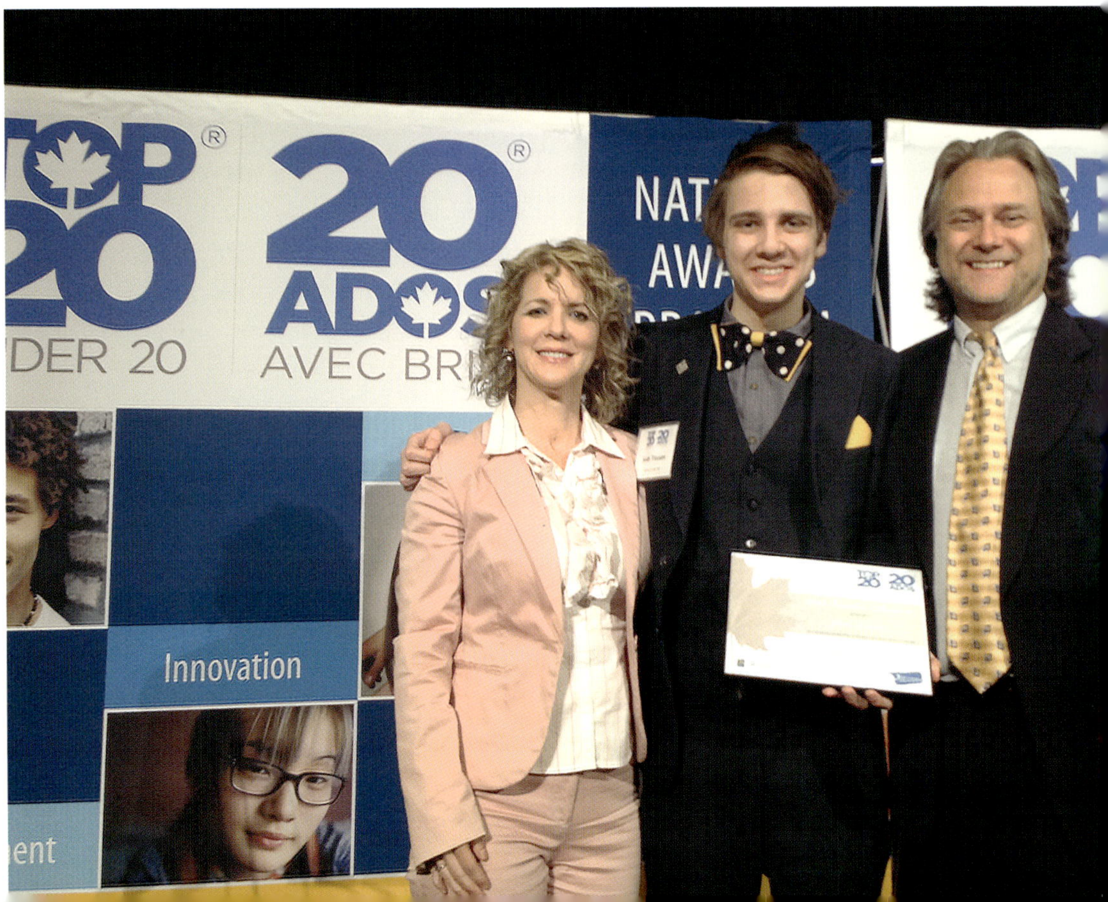

Life After High School

High school was really starting to 'get in the way' of Josh's art, so he was glad to finish two years early. He graduated the week of his sixteenth birthday from Cardinal Newman Catholic Secondary School, located a stone's throw from his home. He earned Academic Excellence, a Specialist High Skills Major in Arts and Culture, and a regional art award. His principal invited him to do a solo exhibition at his convocation. Many of the teachers and students were becoming his biggest fans, in spite of him only being there for two years as a part-time student (part-time home educated through high school).

The year after Josh graduated, the principal, teachers and students jumped on board with the media campaign to get a painting of Josh's voted into the National Gallery of Canada. It was a nationwide competition, and with thanks to his high school and fans across the country Josh received the second highest number of votes and his painting was hung for a month-long exhibition... but not before a teacher from his high school had purchased it halfway through the voting period. This man was only too happy to have his painting hung in the exhibition at the National Gallery in Ottawa.

Josh invited his former principal and guidance counselor to be among the limited number of guests he was allotted for the Diamond Jubilee award ceremony. Later, the school invited Josh to exhibit his work and speak at an arts banquet. Even now, when Josh pops into the school to drop off his yearly open house posters, he inevitably gets pulled into an Art Class by one of the teachers to speak to the students. This past year, the head teachers from the Science Department graciously allowed him to borrow an expensive full-sized skeleton model for the weekend, to get reference photos in his studio for his painting *Can These Bones Live?* (see p. 183).

After high school, people started asking what Josh was going to do next. With his dad's help, they carried in Josh's art to the National Portfolio Day at Ontario College of Art and Design in downtown Toronto. Josh's work was evaluated by the top schools from Paris, New York and Chicago. He received the highest praise and was accepted to go to all of them based on his portfolio alone. However, true to what Robert Bateman had told him, they all made it clear that he would have to start over from zero – they would deconstruct him and remake him into the current style of the art establishment. Josh didn't want that, so he left rather disillusioned, and disregarded the glossy promotional packages that started arriving in the mail.

Next, he and his dad took his portfolio to Redeemer University College in nearby Ancaster, Ontario. They basically said the same thing as the other art schools. They also suggested that Josh was beyond their program and should probably go somewhere else. It shouldn't have surprised him... when he was *thirteen* a professor who taught art at the highly respected Sheridan College near Toronto told his parents that Josh was painting at a third year university level, and at *fifteen* professional artists at the Bateman seminar said Josh was like them after art school at 25-30 years old. In spite of many recruitment packages Josh received in the mail from these art schools, he decided he likely wouldn't go to any of them.

Upon graduation from high school, Josh began working full-time as a professional fine artist, since he was already making an adult's income from his paintings and limited edition giclée prints. Eschewing art school, he endeavoured to follow the sage advice of his mentor Robert Bateman: "Get a meal ticket and *just paint your little heart out.*"

Josh's parents, still thinking he needed something to fall back on, encouraged him to take online college courses in graphic design, which he did. He was soon approached by a local production company and signed a year-long contract as their graphic designer (clients did not realize the work was being done by a teenager). But it was not very long before the paintings would become his 'meal ticket' and, like his photography, the graphic design would be crowded out by the demand for his fine art. Except for large paintings that took longer to sell, all of Josh's paintings were going very quickly, and he now had a waiting list of over twenty commissions.

At Julie's insistence, Doug dragged Josh to one last portfolio review, with professor and master artist Judy Major-Girardin at McMaster University's School of the Arts in Hamilton, Ontario. Like all the others, she highly regarded Josh's skills (in fact, she later wrote on a recommendation for him that she had been "blown away"). But *different* than the others, she respected that Josh was already an emerging professional artist with his own style, which was surprisingly okay with her compared to the other art schools that had frowned upon this.

It just so happened that this same professor was going to be the master artist mentor for a program funded by the Art Gallery of Burlington and Ontario Arts Council, called the New Generation Emerging Artist Mentor Project. Josh had already heard about it, and when he brought up the subject Major-Girardin encouraged him to apply, even though he did not have the required three years of post-secondary art school. She said that if it were up to her, having seen his portfolio she would choose him. Although Josh felt very flattered he did not count on getting in, as he knew there would be many other artists applying for a handful of coveted spaces.

That professor *did* end up choosing Josh as one of nine artists – he was sixteen and all of them were much older and more established than him. They were also *all women* so he got used to being around more female artists, as he had at the Bateman seminar. They accepted him like a son or little brother, but came to respect him as a colleague when they observed his work over the year, and in the years that followed. Older female artists became Josh's best supporters, whereas many male artists acted like they begrudged him, seemingly threatened by this young upstart. In the years after Bateman it was difficult to find male mentors, but Josh eventually met a few through the International Guild of Realism, and by reaching out to specific contemporary realist artists from Canada and the United States whose work he admired.

As he had at the Bateman seminar, during the year in the mentorship Josh learned a lot from the professor and the other professional artists. He appreciated their generosity in sharing information. Still too young to drive by himself, and having moved to Stoney Creek, Julie drove with Josh to the Art Gallery of Burlington. While he was in his monthly sessions, she would sit in on helpful artist information seminars offered by the gallery, taking notes for Josh and sharing them with him afterwards.

Josh was like a sponge, soaking in and acting upon everything he would learn. While he noticed many other artists had good intentions but seemed to struggle at getting around to such tasks as website development and guild submissions, Josh succeeded simply by *doing* what he was told. With that success came criticism from some artists who felt Josh was too self-promoting. But he was merely putting into practice what he had learned. Both he and Julie absorbed so much that year, and will be forever grateful to the gallery for all they gained there. In the years afterward, the staff, especially the Director of Programming who had given a fourteen year old his first gallery exhibition, would quietly relish the knowledge that they had discovered, equipped and launched emerging artist Josh Tiessen. Always careful to give back, Josh donated his painting at their yearly auction.

During the mentorship year, one day after class when Julie had come to meet Josh, she asked the professor about his work in progress called *Forgotten Fountain*, which he had brought in for critique (see p. 107). He always seemed to get such positive feedback from the professor, and Julie feared she may be 'going easy' on him because he was young. She wondered whether his painting was correct in perspective with its 2-tiered circular fountain bowls. The professor reassured her that she should trust Josh, as he had a special ability for depth and perspective.

From that point on, Julie never questioned her son's perceptions, even as he branched out to architecture. This had started the year before with *Behold The Door* (see p. 109), and *Not About The View* (see p. 111), which he completed that year for the exhibition. Josh became increasingly engrossed in textures, and Major-Girardin would write in the exhibition catalogue, "surface textures are the strength and unifying force of Josh's work."

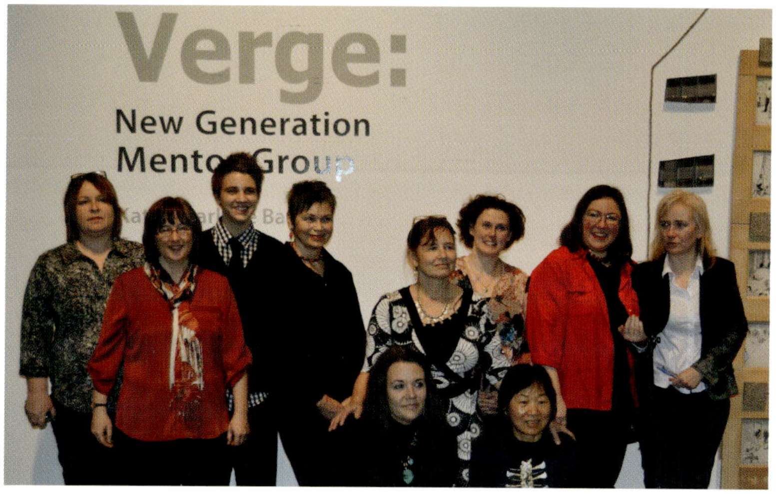

The mentorship culminated in a group exhibition which they called "Verge" (Josh's idea) in the main gallery space. Collectors came to see the work of these up-and-coming emerging professional artists. Josh stood out, still an awkward sixteen-year-old, among a group of women close to his mother's age.

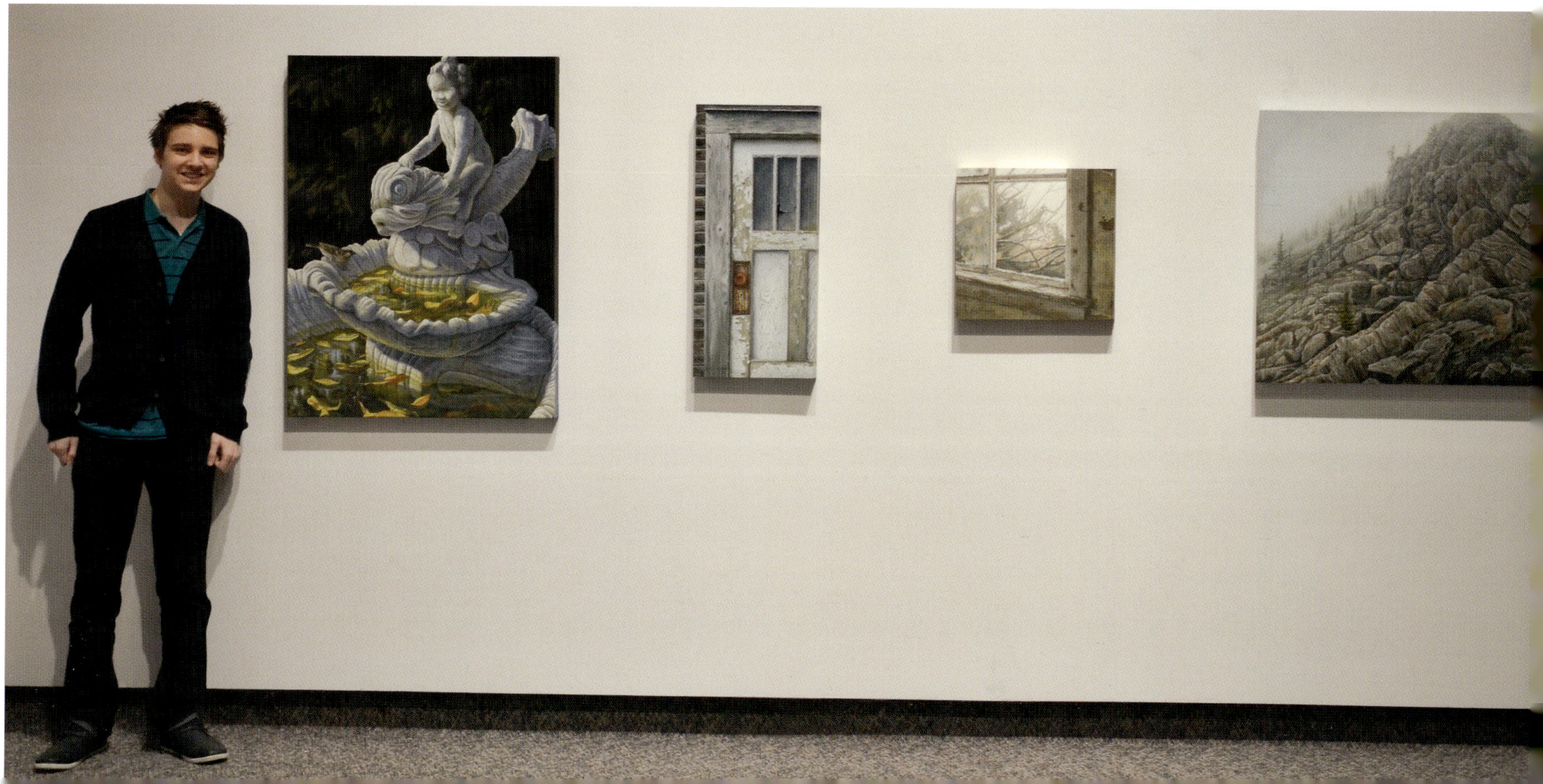

After observing how his work had matured over the course of that year, the professor told Julie that Josh wouldn't need to bother going to university art school (even though she taught at one). She felt he was already beyond anything they could teach him. His parents took this as the definitive word, and after that they put the subject to rest.

As with his life up to that point, Josh's post-secondary education would continue on a non-traditional path – more like the European model of being mentored under master artists. With all his exhibitions, speaking and charity events, although Josh had a strong desire to travel for university, Major-Girardin suggested it would not be practical to take four years out and lose momentum from the rare trajectory he was on. Instead, he found an accredited bachelor's degree program at Emmanuel Bible College in Kitchener, Ontario, that he could complete mostly through distance education.

The college would accept Josh's graphic design and fine art courses for transfer, plus non-formal educational experiences like master artist mentorships, toward a Bachelor of Religious Education in Arts and Biblical Studies. Josh felt this would be the perfect fit for him. Studies in such areas as Church History, Theology and Philosophy would add depth to his work as a fine artist, and enhance the writings he composed to go with his paintings. Major-Girardin affirmed this decision, as well as the ambitious student's long-range plan to continue on to a Master of Fine Art.

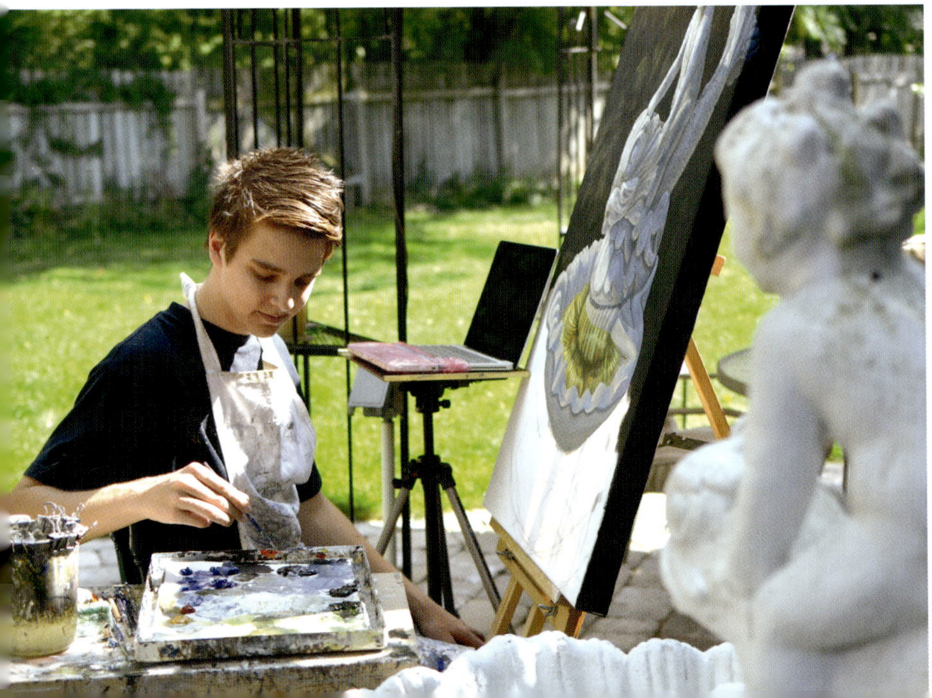

Enrolling in college, Josh was able to use for field study credits the volunteer work he was already involved in at a large arts-focused church, Bethany Community Church in St. Catharines, Ontario. At the invitation of the Creative Arts Director, he had designed a logo and joined the planning team for the new enKindle Arts Festival. He would go on to establish and curate The Bethany Gallery, chairing its leadership team, hosting quarterly exhibitions and artists nights. Josh would also later receive credit for the year-long Echo Educational Internship Program at his church. It included college classes and study in Europe, which also facilitated visits to major galleries so Josh could study the works of the European masters firsthand.

At twenty-one, Josh is now over halfway through his bachelor's degree, working at it very part-time in addition to his demanding full-time schedule. He diligently studies from home on the days his studio gallery is closed, and enjoys interacting with professors long-distance. His only regret is missing out on the campus experience, as he always longs for more intelligent discussion than even his theologically-educated parents can provide him. He looks forward to commuting to the college in the future, to finish up the final year of his bachelor's degree.

At the rate he is going, taking one or two courses at a time, it will likely take Josh double the usual duration to get to a post-secondary degree. After his bachelor's, Josh now has aspirations to start a master's degree in Theology, Art History, "or both," says he. The only barrier is his prolific art career, which contrary to the norm started before he went to school to train for it. Some people, particularly those closely associated with the art establishment, are bothered by this. They feel Josh should have jumped through the hoops and attended art school *first*. But as Judy Major-Girardin assured Josh, "there is not *one way* to conduct an art career, and not *one textook*." The reality is that there are few art programs or books that give much direction on how to establish and build one's career as a professional artist. This likely accounts for the large volume of questions that Josh receives from other artists who have finished undergraduate and post-graduate degrees in fine art, yet have little idea what to do next. They are bewildered by how Josh has reached this level of success at such a young age, and they often write or approach him at exhibitions asking for his advice.

Regional and National Recognition

Josh was distracted by speaking engagements and exhibitions while trying to finish the last couple months of high school. In the midst, he suddenly remembered (notoriously at the last minute) that he wanted to apply for Summer Company, a grant program funded by the Canadian Government for young entrepreneurs. He emailed on a Thursday to ask when the deadline was. The response came on Monday at 4 p.m. saying it was due at midnight that day. With advice from a couple accountant friends, Doug had already helped Josh set up financial records for Josh Tiessen Studio Gallery, which Josh had unofficially established the year before. While the two of them developed a business proposal, Julie itemized all of his supplies and catalogued his inventory. The three of them worked all evening, praying as Josh uploaded over a dozen pages at 11:50 p.m.!

The next afternoon, the local branch of Summer Company, operated out of the Small Business Enterprise Centre at Hamilton City Hall, emailed Josh very impressed with his art and his business plan. They had reviewed his whole application and spent time on his website. Realizing this was the young artist they had read and heard about in the news, they seemed eager to put forth his name. Josh went in for an interview the next day and was chosen out of hundreds of applicants.

The program ran for four months, with seminars by industry professionals: lawyers, insurance brokers, marketers, etc. They helped Josh get a business license, business bank account and insurance, giving him the expertise to take his business to the next level. His parents saw this as a godsend, as the business side of things was getting a little beyond their ability to help Josh, having never run a business of their own.

As usual, Josh picked up everything very quickly and ran with it. The mentors in the program were thrilled after the first month when he exceeded his sales projections for the whole summer. By the end of the year Josh had turned a decent part-time job into a full-time adult's income and, humble as he was, finally convinced himself that he might actually be able to make a career as a fine artist.

When Josh was fifteen he found an online competition called, "So you want to be an artist?" which was being run by the National Gallery of Canada in Ottawa. He wanted to enter, but he was too young so he had to wait until the following year. He almost forgot about it by the next year, only remembering when there was a couple weeks left to the deadline. There were strict size limitations and he only had one small study painting that would qualify... but it sold at an exhibition the day after he had it framed. With only *one week* left, he set out to do another small but highly rendered painting. He planned to portray a close-up section of an old door with peeling paint (a third in his series). In a nod to the art establishment, there would be an abstract geometrical quality about it, causing the viewer to draw closer in order to ascertain what it was.

Like usual, Josh had his own reference photos, which he had taken on the old abandoned homestead. He happened to tell his picture framer about his plan when he was picking up a painting, and she went to the back of her shop emerging with an old tarnished doorknob that she thought he could use. He propped it up on his easel and started sketching. A week later, with less than an hour to spare he photographed his finished work, calling it *Overshadowed* and writing a description to go with it (see p. 121). He uploaded it onto the competition website less than thirty minutes before the midnight deadline.

It turned out that the competition was based on Facebook votes, and when the 200+ images went live on the site the next day the race was on. Each person could only vote once a day, and only through Facebook during the month-long voting period, so it was up to each contestant to solicit more votes from their fans. Following the other competitors, Josh got busy posting on social media and spreading the word through small posters he made and hung around town – feeling rather sheepish as he always did about promoting himself, and questioning whether he would have gone into the competition had he realized it would morph into a social media race. Josh felt very uncomfortable about it all.

As alluded to earlier, although Josh had already graduated, his high school principal, who had become one of his biggest supporters, got wind of the competition and went on the morning announcements several times urging the teachers and 1600 students to vote. He also sent out a memo for all the teachers to post the voting link in their classrooms. Relatives, friends, acquaintances and Josh's collectors from across Canada and around the world also jumped on the Josh bandwagon.

The voting race turned into an intense battle for the top twelve places, with running totals for votes being updated online every day. It became clear to contenders like Josh that they would have to get the word out further. Local and regional newspapers eventually got into the game, and reporters came to Josh's studio gallery to do interviews about him in the competition, resulting in several articles. A couple of them were coloured half-to-full-page spreads. A regional morning show urged their viewers to "Vote for Josh" and aired a time-lapse video of the painting, which Josh had made to promote it on YouTube. By then many people in the area knew Josh and loved his art enough to vote for their hometown boy.

Josh was so relieved when the race was finally over, and was happy to secure a place in the top twelve whose works would be displayed in a month-long group exhibition at the National Gallery of Canada. He and his family drove five hours to Ottawa to see the exhibition,

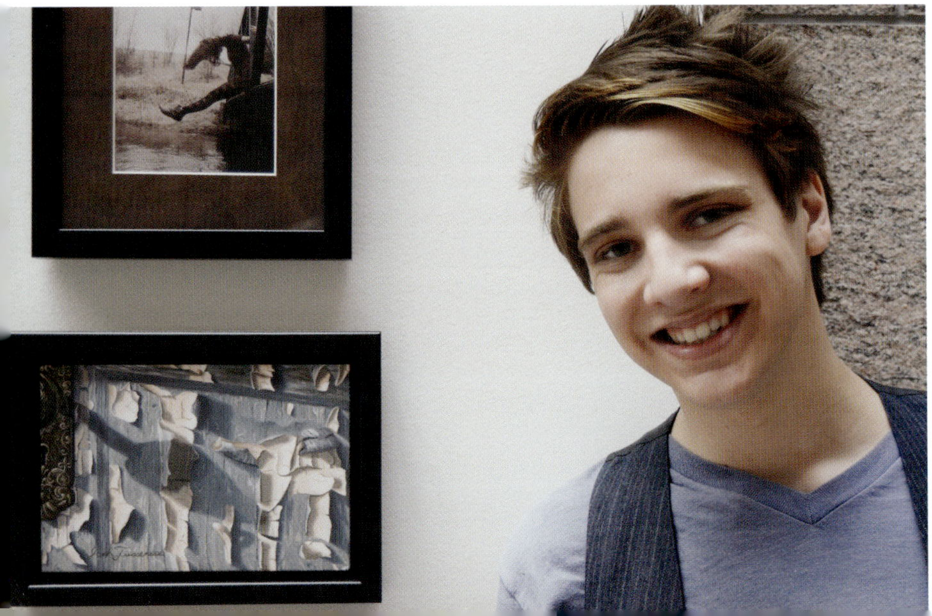

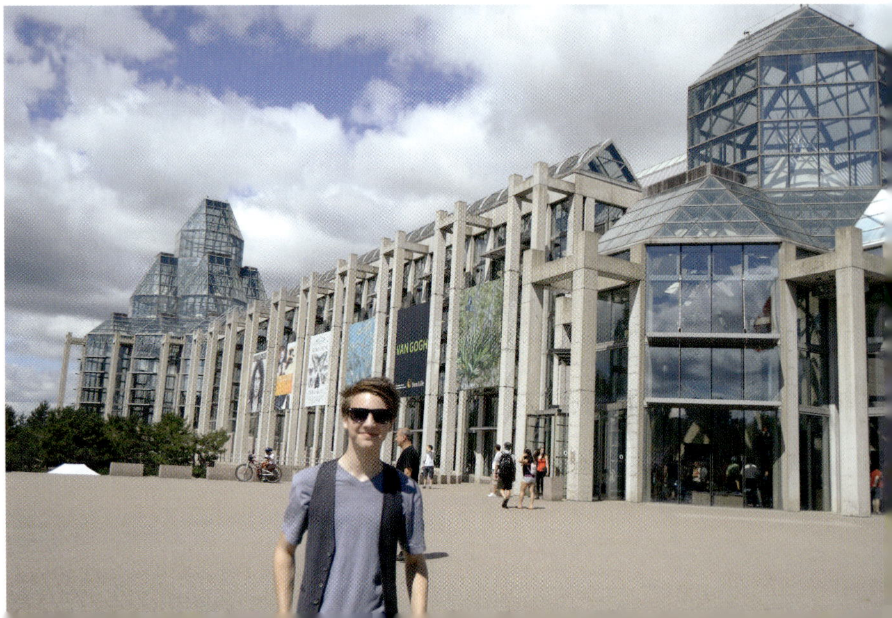

hung adjacent to the Van Gogh exhibit. A panel of four judges chose the top three, of which Josh's painting was not one. That didn't matter as much to him anymore, since he had pre-sold the painting two weeks into the competition for a higher price than he'd ever charged for a small painting (thinking it probably wouldn't sell). Exhibiting his painting at the National Gallery enhanced Josh's reputation as an emerging artist and opened more doors in the months and years to come.

By that Fall, when Josh was seventeen, plans were coming together for him to do an art performance during the yearly Brott Music Festival at Hamilton Place Concert Hall, with a symphony orchestra led by acclaimed conductor Boris Brott. They had flown in performance artists from across Canada, but this particular year they wanted to showcase a local emerging artist. Brott's assistant discovered Josh on Twitter.

Josh had never been on Twitter up to that point, as he found it enough work to develop his website and post on his Facebook artist page. He was at a community business breakfast where a regional executive for the Canadian Broadcasting Company (CBC) had spoken about social media networking. Afterwards, Josh approached him to thank him for the media coverage CBC had given him. The man wanted to connect with Josh on Twitter, but Josh said he was just on Facebook... to which this much older man said, "Oh, you're old school." Not to be outdone by an 'old guy' Josh came home that day and set up a Twitter account. It was shortly thereafter that Brott's assistant found him. When she raised his name at a planning meeting, Boris and his wife Ardyth remembered seeing him in the newspaper. They looked up his website and were convinced they should try to get him.

One day Josh's mother heard him answer a call on the speaker phone while he was painting. She stopped dead in her tracks when she realized it was the symphony conductor Boris Brott telling him to "just call me Boris." He asked if they could commission a painting and have Josh paint it alongside the symphony, as a performance piece during a series of educational concerts for children. Josh, being from a different generation and not having lived very long in the area, had no idea who this man was. He proceeded to say that he had only done a couple art performances and it really wasn't his thing, since his high realism art could not be completed in an hour.

Both Julie and Doug were now in the background mouthing, "just say yes." Josh eventually got their hint, and with Boris gushing that his art was remarkable, he loved his style and really wanted him, Josh started brainstorming about how he could make it work. He suggested doing most of the painting in his studio and creating a time-lapse video (as he had done before) to be shown on a large screen while he finished the painting live on stage with the symphony. Near the end, he could be filmed signing it, and that could be projected onto the large screen for all to see. Brott loved the multi-media idea. The art performance turned out to be a big hit with the hundreds of children, teachers and parents in attendance for the two concerts.

At the end, Brott interviewed Josh on stage. Josh had the opportunity to do one of the things he loves the most: inspire and encourage children to be creative. When Boris asked about his childhood, Josh recalled his life in Russia, unbeknownst to the maestro who had chosen the Russian story and music *Peter and the Wolf* for the performance piece. Since he'd done stints as a guest conductor in Russia, Brott tried out the few Russian words he knew. Josh went along with him bantering in Russian, having been fluent in the language until he returned to Canada at six.

Afterwards, Josh had an exhibition of his work hanging in the portable studio gallery Doug had made him as a labour of love the previous summer. They set it up in the large foyer of the concert hall. Josh sat next to it, interacting with the children who crowded around to see his *Peter and the Wolf* painting up close (see p. 65). They were all intrigued by the fact that the duck, which was originally in the painting, had been gradually painted over

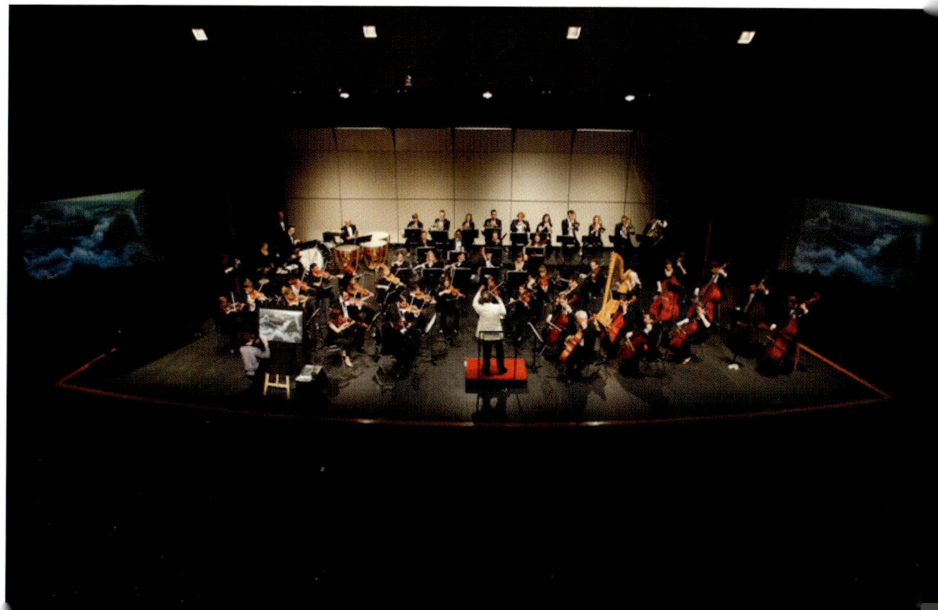

Photo by Ron van Someren

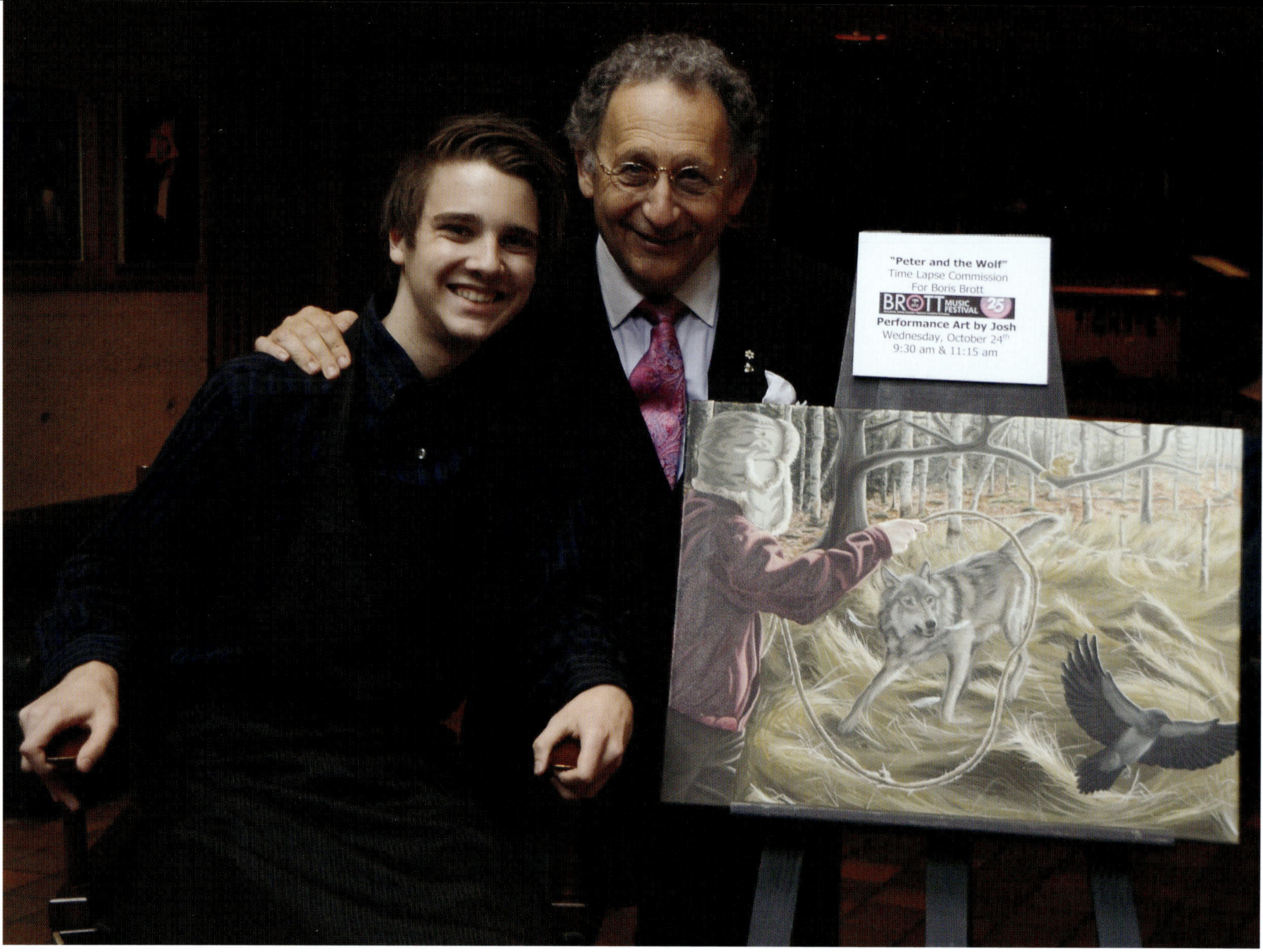

with the wolf who gobbled him up. Only a few swirling feathers remained. The Brotts loved the painting, and hung it in the Brott Music Festival office for all to see.

A few months later, Boris and Ardyth took the Tiessens out to dinner at a private club and formally invited Josh to do another art performance the next year. This time it would be for the adult symphony *Scheherazade*, as part of the Brott Music Festival season. When Josh asked about their budget for the painting, they simply told him to "dream big," so he did. They didn't know Josh very well yet, and were a little taken back by the elaborate plans he drafted for several large moveable plexiglass panels to come together like a puzzle and make a larger painting.

Due to their limited budget as a non-profit organization, they had to settle on another painting and time-lapse video similar to what Josh had done for the children's concerts. They assured him that this was what they had loved so much the first time. But for Josh, to do anything *twice* does not afford the challenge he so thrives on. Nevertheless, he enjoyed providing the experience for adults at the symphony. They, too, were enthralled by it, and by the rest of the young artist's work exhibited in his portable studio gallery. Josh felt even happier with the painting he produced (see p. 66), which had grown significantly in refinement since the first one. Again, the Brotts proudly displayed it in the Brott Music Festival office.

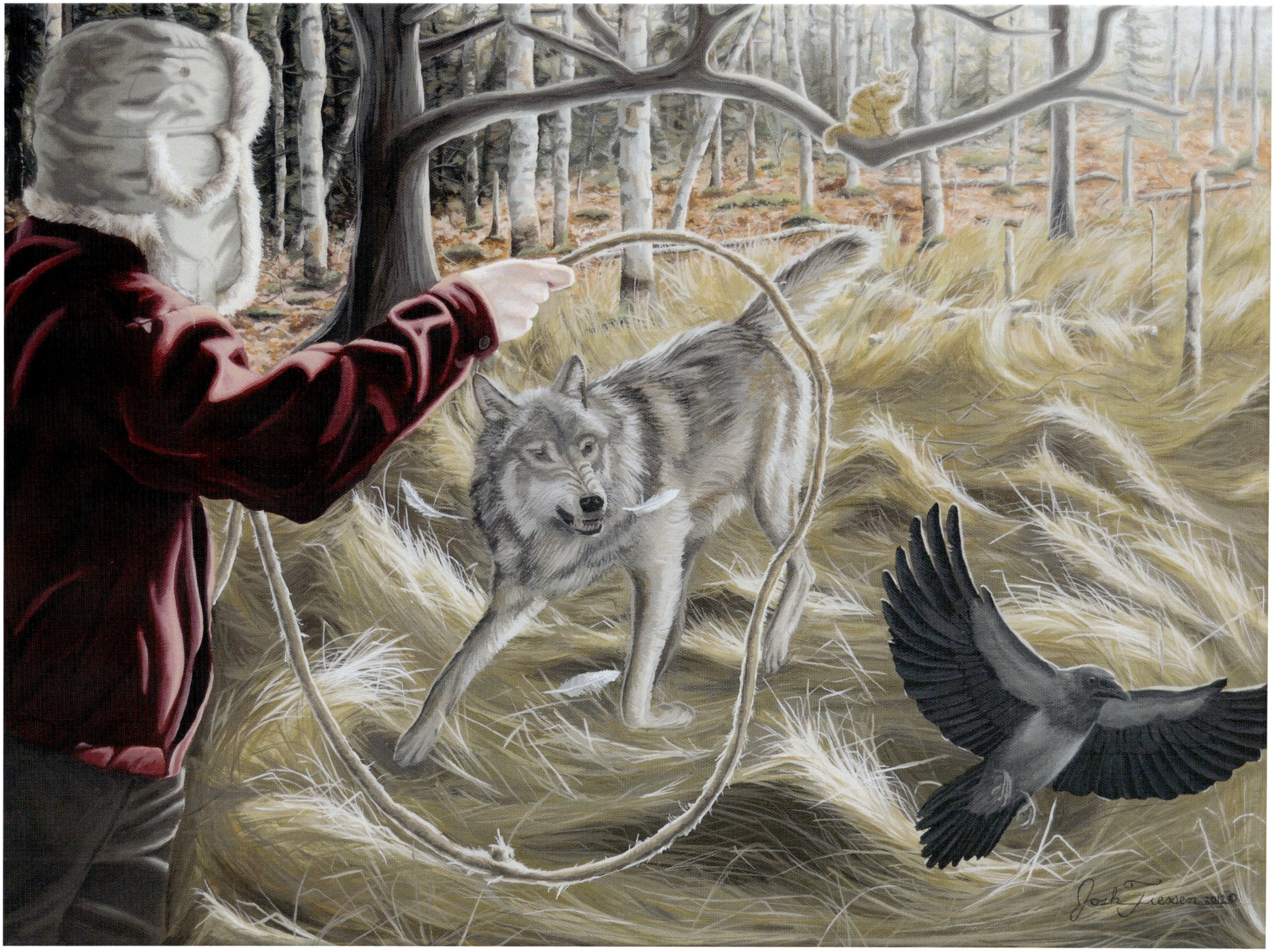

PETER AND THE WOLF
Acrylic on Canvas 18" x 24" 2012 (Age 17)

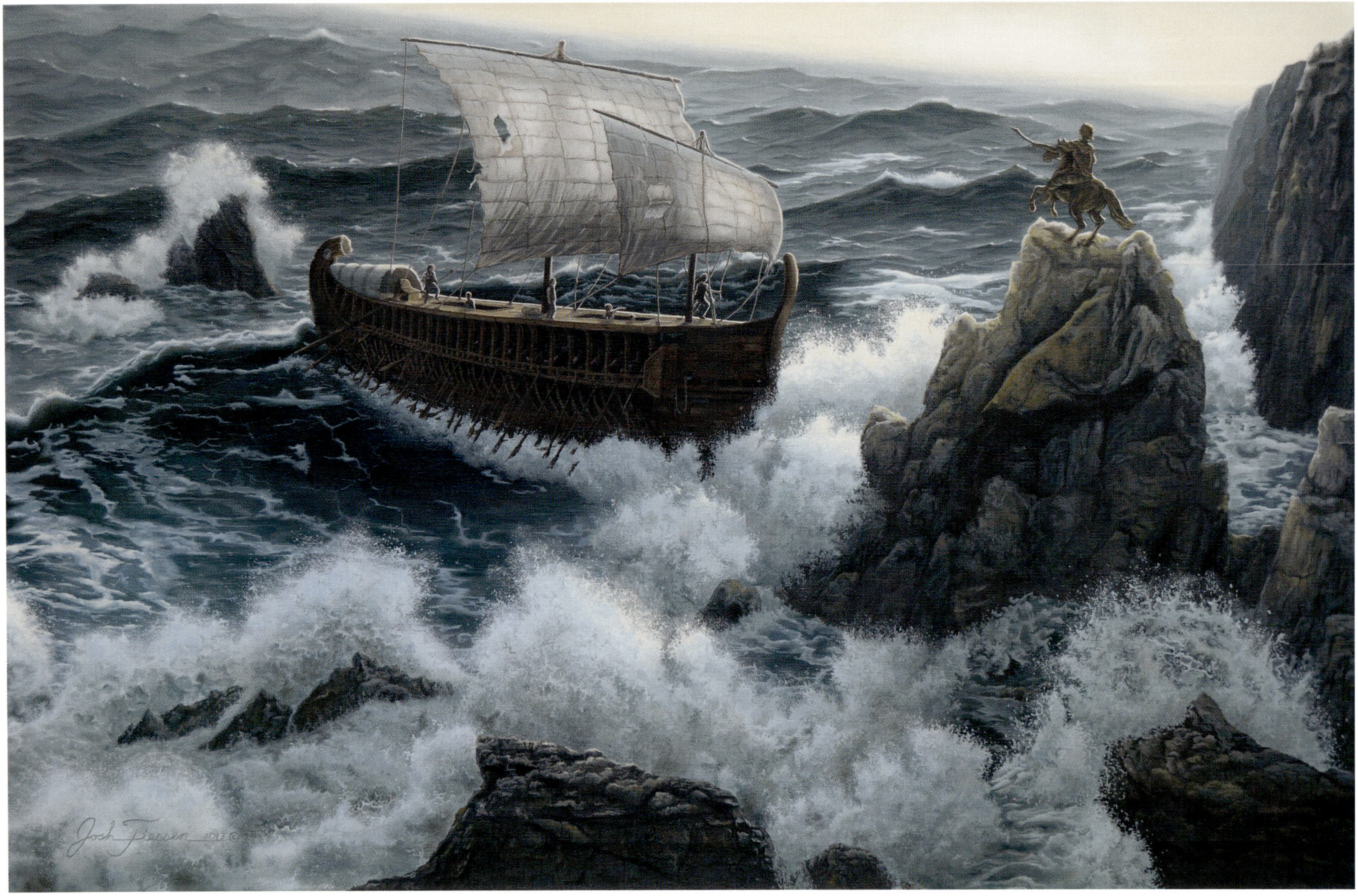

SCHEHERAZADE 4TH MOVEMENT
Acrylic on Canvas 24" x 36" 2013 (Age 17)

International Honours and Local Challenges

Another day while Josh was painting at his easel Julie handed him the phone, and what the person said on the other end rendered him absolutely speechless. He sat with his mouth hanging open in shock, as the person explained that he had been nominated by a Member of Provincial Parliament and selected by the Government of Canada to receive a one-time award being given to outstanding Canadians across the country. It was called the "Queen Elizabeth II Diamond Jubilee Medal," being awarded to him for his artistic accomplishment and philanthropic work. When Josh attended the ceremony and met the other fourteen local recipients, most of whom were three to four times his age with a lifetime of achievement, he felt terribly unworthy. However, with four of his large original paintings displayed at the front of the packed hall and a glowing speech about him given by MPP Paul Miller, it became clear why this young man was considered worthy of the honour, one of many other awards and honours he'd already received in his young life.

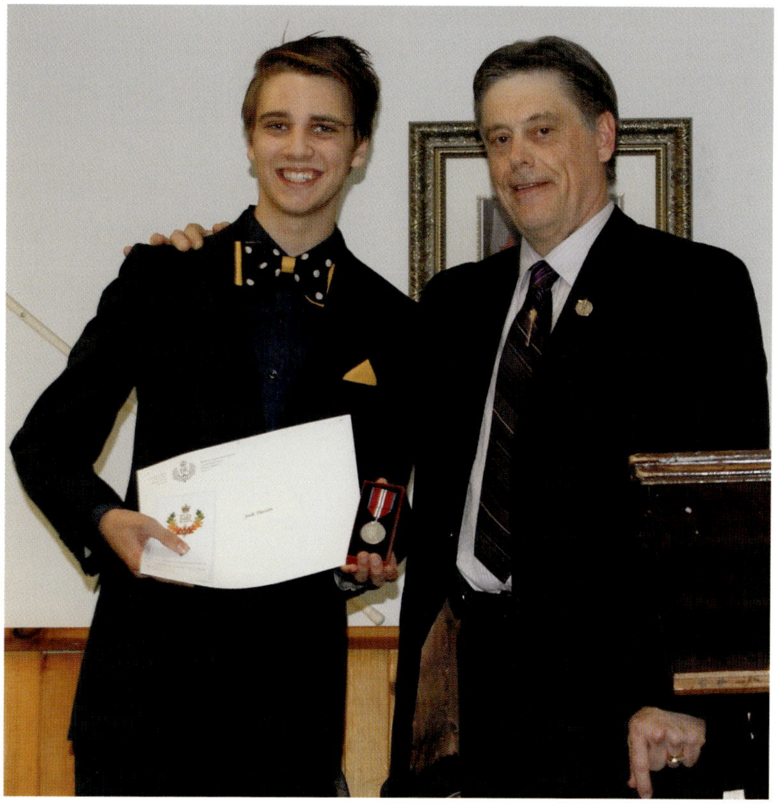

The year 2012 was a whirlwind for Josh. It began with him being juried in as the youngest member of the International Guild of Realism (IGOR), meaning that

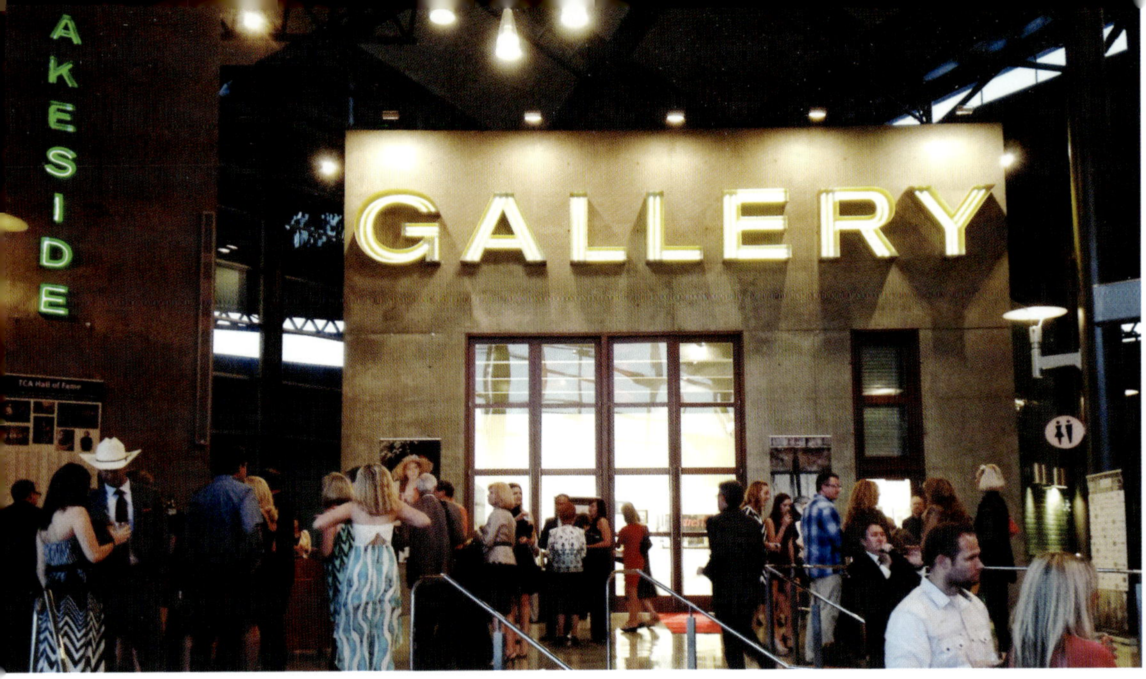

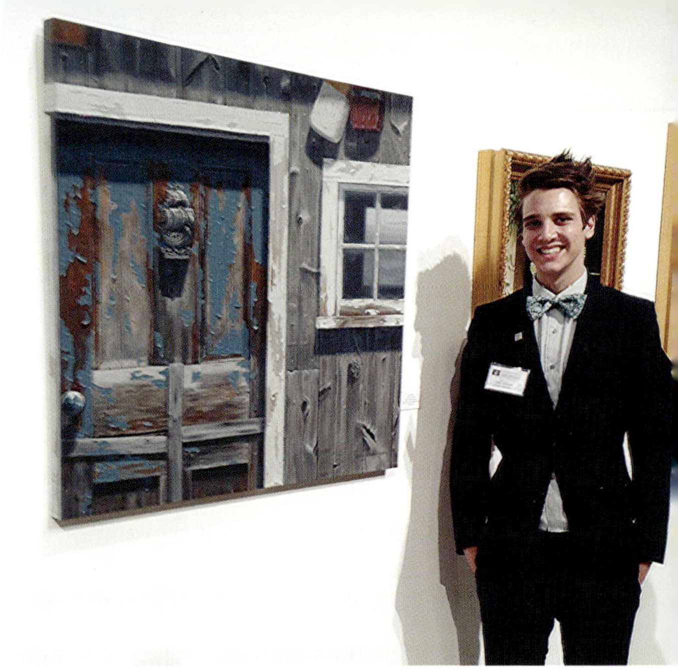

at seventeen he was now ranked among the foremost realist artists in the world. His paintings would be juried into their yearly exhibitions by prestigious American galleries, and join a travelling "Masterworks" museum tour throughout the United States. Within two years, at nineteen Josh would garner his first international award from IGOR, "Creative Achievement Award" for his painting *Ahoy Sleeper* (see p. 161). The guild is very proud of young Josh, their "Canadian phenom" as they call him.

2012 ended with Josh being juried in as the youngest member of the elite guild Artists for Conservation (AFC), the world's top nature and wildlife artists devoted to conservation. His paintings would be juried into their yearly *International Exhibition of Nature in Art*, a virtual exhibition and coffee table book. In between these guild honours, throughout the year Josh was juried in as the youngest exhibitor at numerous art festivals, and it was becoming a familiar theme in his life.

One of the most prestigious festivals was in the Niagara Region. The previous year had been Josh's first to apply, and he was rejected. However, at the last minute an artist had fallen ill and Josh was asked to fill her spot. The committee was positively dumbfounded by Josh's art and the crowds around his booth. The next year they invited him to be a featured artist and moved him up to the front of the hall. His painting appeared on their promotions, and he was featured on their website and in the media. Awards, honours, press and media were now rolling in at such a rate that Julie struggled to keep up Josh's artist CV.

As a teenage emerging artist Josh was defying the odds and breaking age barriers, in a field where thirty is considered entry level and where it takes until forty or fifty to be considered an established artist. But it wasn't all smooth sailing, as there were still some carefully guarded groups. Artists at the Bateman seminar had recommended Josh start applying to the Society of Animal Artists (SAA) since it would likely take him years to get in. They were right – after trying four times over the course of six years the society recently accepted him as an associate member.

The old guard of Ontario's premiere wildlife art festival refused to jury Josh in, even after he won top awards in their amateur competition. It was apparently held by the 'gatekeepers' that allowing in a teenager would lower the bar, which they had set high with the youngest exhibitor over thirty. This did not dissuade Josh. He kept trying for three years. Other artists from the festival asserted his art was better than some of its long-time participants. These supportive artists had seen Josh's work at other juried festivals, suggesting he apply to the wildlife show, shocked to discover he'd applied but had not been accepted.

After the third try, Josh received the most insulting acceptance letter he's ever gotten: tentatively allowing him in but giving his art a detailed negative critique, saying it was merely a copy of his mentor Robert Bateman. They made it clear he would only be permitted in on a probationary basis. Josh wondered if they thought he would be so intimidated that he wouldn't come, but he was undaunted and even offered to fill one of the artist speaking slots. The organizers received such positive feedback about his art and speaking that they invited him to speak again the next year. After that, due to yearly international exhibitions he was being juried into in the United States, which posed a scheduling conflict, Josh was no longer available to attend the local wildlife festival.

Josh faced other challenges that appeared to be related to his age. He submitted work to five local art galleries and was rejected by all of them, stating or implying that he should wait and try again in a few years when he was older. But by the time a few years came, his own studio gallery was thriving, being voted in yearly as the #1 gallery in the area (ironically, over the ones that had rejected him). He was also being approached by larger Canadian and American galleries that would start representing his work. His paintings became in demand elsewhere, such that he never got around to applying to any more local galleries.

Josh had been exhibiting since he was eleven in the Niagara region and Greater Toronto Area, selling most all of his paintings and adding to his long list of commissions. But he had never done any exhibitions in Toronto. The professor who had mentored him suggested he apply to a large expo-style art show. Other artists agreed that Josh should start applying, since it could take several years to get in. Josh got accepted on his first try.

In February 2013 he set up his exhibition at the upscale originals-only show, called The Artist Project. One of his biggest challenges was having enough original paintings for shows that would not accept prints of any kind, not even his limited edition giclées. As he had done before, Josh borrowed back paintings from his gracious collectors. He explained that the provenance of an original painting, in other words where it has been exhibited, increases its value. The prices on Josh's new paintings went up by almost double before the show – still modest by American standards for the international exhibitions he had started to be juried into, and also appropriate for the more conservative and much smaller Canadian art market.

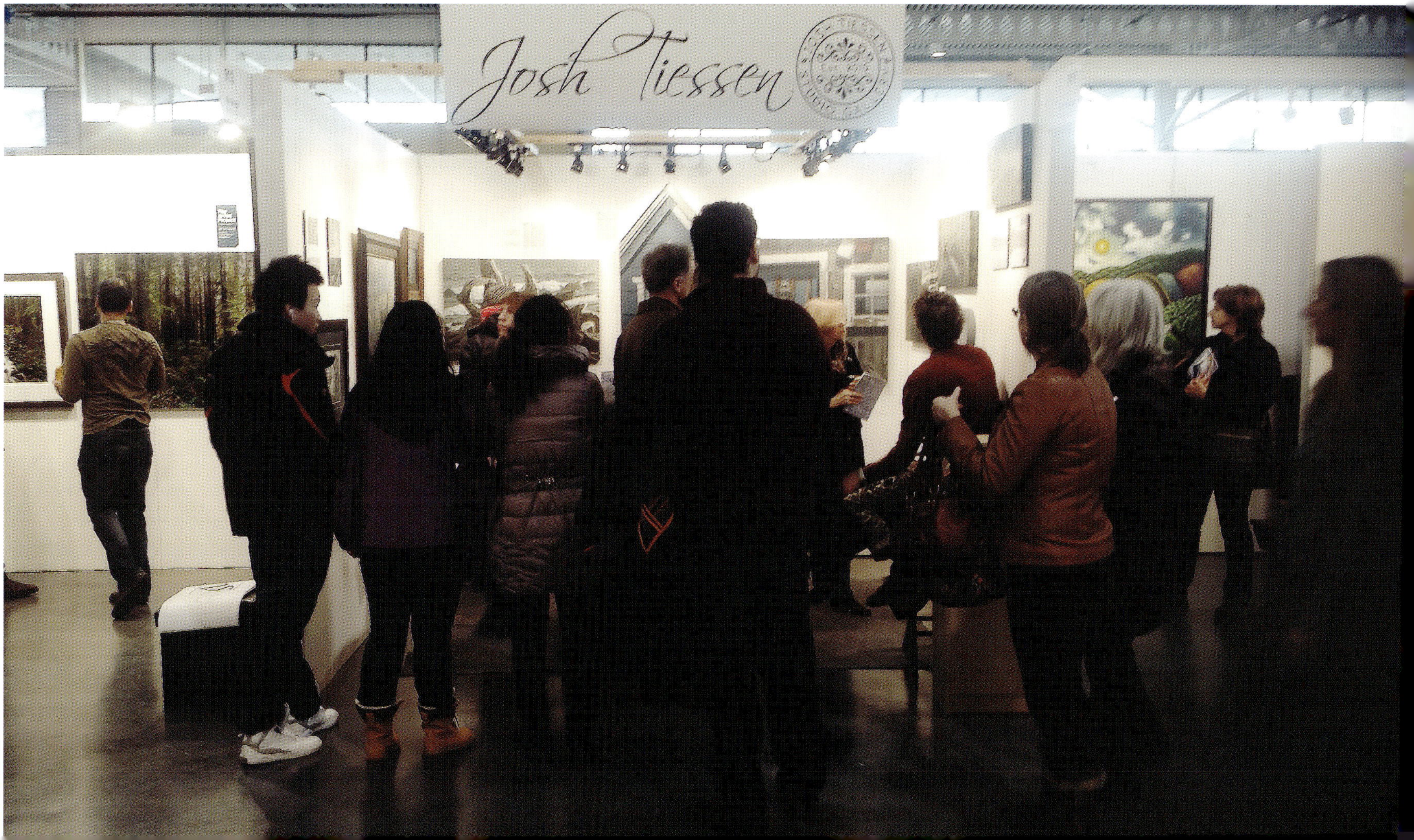

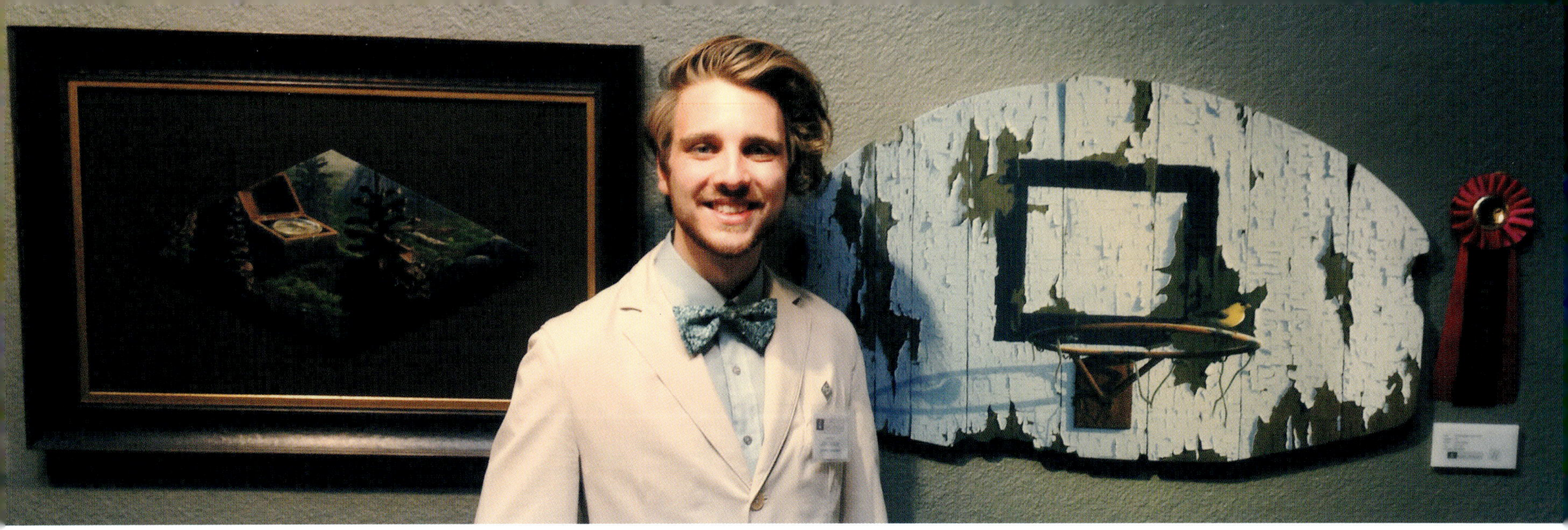

The Toronto show was a risk for an emerging artist, as the cost to do it was upwards to $3,000, about ten times more than other shows in the region. On the opening night Josh was elated when a painting was purchased by one of the city's largest private collectors (which he only knew from another artist who told him after the couple left). When they returned at the end of the show to pick up their painting, they said it would be hung across from a Group of Seven original... Josh later visited their home to borrow back the painting, and sure enough it was.

By the end of the weekend, out of 200 artists the organizers approached Josh saying they had so much feedback about him that he'd emerged as the "superstar of the show." A similar thing had already happened at several other shows. Word would get around about this young artist, and his booth would be swarmed with people who were sent by admirers to see his work, including other artists who were mostly very supportive and kind.

Josh did the Toronto Artist Project for three years, being featured by the city's most popular social media bloggers and interviewed on national television. After the third year, the demand for his paintings at international exhibitions, plus direct sales from his gallery to Canadian and American collectors, meant he did not have enough paintings available for sale to do the show in Toronto.

In order to focus on what he loved the most, namely painting new original works of art, eventually Josh had to cut down on more of the festivals and shows he used to do, limiting them to a few high-end juried events each year. While the early exposure was immensely helpful to his career, collectors increasingly came to him at his own Josh Tiessen Studio Gallery. International collectors began purchasing Josh's art directly from his web store. His original paintings and some fifty limited edition giclée print series are now shipped to homes and businesses around the world. His yearly Studio Gallery Open House the second weekend of December (now in its seventh year) brings collectors from all over the region and beyond. It remains his largest grossing exhibition each year.

As stated, Josh has sold almost ninety works of art to date, with his largest oil paintings fetching into the twenty thousands. The commercial galleries have come knocking, but Josh has been very selective, limiting the number of galleries besides his own where he exhibits and sells his work. Among the few galleries that represent him are some of the most well respected in Canada and the United States. These gallery owners and curators understand the gravity of Josh's talent in respect to his age. At the same time, they recognize that the quality of his work speaks for itself regardless of his age. They are proud to represent his innovative body of work.

Being exhibited by major galleries in the United States has attracted attention from the top fine art magazines, which have featured Josh's art numerous times. He remains humble and grateful for every collector, guild, gallery owner, curator and magazine editor who has promoted him as an emerging professional artist in the renaissance of contemporary realism now underway in the 21st century.

Final Piece of the Puzzle

A few weeks before the first Toronto show, when Josh was seventeen, his parents received a phone message and email from Dr. Joanne Ruthsatz, a psychology professor from Ohio State University. She had studied child prodigies for fourteen years and was a recognized global prodigy expert who had published academic studies and appeared on national television. She informed the Tiessens that art prodigies are the rarest, especially *male* art prodigies, and that she was delighted to discover Josh in a *Huffington Post* (New York) article from the previous summer called, "10 Art Prodigies You Should Know." It featured children and teens from around the world. Josh was the sole Canadian. He had only found out about the article when Doug's cousin emailed congratulating him on it. Josh looked it up online and felt humbled to be included with others who were making up to *hundreds* of thousands of dollars from their art. He was still selling his for modest prices as a yet-undiscovered prodigy artist (even so, a few Canadians had questioned his prices when he raised them).

In the weeks after the article was published online, including videos pulled off YouTube about each of the ten art prodigies, Josh was astonished to see his video had the most views and was consistently ranked first among the ten. Spinning off the article, Josh was contacted by *HuffPost Live* (Los Angeles). They conducted a live half-hour webcam interview with Josh and his mom for the show, where they featured him along with an adult drumming prodigy and another psychology professor in a segment called, "Post Childhood Prodigies."

Dr. Joanne Ruthsatz, having read the *Huffington Post* article and studied Josh through his website and YouTube channel, was convinced that he was indeed a prodigy – in fact she claimed he was the *only known male art prodigy in North America*. She asked Doug and Julie if they would consider allowing her to visit, in order for her to study and do tests on Josh. The Tiessens were a bit skeptical.

During a conference call to further discuss the matter, Dr. Ruthsatz asked about their second son, discovering that Zac was a musician and composer. Watching him on YouTube afterwards, the professor suspected that *he too* was a prodigy. She called right back saying she was even more eager to visit the family as soon as possible, to test both boys. Josh only had a small window of time while he was booked off public events to paint toward the Toronto exhibition. Trying to protect his time, Doug and Julie were hesitant but agreed to her coming for one day the next weekend. Zac was leery but relented and booked the day off work. With the worst blizzard in five years on its way the professor was undaunted, braving the six-hour drive from Ohio up to Canada.

The foremost child prodigy expert told them over lunch, that in the first five minutes of meeting Josh and Zac it was confirmed to her that they were *both prodigies*, two in one family, an extremely rare find. The Tiessens were all still skeptical, wondering how she could tell. She spent the day 'snowed in' with the brothers doing interviews, DNA, IQ and AQ (Autism) testing. Neighbours ribbed their parents who were out shovelling snow on their own, asking why their two young men were not helping, and whose fancy car from Ohio was parked in their driveway.

Without yet tabulating their scores, over dinner the professor told them that both boys were on the high end for intelligence and also for autistic tendencies, which would explain their extreme focus and attention to detail. As with all the other prodigies she had studied, Dr. Ruthsatz observed that Josh and Zac did not have the social-behavioural deficits usually associated with autism.

The professor left the next day, saying she felt blessed for meeting such remarkable young men who, like all prodigies, were mature beyond their years (interestingly, others had also said the same). Josh had long been called a prodigy by the press and media, but the family hadn't really taken it seriously. Doug and Julie now struggled to get their heads around the idea that their two sons had been officially labelled *bona fide* prodigies, especially since Dr. Ruthsatz told them that *prodigies occur only 1 in 5-10 million of the population*. With the Tiessens' permission, she added Josh and Zac to the elite group of (then) twenty-four prodigies she was studying worldwide.

Ruthsatz was not only impressed by the Tiessen brothers' maturity and the body of work they had each produced to date, which she deemed to be at an advanced professional level, but also with what turned out to be high IQ scores once tabulated. She wrote back saying that, like all the other prodigies in her study group, they were both in the 99th percentile for "working memory." Zac scored high in every category and so did Josh, with the exception that he fit the profile for the artist prodigies with regard to visual-spatial skills that are ironically low.

At the professor's request, the Tiessens had surveyed their relatives on both sides but had not found any autism in their blood relations. This was apparently the case for about half the prodigies from the study group. In an effort to discover the sources for their exceptional abilities, during her visit Dr. Ruthsatz had delved into each of their histories, especially interested in the larger narrative of the Tiessens' life in Russia. When she asked his parents if they remembered how far back Josh's art ability went, they responded candidly, "he just came this way." Ruthsatz laughed, as this answer was apparently all too familiar among prodigy parents. Since the talent seemed to be in Josh from birth, she pressed further back, asking if there had been any pre-term labour or a trauma during pregnancy. Julie answered, "both." The story then came out about her difficult pregnancy with strong contractions from the second month. Dr. Ruthsatz told them there were other prodigies whose mothers had pre-

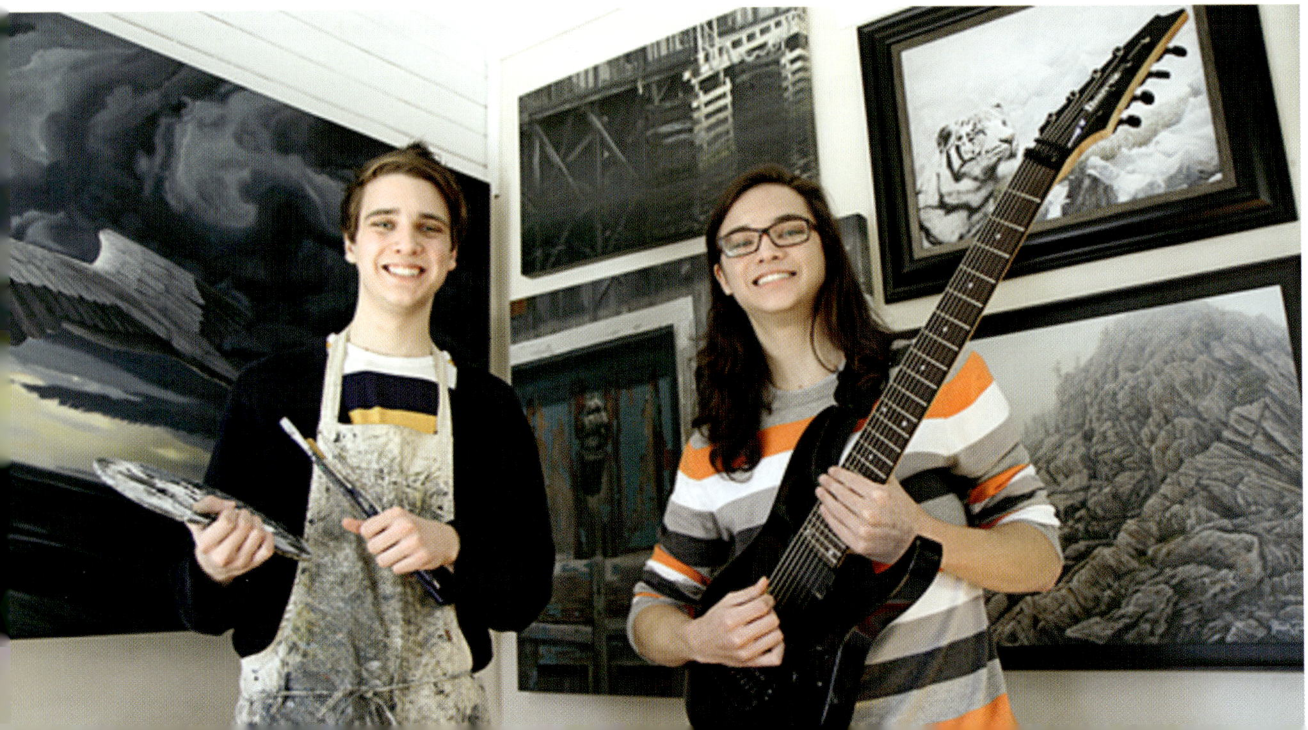

Photo by Cory Ruff

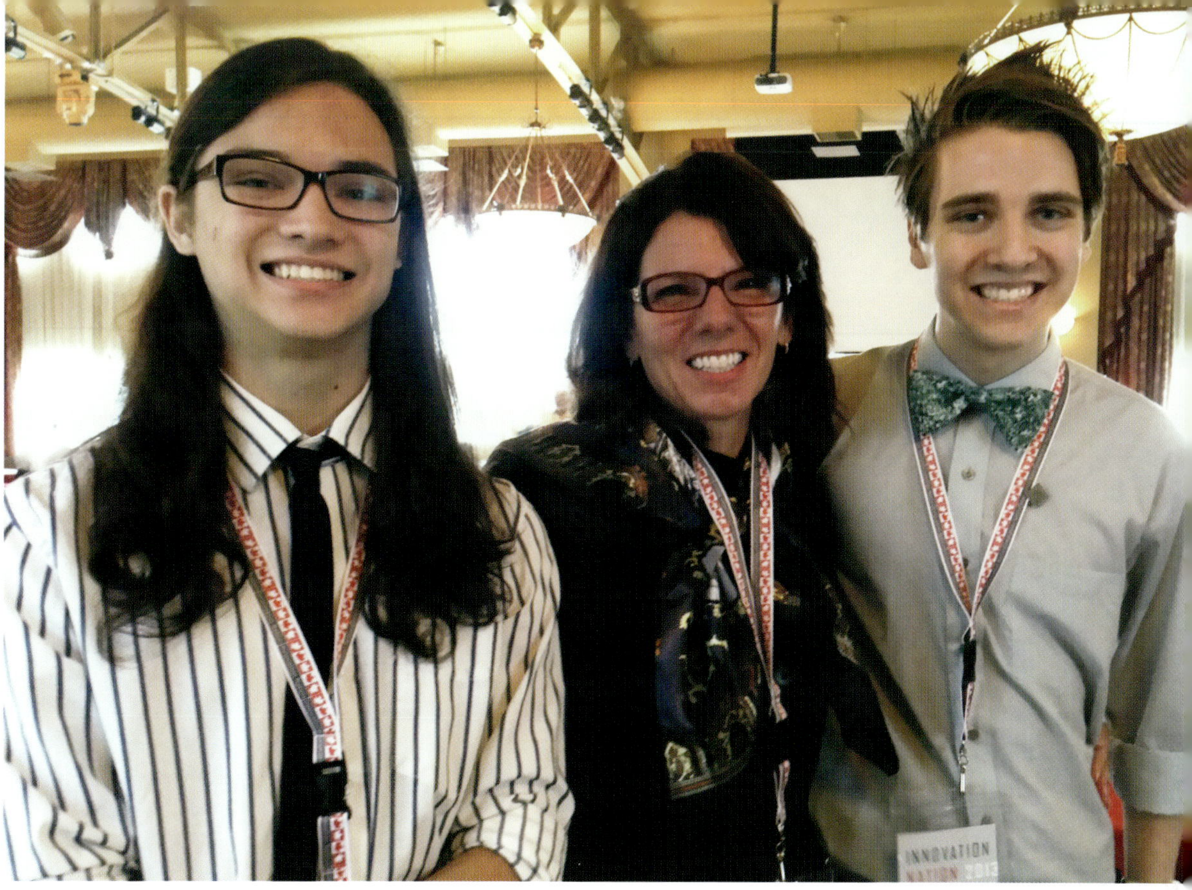

term labour, and *that alone* had been sufficient to cause a brain injury. Julie went on to tell her about the Moscow guest flat incident and her fall a little over a week before Josh's birth. Ruthsatz explained it was possible that a prenatal left-brain injury had precipitated an overcompensation in the right hemisphere causing the artistic prodigiousness.

Finally, after seventeen years of life with this unusual child, they had a feasible explanation for why Josh had been born an art prodigy, when neither of them were artists nor were there any among their predecessors.

Dr. Ruthsatz, or "Joanne" as she insisted they call her, visited a couple more times and is still often in touch with the family. It was she who urged them to write down a detailed developmental history, which formed the basis for the story you have just read. Collectors had requested a coffee table book with Josh's story and art, but the Tiessens had never gotten around to it as there were so many other demands on their time with all his exhibitions and public appearances. The professor's insistence, coupled with a back spasm that took Julie off her feet for two months, were the impetus she needed to get on with it. Drawing on many sources, from an official report to their mission organization about the Moscow incident, to dozens of articles written by the press about her son, Julie pieced together a surprisingly long history of the teenager's short life.

After meeting the Tiessen brothers, then reading their developmental histories Julie later sent her, it became obvious to Dr. Ruthsatz that they likely carried what she called the "prodigy gene," closely related to the autism gene. Months later, when the DNA results came back it was confirmed. Through reading more of the professor's published academic papers, the Tiessens would come to understand how this gene could have protected their sons from the negative effects usually associated with brain injuries, and unleashed the prodigy in each of them. Recently, this information was made available to the general public, in a book co-authored by Dr. Joanne Ruthsatz and Kimberly Stephens. The book is called, *The Prodigy's Cousin: The Family Link Between Autism and Extraordinary Talent*. Based on the histories Julie had sent, and further interviews with the Tiessen family conducted by Stephens, Josh and Zac's stories are explored in Chapter 8, "Another Path to Prodigy." This fascinating book is like a detective story, scoping out each case, then in scientific detail examining how it is that prodigies like Josh came to have their extraordinary talents.

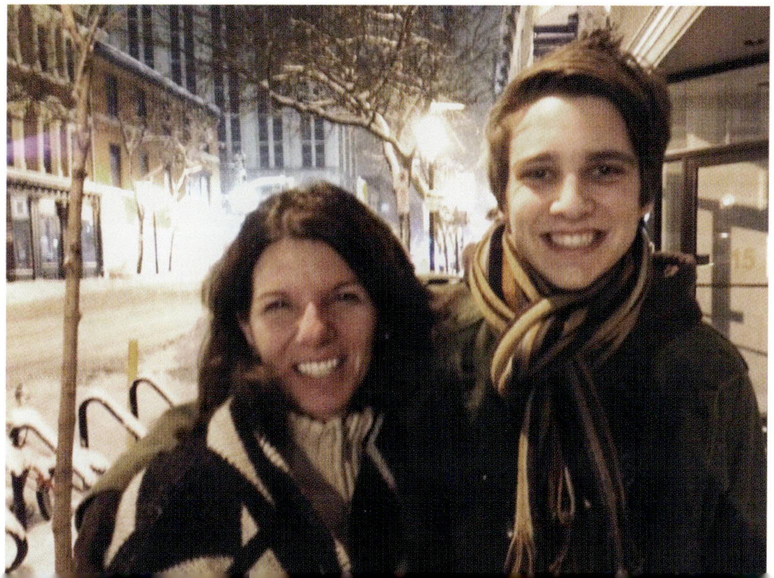

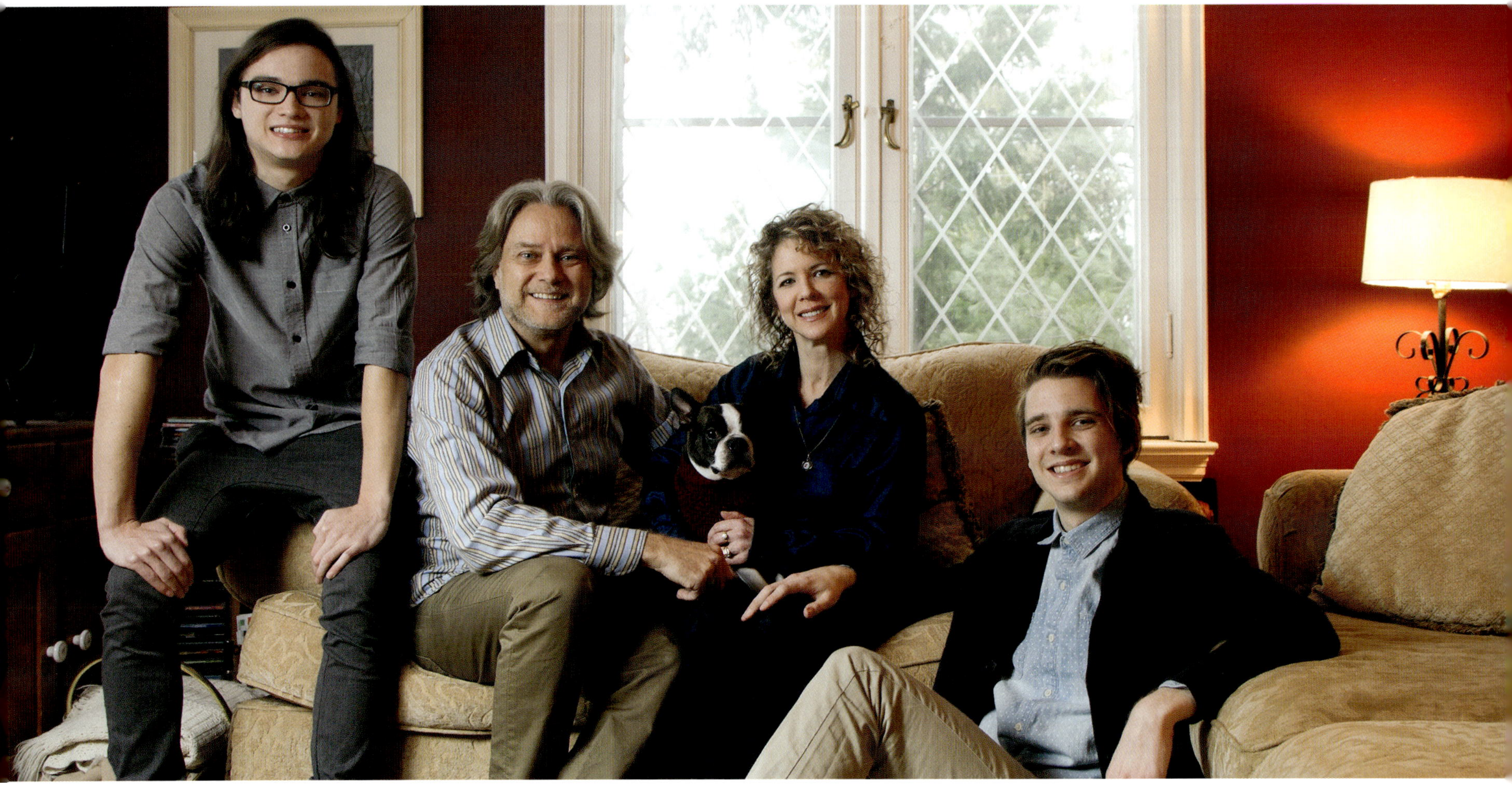

Photo by Peter Power

Postscript: Family Tragedy

After the life of adventure Josh had grown accustomed to in his early childhood, the Tiessens eventually had to stop travelling overseas. Doug had worked sick for several years and was finally placed on a medical leave by his physician, from his position as Assistant Vice President of Global Ministries for the mission organization. Eighteen specialists and almost a decade after he had fallen ill, in 2008 Doug was diagnosed with Chronic Lyme Disease (CLD), which he had contracted from the mission guard dog that had come with the last house they lived at in Krasnodar, Russia. Its owner would take it hunting, and the dog would return covered in pheasant ticks. Doug carefully removed them to protect his family, knowing the insects could carry some sort of disease... not realizing that he was being infected himself, likely by nymph-ticks the size of grains of sand.

Julie started getting symptoms a few years later and was diagnosed with CLD in 2011. Most tragically, a year later it was discovered that Josh and Zac also had severely compromised immune systems, with Lyme being the only explanation. It is not conclusive whether each family member contracted the disease from the hunting dog in Russia, or whether they contracted it living with each other. Regardless, the disease started taking its toll, and symptoms for each of them were compounding. Desiring to keep his personal and professional life separate, Josh rarely mentioned his health struggles, and people who saw him at his exhibition openings never knew.

With no treatment for Chronic Lyme Disease available in Canada, a small army of family and friends from the Tiessens' church formed a committee and launched a campaign to raise money so the family could be treated in the United States. Editors of the local and regional newspapers, who by then were very familiar with the Tiessen brothers, sought to help by writing articles.

Over $280,000 has been raised to date for the family, of the $350,000 goal, and the YouCaring campaign is ongoing. In the summer of 2015 the Tiessens were all treated at a clinic in Florida, each on daily IV infusions and upwards to 100 pills and supplements a day for eleven weeks. The treatment proved effective in halting the downward progression of the disease. The Tiessens would now have a fighting chance at a healthier future, especially for Josh and Zac who have their whole lives ahead of them.

Even during treatment, which was stronger than chemotherapy and for which Josh had a PICC line inserted in his arm, the intrepid artist could not be stopped. Slowly but surely he completed a large painting, entitled *Whale Hymn* (see p. 179). Shortly after returning to Canada last Fall, it sold through his web store to an American collector for the highest price he'd ever received. Of course, Josh Tiessen's story is far from done. But the foundation has been laid in his first decade as an artist, for a successful career in a difficult field. With his health now restored, he is poised and ready for the decade ahead. Josh has the rare privilege of doing what he loves and making a living from fine art. This, in turn, gives him a platform and enables him to do the *other* things that he loves – being generous through his philanthropic work, speaking, teaching, mentoring and inspiring others – thereby making a difference in the world through his art.

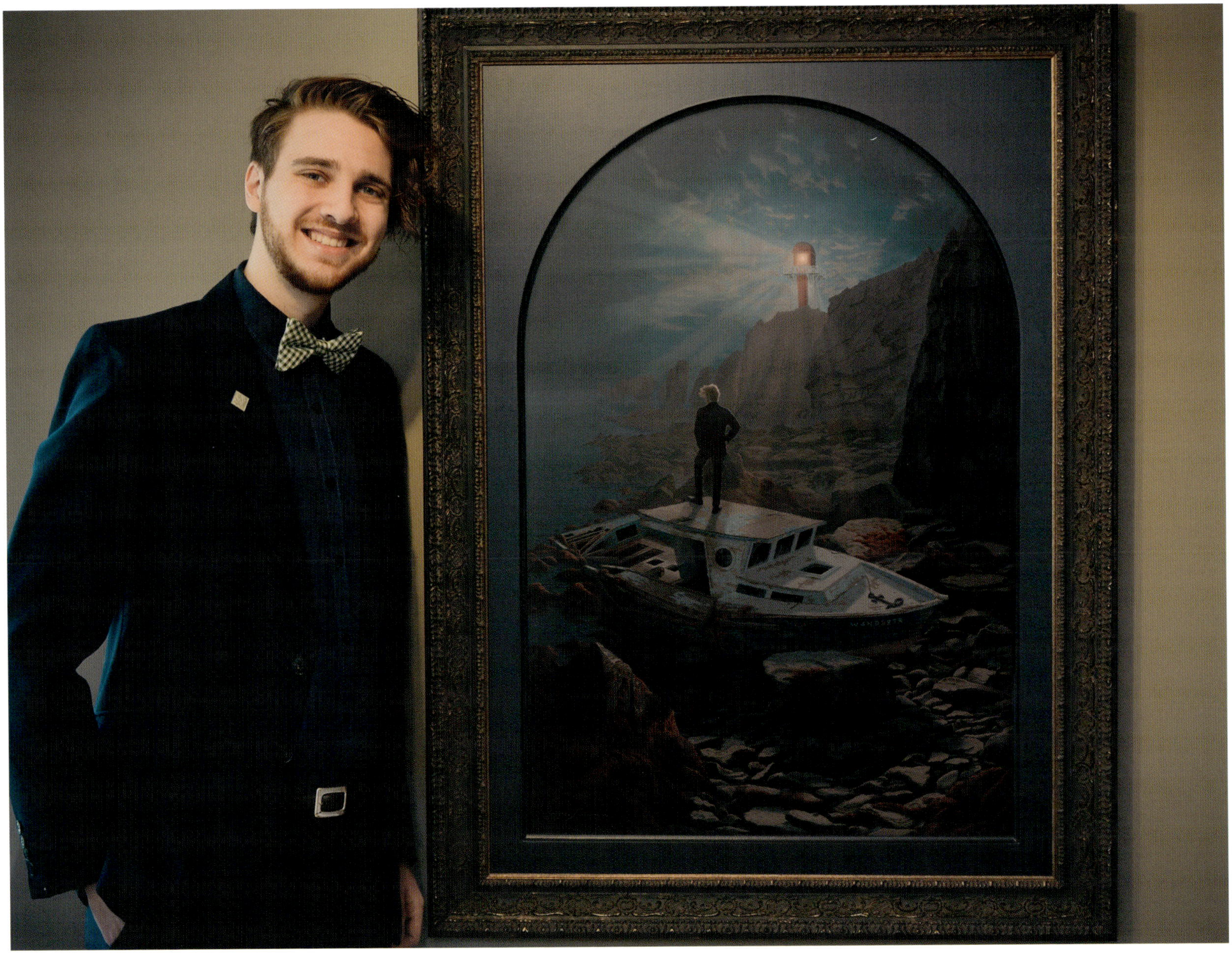

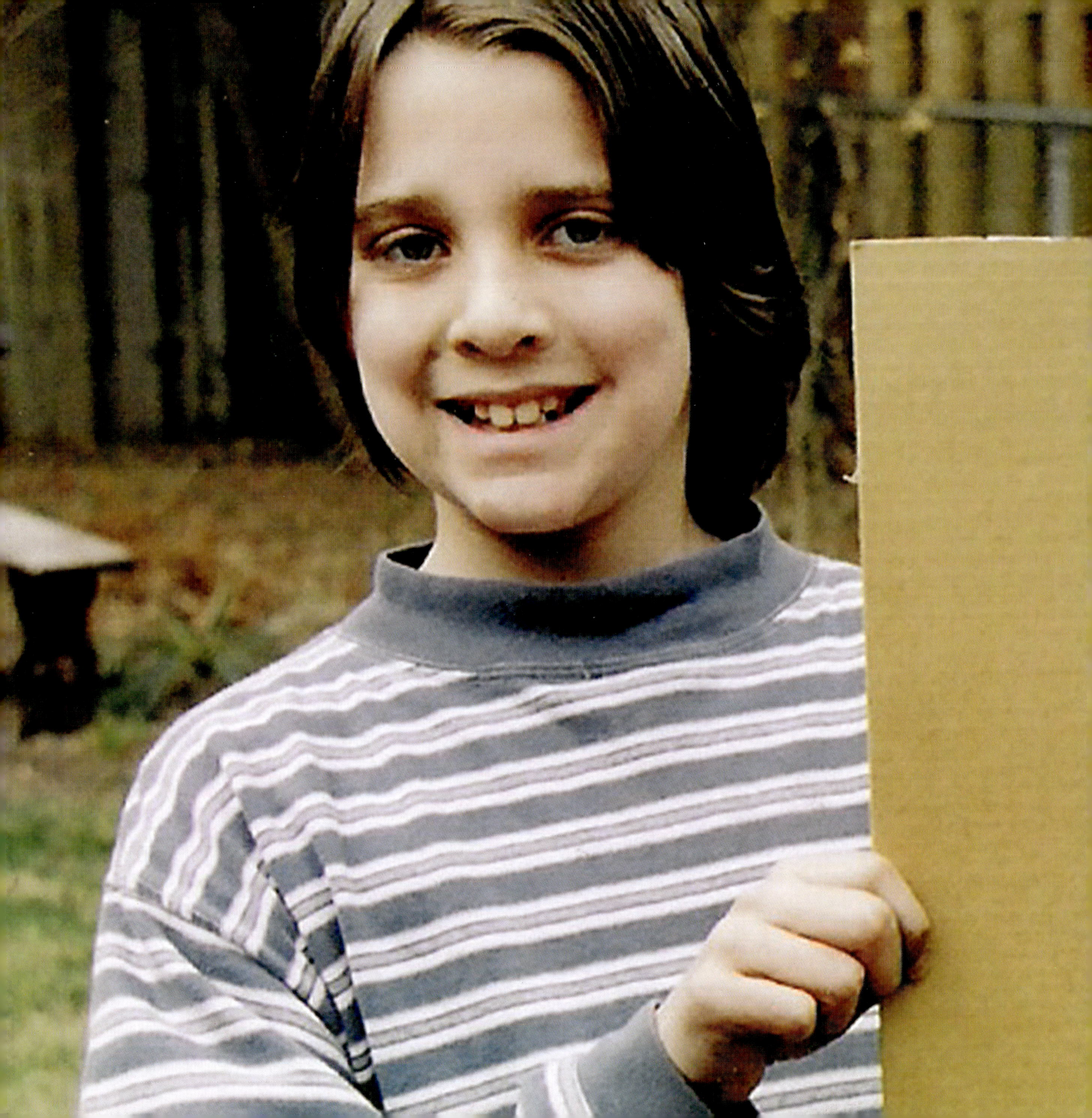

EARLY WORKS

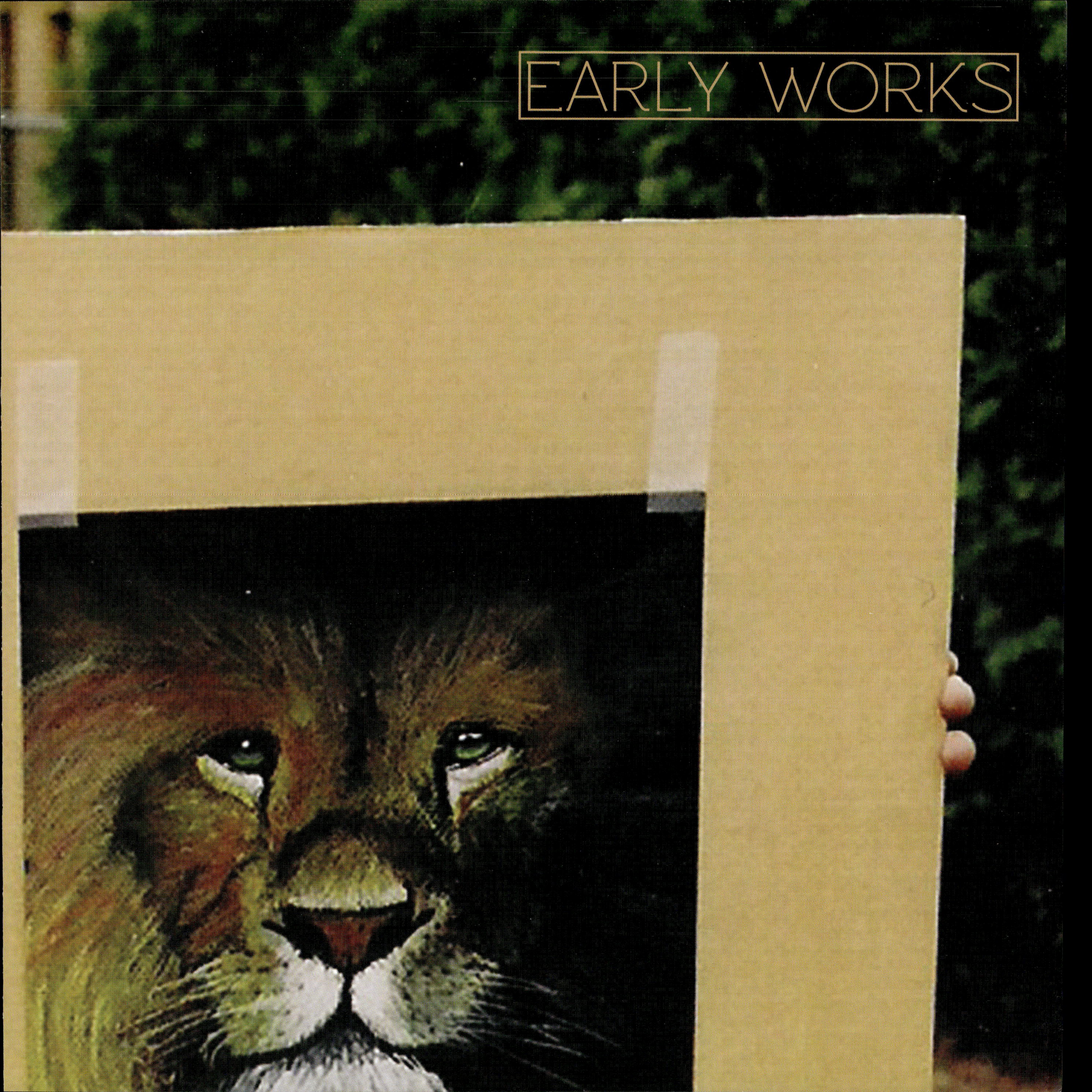

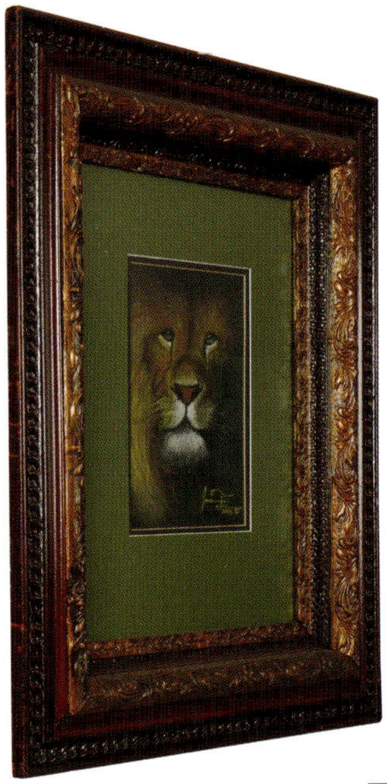

ASLAN

This was my first chalk pastel, done under the guidance of wildlife and animal portrait artist, Valerie Jones of Burlington, Ontario. People thought it was so good that they didn't believe I could have done it on my own as a ten year old. But I did, and Val took photos to prove it, truthfully telling everyone how she has never touched any of my pieces. She would show me things on the side, like how to do eyes, but she always gave me complete freedom to do my own work. I was inspired to draw this subject from the Chronicles of Narnia book series by C.S. Lewis. I have always loved *The Lion, The Witch and The Wardrobe*. The lion named Aslan is a great metaphor for Christ. My favourite quote from the book in reference to Aslan is, "He's not a tame lion, but he's good." My desire was to illustrate this through his fur and eyes in this picture. I don't think I could ever give away or sell the original.

Chalk Pastel on Paper 12" x 9" 2006 (Age 10)

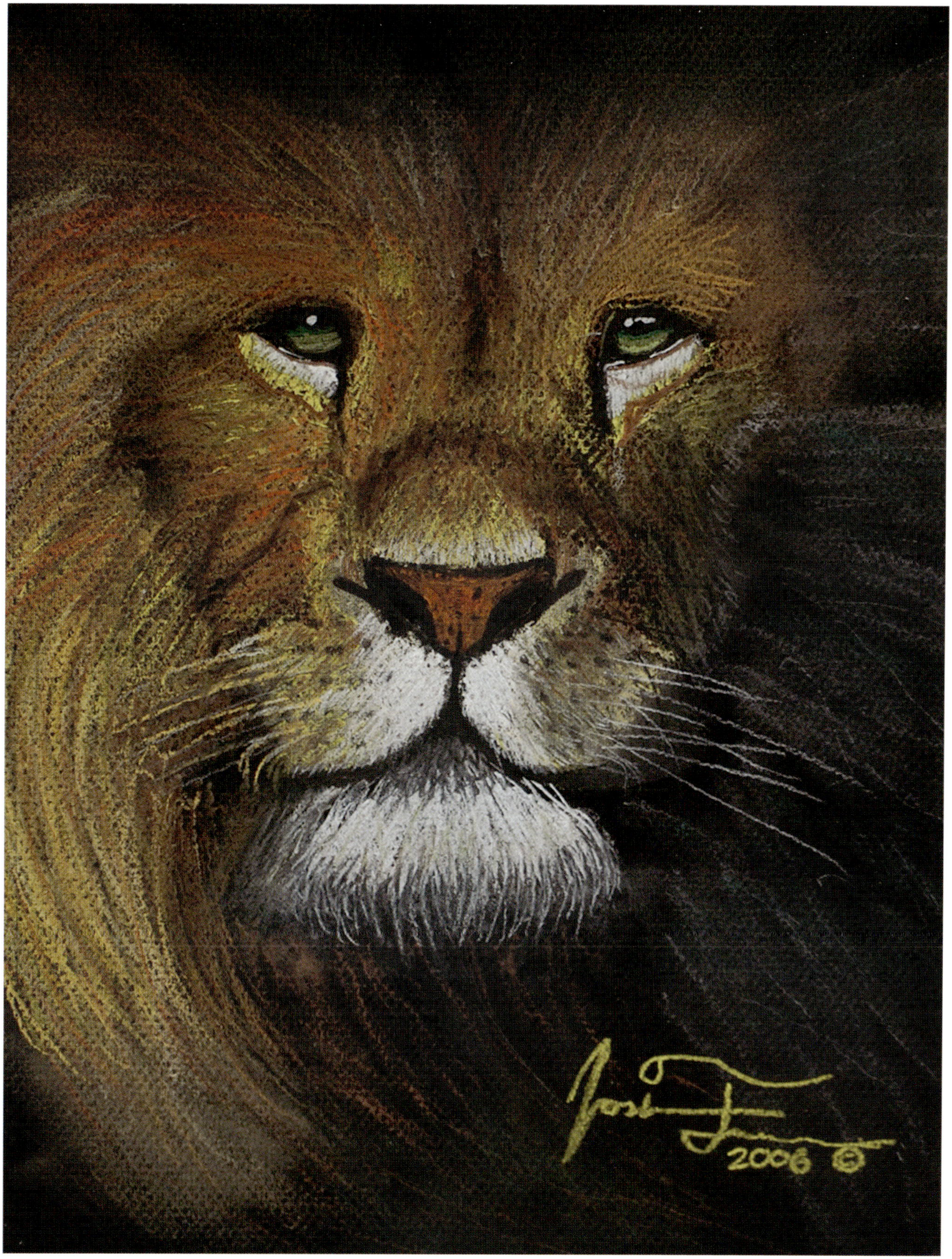

RED SQUIRREL

At the time I did this chalk pastel at age eleven we were living in a rented home, which sat next to a ravine on 32 acres of land. My brother Zac and I enjoyed building forts down in the woods and mucking around in the stream. We loved to watch the squirrels scurrying through the trees, hiding nuts in hollowed-out trunks. I was inspired by a photo in a children's wildlife magazine and decided to draw this Red Squirrel. Before I hung it for my first exhibition in the Artway on Two at Joseph Brant Hospital it was sold... to my grandmother. At her request, I had already done a portrait of her cat Miss Sally, and I gave that to her as a gift. When she saw this squirrel and said she would like to buy it, I offered to give it to her too. However, she insisted on purchasing it so I gave her a good deal. She proudly displays it in her dining room, showing photos of this and the rest of my pieces in a purse album she carries wherever she goes... typical grandma!

Chalk Pastel on Paper 16" x 10" 2007 (Age 11)

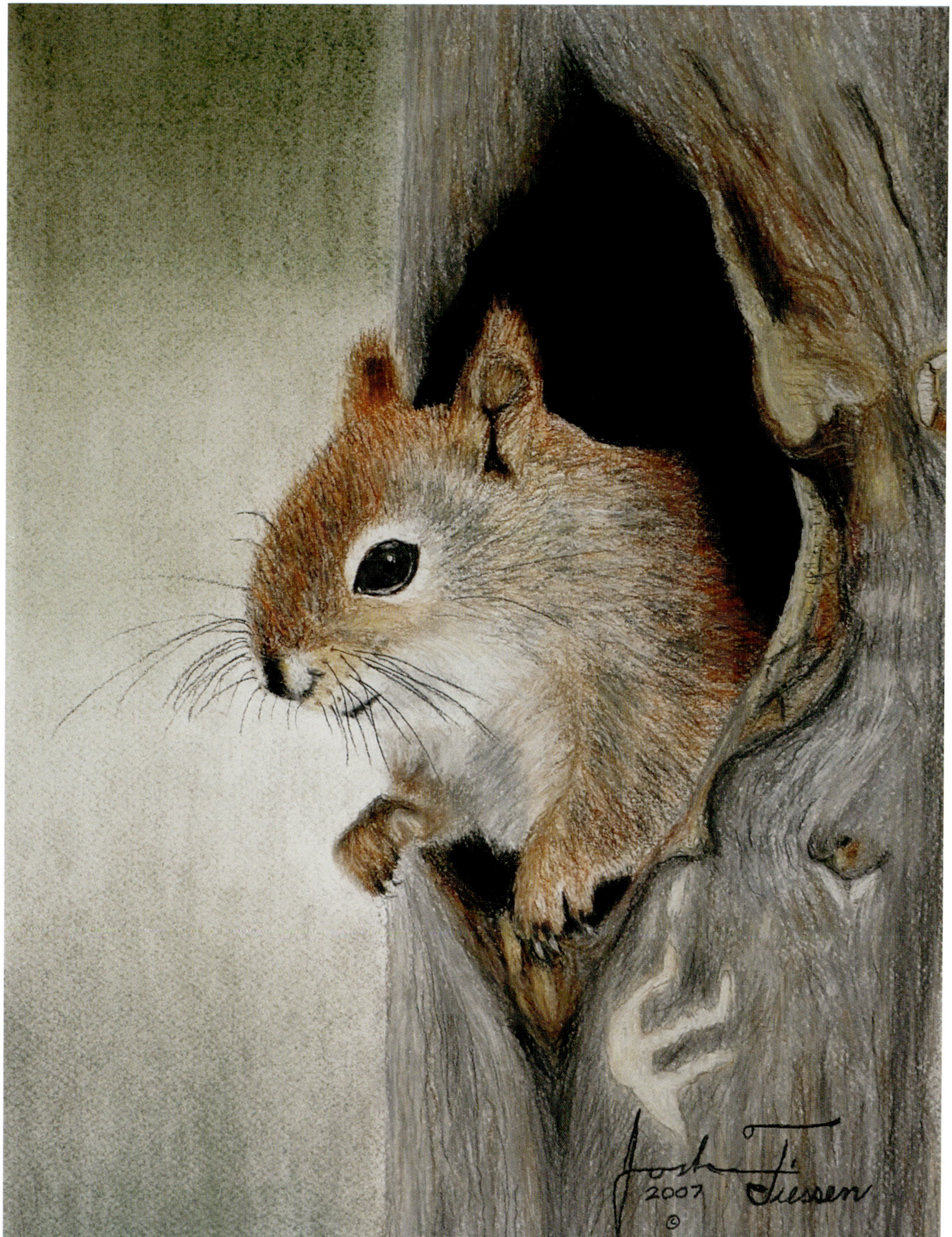
2007
©

PERSEVERENCE

It was the dead of winter and a friend had loaned us the DVDs for the entire BBC series of *Planet Earth* and *Blue Planet* that we had missed while living in Russia. We watched them almost every day during lunch for a month, as we were so captivated by them. Before that, my understanding of penguins had come mainly from the movie *Happy Feet* which, as I discovered from the BBC series, was surprisingly accurate. I became very interested in the *March of the Penguins* and was amazed at the perseverance of the fathers through the harsh dark stormy season to huddle together protecting their one egg each, as the mothers are off feeding in the ocean. The dads carefully balance the large egg on their feet under their pouches to keep it from freezing in the snow. The group works together taking turns on the outside with backs to the unrelenting 40 mph winds. Through instinct they know how to do this and are determined to persevere, as they were hard-wired for it by their Maker. In this painting I wanted to show the harsh weather conditions by using bold expressive brush strokes, which depict the swirling wind and icy snow.

Acrylic on Canvas 16" x 20" 2009 (Age 13)

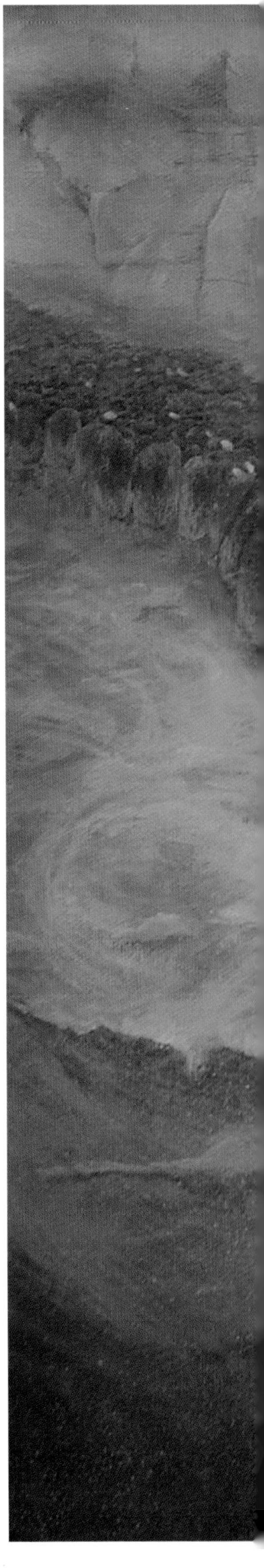

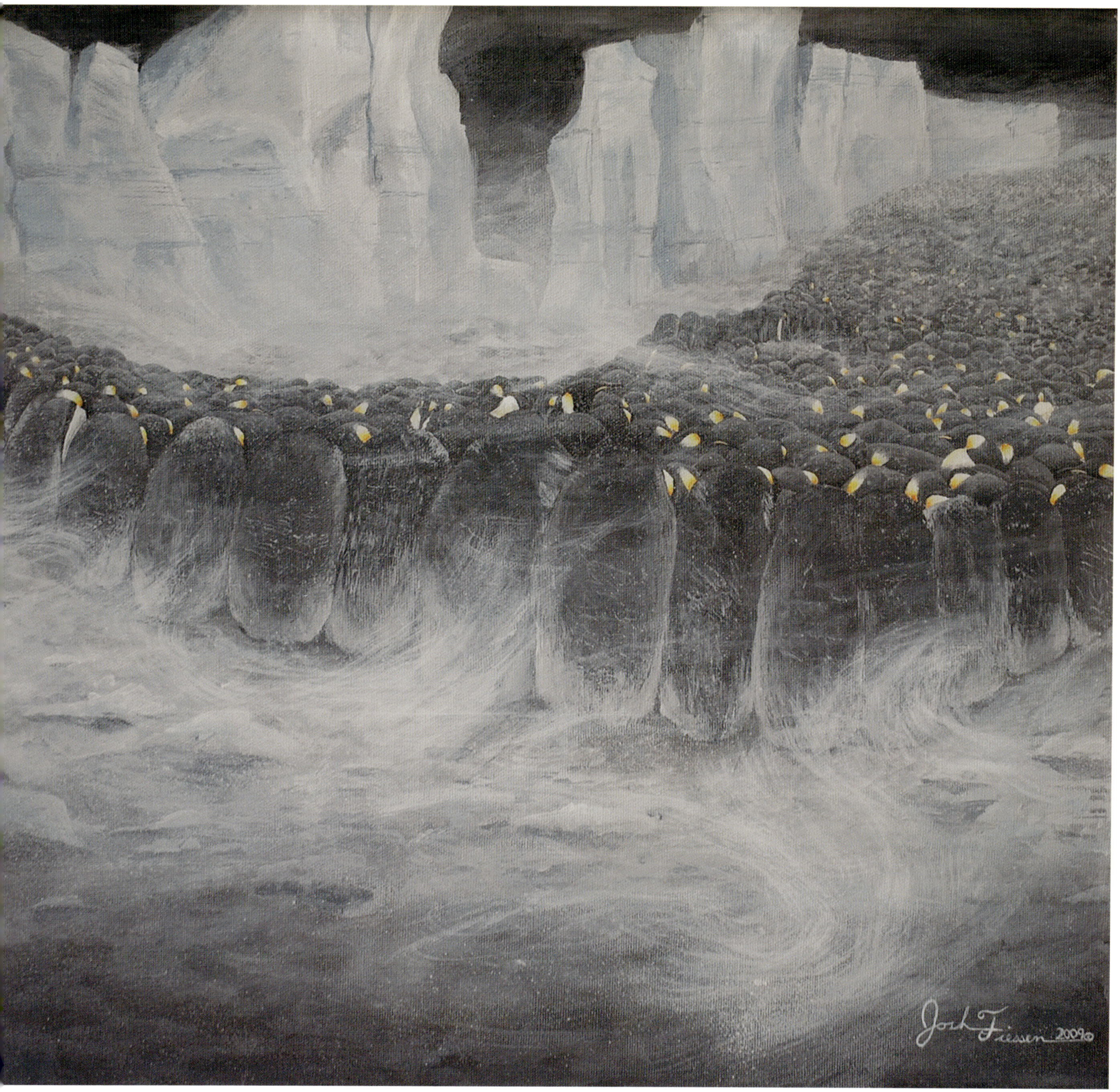
Josh Friesen 2009©

A WINTER'S REWARD

Following the harsh winter, on the successful completion of the father's difficult task of protecting the egg, the penguin mother returns just as the baby hatches from under the dad's pouch. What a wonderful reward for their efforts! This scene of the little penguin family is repeated as far as the eye can see, and we are treated to it in the comfort of our own homes because of the dedication of scientists and videographers who captured it in the barren icy landscape of Antarctica. Starting with a blank canvas, I completed the main colour blocks for this painting during a "Celebration of the Arts" at my church, Paramount Drive Alliance Church in Stoney Creek. Since they had seen it being painted, a few people who were there wanted to purchase the original, but of course only one could. Others requested prints and I was happy to make these available for the first time, so that more people could enjoy my art in their homes.

Acrylic on Canvas 20" x 16" 2009 (Age 13)

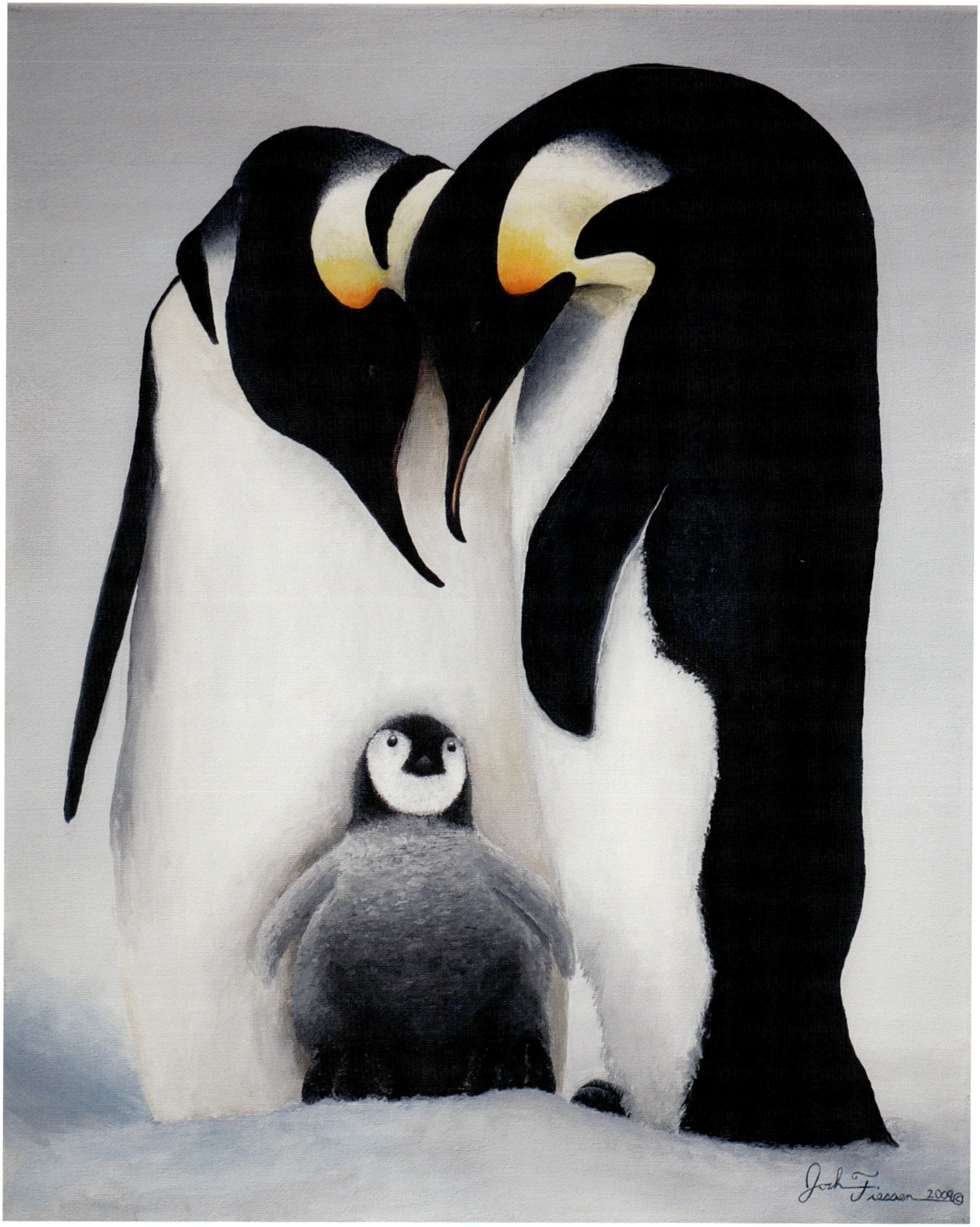
Josh Friesen 2009©

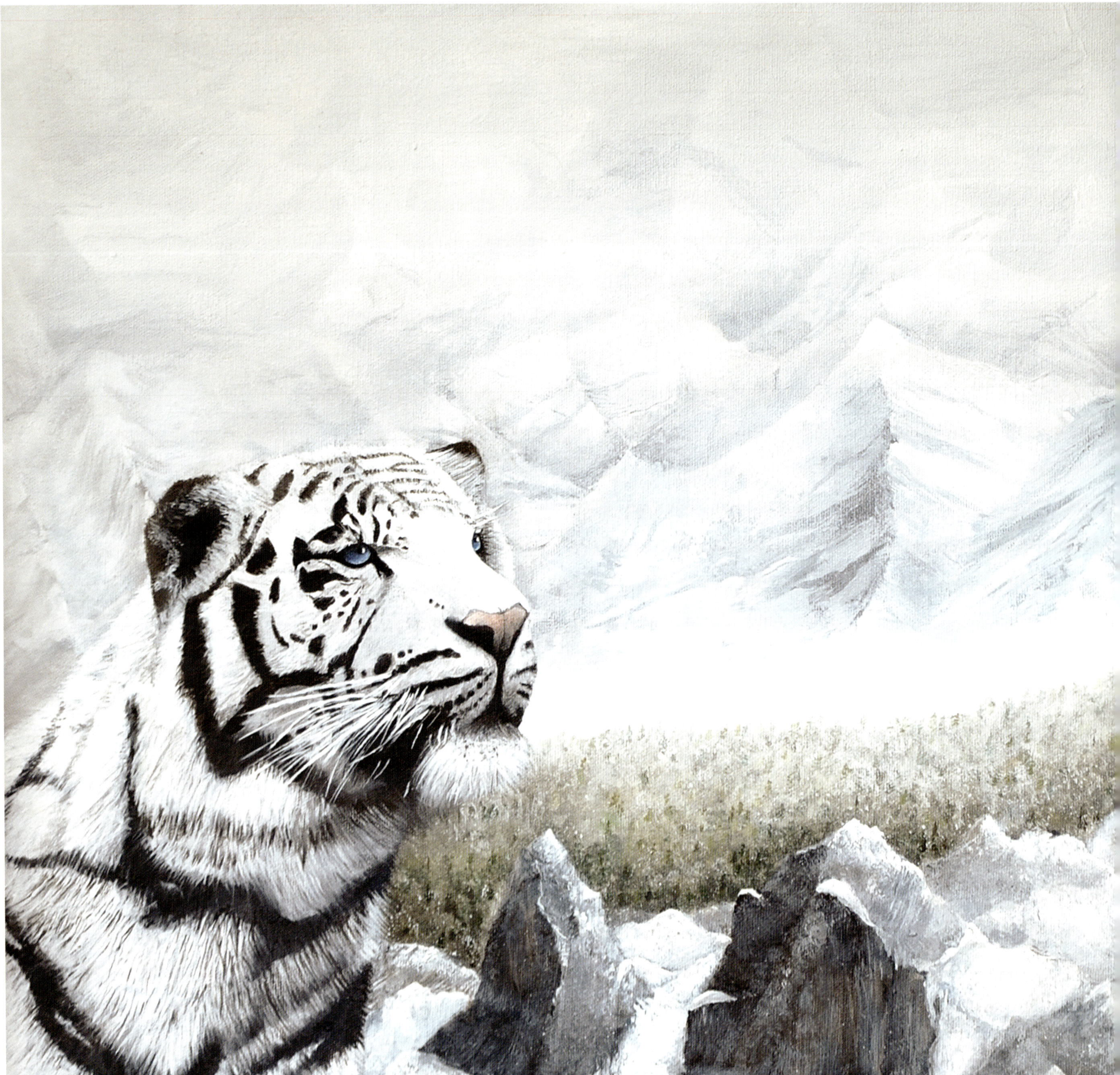

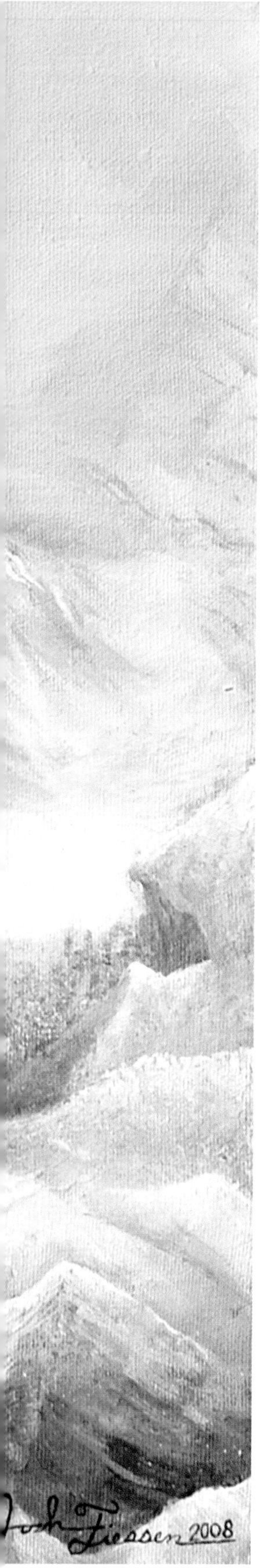

SNOW WHITE

I spent the early years of my life living in Russia, where we went to every travelling zoo and circus that came to town. The rules were more relaxed there and we could watch from six feet away, as the animals paced in their wide-barred cages. It was bittersweet, as we always felt bad for the animals in their cramped quarters and did our best to urge the keepers toward their better care and comfort. It wasn't until we moved to Canada that I realized what a privilege it had been to see those animals up closer than we ever get to see them here. In particular, the White Tigers and Snow Leopards had made a strong imprint on my mind, and I later painted them seeking to show their strength and graceful beauty. In this painting I tried to highlight the tiger's stripes against the snowy mountains in the distance, and show how the tiger could fit into a northern environment. I wanted the only distinct colours in this painting to be the pink nose and the bright blue eyes. I entitled it *Snow White*, with the intentional irony of juxtaposing a fairytale character and a wild animal.

Acrylic on Canvas 16" x 20" 2008 (Age 13)

Breakaway Magazine Art Competition (ages 13-19) Honourable Mention (4th Place)

ELEPHANTS AND EGRETS

Since we had become acquainted with several South African families, my mom decided that our geography study on the continent of Africa would focus on South Africa. As usual, we brought home stacks of books and DVDs from the library. My brother and I were given the assignment of interviewing our South African friends. Some of them gave us photos, and I was immediately attracted to the elephants and began sketching their wrinkled trunks and large ears – bigger, I found out, than their Asian counterparts. I had a composition forming in my mind, which would prove to be very challenging for a twelve year old. With the elephants complete, I then searched for the kind of birds that I had seen flying among them and found that they were Cattle Egrets. I finished the painting in time for my exhibition at The Wine Village "Fiesta," for which I had been chosen out of dozens of local artists and was the youngest of the five that exhibited there (I had just turned thirteen). Following that, the painting was featured by the Cable 14 guy who discovered me at the Fiesta and came to my studio (then in the garage) to do a piece on me for their *Urban Cut* television show. However, I was never entirely happy with the painting, and a year later I started correcting some of the problematic areas and pumping up the colours which had been quite pale... and ended up basically repainting the whole thing! I was much happier with this new improved version, which I finished just in time for my exhibition at the Art Gallery of Burlington. The paint was still drying on the signature I had completed the morning we hung it on the wall there, and within an hour it was sold to some South Africans.

Acrylic on Canvas 30" x 24" 2008-10 (Age 12-14)

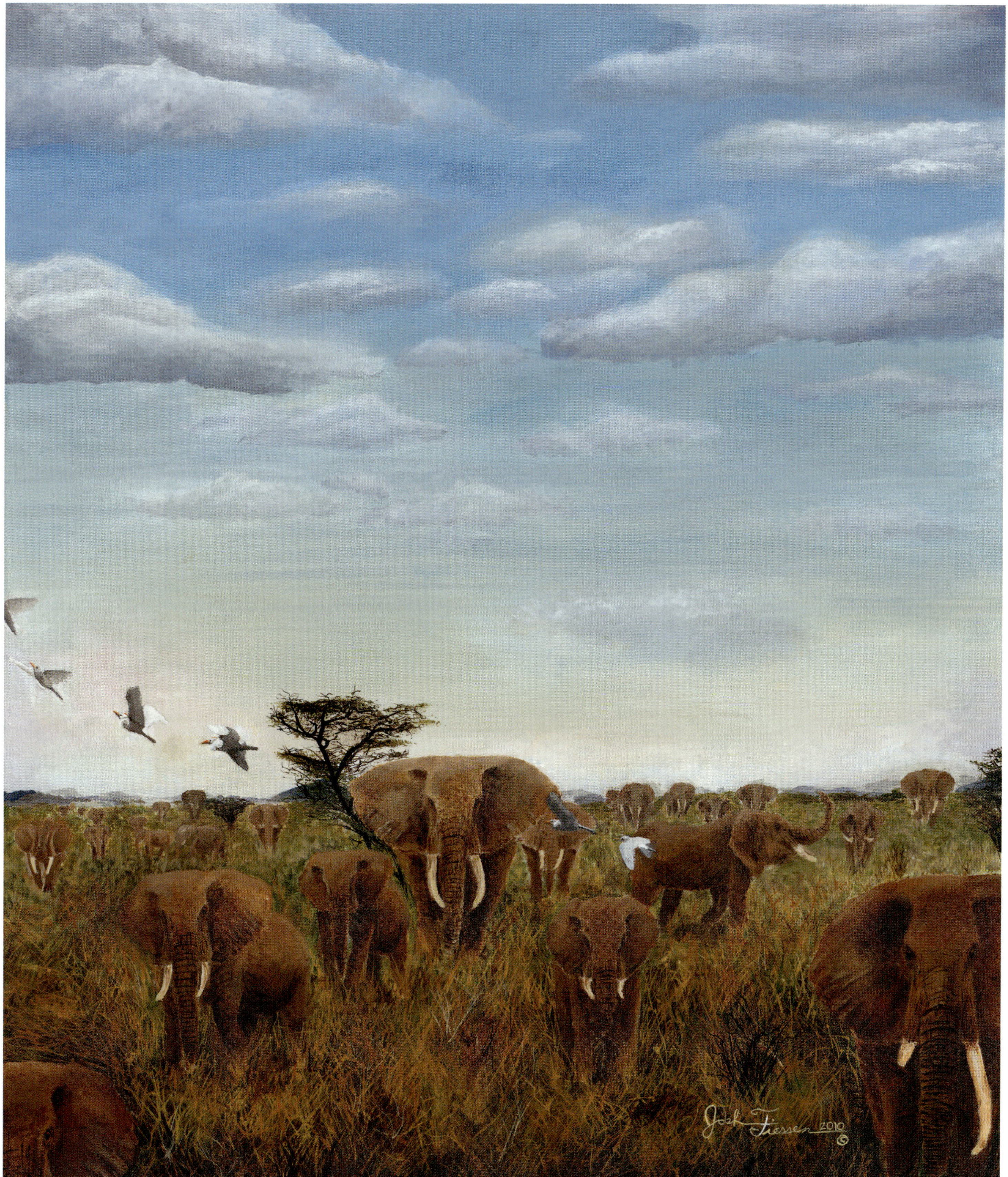
Josh Friessen 2010 ©

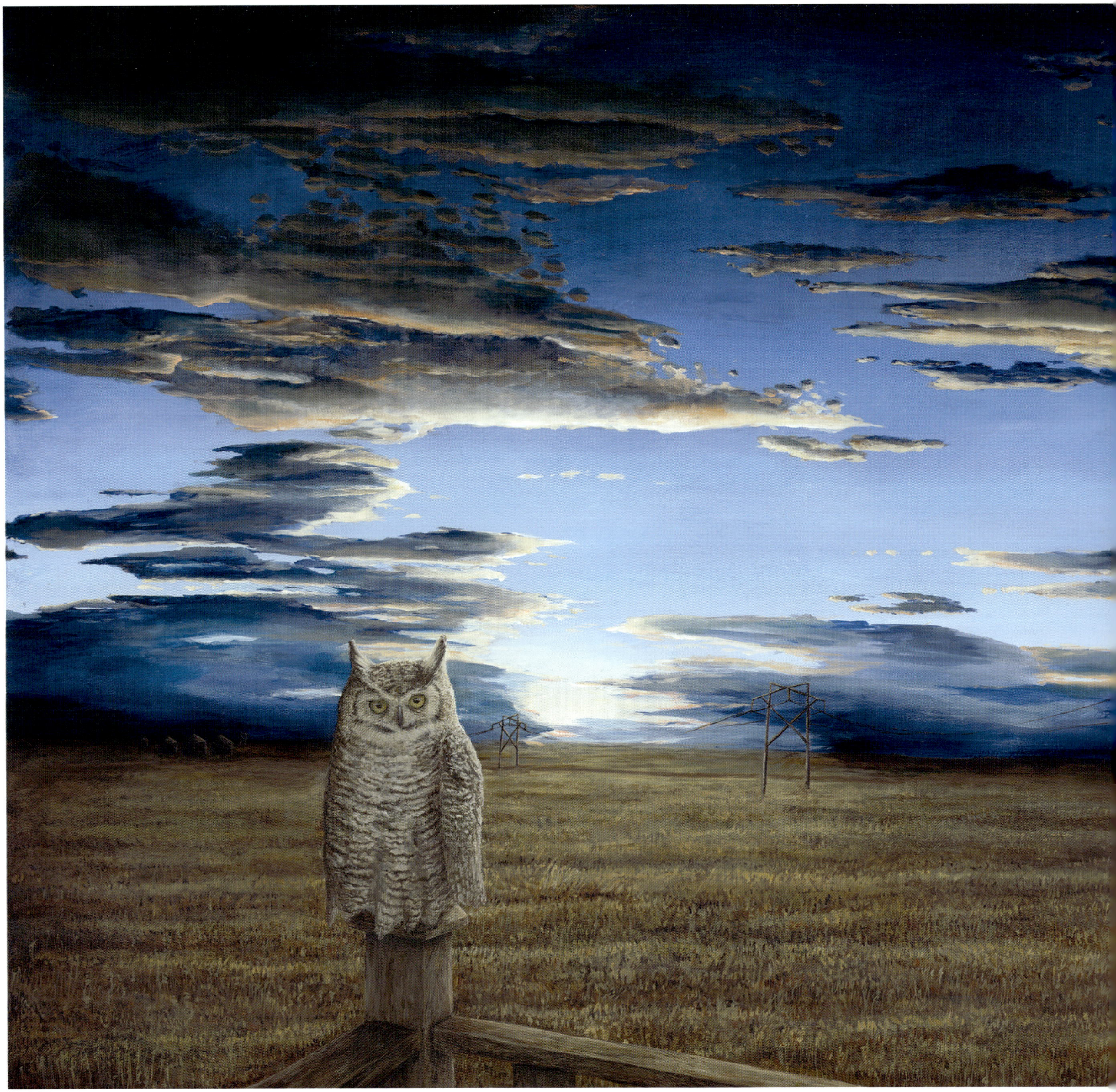

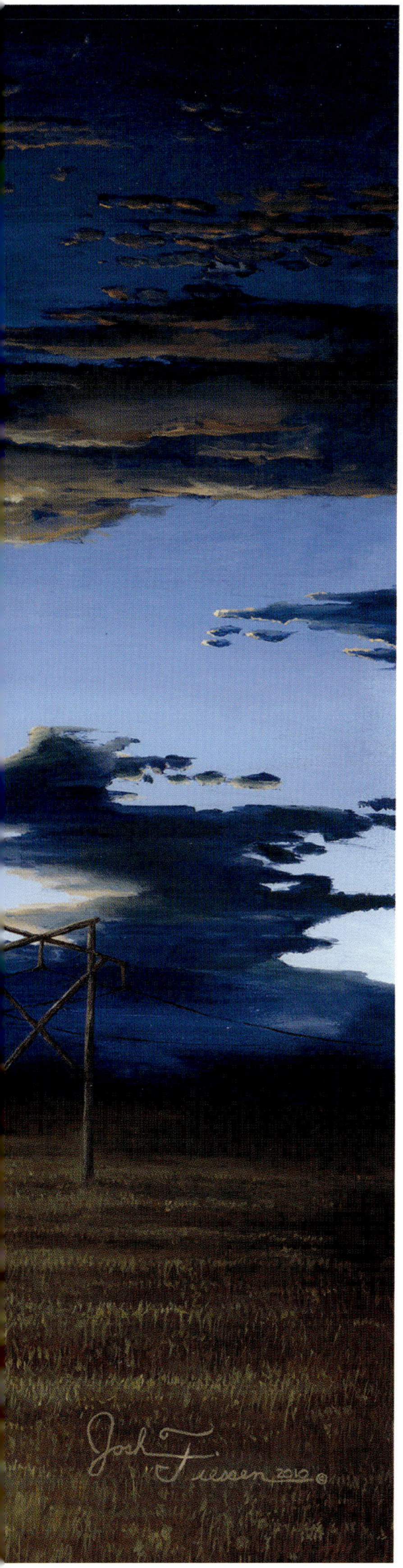

SASKATCHEWAN DUSK

I enjoy visiting my Uncle Daryl and Auntie Diane's farm near Wilcox, Saskatchewan. They always take us for drives in the evening to examine the progress of their crops and allow us to experience those amazing big sky sunsets. I love the way the endless fields of golden wheat turn to copper as the sun goes down. I was gathering photos and planning a painting to show the expansiveness of the prairies when my cousin Kyle, who also farms there, emailed me some photos of a Great Horned Owl on their porch railing. It had one droopy eye and stood uncommonly still as he took many photos of it. So it didn't surprise him when he found it dead in the field later that day – seemingly of old age rather than any visible mishap. In my painting I wanted to portray that this owl was indeed on its last legs. I could have painted a young perky owl without any imperfections, but I wanted to stay true to the reality of this scene. The owl reminded me of the final time I hugged my Grandpa Cairns as he was on his way out our door. I told him I loved him, and I noticed his eyes were heavy as he pulled away. He knew it and we knew it, his heart was winding down. It was dusk and he was weary. His eyes told me that he was sorry but this would have to be our last farewell. And it was. The patriarch of our family was gone. In nature and in our own lives sickness and death are inevitable, so we must take the time to enjoy each person and animal that God brings our way even for just a short time.

Acrylic on Canvas 36" x 48" x 2" 2010 (Age 14)

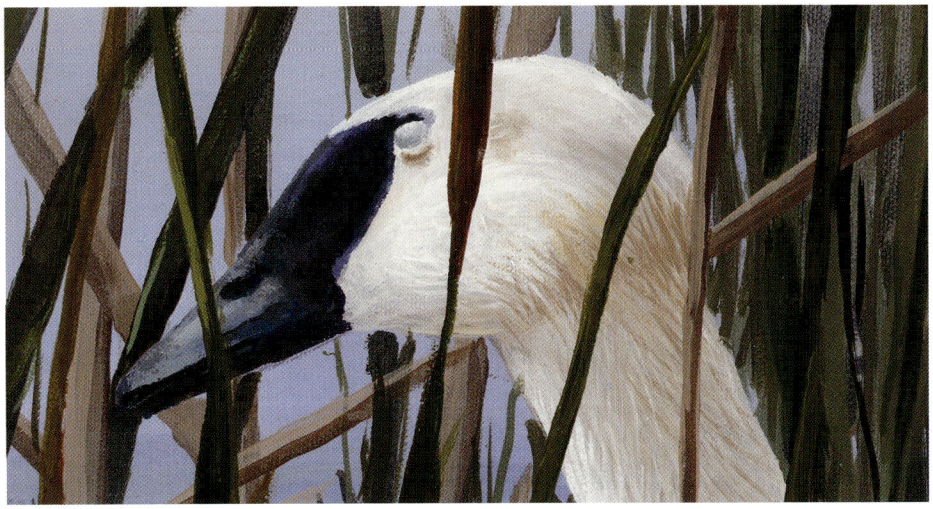

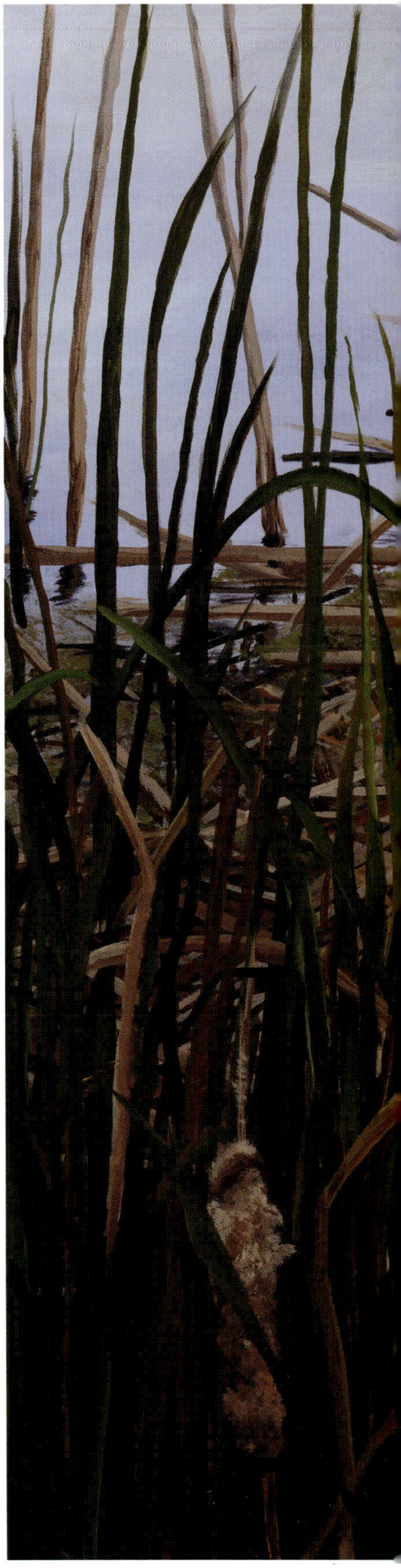

NESTING TRUMPETER SWAN

I have not liked school field trips that I've been on because I find by the time we get there it's almost time to go home. However, I have loved going for day trips with my family and our friends. This way I can spend as much time as I want taking lots of photos. We always arrive when the doors are opening and leave when the lights are going out. A day at the Toronto Zoo was no exception. We lingered in the late afternoon sun for almost an hour on a raised deck above the large wetland area. I was trying to get the perfect photo of a Red-winged Blackbird that kept flying over the pond, when I spotted her... a young nesting Trumpeter Swan almost hidden among the cattails. I took many photos as she lay there in perfect repose, eyes closed, completely calm. Then we figured out why. These swans mate for life, and it was the male we had seen off in the distance circling the area and dutifully keeping watch that enabled the female to rest without worry. If only we could trust like that. I took a different approach with this painting, hiding the swan in the reeds and cattails, creating a mood of mystery for the viewer to figure out the scene.

Acrylic on Canvas 30" x 40" x 2" 2010 (Age 14)

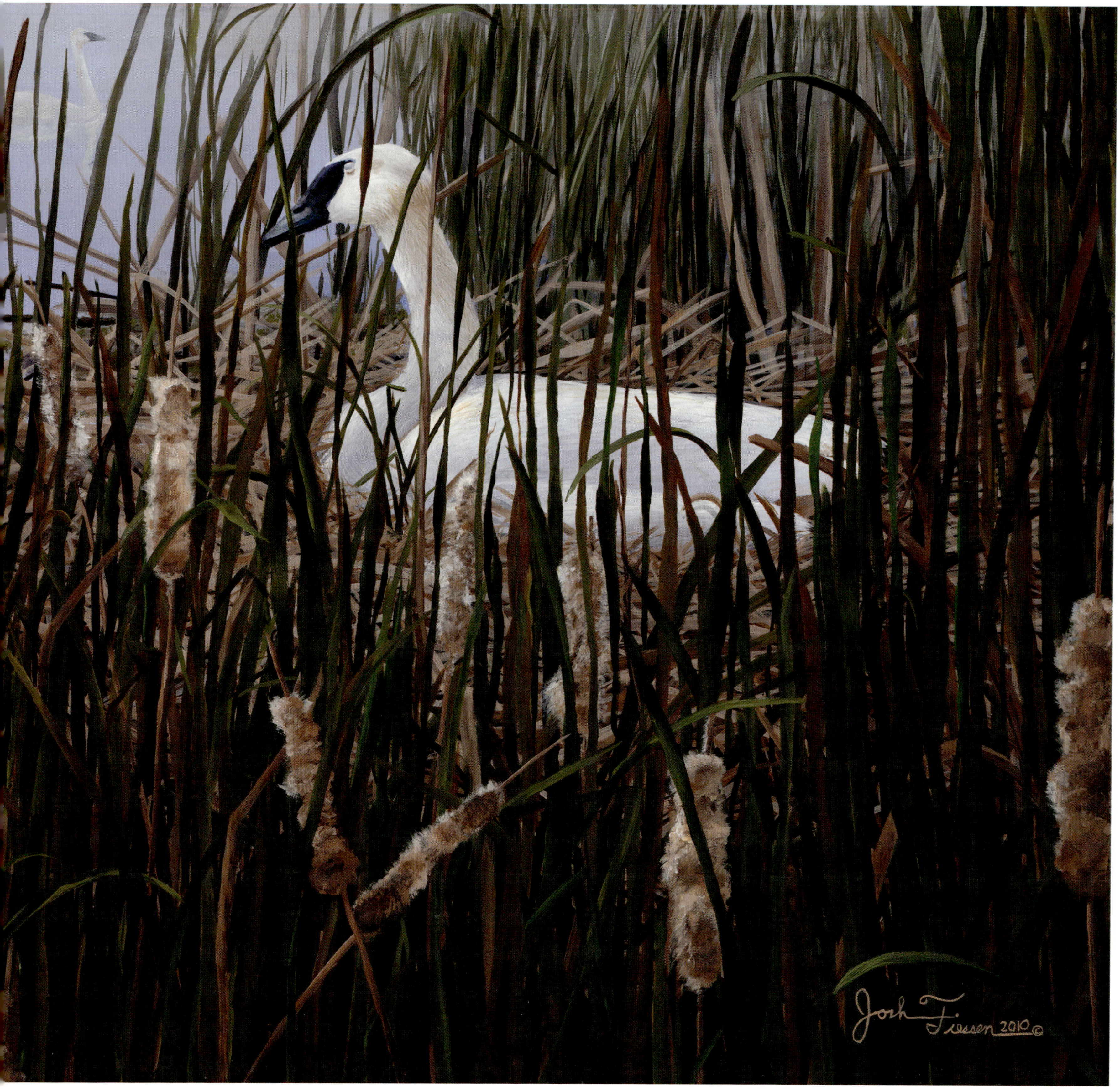
Josh Fiesen 2010 ©

SNOW LEOPARDS

I have always loved the elusive and mysterious Snow Leopards who live in the Central Asian Mountains. They have unbelievably thick, three-meter-long tails that I wanted to emphasize in this painting. None of the reference photos I had taken at the African Lion Safari or the Toronto Zoo had these animals from the back, but I was determined to show the one in this awkward pose so that the tail could be seen in all its power and glory. It is as if he has heard something, and has halted from following the other to take a backwards glance. When I later pondered this painting, I realized that for me the leopard on the left symbolizes people who always have their gaze on the future, while the one on the right represents those who are fully alert to living in the present. Sometimes I spend too much time pondering (and worrying) about the future and am not able to fully engage in the interesting things that are happening around me in the present. This was painted during a time of my life when I was worrying about the future, but needed to stay in the moment and be thankful for what I was experiencing in the present. I kept track of the hours it took me to complete this painting and I recorded up to eighty hours, but later I kept going back to it over and over for a month, so it probably amounted to much higher by the end.

Acrylic on Canvas 36" x 48" x 1" 2009 (Age 14)

ACSI Fine Arts Festival "Excellence and Displayed Competence in Painting" Grade 9
"Outstanding Artistic Execution in Painting (Best in Show)" Grades 9-12

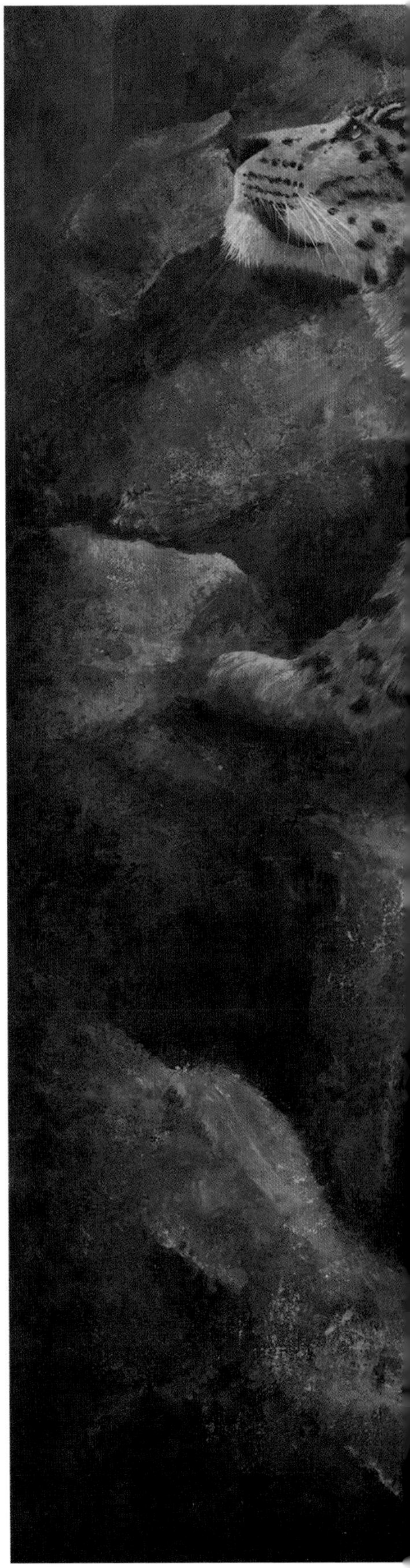

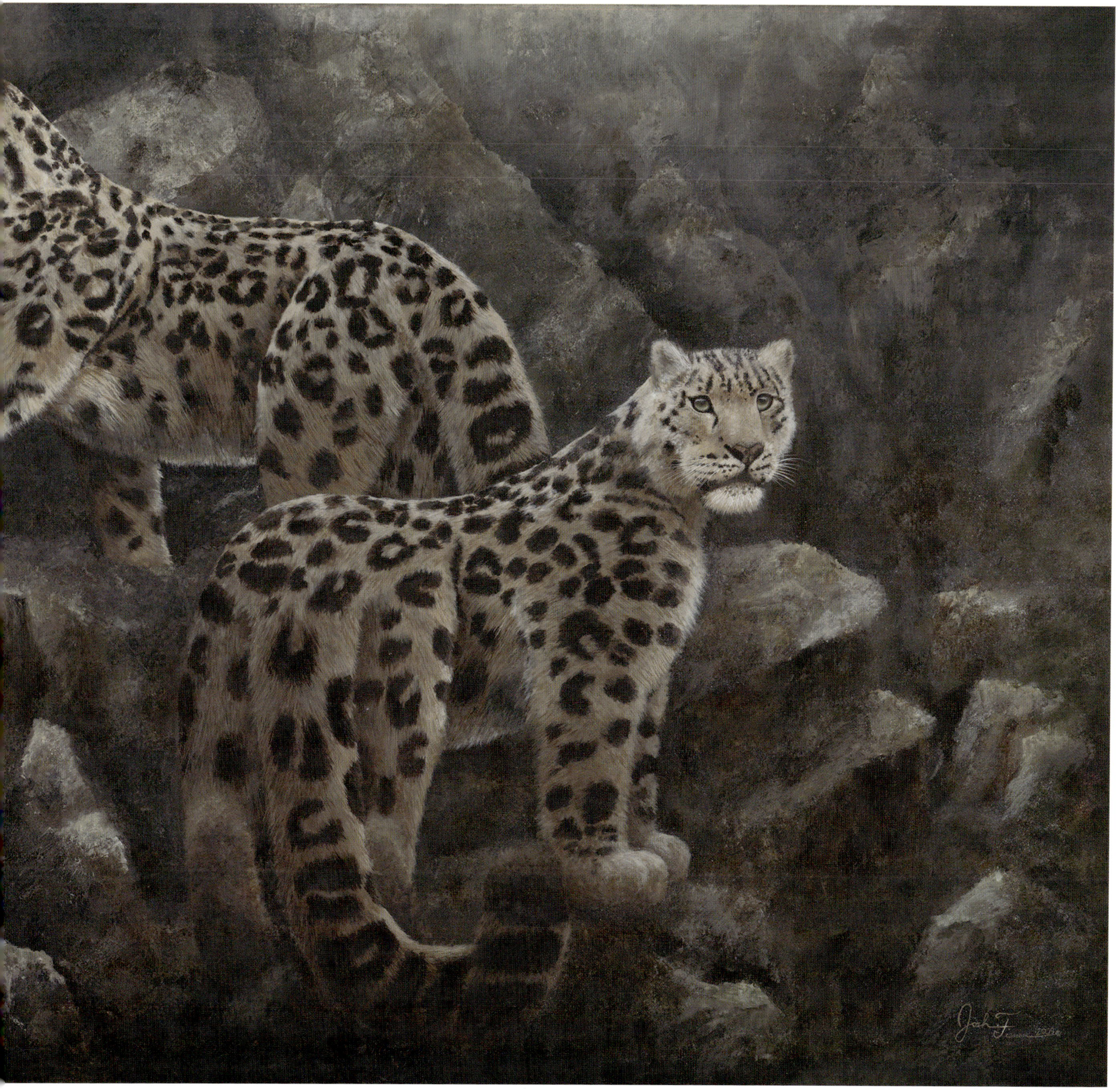

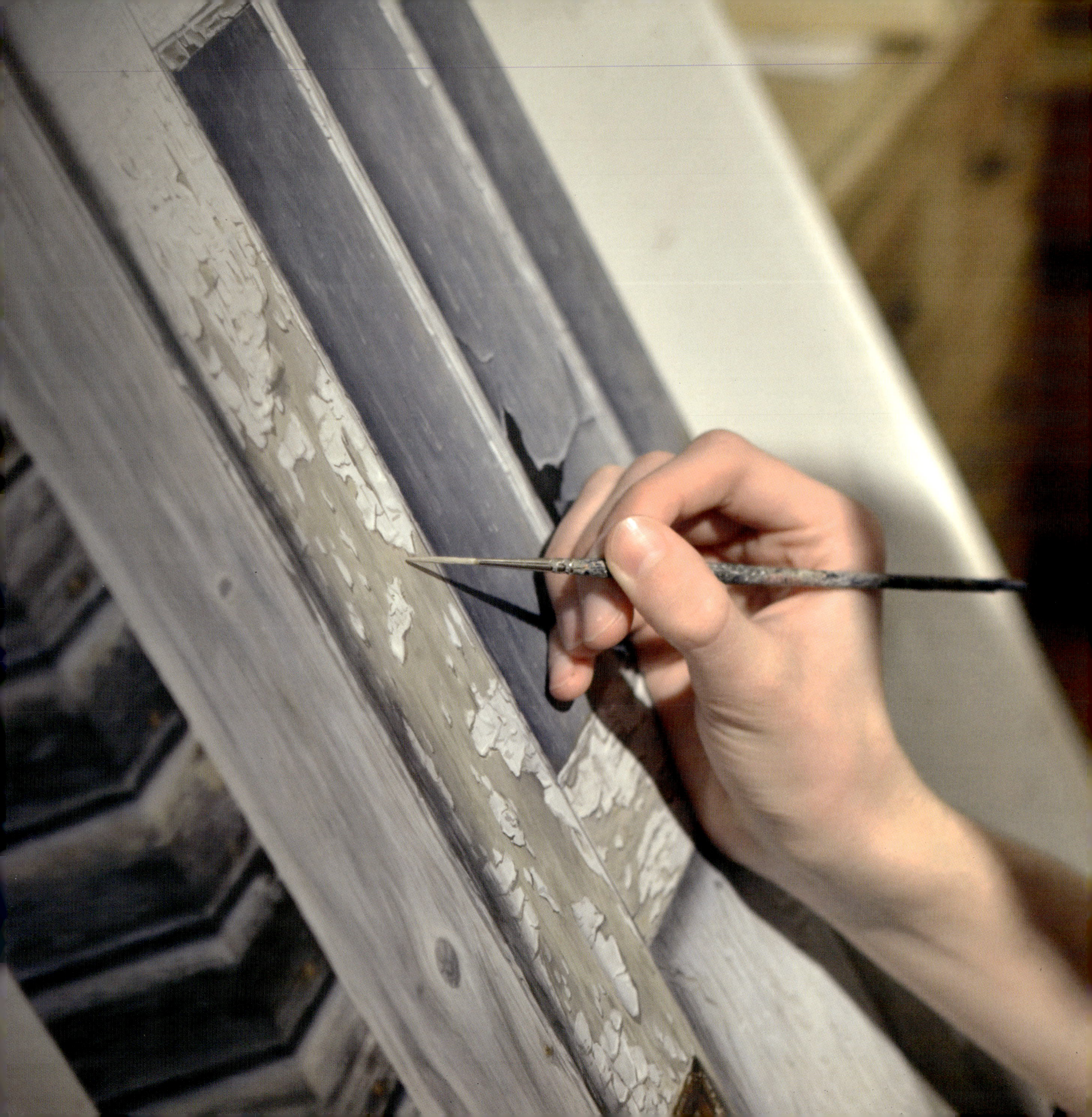

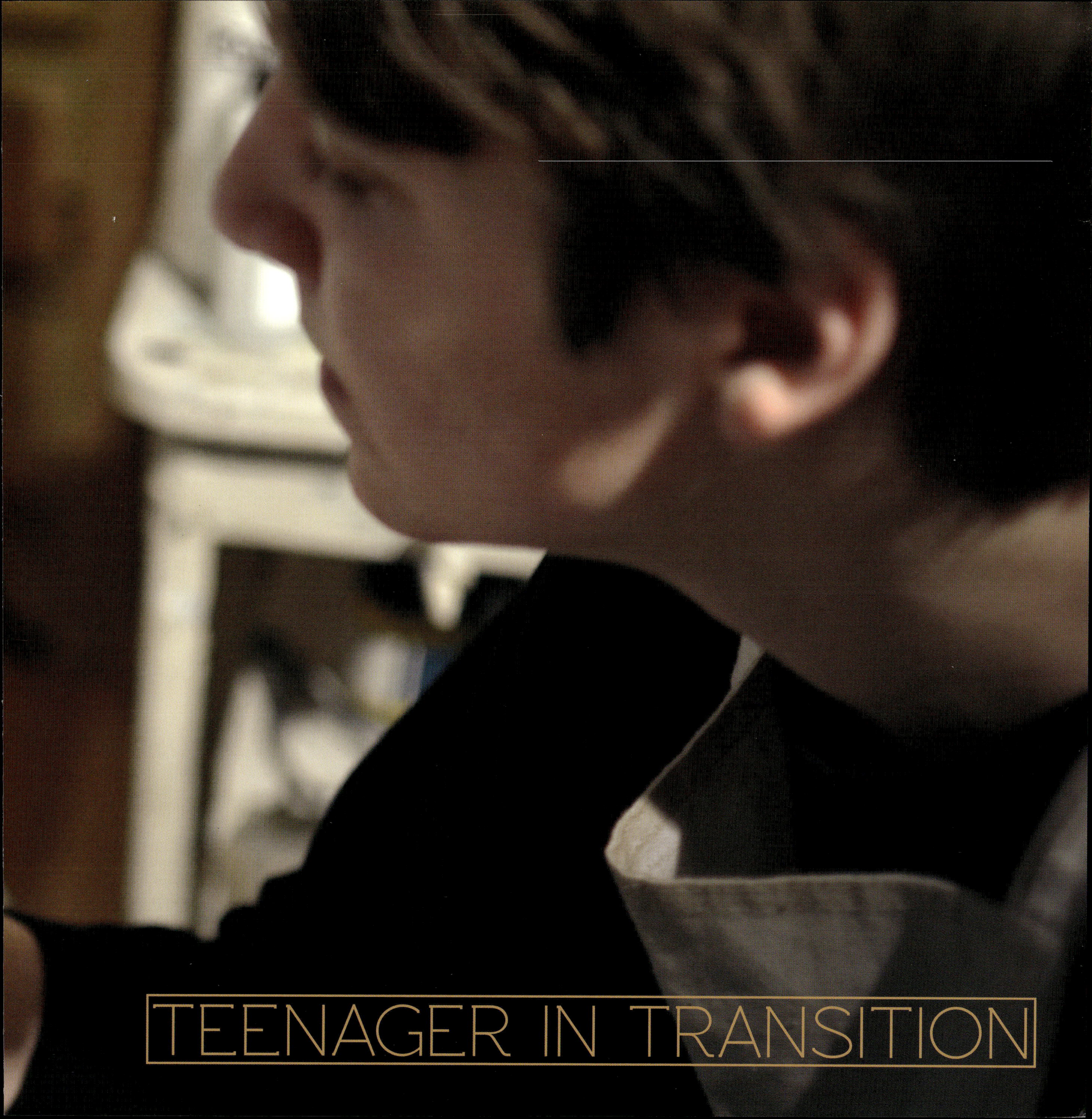

TEENAGER IN TRANSITION

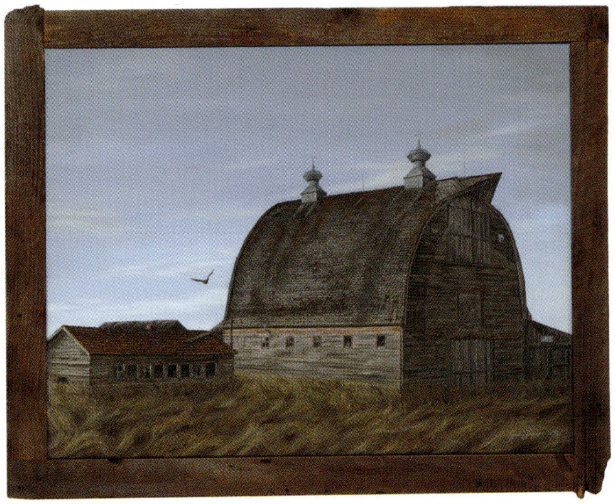

UNABANDONED

This unique old barn stands on some land that my cousin Kyle farms near Wilcox, Saskatchewan. He and my Uncle Daryl took us there when we were visiting in the summer so I could photograph it. I was still taking pictures when my dad went with them into the barn. Up in the rafters they were surprised to discover a huge Great Horned Owl staring down at them. I only caught a few fleeting shots as it flew out an opening in the back, and off into the expansive prairie sky. The next day we returned and the same thing happened. What seemed like it had been abandoned was actually not abandoned at all. It reminded me of the times when I feel lonely and empty, like no one is there. But I know that I will never be alone, because God is always with me. I used all my photos as references for this painting. Someone commented on how tedious it must have been to paint every last shingle, and others have noticed the small details and their shadows. Many appreciate the feelings of nostalgia that this painting conjures up.

Acrylic on Canvas 27.5" x 35.5" 2010 (Age 15)

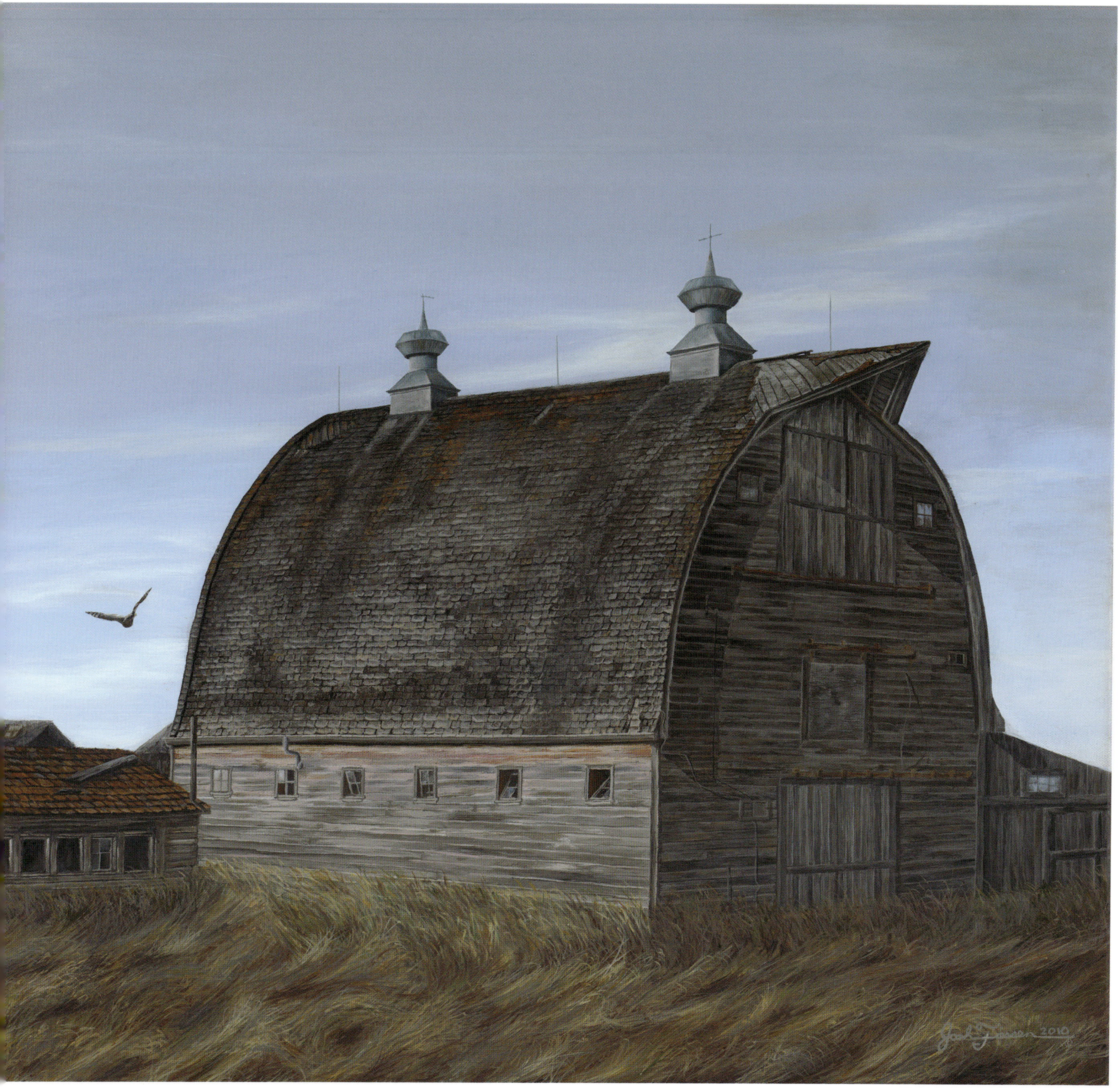

SOLITUDE

The word solitude is often associated with misty mornings and mountainous regions. It is the remoteness from human activity and isolation that is central to the meaning of this painting. I wished to demonstrate this by the two secluded Bighorn Sheep that are camouflaged, giving a sense of the scale and vastness of the mountain. I was in Banff, Alberta, where I took the reference photos for this painting on a misty, hazy day when the sun was absent and so was the horizon. Although humankind is slowly encroaching upon these amazing landscapes, there are still untouched places like this in our vast country of Canada. I wanted to show through this painting how the beauty of the natural world is still present and should be respected and preserved. These are the places where I feel like I am in a dream, where time stands still in the quiet peacefulness of environment and landscape.

Acrylic on Masonite 30" x 34" 2011 (Age 15)

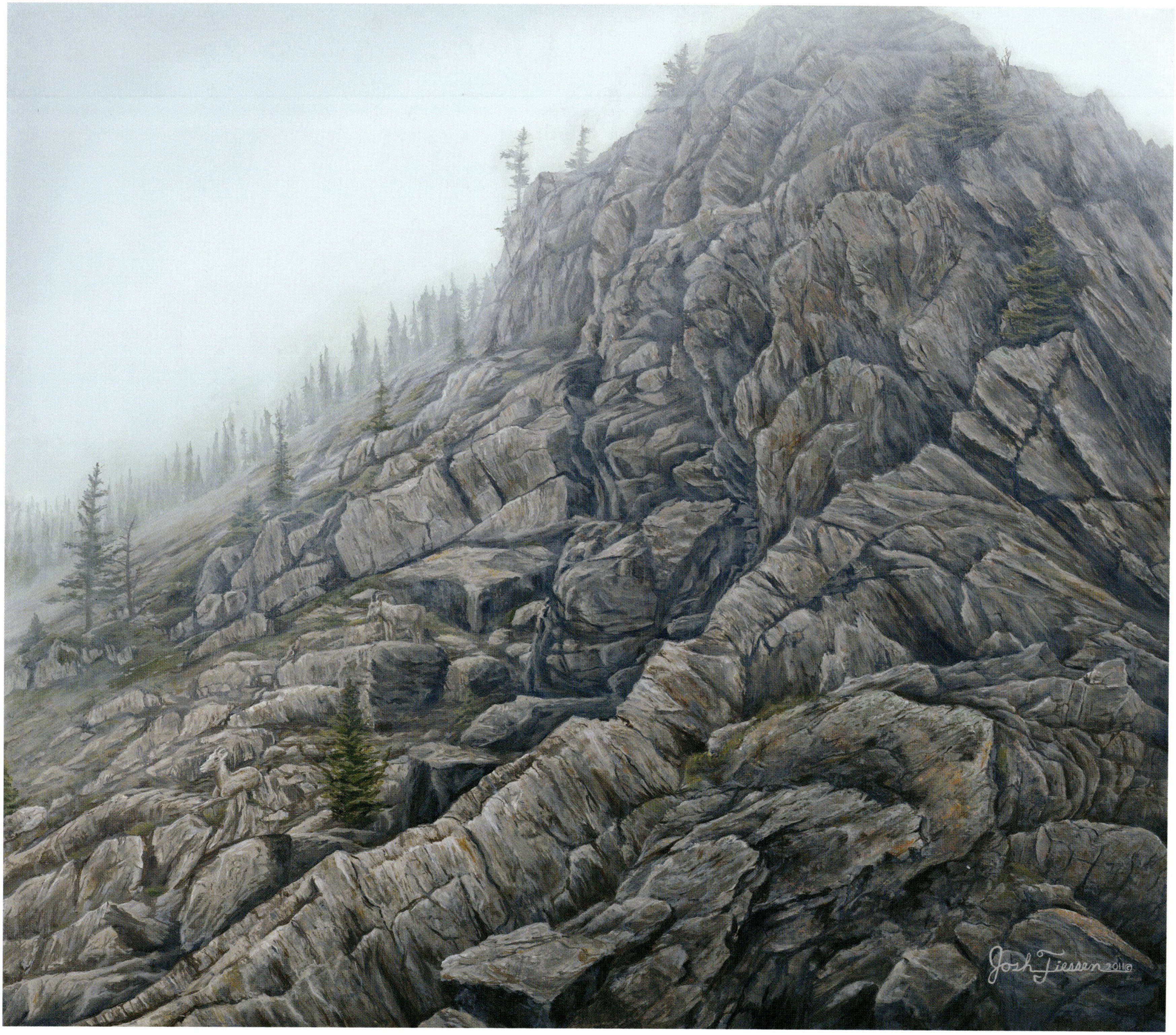
Josh Tiessen 2011©

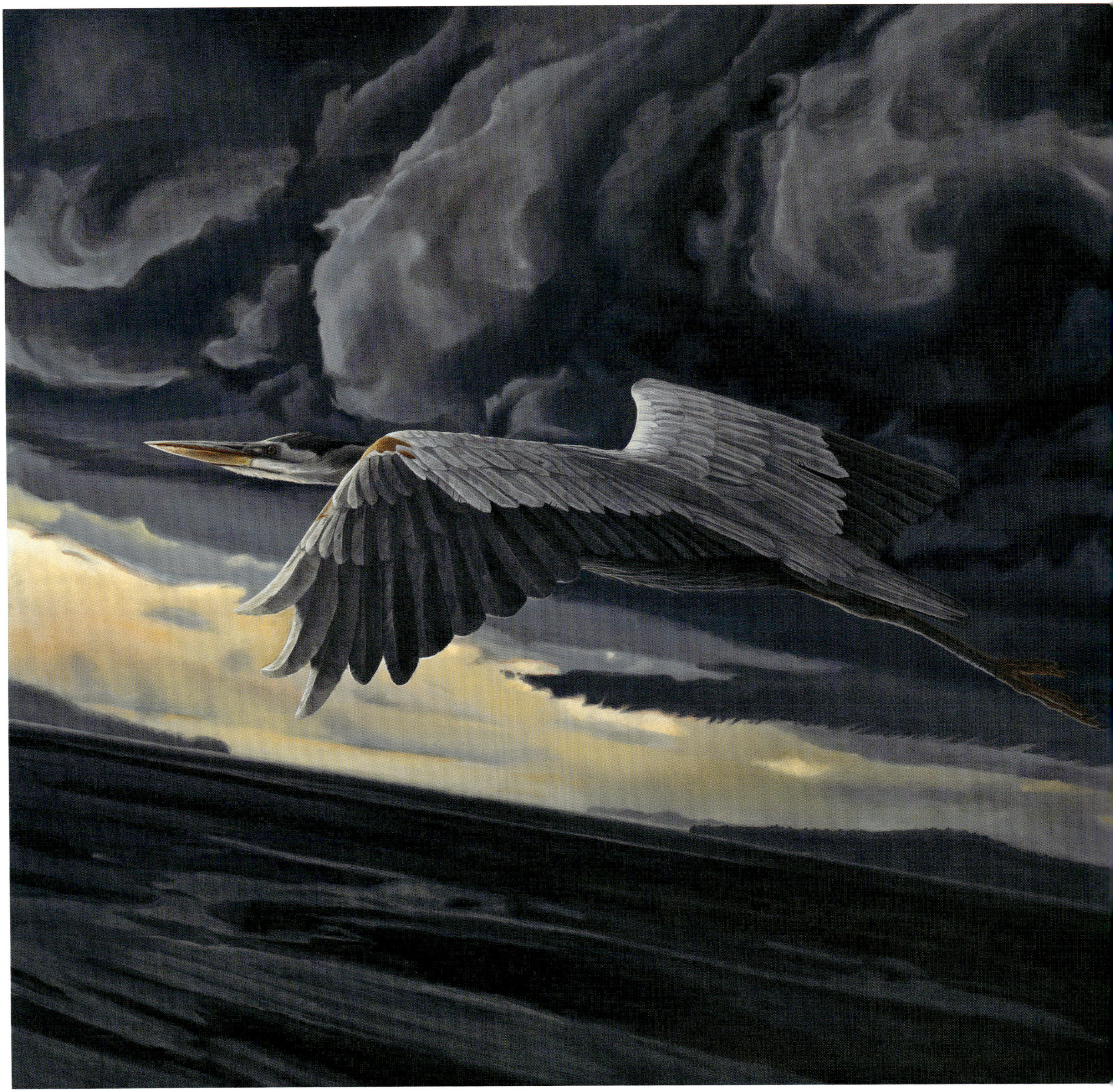

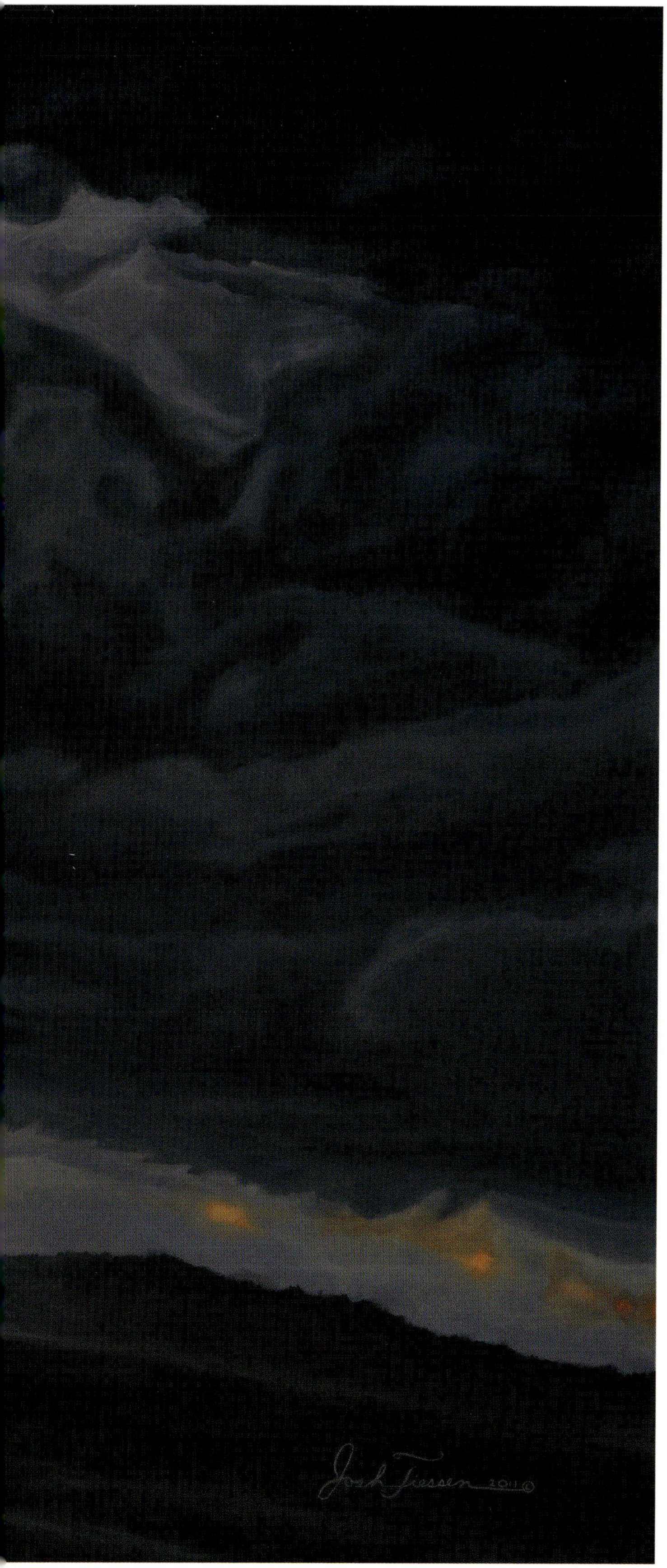

GLIMMER OF HOPE

This piece is the largest that I have completed to date. For reference, I used photos that I took of a Great Blue Heron in flight and stormy clouds, while I was in British Columbia on Cortes Island being mentored under Robert Bateman. A year later, just before starting this painting in the Fall, I had the rare opportunity to take photos of this amazing bird up close, as I happened upon one down on the shore of Lake Ontario not far from where I live. This helped me better understand the patterns and colouring of the feathers and face in particular. I used over twenty photos in order to achieve high realism detail. Compositionally speaking, I decided to put the horizon on an untraditional slight angle, as I felt this gave it a more dynamic sense and created greater aesthetic appeal. The swirling clouds add further motion as the heron flies toward brighter skies, keeping ahead of a turbulent storm. For me, the slight glimmer of light reflected on the heron represents hope within the darkness of the tempest. Although it appears that the heron is about to be engulfed, with no certainty of a way out, the light ahead evokes the metaphor of coming through one of life's storms and looking toward a brighter future. My family has faced a lot of storms, but our faith in God has given us that needed glimmer of hope to pull us through.

Acrylic on Canvas 40" x 60" x 2" 2011 (Age 15)

FORGOTTEN FOUNTAIN

When my family came back to Canada from Russia (where I was born and lived for the early years of my life) we moved into a house in Burlington, Ontario on the property of CAMA Woodlands Nursing Home. The house and gardens used to be part of that, but had been neglected for many years. So we set out to recover the old gazebo and surrounding flowerbeds. When my mother started cutting back a gigantic circular hedge, my brother and I found an entryway to the inside, where we discovered an old forgotten fountain! The little boy on the fish had toppled over, but we were delighted at our discovery. My mom trimmed the hedge way down so it could be seen, and my dad helped us put it back together and clean it up. For Mother's Day we refurbished it and put in a pump from my grandpa's old fish tank so the fountain would work. My mom was thrilled, and we all enjoyed it so much that we hauled it to the house we moved to in Stoney Creek a few years ago, and I can see it from my studio gallery windows. In the Fall, I took photos of it with the fallen peach tree leaves and murky water. The photos had two Blue Jays in them, but I later took more with House Sparrows, which are a common everyday sight. After 200 hours of painting it from August to October (see my time lapse video on YouTube), the water once again looked green and the peach tree leaves had fallen into it just like the year before. The sparrows that use it as their birdbath are humble, sometimes forgotten birds just like this fountain was, but I wanted to celebrate both of them in this painting. I liked the baroque revival style of the fountain and the challenge of this work, as it incorporated a statue of a human figure, perspective of roughly circular clamshells, water with reflections, and colourful cast shadows creating interesting shapes.

Acrylic on Canvas 40" x 30" x 2" 2011 (Age 15)

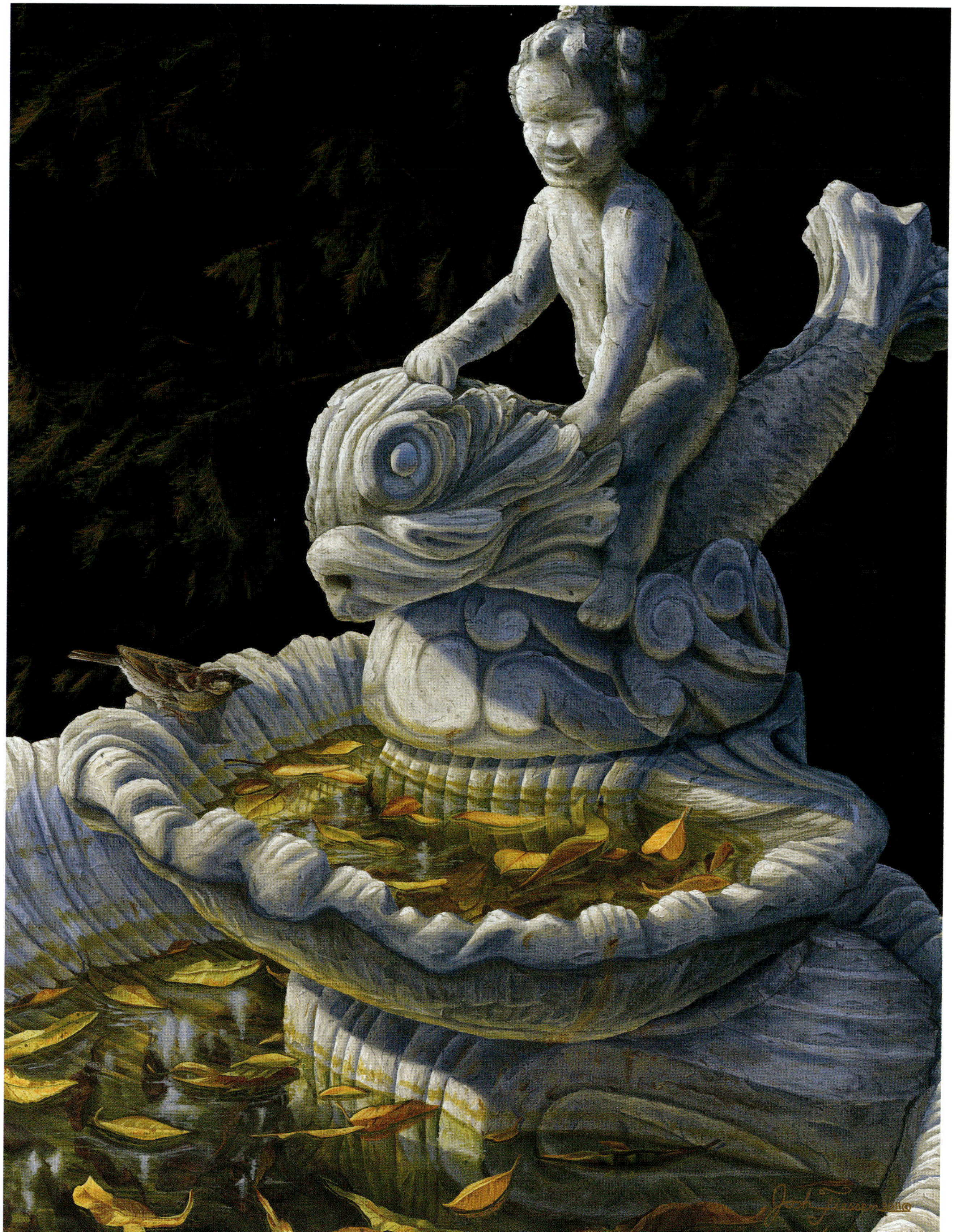

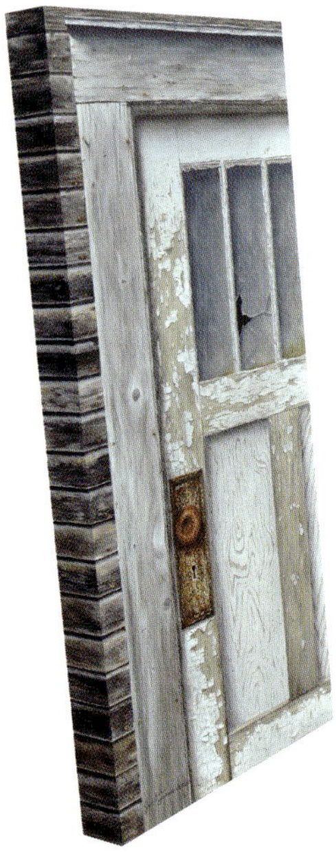

BEHOLD THE DOOR

I have been captivated by the peeling paint on abandoned farmhouses, which inspired my photographic series called "Watching Paint Peel," and later this painting. This piece is a composition based on several of my photos rather than being a photorealistic representation of one specific door. I took artistic license to enlarge some elements for emphasis. As I painted I thought about how, just like this old farmhouse door, we weather, fade and shatter over the years from the harsh elements of life that slowly deteriorate our outer and inner beings. I wanted to communicate a deeper theological meaning through this piece: that even though our souls have become filthy because of sin in this world (both ours and that of others) the God who created us looks past our ugliness and offers inner beauty and joy to all those who will believe in Him and accept his gracious offer. *Behold The Door* stands as a metaphorical depiction of the entrance to our soul when Jesus (God in flesh) comes to our door and knocks (Revelation 3:20). The question is, will we let Him into our lives or keep the door tightly locked?

Acrylic on Masonite 30" x 14" x 2" 2011 (Age 15)

ACSI Fine Arts Festival "Exceptional 2-Dimensional Piece of Show (Best in Show)"

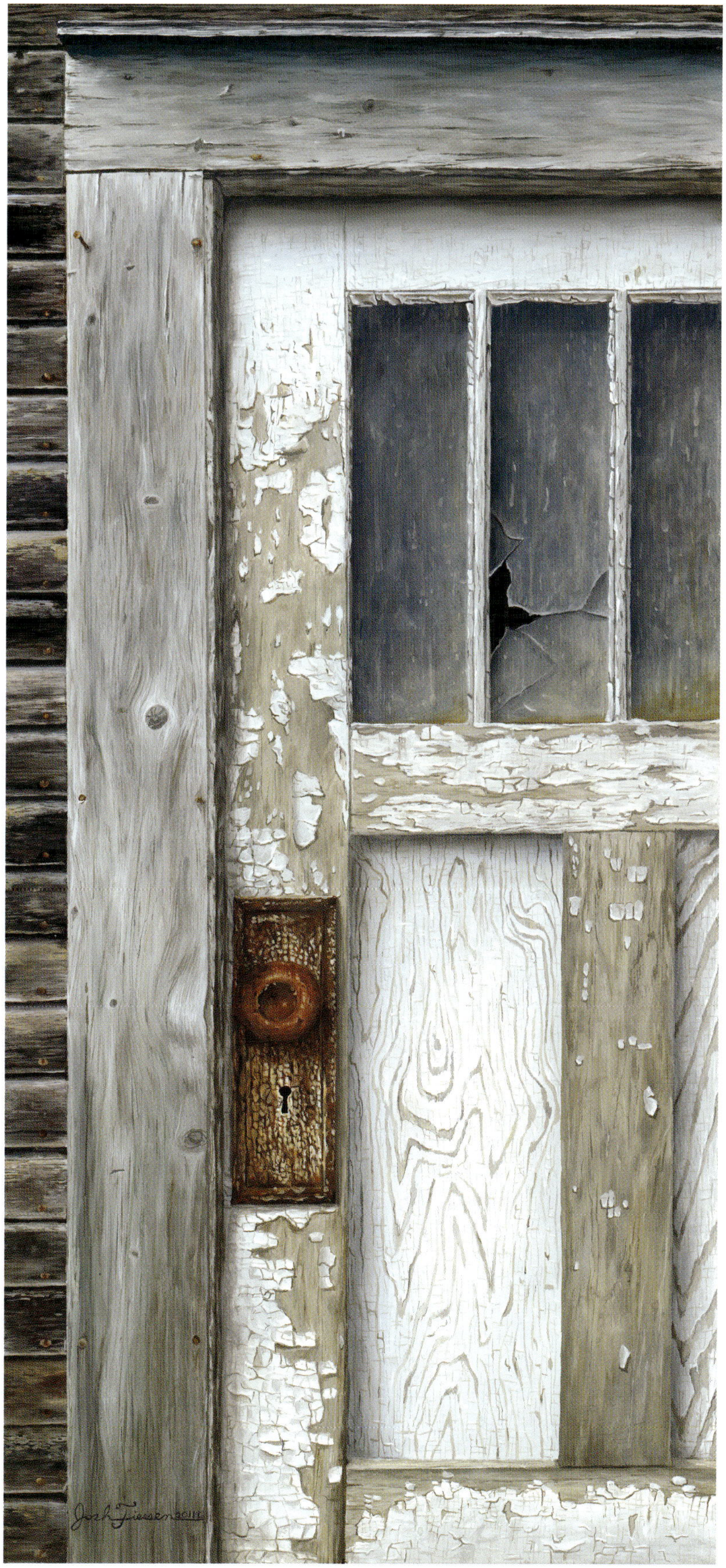

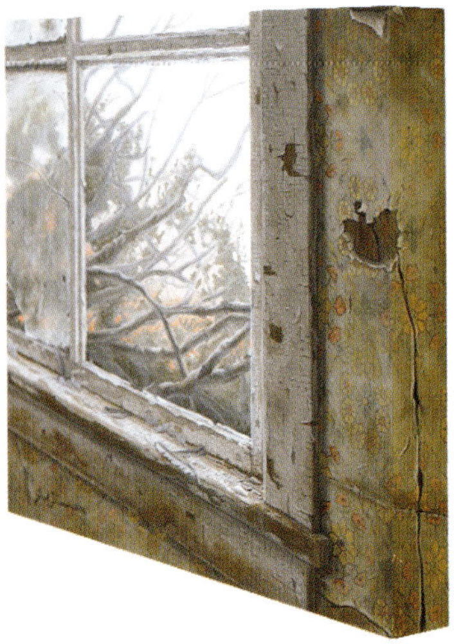

NOT ABOUT THE VIEW

A painting of a window often draws the viewer to look out into the distance, but rarely does it encourage the viewer to see inside. In this piece I wished to direct the observer's attention to the inside of the window – the window frame, windowsill and wall. The viewer is encouraged to ponder the mystery of the scene and ask questions like, why might there be feathers on the windowsill? Who used to live here and when? What is this architectural relic of the historical past saying to us? If these walls could speak! These and other questions are important to unravelling the meaning of this piece. The viewer's background experiences will inevitably contribute to their emotional response to this painting. As for the technical aspects, similar to my previous painting *Behold The Door*, the first painting in this series, I was fascinated by the weathering effects of natural elements on architectural structures which occur over time. Again, the eye is drawn to the peeling paint, and added to this are the dirty, broken and missing windowpanes, plus the intricacy of peeling vintage wallpaper from the past century. This pattern is reflected in the design that the old Caragana bush creates against the sunset.

Acrylic on Masonite 16.5" x 18" x 2" 2011 (Age 16)

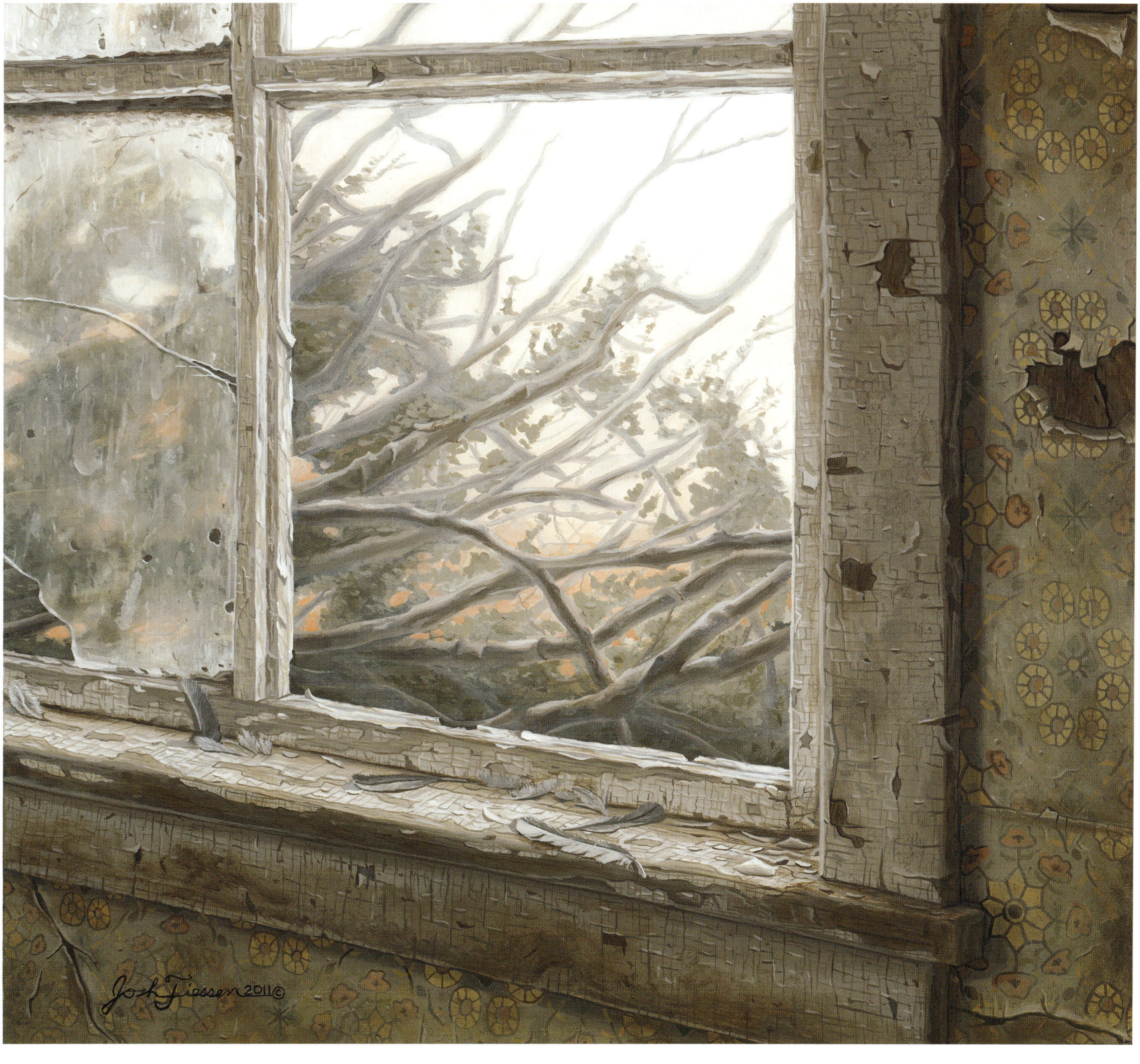
Josh Tiessen 2011©

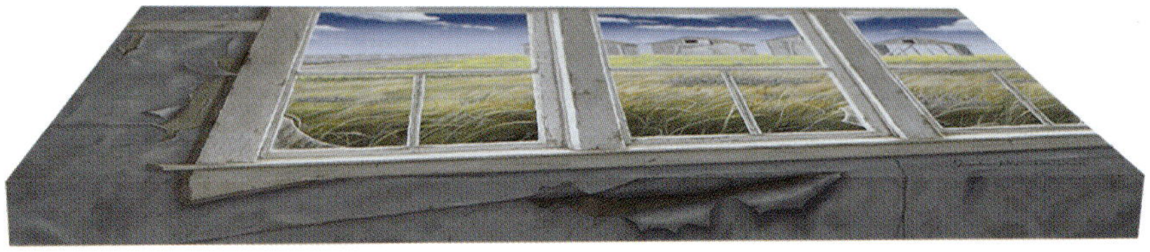

PRAIRIE PONDERINGS

I have witnessed a variety of feelings and responses from those who have stood and pondered this painting. For some it represents a sentimental place that reminds them of their childhood, but for others it is just an old dilapidated homestead. Many have said they experience a sense of joy in viewing this composition, which pulls them into the beautiful scenic view of the prairies where an old farmhouse window frames the flat landscape. The faded inside environment contrasts the bright blue and white-clouded sky, purple flax and yellow canola fields separated by a trampled dirt road leading out to the endless horizon. The painting evokes a different pace of life, a calm from the busyness, which city-dwellers sometimes idealize and long for: old granaries, teetering fence posts, peeling wallpaper, worn paint on windowsills, and what remains of windowpanes that once were... all marking the seasons that this old house has endured. Beauty can be found in this scene for those who are able to appreciate the intricacy and complexity of each element, which together give this painting its appealing character.

Acrylic on Masonite 24" x 32" x 2" 2012 (Age 16)

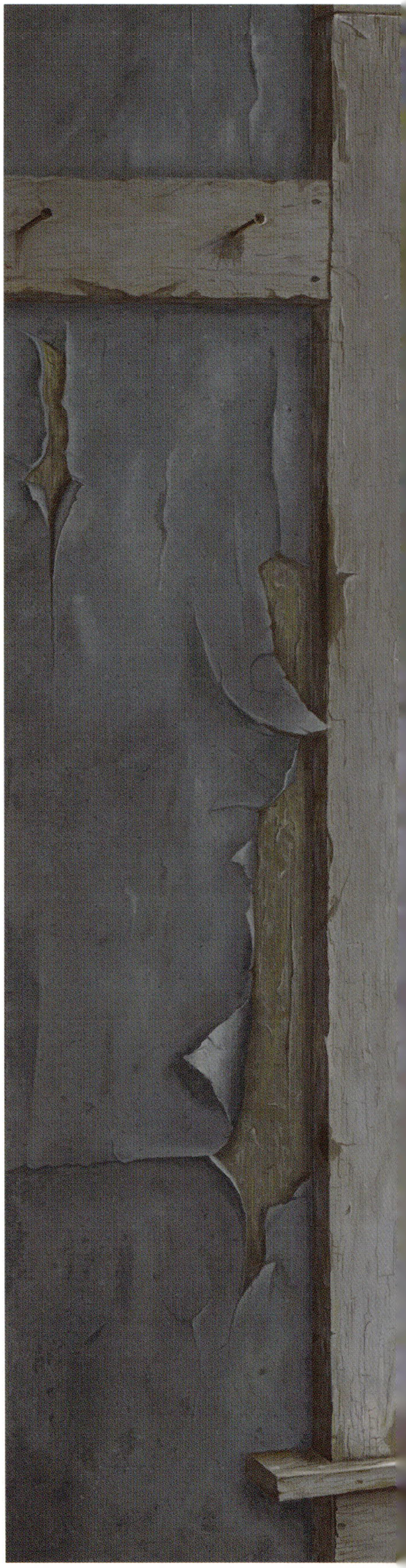

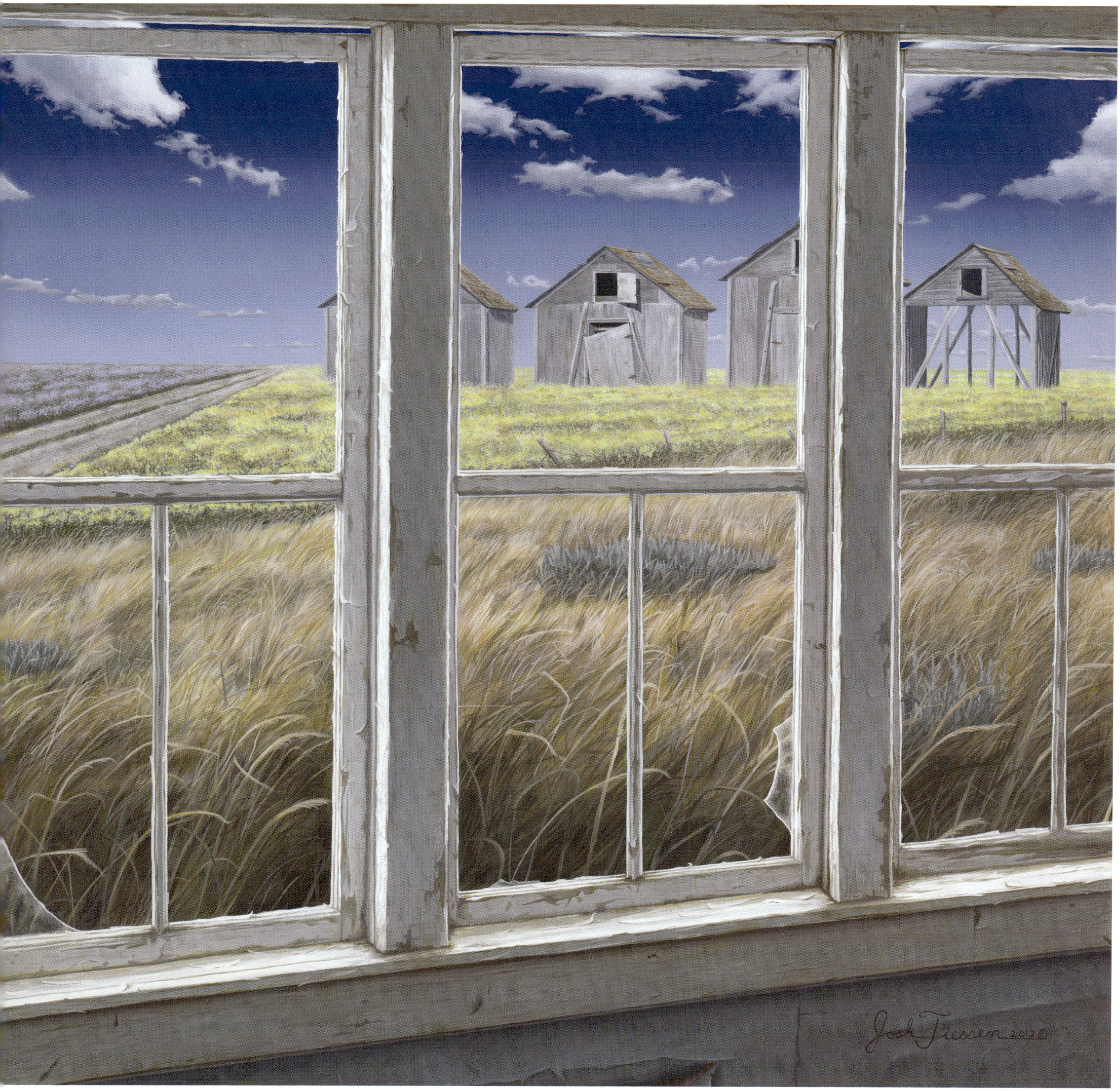
Josh Tiessen 2012©

GUARDIAN OF THE KARST

When I was being mentored under Robert Bateman, he advised me to join and support local groups that are making an effort to preserve nature. So I decided to join FOTEK (Friends of the Eramosa Karst), which is a group that has supported a new conservation area above the Niagara Escarpment in Stoney Creek. After I joined FOTEK, the board saw my website and asked me to be the featured artist with an exhibition at their annual Dinner and Dance Fundraiser, and donate one of my prints for their raffle. The whole board took my family on a personal guided tour of the Eramosa Karst. So, what is a 'karst' anyhow? I found out it is a geological term for a landscape that has an underlay of limestone, which over the years has eroded and dissolved, creating ridges, fissures, sinkholes and caves. I was intrigued by this and took many photos of the landscape, especially the caves. At one point on our tour I spotted a hawk in the distance, so my brother and I ran to take a closer look at what turned out to be a Red-tailed Hawk, which I took many photos of (holding up the tour for about ten minutes!) But when I sent the board the photos later, they were delighted and encouraged me to do a painting of it for next year's fundraiser. This summer I used the photos I had taken of the rock formations, caves and hawk as references to create this painting entitled *Guardian of the Karst*. I wanted to depict the hawk in a stately pose on the bare branches of pre-snow winter, in front of the entrance to the largest cave. His head has just turned, as if he has suddenly heard or seen something of potential danger. His razor-sharp stare depicts the curiosity and mystery of the moment.

Acrylic on Masonite 13" x 16" 2011 (Age 16)

Buckhorn Fine Art Festival "First Place for Teens (13-19)," and "Future Promise Award"

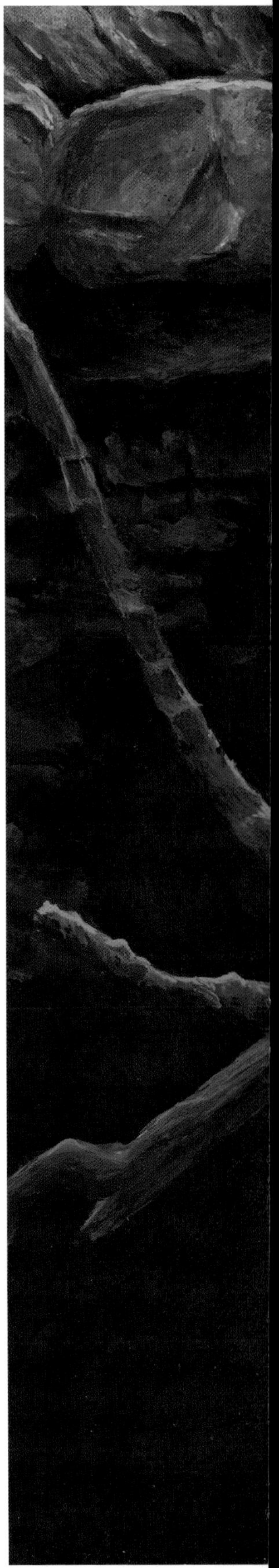

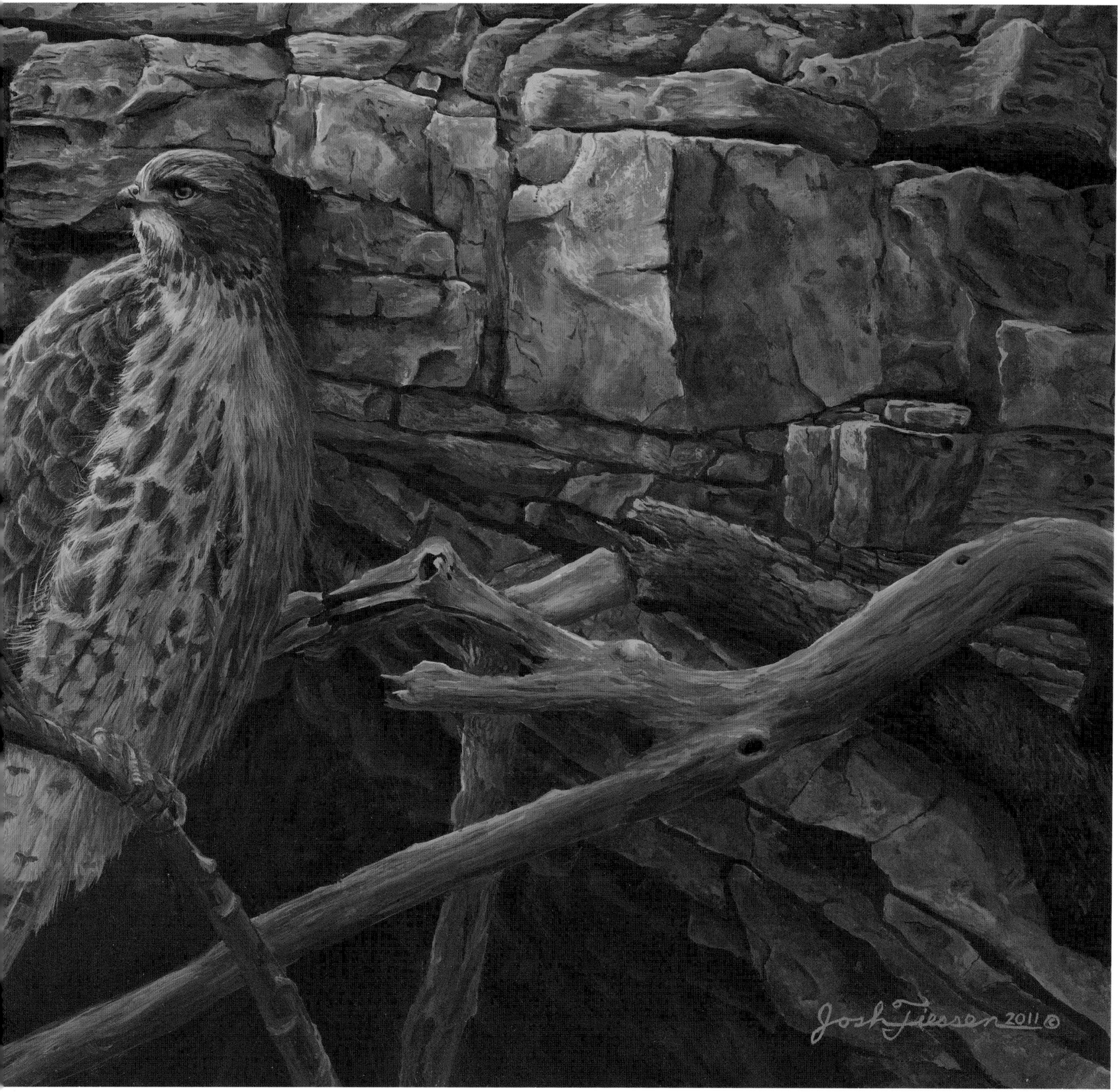
Josh Tiessen 2011©

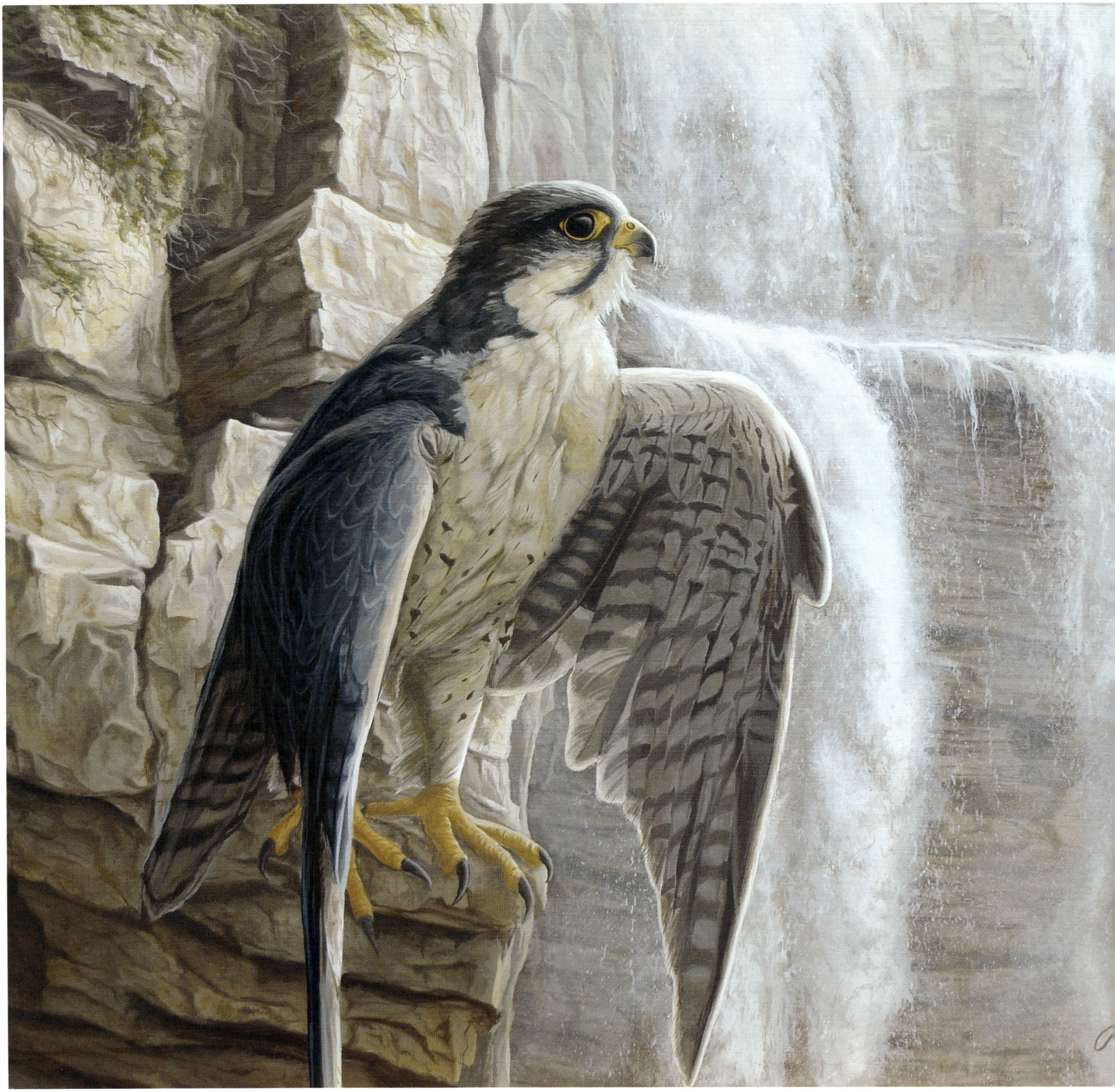

CLIFFHANGER

I had just sold my award-winning *Guardian of the Karst* painting to a collector who was opening a gallery in the South of France. When another collector of mine saw it, she was smitten that it had already sold! So she commissioned me to do another bird of prey, giving me the choice of which species but suggesting one with a bit more colour. I had just taken some great photos of a Peregrine Falcon at a birds of prey show at Ball's Falls Conservation Area. I also took photos of the falls there, and combined them with photos I had taken of Webster's Falls in Hamilton to create the composition for falls and cliffs in this painting. I had never done water like this before, so it was a new challenge that I enjoyed. I thought the title was quite fitting too.

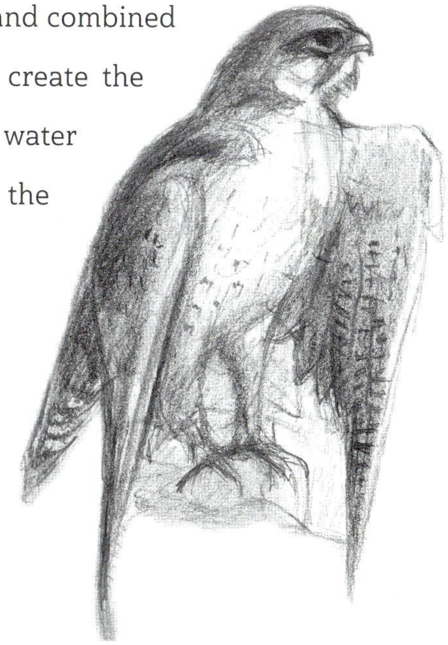

Acrylic on Masonite 13" x 16" 2012 (Age 16)

Whitehern Historical Museum Teen Art Competition "Second Place"

DEEP CALLS TO DEEP

As I painted this piece, a certain portion of prose poetry resonated in my mind. I later looked it up and decided to borrow the title for this painting from it. Psalm 42:7-8 says, "Deep calls to deep in the roar of your waterfalls; all your waves and breakers have swept over me. By day the Lord directs his love, at night his song is with me – a prayer to the God of my life" (*NIV*). There is something about the darkness and endless repetition of waves in deep water that calls forth intensity and power. I hoped to capture a little of that in this small piece as I studied the techniques that would form the backdrop for a future painting (*Creation Longs*, see pp. 124-125).

Acrylic on Masonite 6" x 9" 2012 (Age 16)

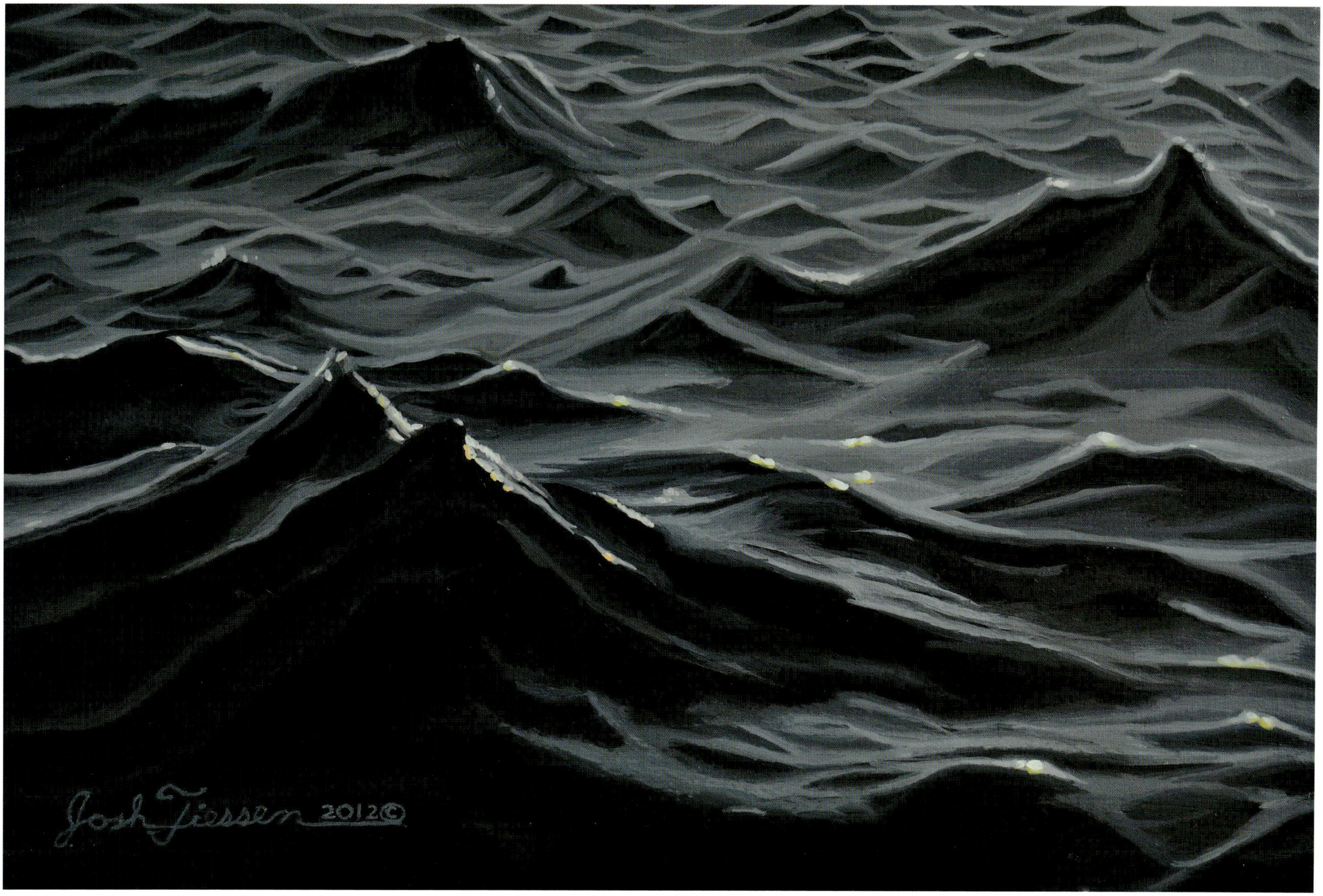
Josh Tiessen 2012©

OVERSHADOWED

When my family was visiting our relatives' farm in Saskatchewan, my uncle and cousin took us over to some new land they were renting for farming. In the middle of it stands an old barn and farmhouse – an abandoned homestead that they figured we would find interesting. I took many photos outside and inside, which I later turned into a photographic series called, "Watching Paint Peel." But it didn't end there, as I started doing paintings based on the photos I had taken of the old barn, the farmhouse door and a window from the inside. Still, I wasn't done. *Overshadowed* is yet another smaller vignette of those relics from the past century. Why do they hold such fascination for me, as a young urbanite from Ontario? It wasn't until this latest painting that I figured it out. I care for endangered species of animals, and homesteads in Ontario such as these have become endangered species too, pushed out to the edges by our urban sprawl. We fail to stop and contemplate the simple beauty of their architecture, and the wisdom of those who once lived there and on whose shoulders we now stand. Before the last of these homesteads is bulldozed by our new millennium, I wanted to pause and ponder as I carefully and lovingly rendered each detail into a high realism memoir. At sixteen, I guess I'm just an old soul after all.

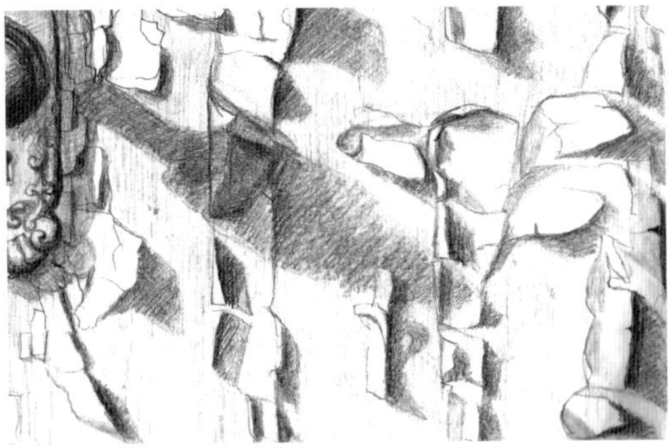

Acrylic on Masonite 6" x 9" 2012 (Age 16)

In the competition "So you want to be an artist?" this painting earned the second highest votes out of 200 entries across Canada, making it into the National Gallery of Canada for a month-long exhibition with the top twelve

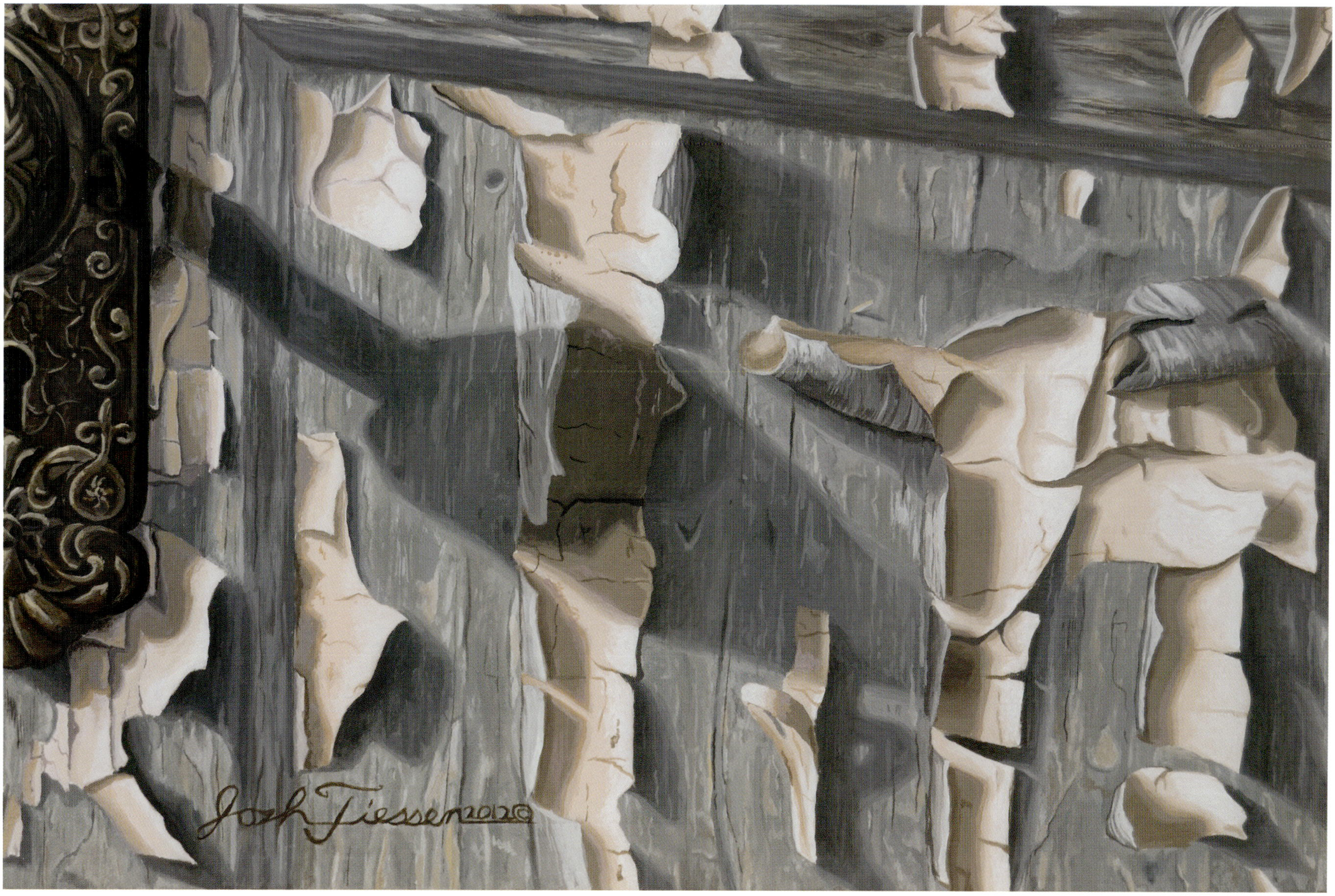
Josh Tiessen 2012©

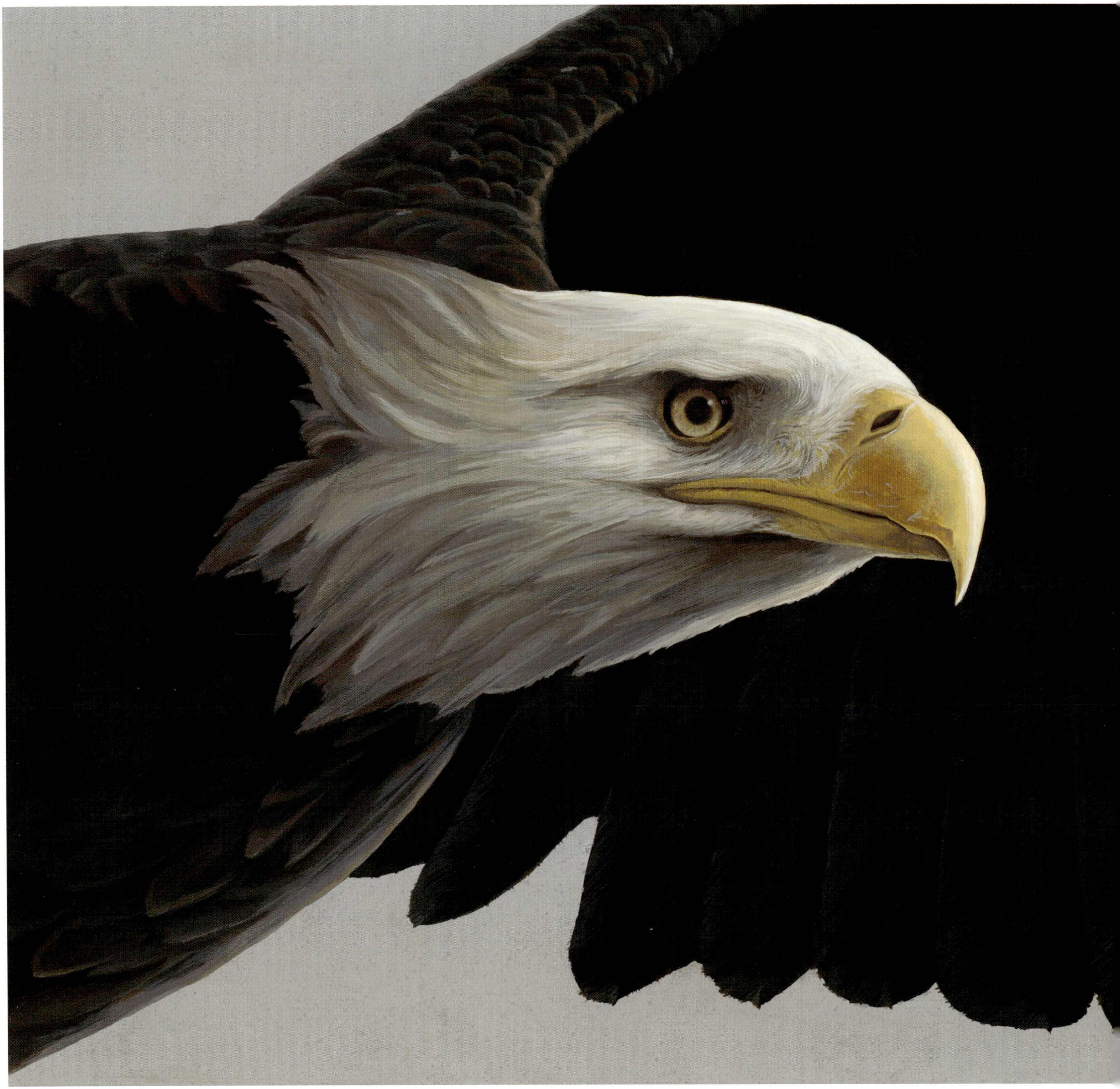

OVERSEER

While travelling down east in the Maritimes, I saw many Bald Eagles in flight and perched in trees. Along the mountainous Cabot Trail and on a boat tour in the Atlantic I was able to take many photographic references from various heights and angles. The tour guide would throw out fish for the eagles to swoop down and snatch with their sharp talons. Eagles have incredible vision, four times the sharpness of humans, able to see prey with clarity from a couple kilometers away. They soar high above forests and large bodies of water, overseeing all the land and animals below. For this composition, I used the dark underside of the wing merely as a background, intentionally highlighting the face as the focal point rather than emphasizing the wingspan as many other artists have already done.

Acrylic on Birch 11" x 17" 2012 (Age 17)

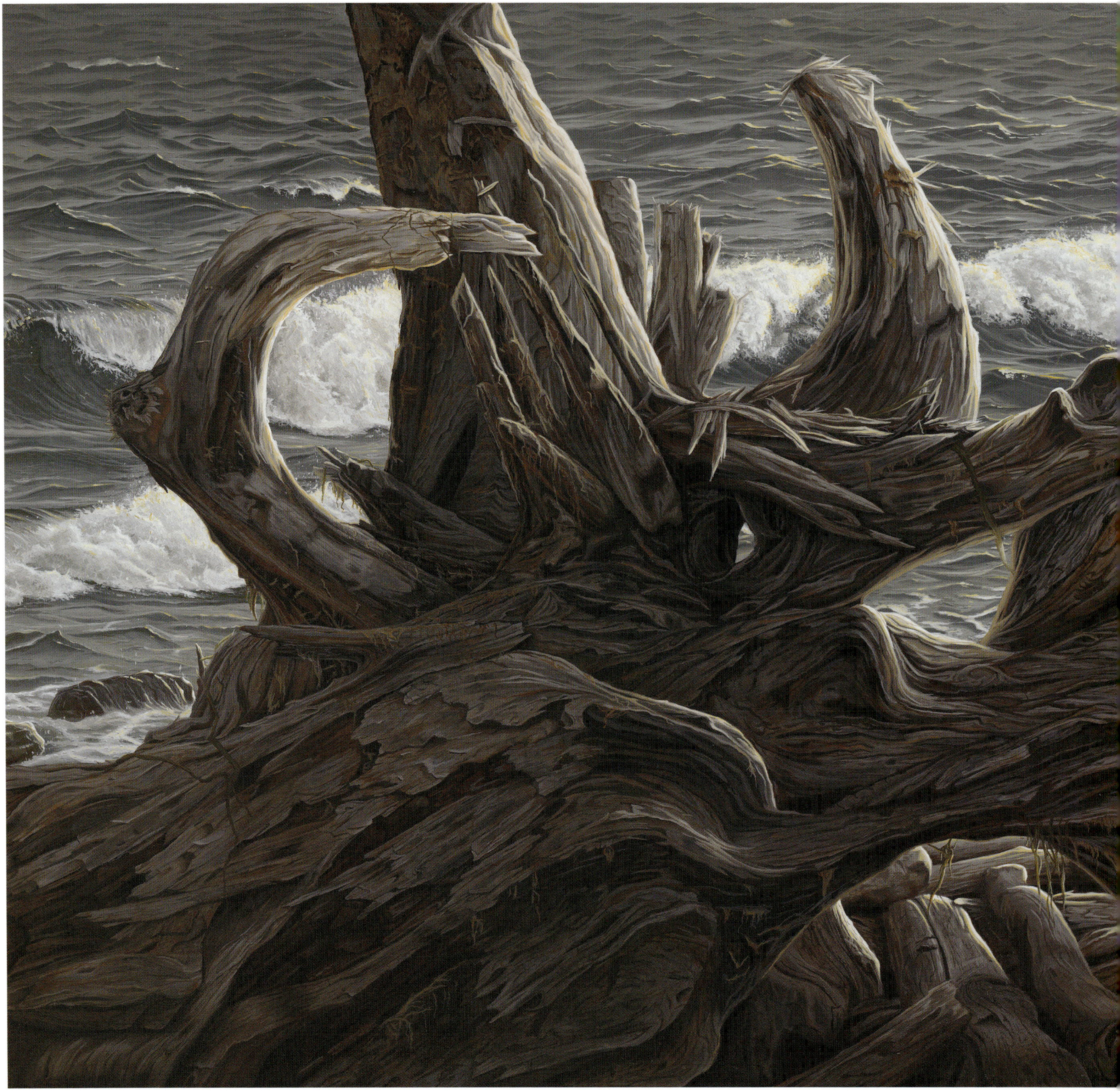

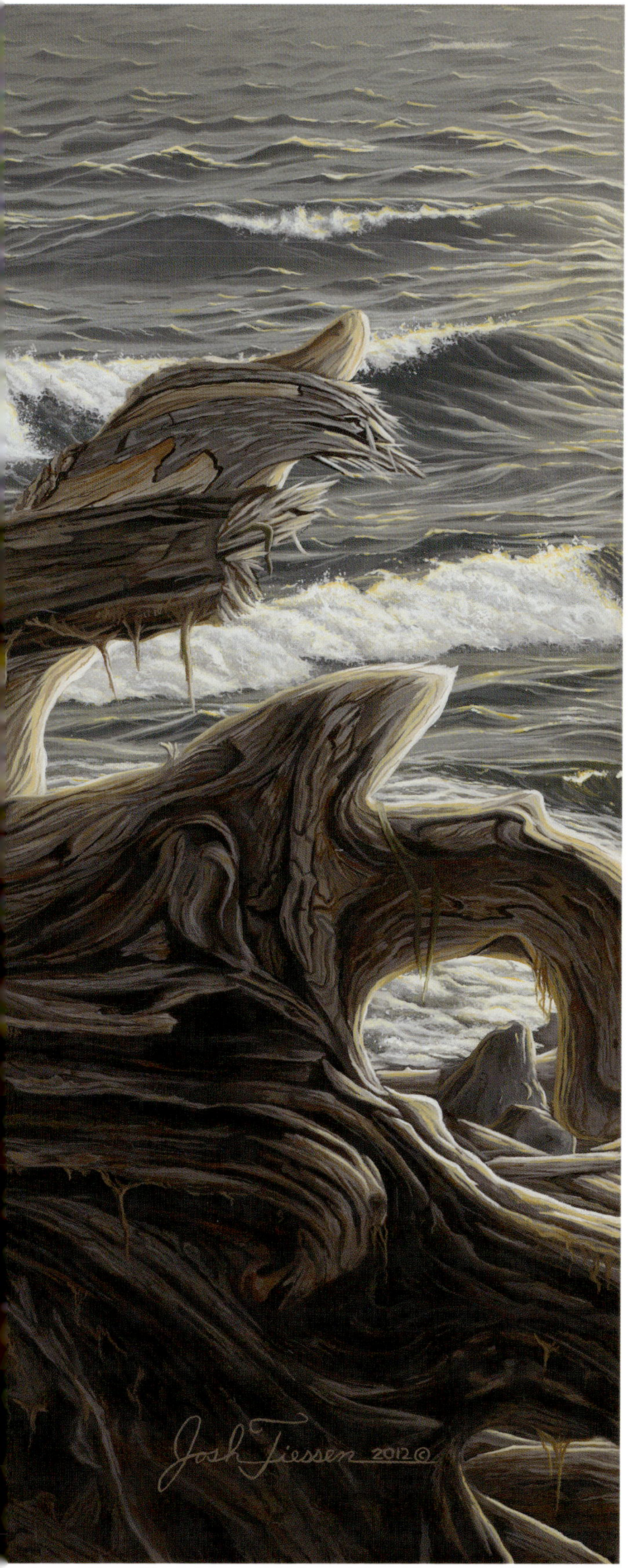

CREATION LONGS

As I painted this, the word "longing" kept coming to me. First I thought of the longing people feel to be by the ocean, or at the lake. Somehow the rhythmic lapping of waves is like therapy that calms the soul. Then, as I was painting the driftwood, which was dead and yet seemed to come alive with the setting sun, I started to think of the biblical concept of how creation longs for a brighter day. "The created world itself can hardly wait for what is coming next" (Romans 8:19, *The Message*). Even people who don't believe in heaven instinctively long for a time when all wrongs against them will be made right and when justice will prevail. For those who do believe in heaven, this gives us hope as we eagerly wait for the Creator to put everything back to how He meant it to be in the first place. For this painting I used photos I had taken on Cortes Island in northern British Columbia, and photos from a couple kilometers down the road from my studio on the beach of Lake Ontario. As always, I used many photos, which I made into a collage on my computer. I then developed my own composition as I began sketching. I was intent on portraying how the motion in the driftwood mimics the motion of the waves.

Acrylic on Canvas 24" x 36" x 2" 2012 (Age 16)

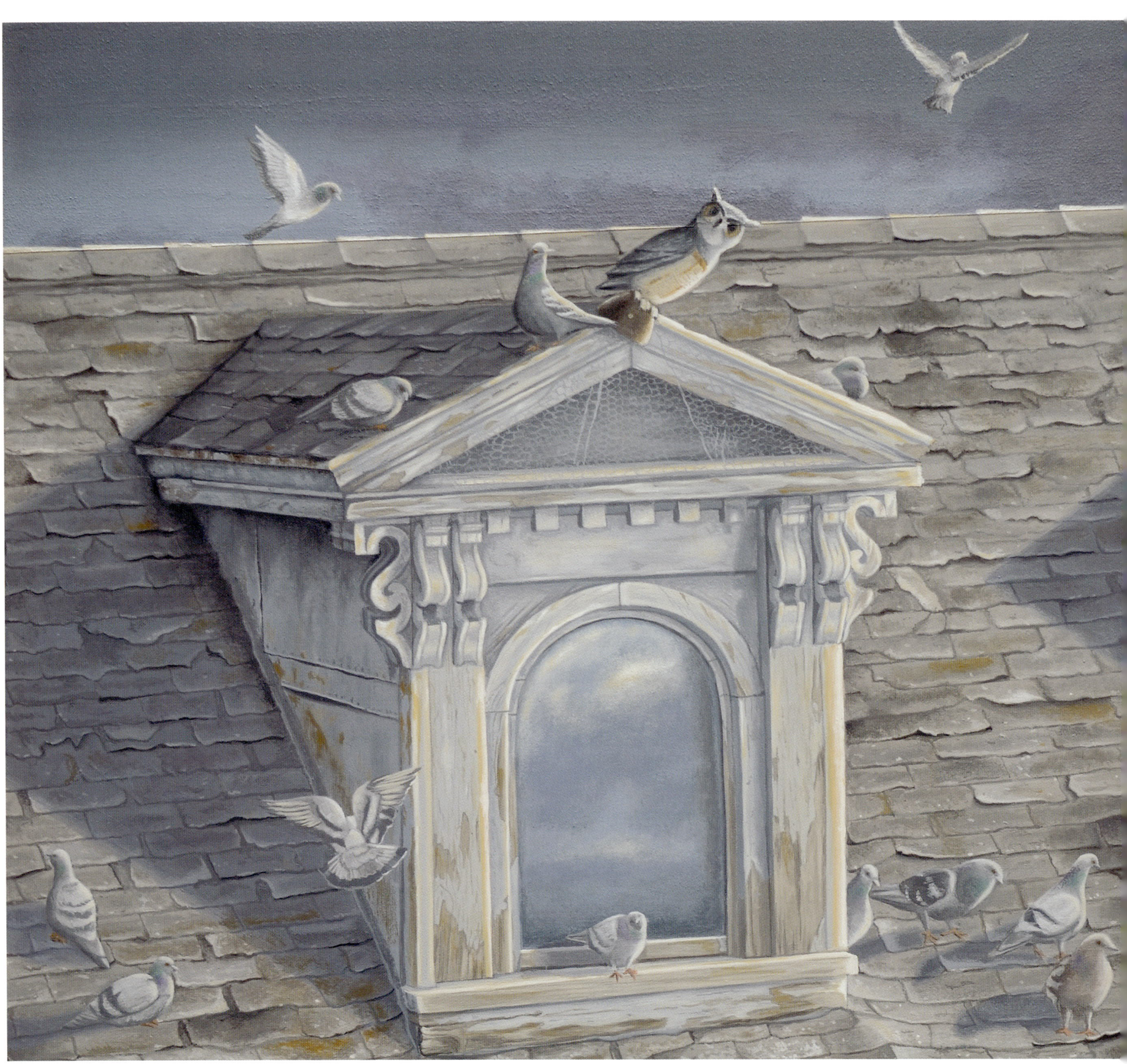

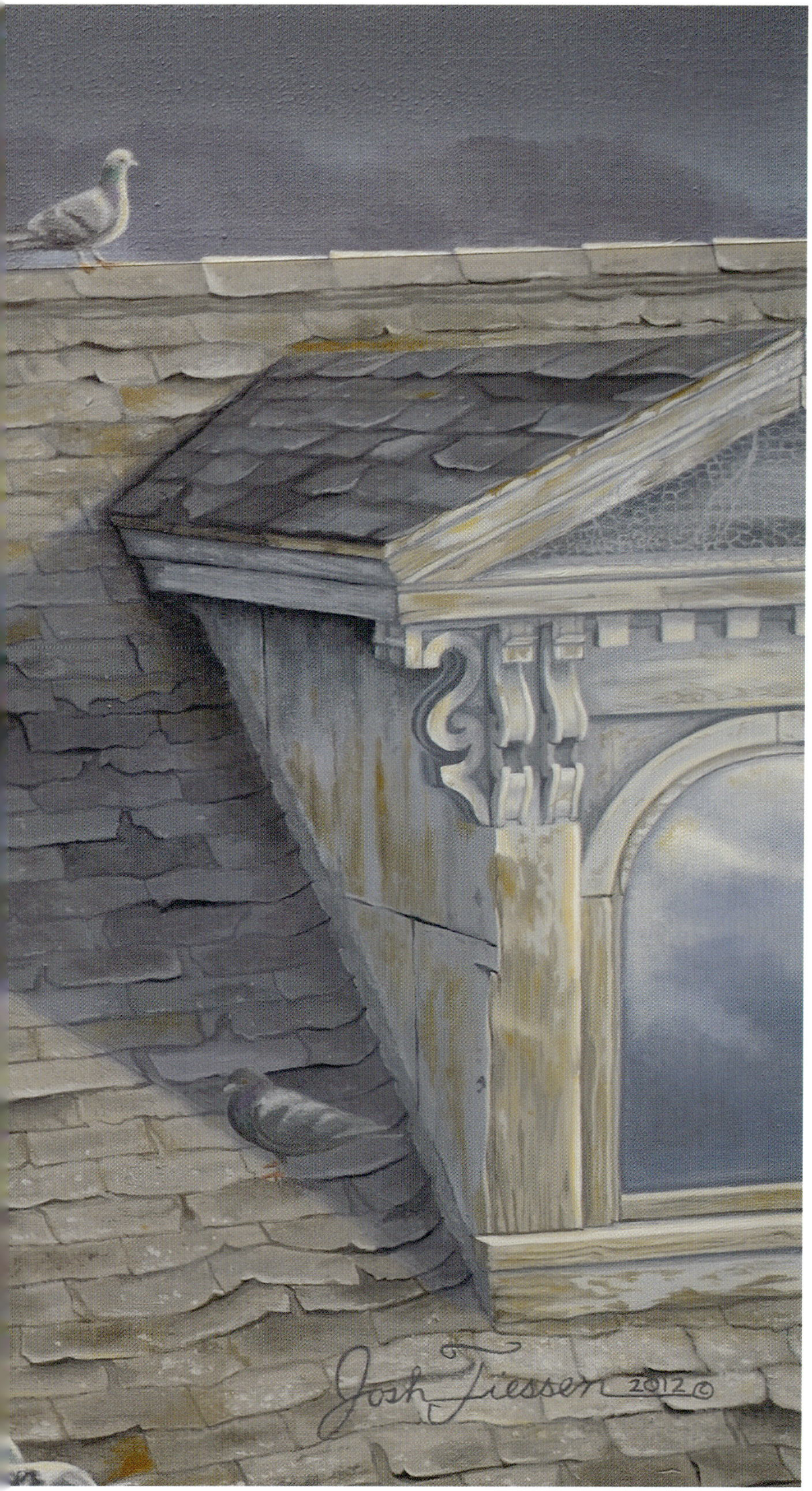

PIGEON PARADOX

As I was walking around downtown Hamilton taking photos of some very old buildings, one of them caught my eye. I looked up and saw a curious scene unfolding. Upon ornate weathered dormers protruding from a loose-shingled roof, a fake owl was perched on the peak surrounded by undaunted pigeons. The plastic owl, set up as a decoy, was unsuccessful in scaring off the pigeons, kind of like scarecrows with birds perched on them. These little guys are smarter than we give them credit for, and probably pushed over the owl themselves! It was not until one brave pigeon went against the status quo, realizing the owl's façade created just an imitation of fear. I found this scene ironic and humorous, and together with the old ornate dormers was inspired to do an original composition of it. I felt this painting illustrated how in life we have perceived fears that turn out to be false; it is not until we face them that we will ever know the truth. It is interesting to see how through the man-made world and the world made by God, metaphors often arise in this relationship.

Acrylic on Masonite 12" x 20" 2012 (Age 17)

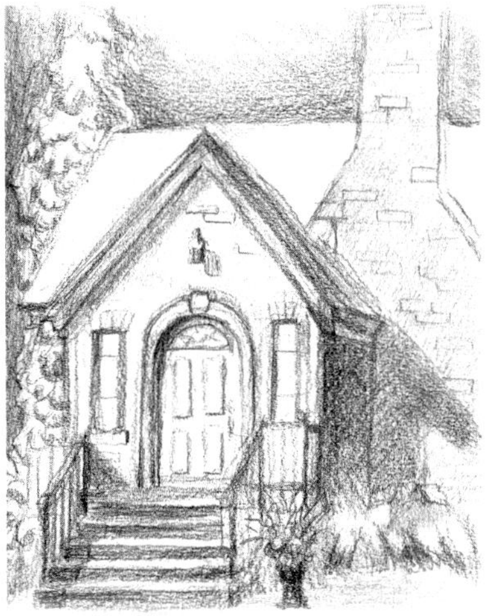

FLURRY HOME

This was a commissioned painting of a home on Lake Avenue Drive in Olde Stoney Creek, close to where I live. I had always admired the house with its tomato-coloured door, and I had even taken a few photos of it for inspiration. When the couple asked me to do this commission I was very interested. Fortunately, I had taken some of the photos on the first and almost only snowy day of last winter, as they wanted it with snow falling. While composing the painting, I felt that the tall Spruce tree and chimney seemed to balance each other. By gradating the sky from light to dark, top to bottom, I was able to create a dense atmospheric feel. The snow coming down added motion to the scene, and with only subtle Christmas accents this painting can be hung for the whole winter season.

Acrylic on Masonite 24" x 20" x 2" 2012 (Age 17)

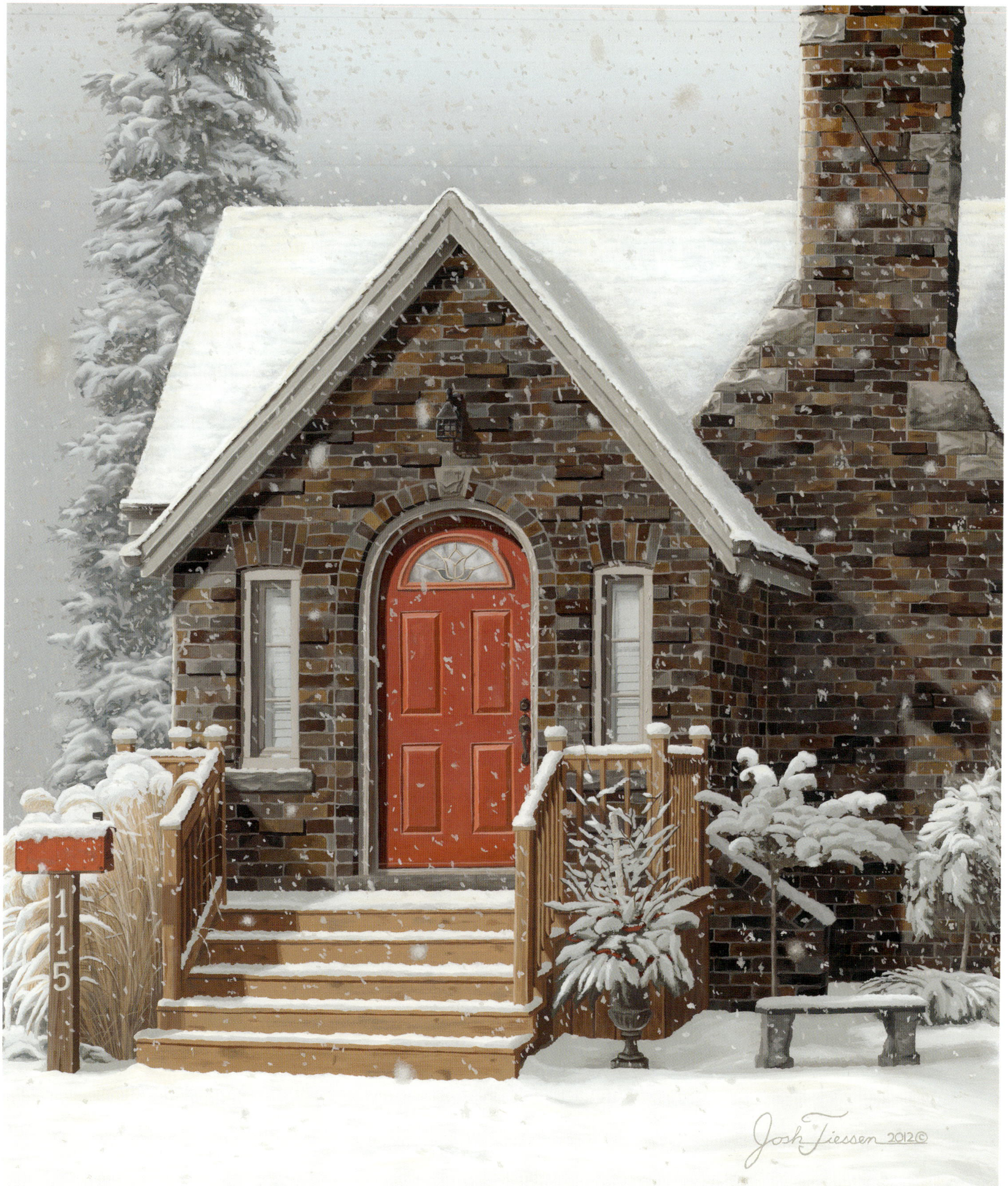
115
Josh Tiessen 2012©

POLAR EMERGENCE

The majestic polar bear rises from the water with a longing glance. Its fur is soaking-wet and yields pearl drops of water. Along with other artists who portray wildlife, I have always admired the Polar Bear, a very popular subject made famous by Coca-Cola. I wanted to present this bear in a unique and fresh way, emerging out of the water in synchronization with the ice. The title *Polar Emergence* alludes to the fact that there is an emergency in the Polar Bear's environment, with ice rapidly melting, forcing him to travel further by water for food. As stewards of this earth and its species, I feel that we should each do something to take action. As an artist, through this depiction I would like to motivate people to an appreciation for this strong and beautiful animal that is beloved by so many.

Graphite and Charcoal 9" x 12" 2013 (Age 17)

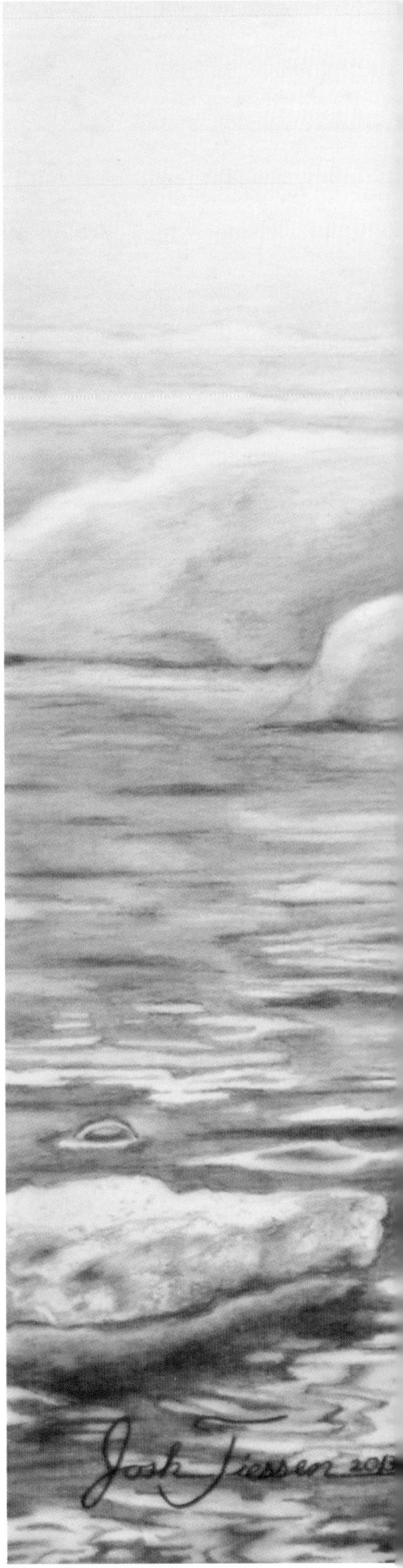

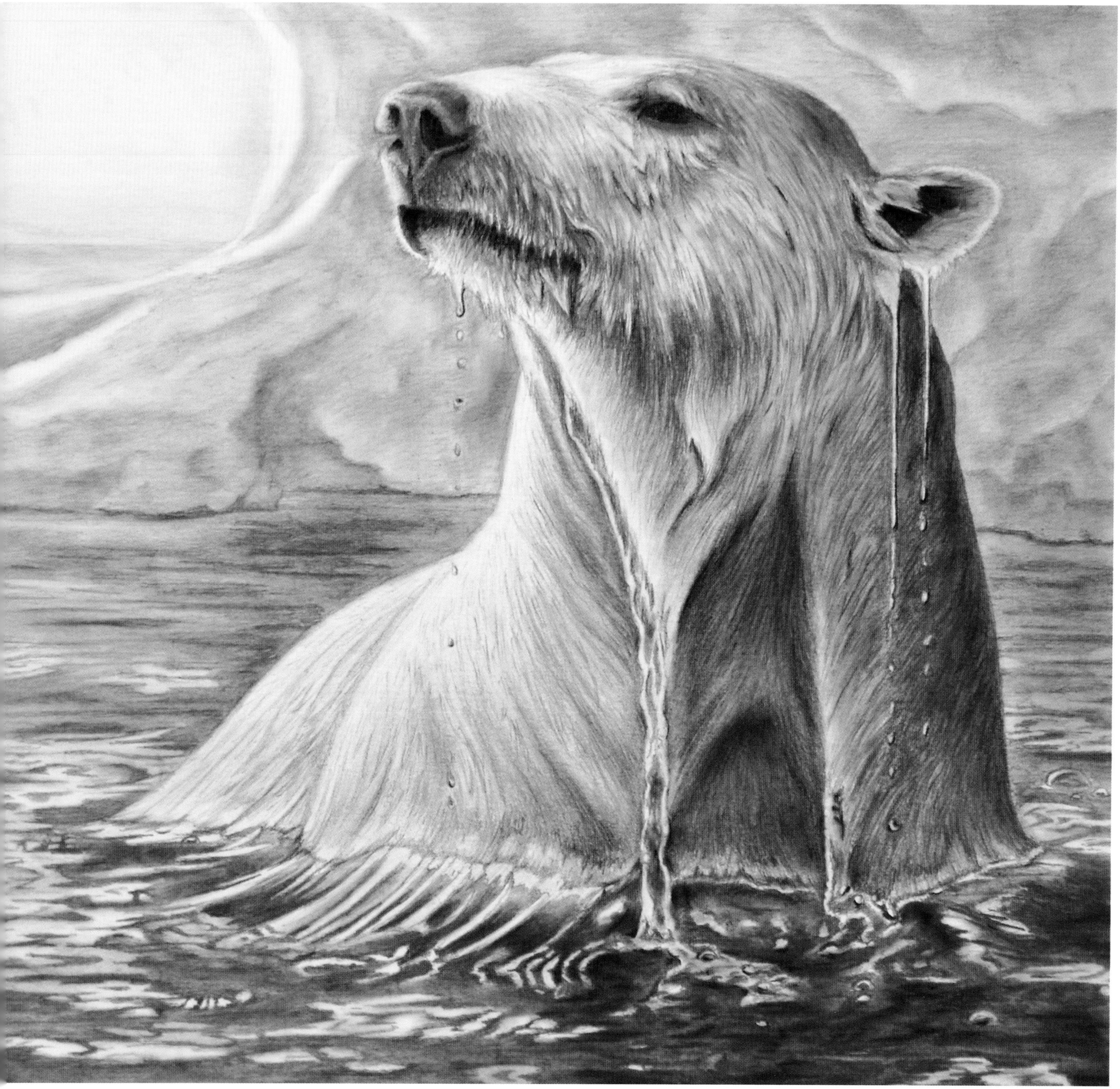

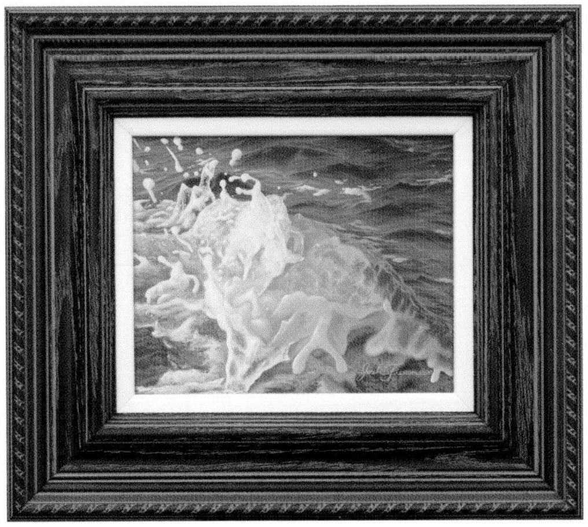

OCEAN'S EMOTION

For me, water always evokes an emotional response. During the time I was working on this piece at age seventeen, I was experiencing waves of emotional ups and downs splashing all around me. While painting I enjoy listening to music and contemplating lyrics. The words "the smallest drop in the ocean can start a wave of emotion" specifically spoke to me [i]. The smallest thing such as a hidden rock can create a sea-foam splash, like in this painting based on many photos I took of the ocean's roaring tides crashing into Prince Edward Island late one summer's eve. Of course, this scene could have occurred on any coast, which is why it has such universal appeal. I find it interesting how people are fascinated by water, something so common that fills 70% of the earth, yet can convey such metaphoric meaning. For me as an artist, depicting water like this highlights its beauty and the necessity of preserving this natural resource. I was on my way out the door to get this piece framed, when a collector from Newfoundland saw it on my Facebook page and messaged me saying he wanted to purchase it. I texted him photos and we picked out the nautical frame together.

[i] *Eternity* by Paul van Dyk, vocals by Adam Young (Owl City)

Acrylic on Birch 6.5" x 8" 2013 (Age 17)

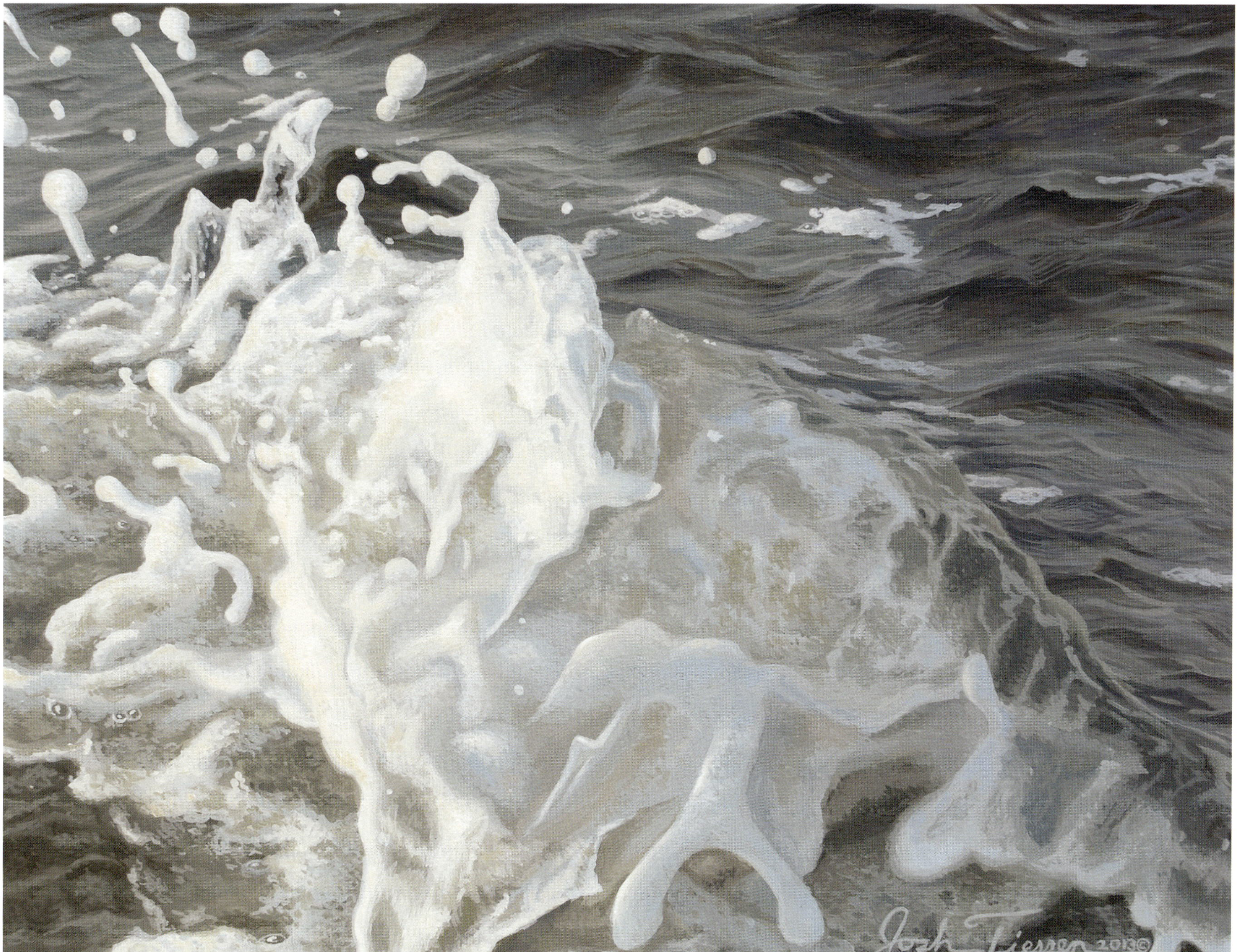
Josh Tiessen 2013©

MONUMENTAL TURNING POINT

The Olde Town of Stoney Creek where I live has a wealth of historical importance. The Battle of Stoney Creek was the turning point in the War of 1812, when the British Redcoats were able to turn the tide of American penetration into Upper Canada. The organizers of the yearly battle re-enactment, held at Battlefield Park just down the street from my studio gallery, suggested I complete a painting for the bi-centennial (200th year) celebration the first weekend of June 2013. They were interested in the limited edition prints for their museum gift shop. A week later, I received an email out of the blue from a former Stoney Creek resident who had moved away because of work but wanted a painting to remind him of his hometown. With a potential buyer for the original, I decided to go ahead. On a couple of occasions when the winter chill let up, I climbed the long stone stairway at Battlefield Park to take photos from various angles of the 100 foot tall monument, the iconic Stoney Creek landmark erected in commemoration of the battle for the centennial celebration in 1913. As I painted, especially contemplating the flags in the stained glass window, I thought of the subtle metaphor of a Cardinal triumphantly perched on the peak of the stone wall and a Blue Jay flying away in retreat. As a young Stoney Creek artist, this painting is my contemporary contribution to honour the people who bravely fought for our freedom.

Acrylic on Birch 8" x 10" 2013 (Age 17)

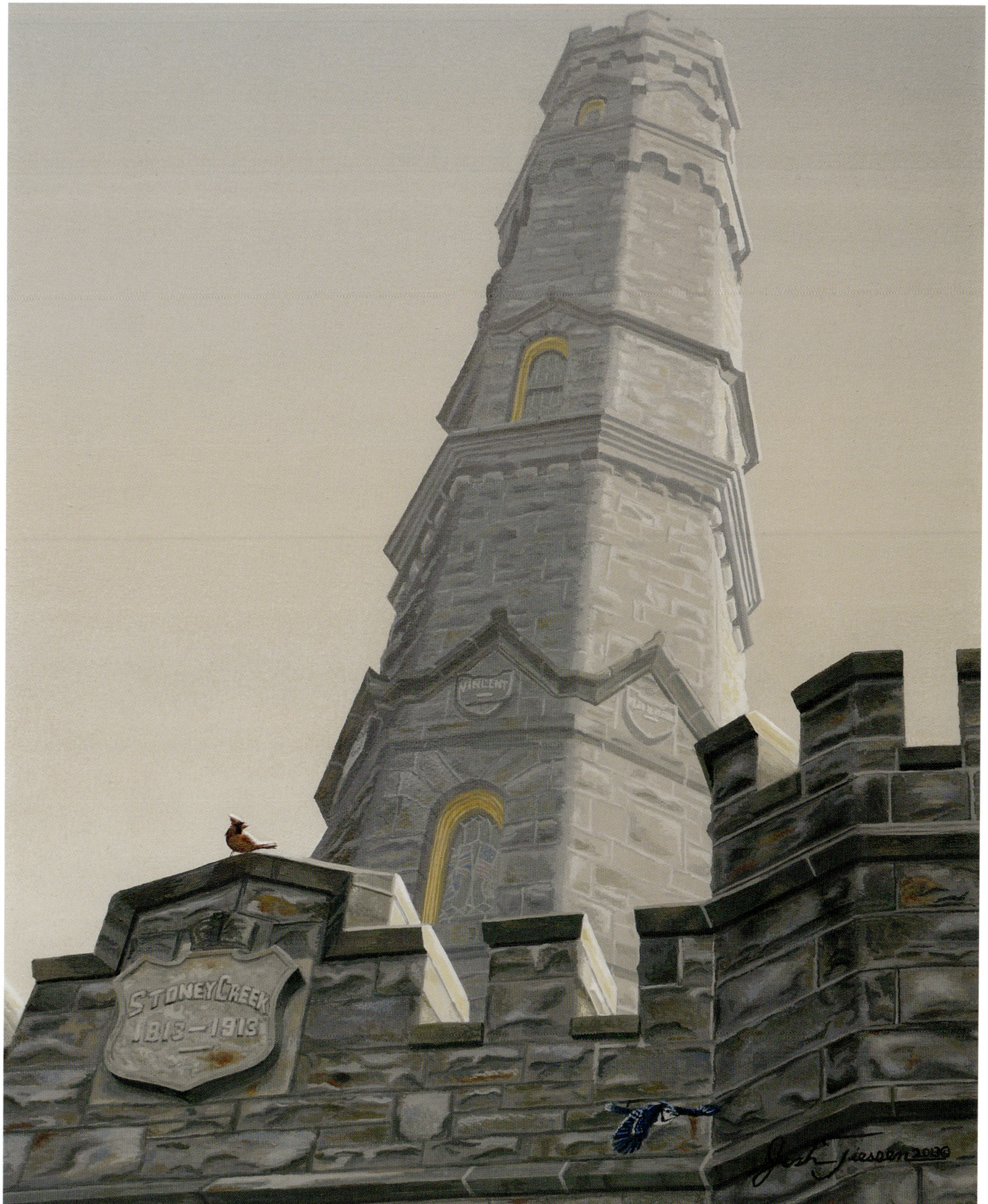
STONEY CREEK
1813 – 1913
VINCENT

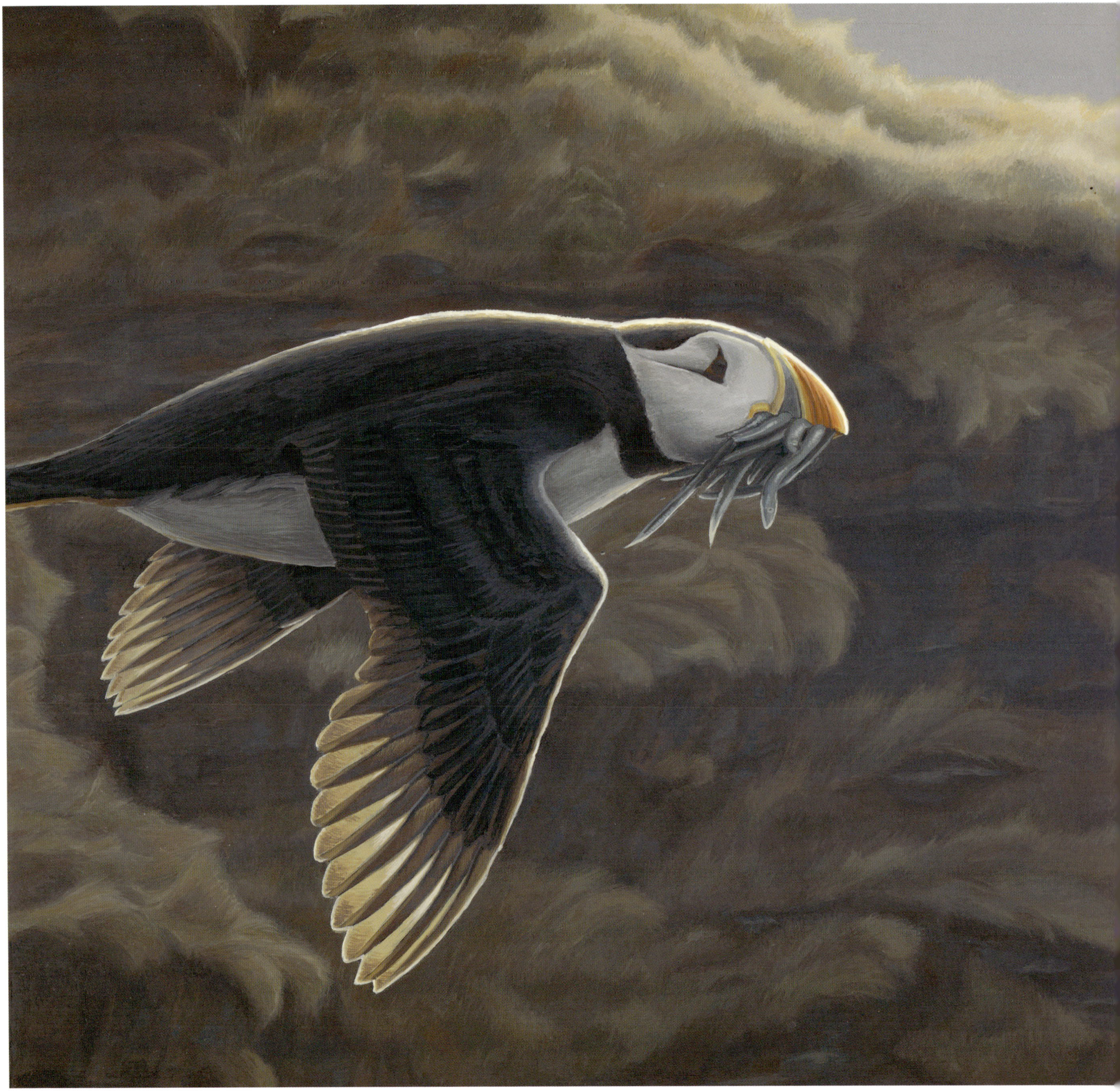

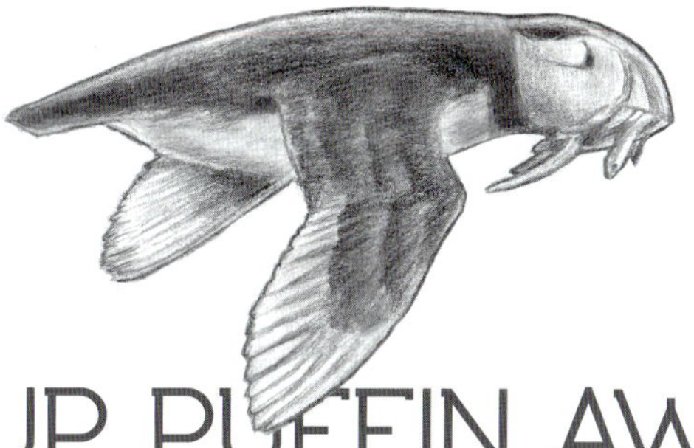

UP PUFFIN AWAY

I have been intrigued with Atlantic Puffins for their bright colours and unique clown-like faces, often called the 'clown of the ocean'. They seem to have an endearing personality, kind of like mini-penguins. On a boat tour through island cliffs off the coast of the Cabot Trail in Nova Scotia, I was thrilled to see these birds up close in their natural environment. It was surprising how tiny they were (about 8 inches tall) and how fast they dove for fish, darting up from the water and back to their homes flapping their wings at 400 beats per minute. It was hard to see them as they were a blur to the naked eye, and only with my telephoto lens was I able to catch them in mid-flight. I expected to see them standing around in groups on land, but as easy prey they disappeared with their mouthfuls of fish into tiny burrows carved into the island cliffs under tufts. The evening light in my painting shows the puffin returning home with a mouthful of fish for the final time after a long day of fishing.

Acrylic on Braced Baltic Birch 10" x 16" x 2" 2013 (Age 17)

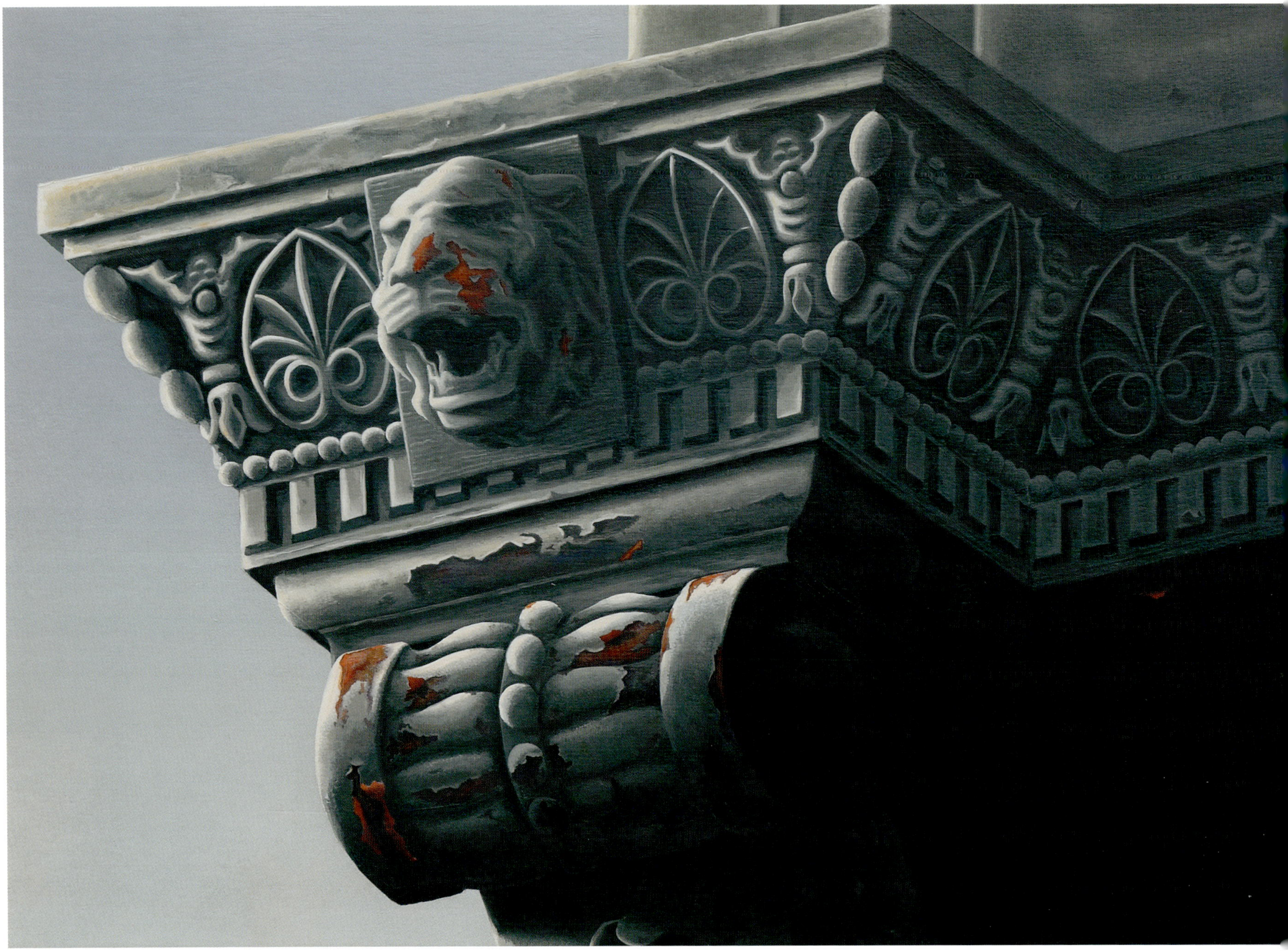

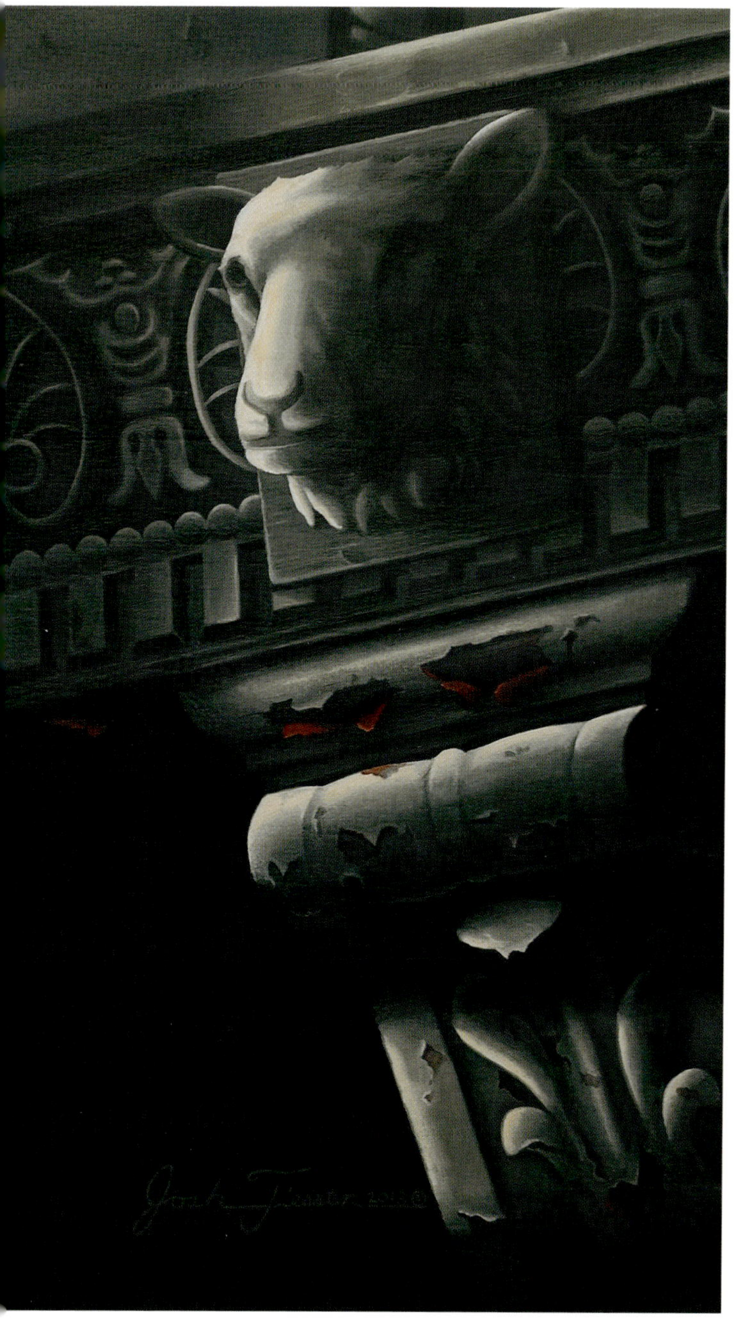

THE LION AND THE LAMB

Fascinated by an old ornate European-style building adorned with lion heads in downtown Hamilton, I was inspired to create this painting. I was also drawn to the weathering of this building indicated by peeling paint, which strangely revealed red paint underneath. The late evening sun illuminating this sculptural surface enhances the contrasts. While most decorative structures use gargoyles or lions traditionally believed to ward off evil, I paradoxically replaced one of the lions with a lamb. The lion, a symbol commonly representing strength and ferocity, together with the lamb, a symbol representing humility and weakness, is an uncommon coupling that may seem strange to some viewers. Biblically, the symbol of a stronger animal such as a wolf, leopard or lion paired with a much weaker animal like a lamb, goat or calf, allegorically portrays a time when there will be ultimate peace and complete restoration (Isaiah 11:6). Metaphorically, the lion and the lamb represent the duality of Christ, who in essence was the perfect and pure Lamb of God sacrificed by crucifixion in place of humankind, but also the mighty Lion of Judah triumphing over death and reigning as King (Revelation 5:5-6). While this information is not intended to be didactic, it is nonetheless the personal meaning behind this painting, but it is up to the viewer to make their own interpretation.

Acrylic on Braced Baltic Birch 12" x 24" x 2" 2013 (Age 17)

SWALLOWS OF MISTY WHARF

A feeling of exhilaration came over me on the misty morning my family explored the coastal drive between Peggy's Cove and Lunenberg, Nova Scotia. I couldn't resist stopping at every little fishing village along the winding road, which meandered around bays and coves with the anticipation of what could be discovered beyond the next curve. Each time I hopped out of the car with my camera in hand, I was accosted by the smell of salty air repugnant with fish and rotting wood. Misty Wharf is a representational place, which is a composite of many similar structures supporting humble little fishing shacks. The mist was gently lifting from the reflective water as the morning sun broke through overcast clouds, sharply illuminating anything in its path. A few Barn Swallows swooped out from their homes below the docks and into the light.

Acrylic on Birch 18" x 30" x 2" 2013 (Age 17)

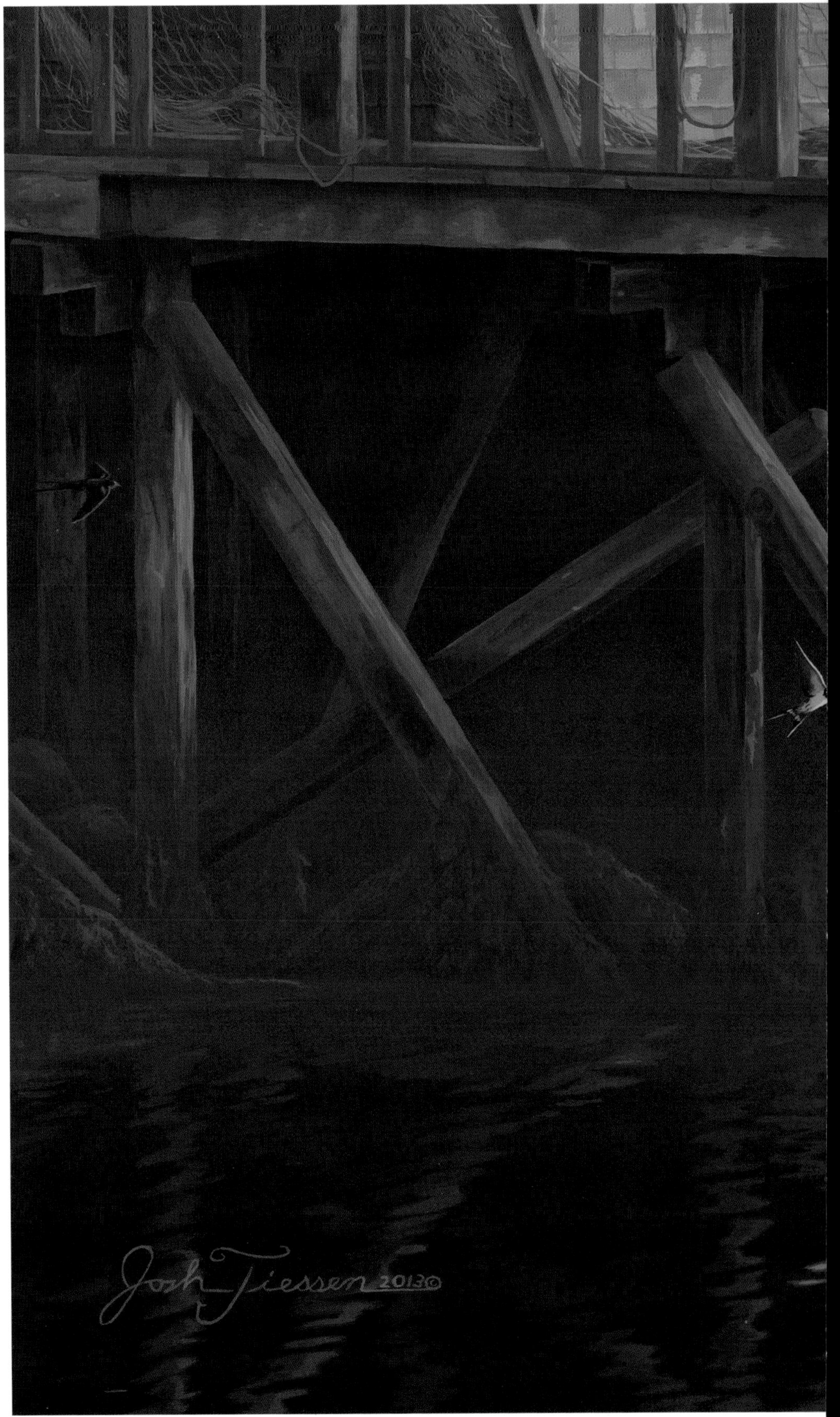

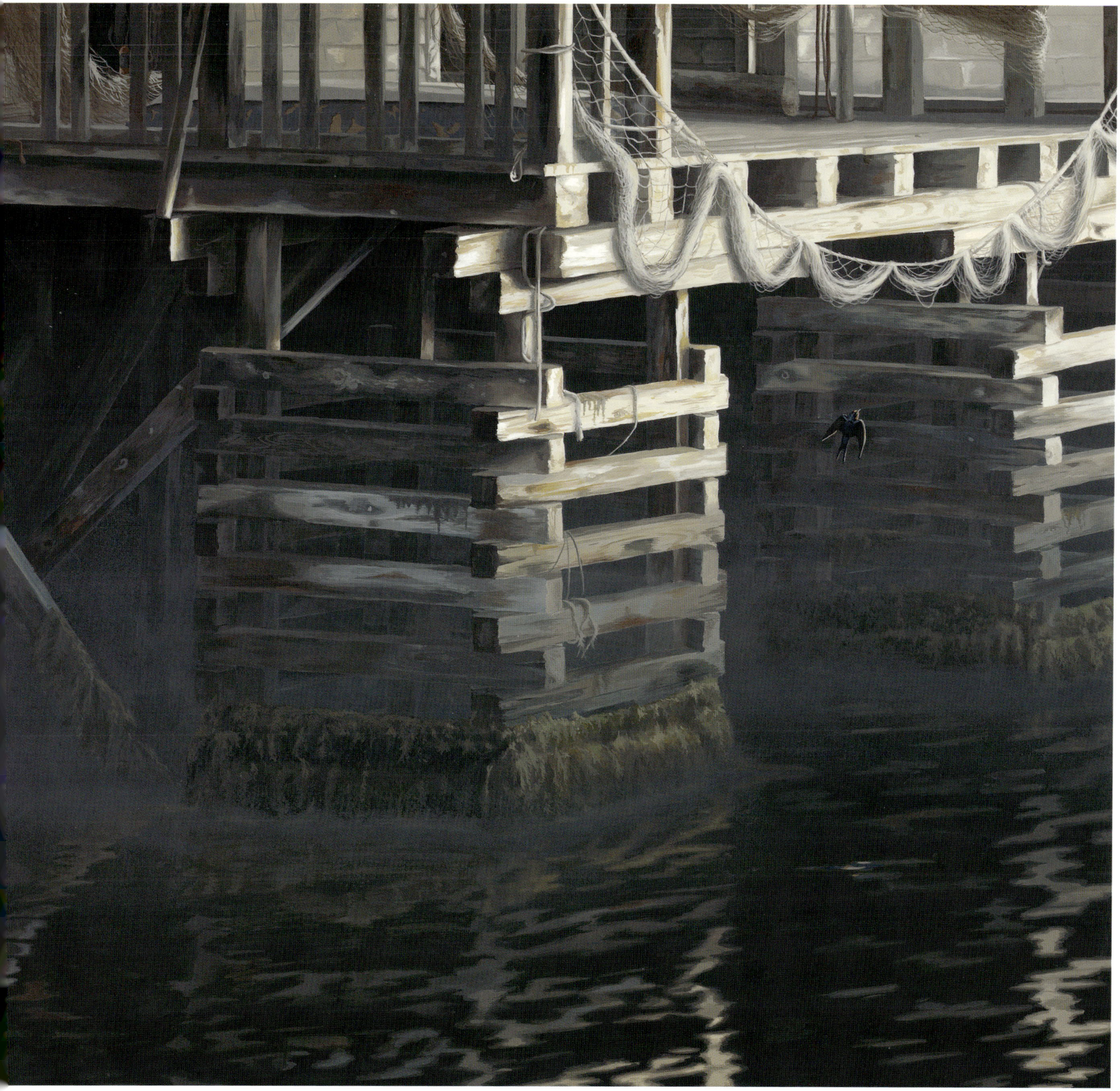

SHIPWRECKED TREASURE

The inspiration for this painting came from the nautical features found in many small fishing towns along the East Coast of Canada. While travelling through the Maritimes, old but vibrantly painted fishing shacks wrapped with fishing nets and lines of multicoloured hanging buoys became a common scene. Poking around taking photos and looking for unique architectural features, I stopped dead in my tracks when I saw this old rustic ship doorknocker. Later, after doing research, I found out that this tall sailing ship was actually the 16th century Galleon, which had been used for exploration trips and in war fleets. Like the fate of many of the Galleons, taking artistic license I felt that this little ship knocker could be figuratively shipwrecked on one of those dilapidated shacks, unable to move but still fairing quite well in comparison to the weathered wooden door it was affixed to. By placing the ship on the left side facing the window on the right, which looked out through another window to the ocean, I felt it could subconsciously summon the thought of it sailing through the window and onto the water. The long shadows, a recurring theme in my work, added some interesting abstract shapes and helped accentuate the texture and the three-dimensional planes. I have always been enamoured by the aesthetic appeal of surface textures such as wood grain and peeling paint. In this painting, although most of the hues are neutral and muted, I enjoyed applying the chromatic emphasis on the door. The teal peeling paint and reddish orange wood seemed to harmonize together because of their complementary relationship, and helped draw attention to the Galleon doorknocker, which in turn subtly reflected those colours.

Acrylic on Braced Baltic Birch 35" x 35" x 2" 2013 (Age 17)

Art Renewal Center International Salon Competition Finalist

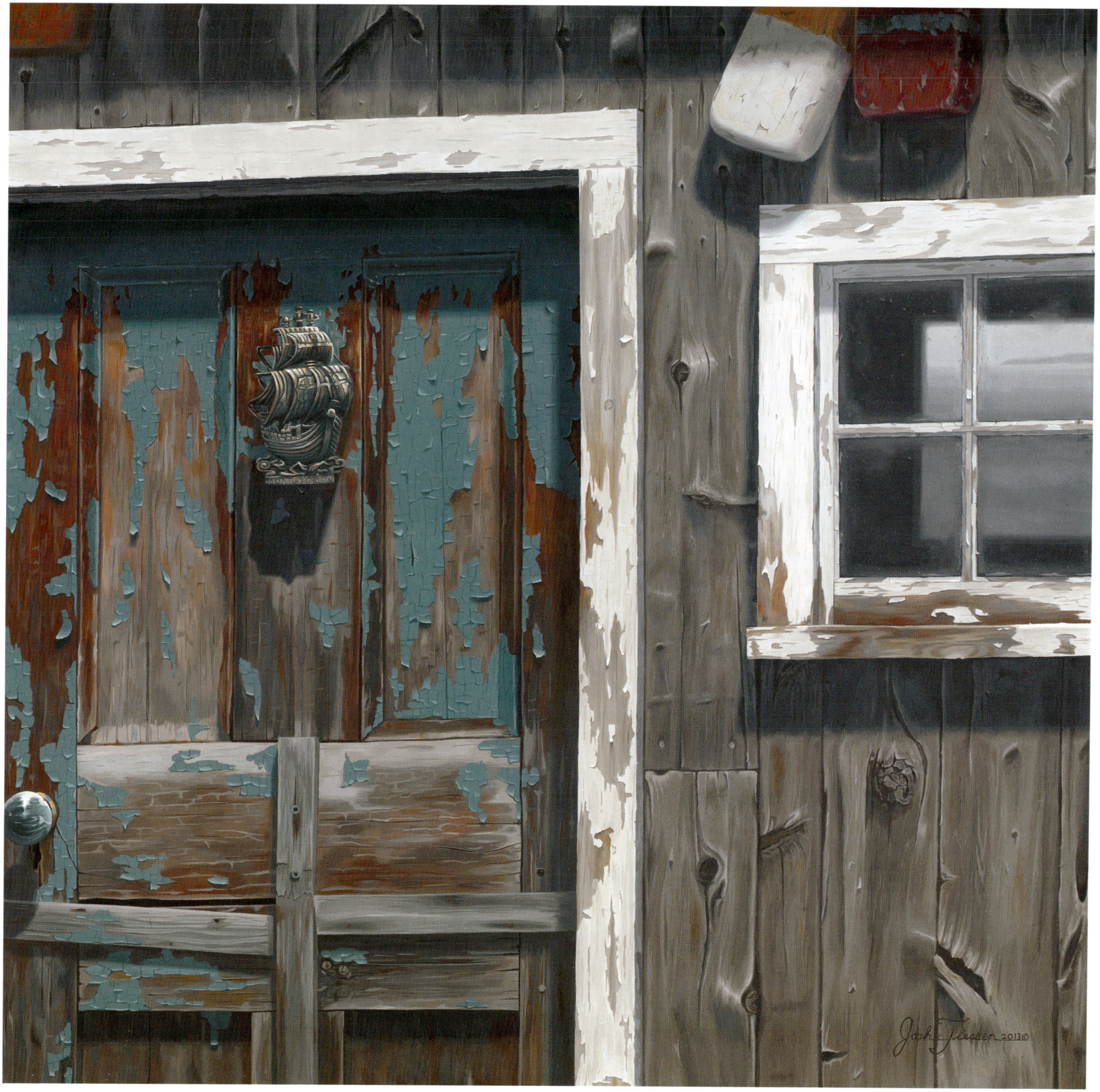
2013©

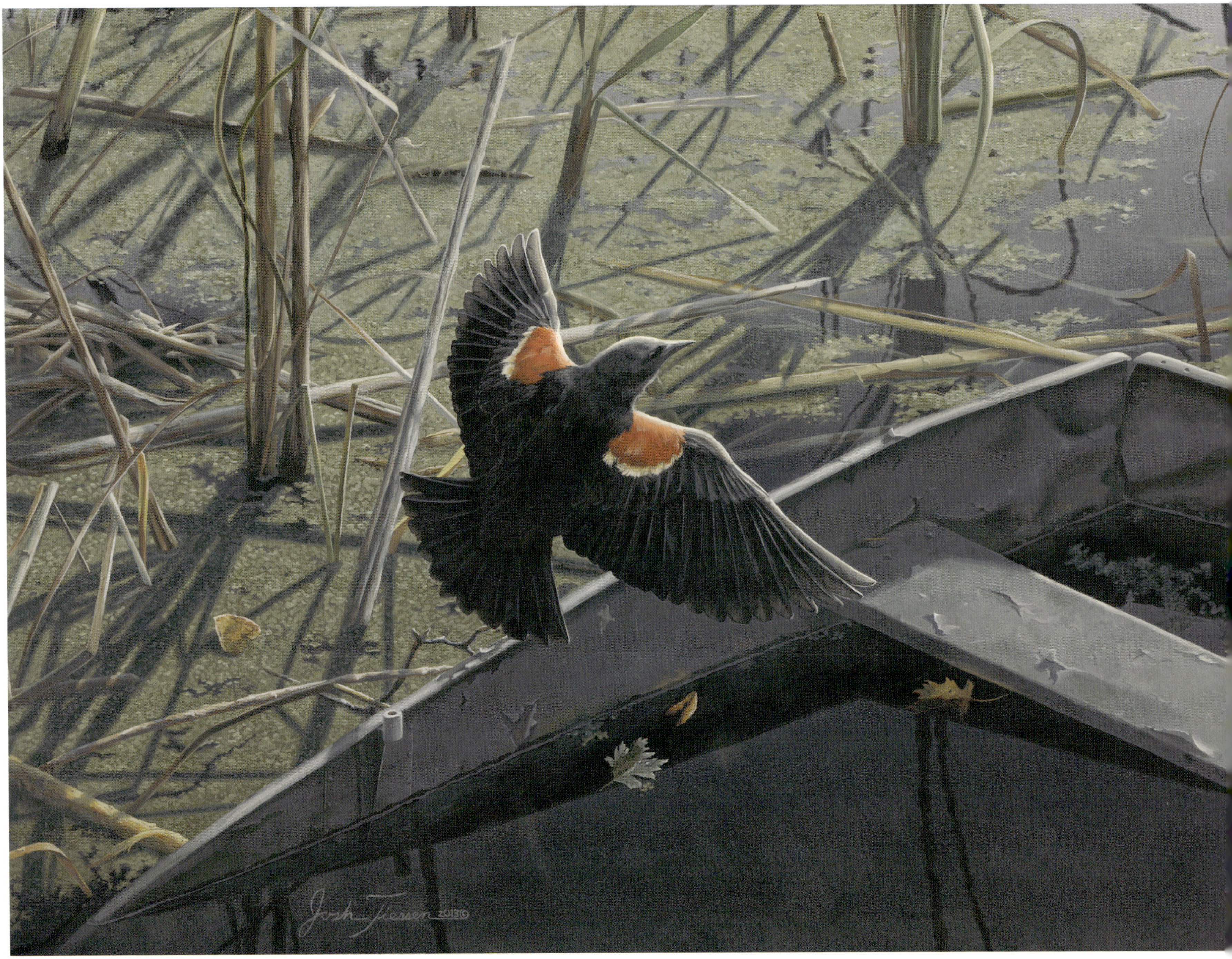
Josh Tiessen 2013©

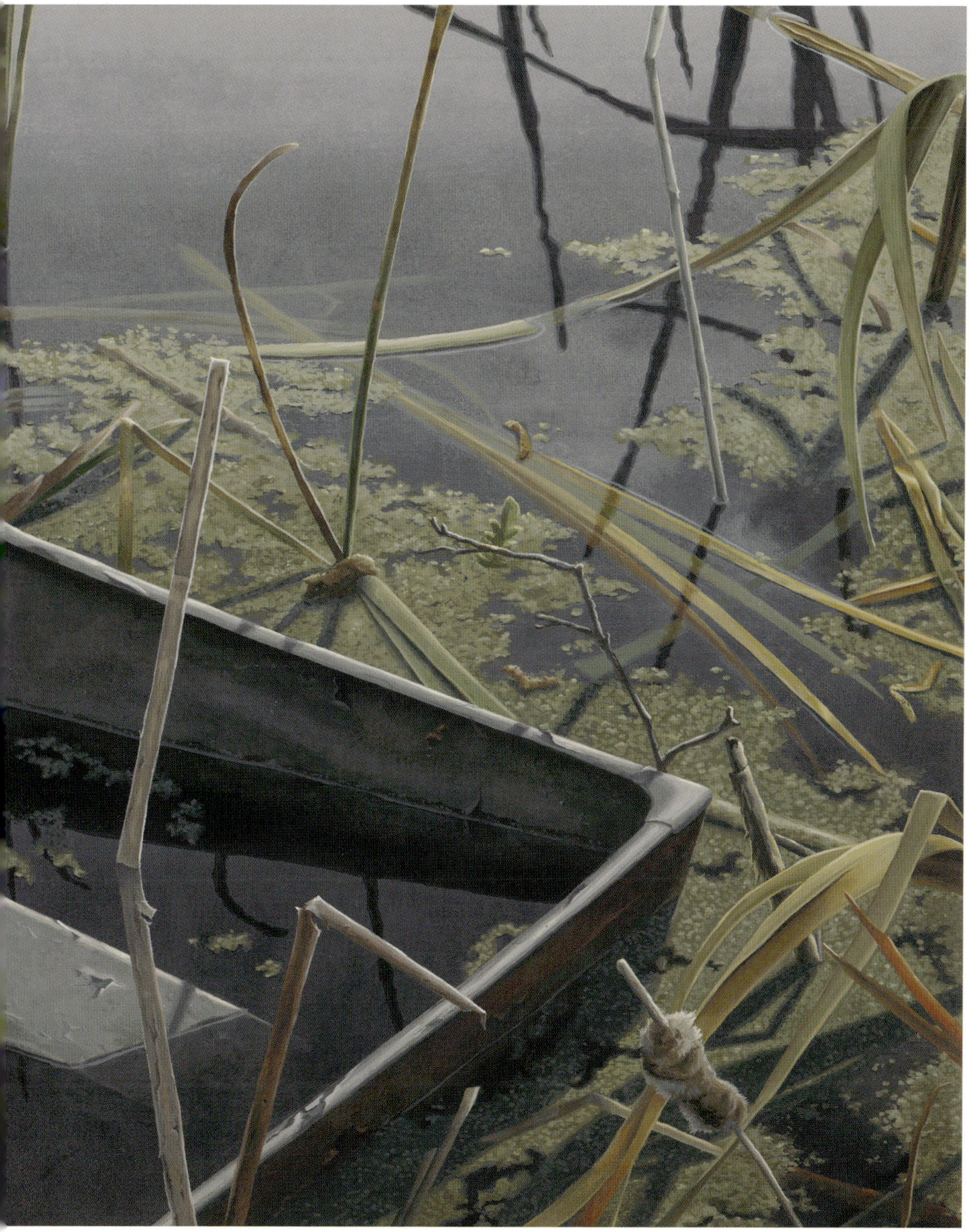

POND'S EDGE

A submerged fishing boat hidden within reeds casting shadows upon a broken carpet of algae became the initial inspiration for *Pond's Edge*. Water refractions and reflections coupled with complex long shadows create abstract lines, allowing for fragmented geometric shapes. The Red-winged Blackbird, which generally inhabits freshwater marshes, naturally seemed to be the perfect subject personifying the explorer, soaring through the thick wetland vegetation. The Toronto collectors who purchased the original loaned it back for the International Guild of Realism "Masterworks" museum tour travelling throughout the United States for a year.

Acrylic on Braced Baltic Birch 12" x 24" x 2" 2013 (Age 17)

Art Renewal Center International Salon Competition Finalist

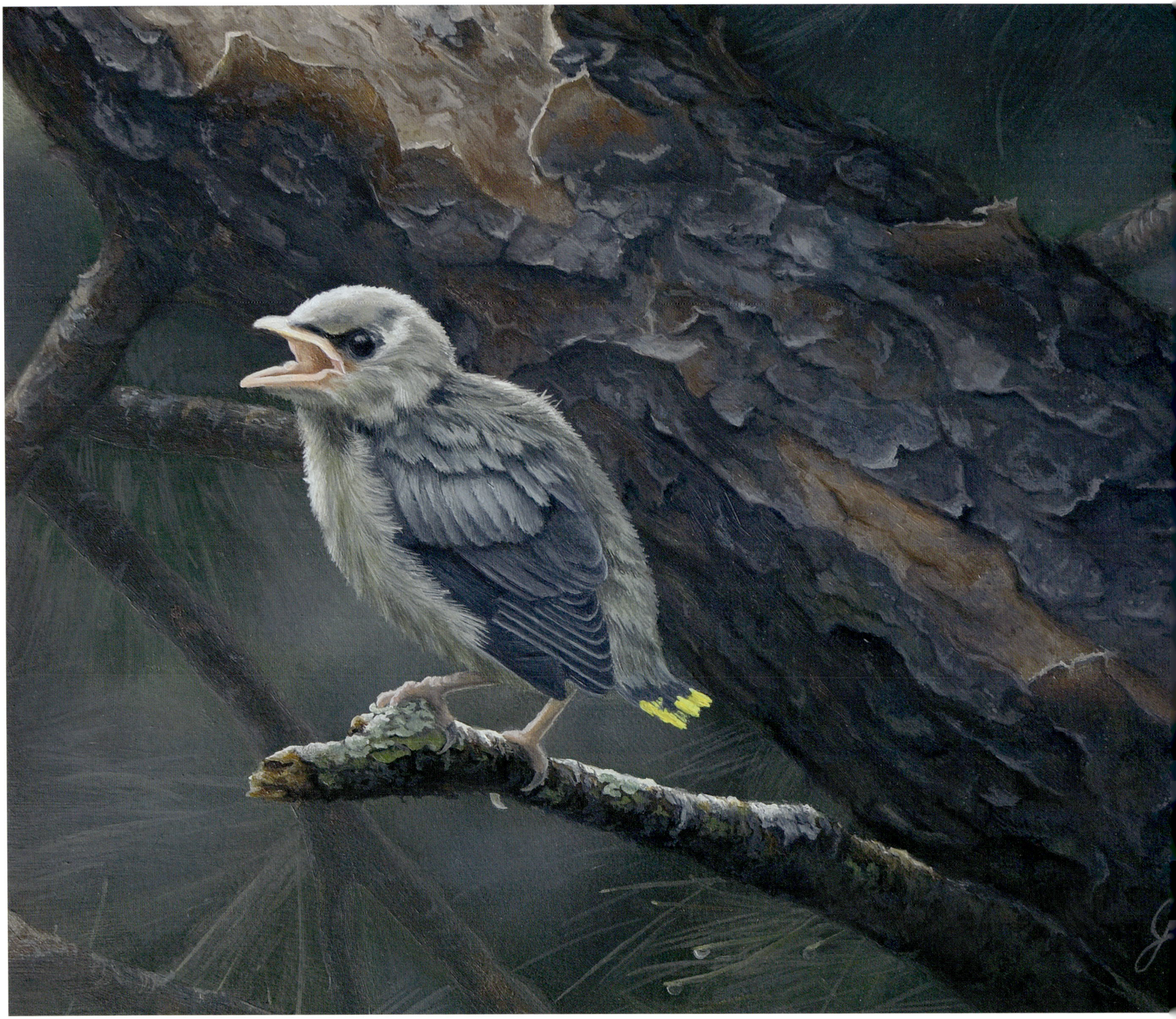

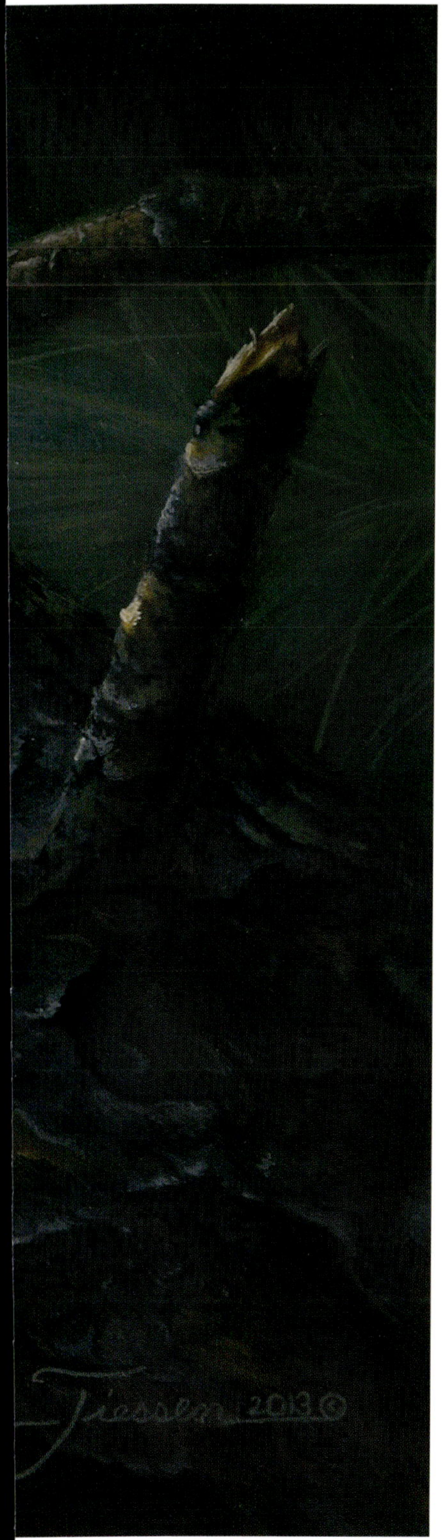

DISLODGED

I joined my family for a couple days at Miners' Bay Lodge, a quaint vacation property in the Haliburton Highlands of Ontario, where families 3-4 generations deep return yearly. The beach was full for the traditional Friday afternoon regatta. With the sky turning indigo, they were trying to get through the water-balloon-toss to the tug-of-war finale, when a wind whipped up the bay and sent everything flying, in what would later be deemed a mini-tornado. Everyone managed to run for cover. Amidst 200 falling trees miraculously no one was hurt and no cottages or trailers were destroyed. A massive cleanup effort was soon underway, with chainsaws buzzing at 100 foot trees now laying across laneways, one that had narrowly missed our car as we were driving out. After that tree was cleared back, those of us cleaning up debris in front of our cabins heard the loud chirping of a baby bird sitting among the fallen branches, seemingly calling *"Mom!"* A colourful Cedar Waxwing eventually returned looking very concerned, and rounded up two other babies while quieting their cries with food. The whole family had been dislodged from the tree, with the juveniles not quite ready to fly. By nightfall, the power outage prevented us from seeing them. We left the next morning hoping they had found another place to start rebuilding their home, even as Miners' Bay Lodge was rebuilding damaged cabins and fallen power lines. It was a reminder to us all of the fragility of life and the temporal nature of our earthly homes.

Oil on Birch 8" x 12" 2013 (Age 18)

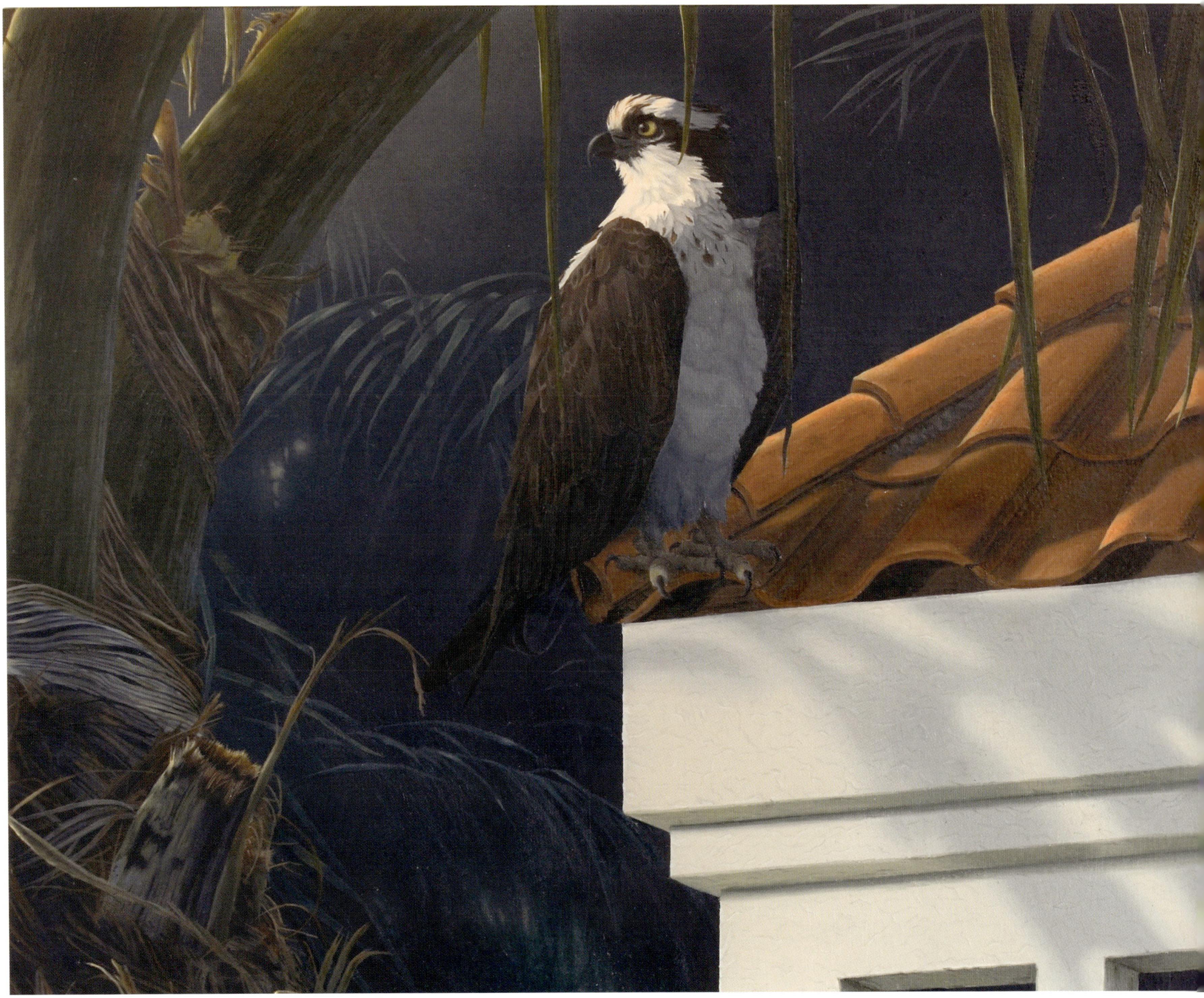

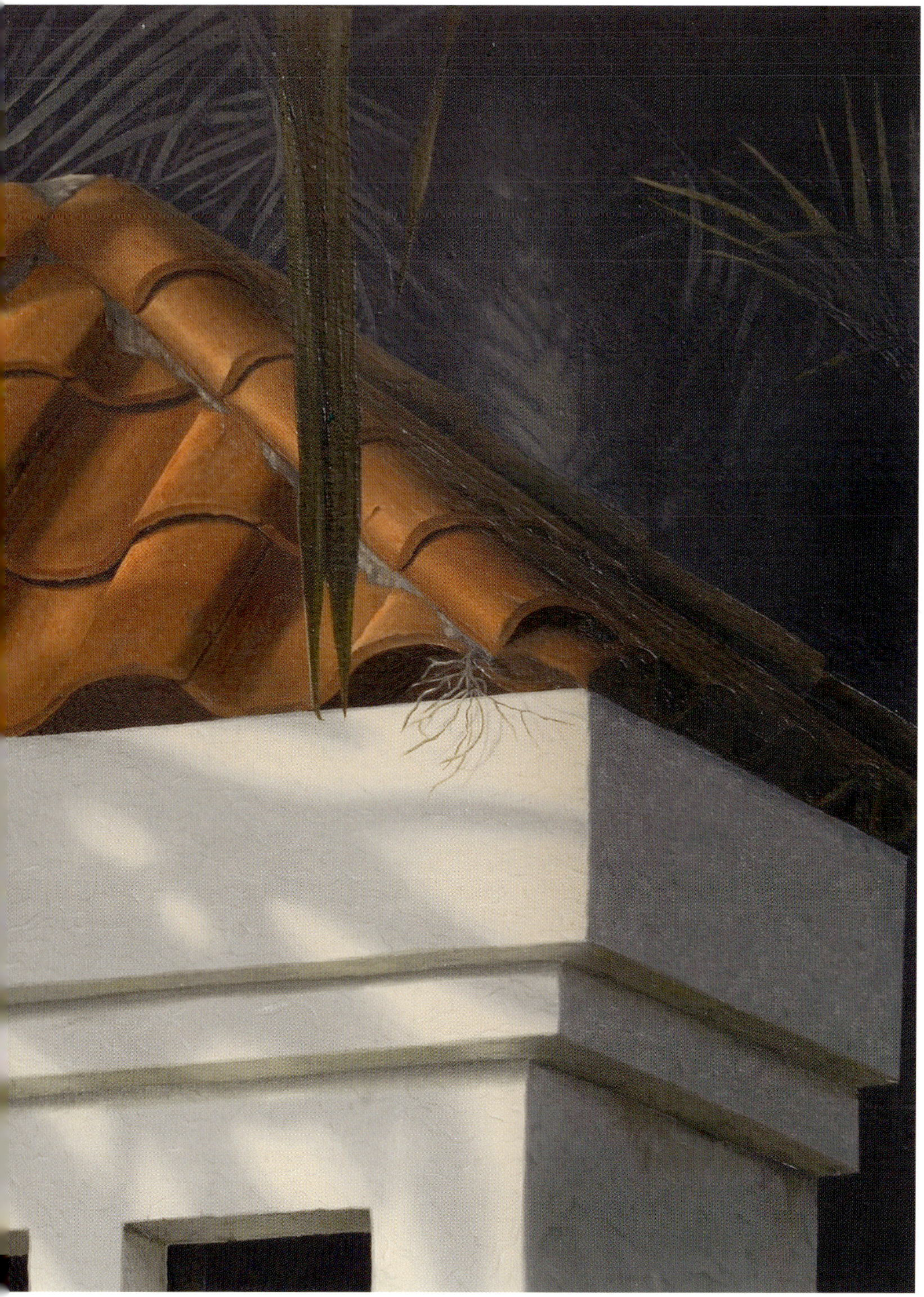

WATCHMAN OF BAHIA DEL MAR

This painting is based on many photographs I took while staying at the Florida condo of some long-time family friends. We travelled to bird sanctuaries and zoos in the neighbouring St. Petersburg area, but nothing compared to our little corner of paradise right around the condo! The resort is on a small island, and this resident Osprey is often found perched on the clay-roofed buildings. Within the shadows of the Royal Palms, he sits keeping watch as the last bit of sunlight disappears behind the horizon.

Oil on Braced Baltic Birch 13.5" x 24" x 2" 2014 (Age 18)

BEAUTY ON THE BRUCE

For those unfamiliar with Southern Ontario, the Bruce Trail is an 885 km hiking path along the Niagara Peninsula, enjoyed by outdoor enthusiasts like our family. This painting was commissioned by friends who live near Felker's Falls along this hiking trail. White-tailed Deer used to frequent their property in the early morning hours, but due to construction and housing development, the deer have become more scarce. Using their photos and my own as references, I captured the scene of a buck and doe meandering through the wild grass field adjacent to their property on a misty fall morning. I've always wanted to paint an old split-wood fence, as I love how organic they feel compared to metal fences, so this was an opportunity to do that. I hoped to infuse a sense of mystery and beauty into the painting through the foggy background and the doe's backward glance, contrasted with the buck's confident advance into the light.

Oil on Braced Baltic Birch 24" x 30" 2013 (Age 18)

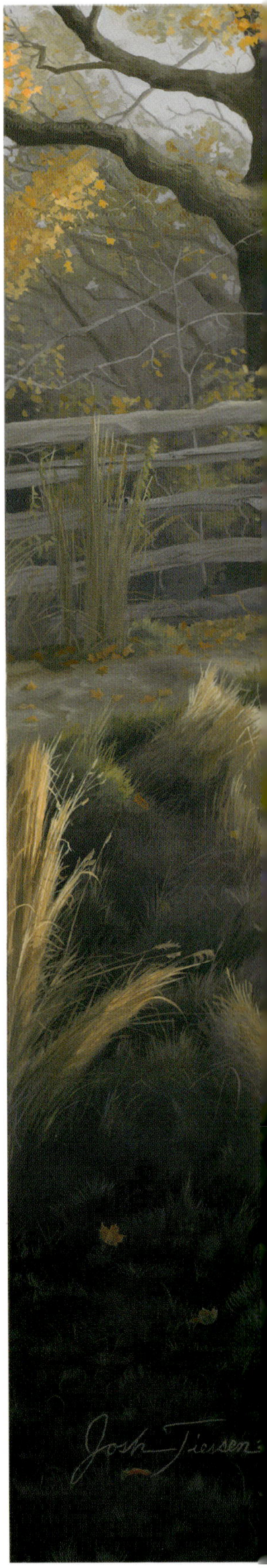

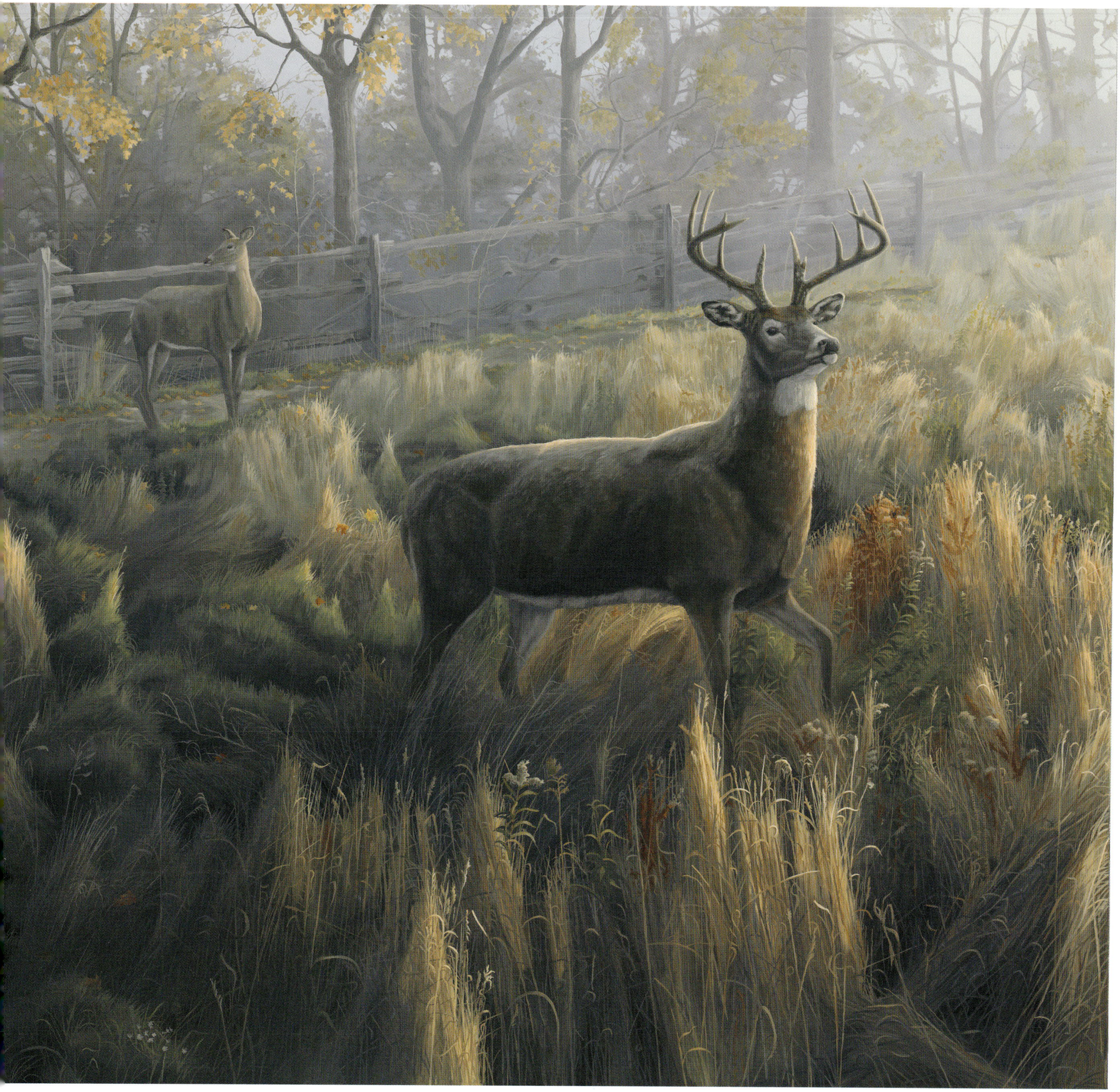

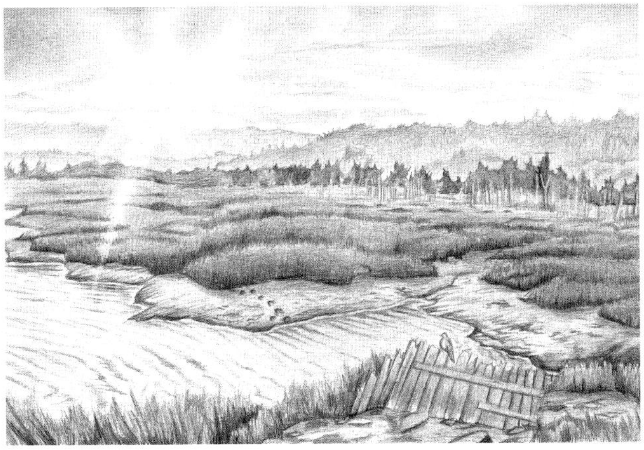

TRANQUIL TIDES

The initial inspiration for this landscape painting came from where my family camped on the edge of the Bay of Fundy in New Brunswick. Every evening we would go out to clod through the mud and witness the tide returning inland. Then we sat on a knoll until the sun set over the distant hills, its last light reflecting on a relic from the past. A collector who visited my studio gallery a short time later requested a small landscape painting based on my photos. When her name finally came up on my long list of commissions we worked together to flesh out the details, including the footprints (reminiscent of an old poem), Mourning Doves, and a specific latch on an old wooden fence. It is my desire that this painting will invoke the serenity of the scene, transporting the viewer to their own personal place of tranquility. The beauty of creation witnessed through the medium of art can be a conduit to 'the peace that passes all understanding' (Philippians 4:7).

Oil on Baltic Birch 8" x 12" 2014 (Age 19)

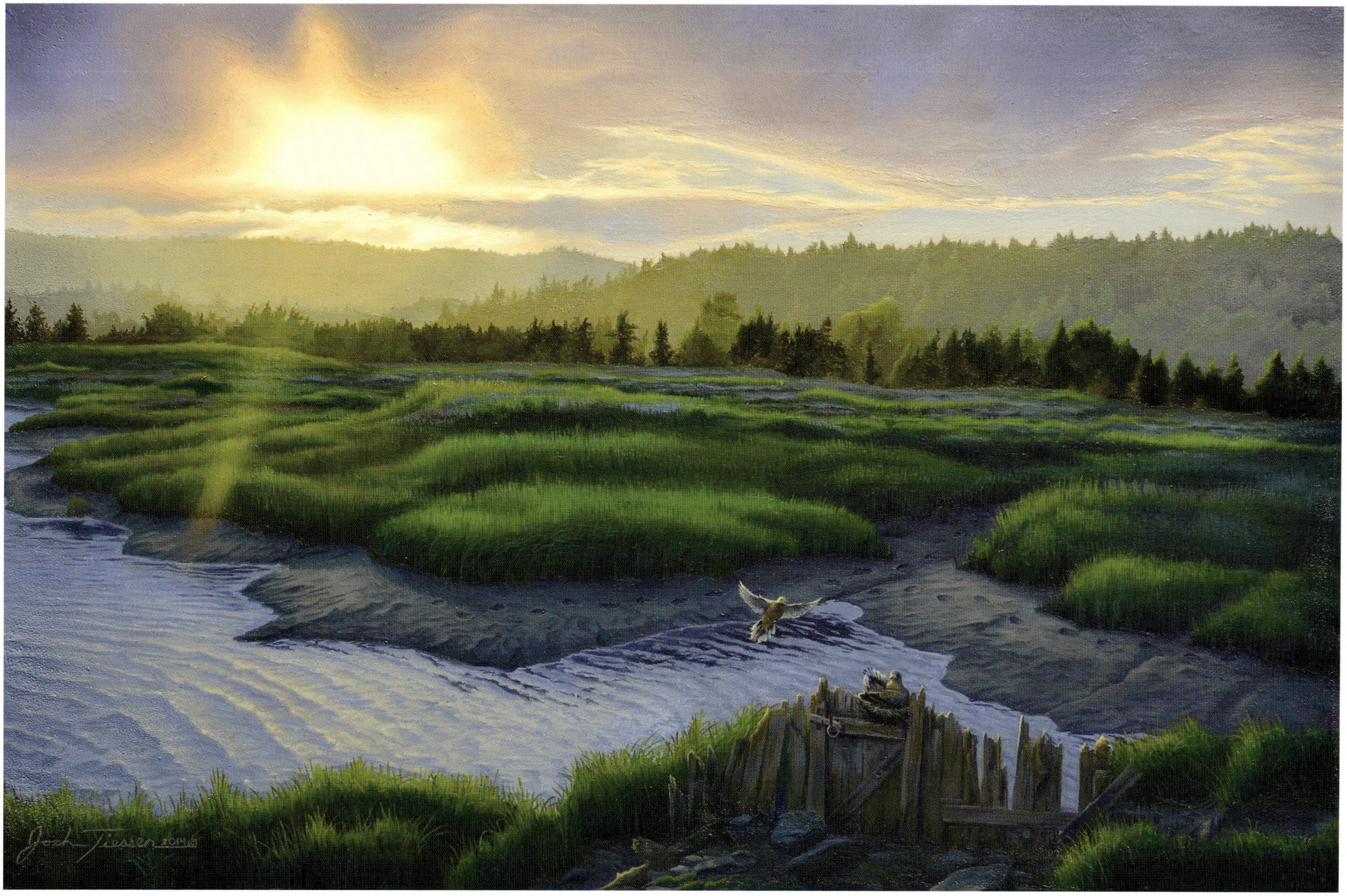

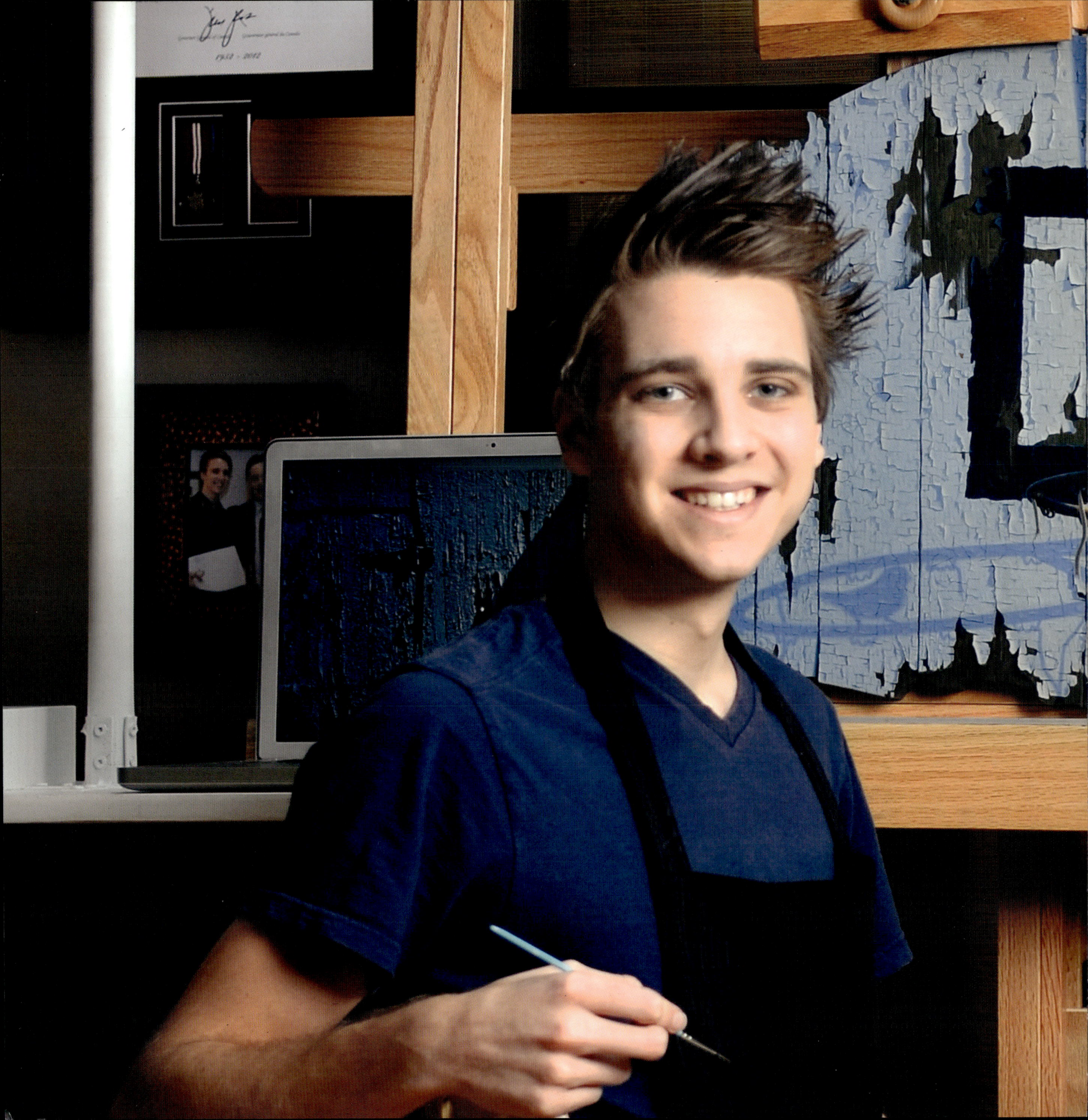

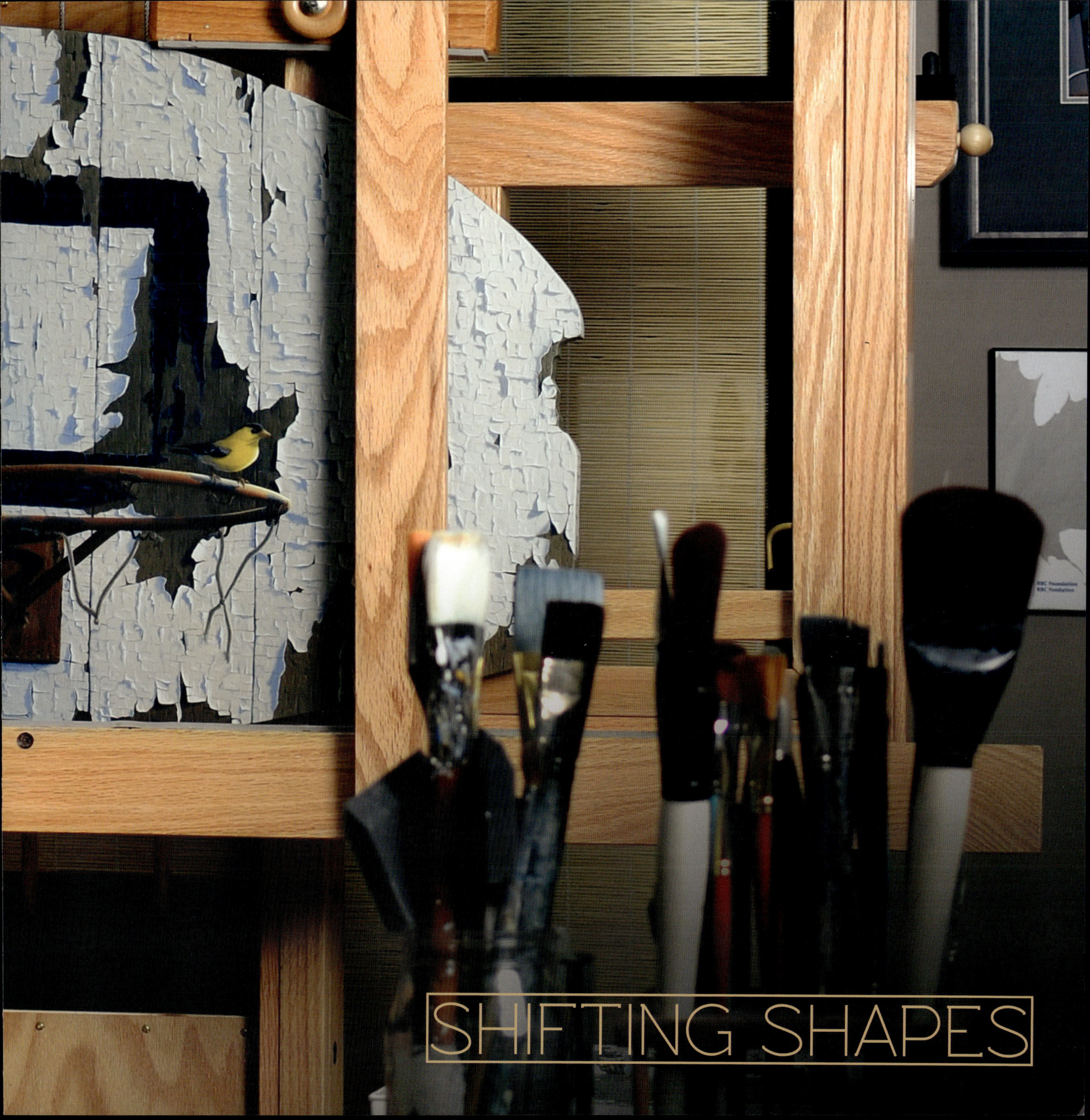

SHIFTING SHAPES

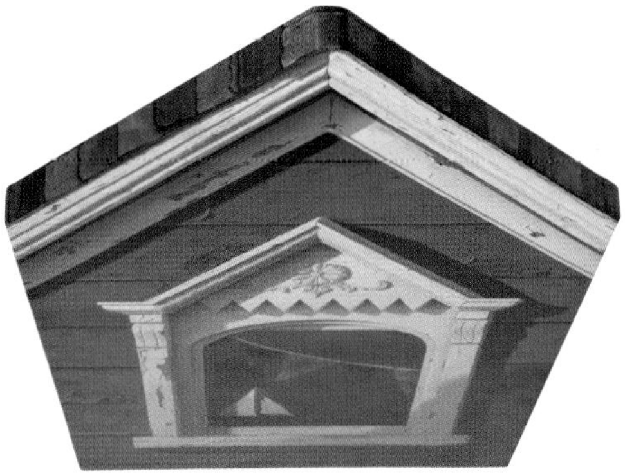

ETERNAL SAIL

Inspired by elements from my Maritime photos, I did a series of imaginative sketches to develop this composition. It is my first diversion from traditional quadrilateral format, as I decided in this case the subject matter would dictate the shape of the piece. I extended the image around the 2" sides, enhancing the three-dimensional effect by painting shingles on top of the peak. I became mesmerized by the repetition of triangles, which I highlighted in the architecture, bunting banner and sailboat. The use of long cast shadows and a half shadow indicates the time is nearing sundown. *Eternal Sail* speaks of loss, celebration and gift, all reminders of eternity unseen. But where did that come from? While years had worn away the coastal home since that fateful day, the memory had not been forgotten. A banner hung, it was to be a joyous celebration until dreadful words fell on a mother's ears: father would not be coming home from sea. So as not to disappoint, holding back tears she proceeded with her son's birthday. The little boy carefully unwrapped his only gift, a toy sailboat crafted by his father. Attached was a penned note, recounting fond memories of sailing together, with words of encouragement and hope. As the young cabin boy matured and eventually became a captain, the sailboat remained in his childhood room. It stood as a reminder that although our voyage will eventually come to an end with the setting sun, when we know the Captain of the Tide our celebration is anchored in the hope of eternity.

Oil on Braced Baltic Birch 48" x 24" x 2" 2014 (Age 18)

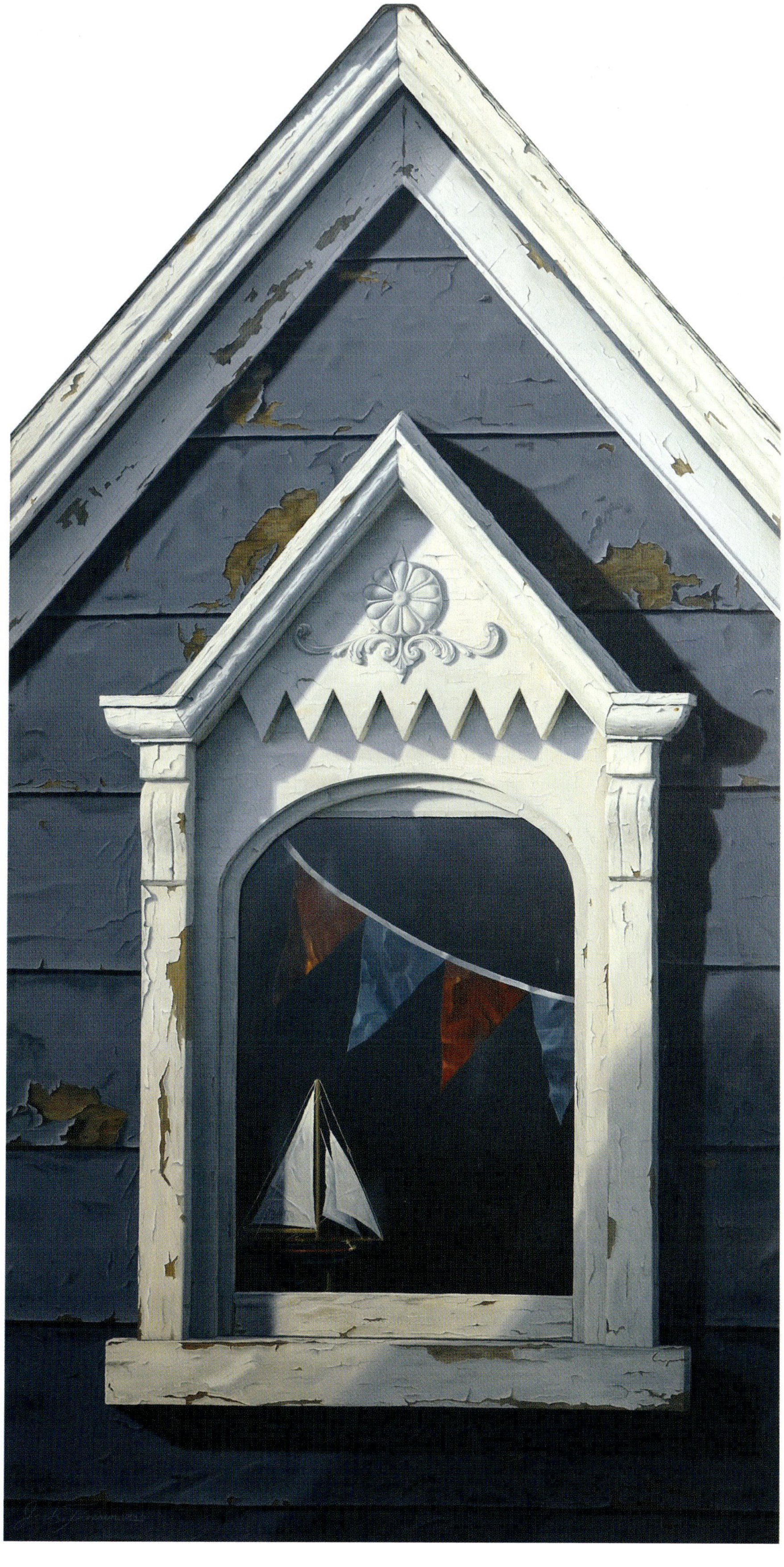

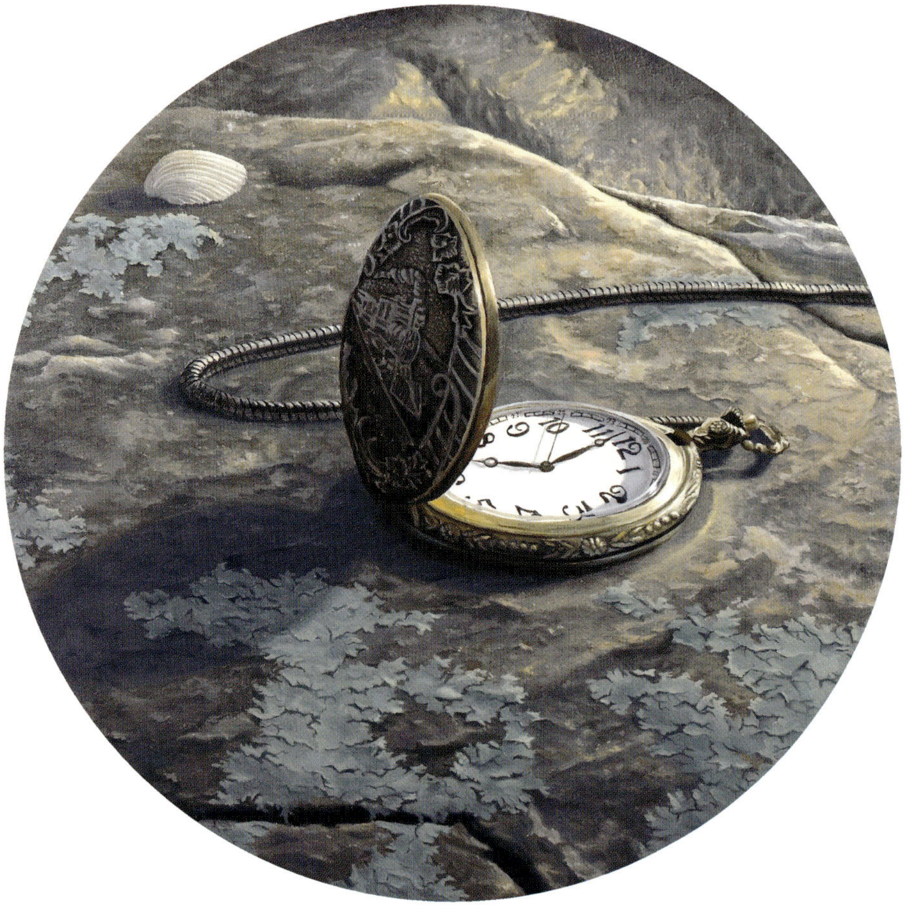
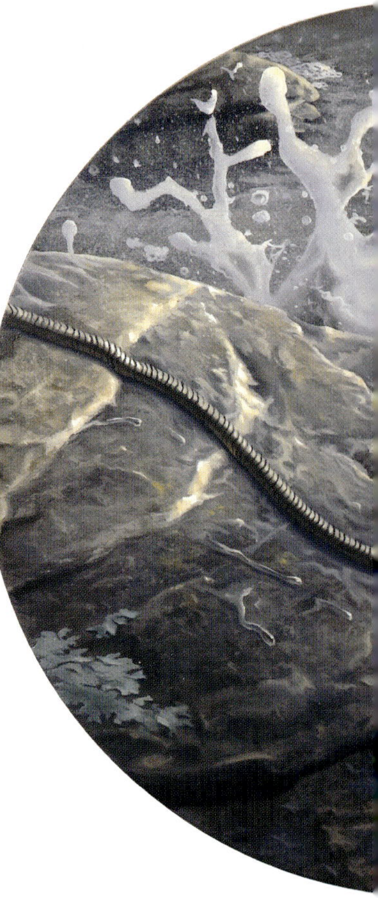

TIME IS MY OYSTER

Passed down from my great-great Uncle Percy, I inherited an heirloom Victorian-style pocket watch, which has become a treasure of mine. I set it among other objects I have collected such as seashells, rocks, and an old trinket box. From this shelf of curious items the idea came to me of juxtaposing the mechanical timepiece with a natural shoreline landscape. While composing the sketches, I realized I had been subconsciously influenced by Salvador Dali's paintings of melting clocks, which I had seen the summer before at the Dali Museum in Florida. This was later affirmed by viewers commenting on my first work in progress photos, saying it echoed Dali in realism. I felt that a circular format would reflect the roundness of the pocket watch, and I decided to continue the composition onto two other circular panels for my first ever triptych (three paintings making up one) on solid red

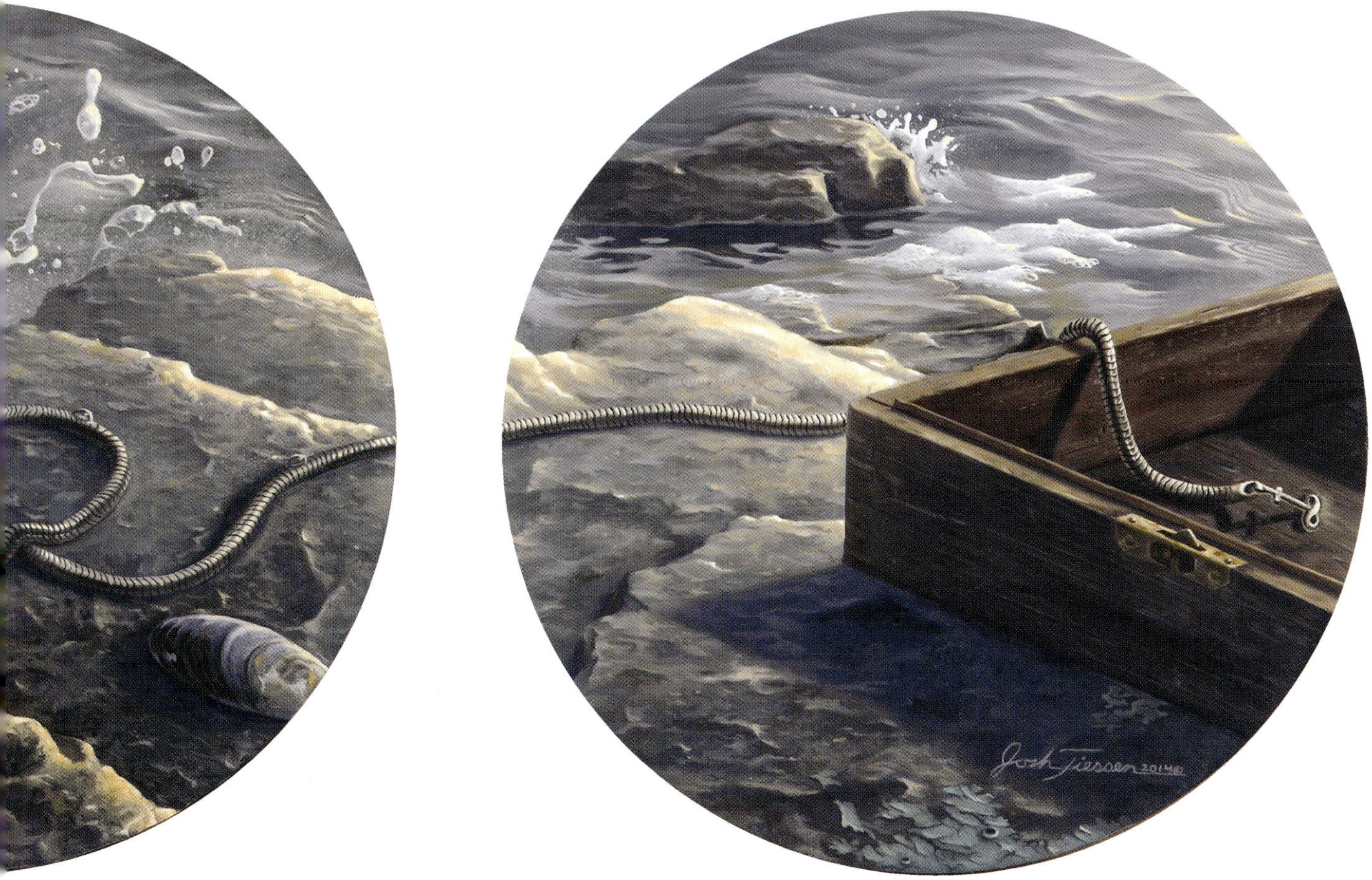

oak panels, the same surface Michelangelo painted on. I did not realize how challenging it would be to paint around the sides of circles, but in the end it proved rewarding for its anamorphic uniqueness. This painting has a somewhat mystical feel, travelling back into history and reaching forward to the future, transporting the viewer to a 'steam punk' world. The title is reminiscent of a Shakespearean proverb 'the world is my oyster', but elicits contemporary metaphors through the commodity of time. While working on this painting the fleetingness of time became a point of contemplation, a reminder of how time is the most valuable currency, something we either lose or master. We only have one life on this earth, then it all ends up in the proverbial box.

Oil on Solid Red Oak, Triptych 9" x 2" 2014 (Age 18)

AHOY SLEEPER

I began thinking about painting an aquanaut, or deep-sea diver, when we were in Florida and some friends suggested we meet at Tarpon Springs, an old Greek settlement known for its sponge industry. On a boat tour I became fixated on an antique diving suit donned for a demonstration of how they collected sponges. I was drawn to the brass surface texture of the helmet, which was even more interesting with the emergence from water. Once home, I did further research on lighting, wet rubberized fabric and brass. I had my dad take photos of me, first in my studio and later emerging from Lake Ontario wearing a round brass planter on my head! The choice of using a circular panel was intentional. In viewing a rectangular piece, there is a left-to-right beginning-to-end, whereas a circle is cornerless, resulting in a type of timelessness and unity. This set the stage for a painting that would come to carry peculiar metaphysical weight. Over the years I have been intrigued by Ephesians 5:14, which states "Awake, O Sleeper, and arise from the dead, and Christ will shine on you" (*ESV*). When reading it, I would always have a strange picture in my mind of a diver rising upon a seaweed shore with a bird flying above. Suddenly, this verse in Ephesians and the visual idea for this painting converged. As I conceptually developed this piece, I began to see the metamorphosis of the aquanaut emerging from the depths of the ocean into an unknown light, with an illuminated Common House Martin ascending into the sky. By excluding the face and skin colour, the figure becomes a metaphoric archetype for spiritual transformation, arising from deadness of soul into new life in Christ, which is available to everyone.

Oil on Braced Baltic Birch 35" x 2" 2014 (Age 18)

International Guild of Realism 9th Annual Juried Exhibition "Creative Achievement Award"
Robert Lange Studios, Charleston, South Carolina

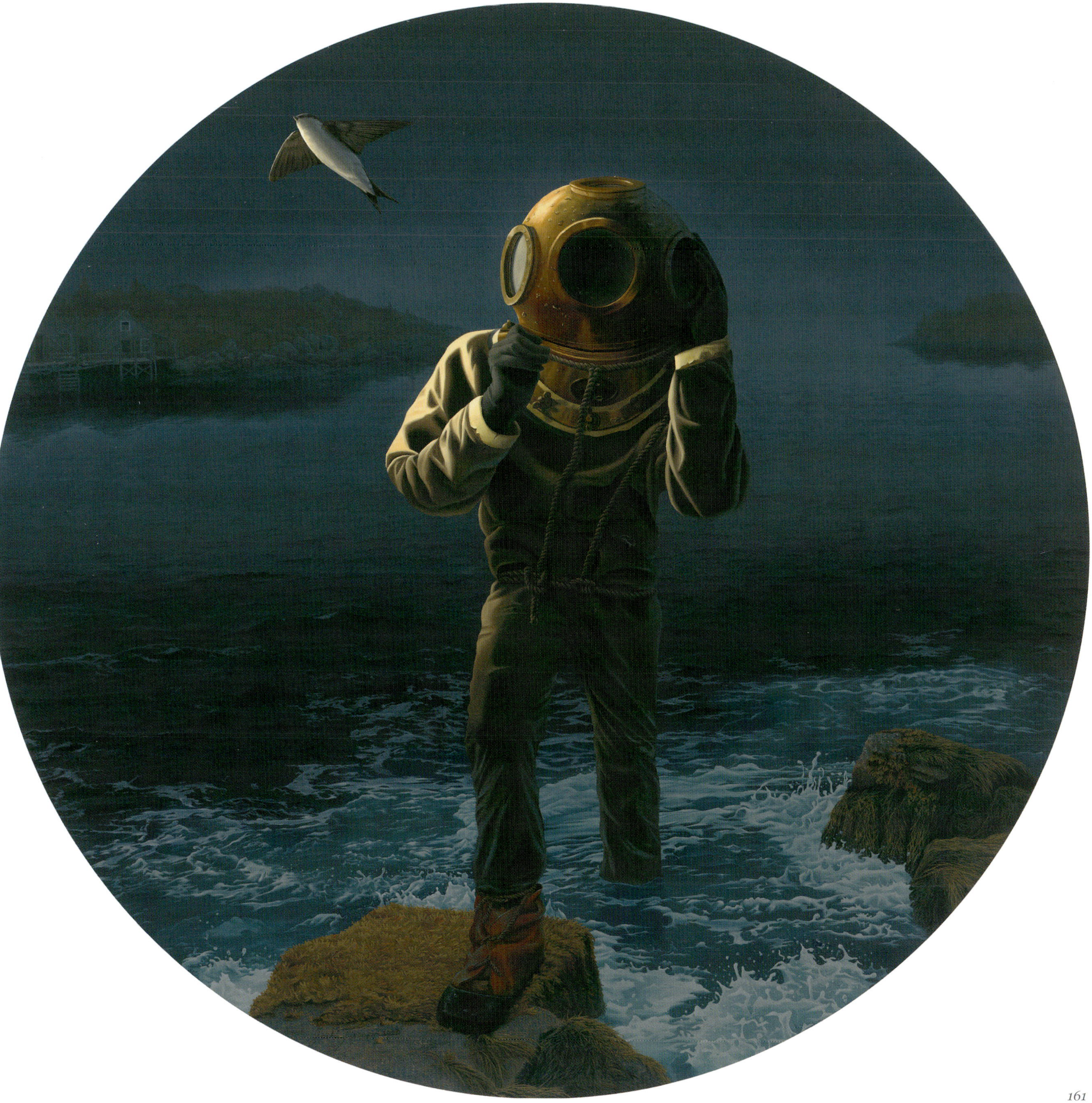

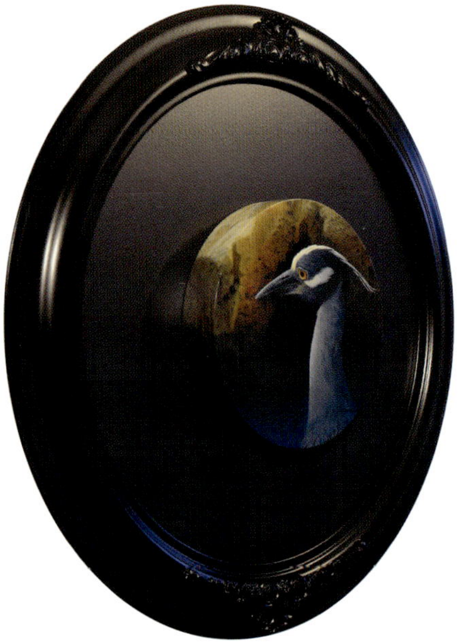

REGAL BLUES

Inspired by my trip to the gulf coast of Florida, for this painting I wished to capture in an anthropomorphic way the noble quality of this Yellow-crowned Night Heron, whose countenance indicated a somber look of contemplation. I hadn't given much thought to how it related to me personally, until a fellow artist saw this painting hanging at the Art Gallery of Burlington and said the bird reminded her of me, both in its physicality and personality. It was then that I realized, in spite of efforts to stand tall and stay strong, I had been feeling introspective and even a little blue when I painted this. In choosing the classic cameo frame, perhaps I was completing this self-portrait. It's fascinating as artists how much of our own person we infuse subconsciously into our work, sometimes revealing more of ourselves than we intended to the keen observer.

Oil on Masonite 9" x 2" 2014 (Age 19)

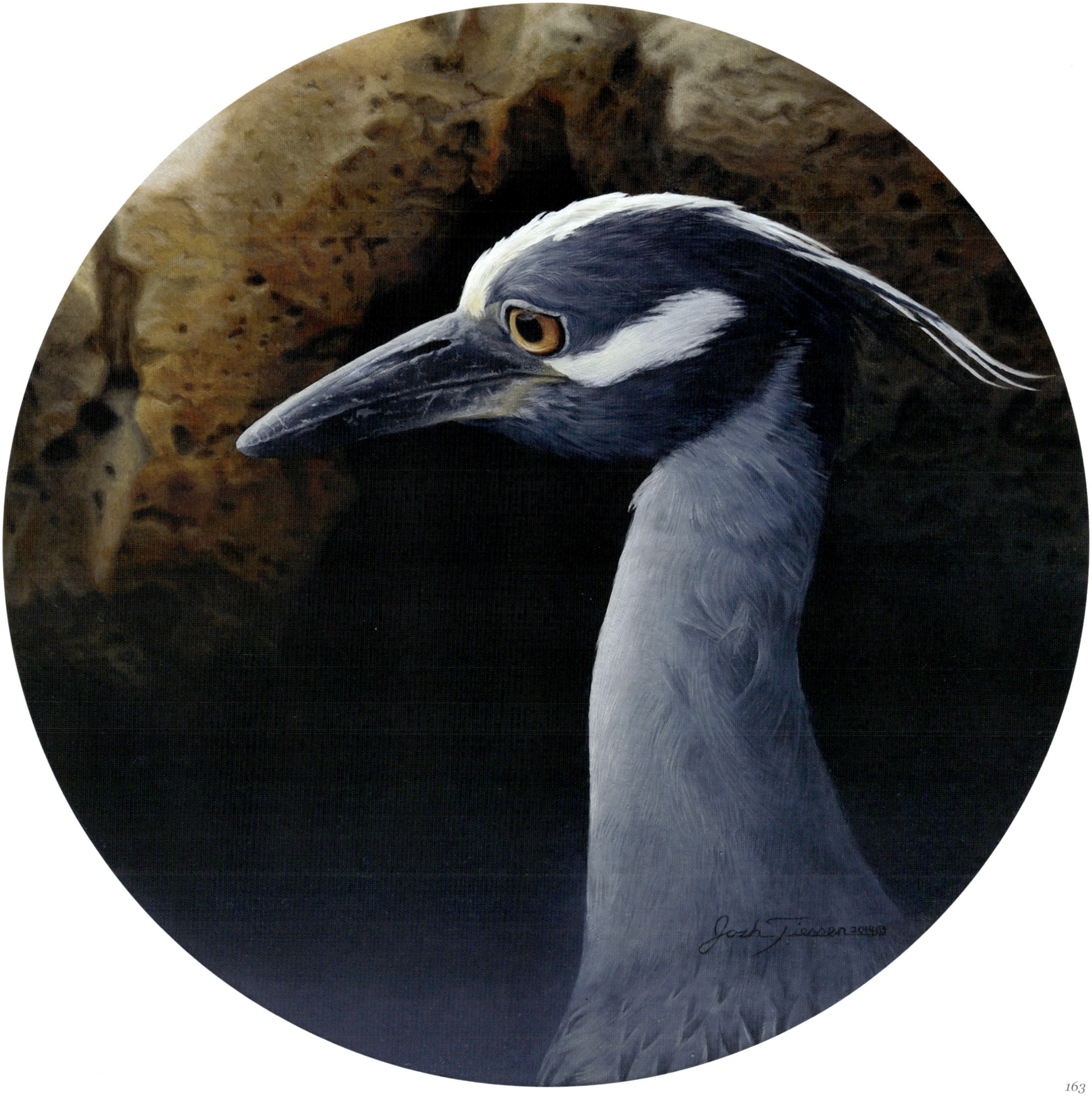
Josh Tiessen

CONFLUENCE

As it may be guessed from their presence in many of my paintings, I'm a bit of a birder. Florida is known as a bird paradise, so I was thrilled when friends offered their condo for a vacation there. I researched birds before we left, and was particularly interested in the Roseate Spoonbill because of its unique platypus-like bill. We travelled to nature reserves in search of this elusive beauty, and the day before we left Florida I finally spotted one, but had to follow it into someone's backyard just to get a few fleeting photos. On the next year's trip back to our friends' condo on Isla Del Sol we took our bikes. To my surprise, on the first evening biking the island golf course, there on a pond was the Roseate Spoonbill! We returned many evenings and were treated to the delightful sight of this bird landing and taking off from the water, and I got dozens of great reference photos. Later, as I sketched, I tried to create a dynamic composition showing the whimsical confluence of motion between the bird's wings and the splashing water. I normally don't paint in such vibrant pink and magenta, but I loved how striking these colours appeared against an indigo backdrop at nightfall.

Oil on Braced Baltic Birch 11" x 2" 2015 (Age 19)

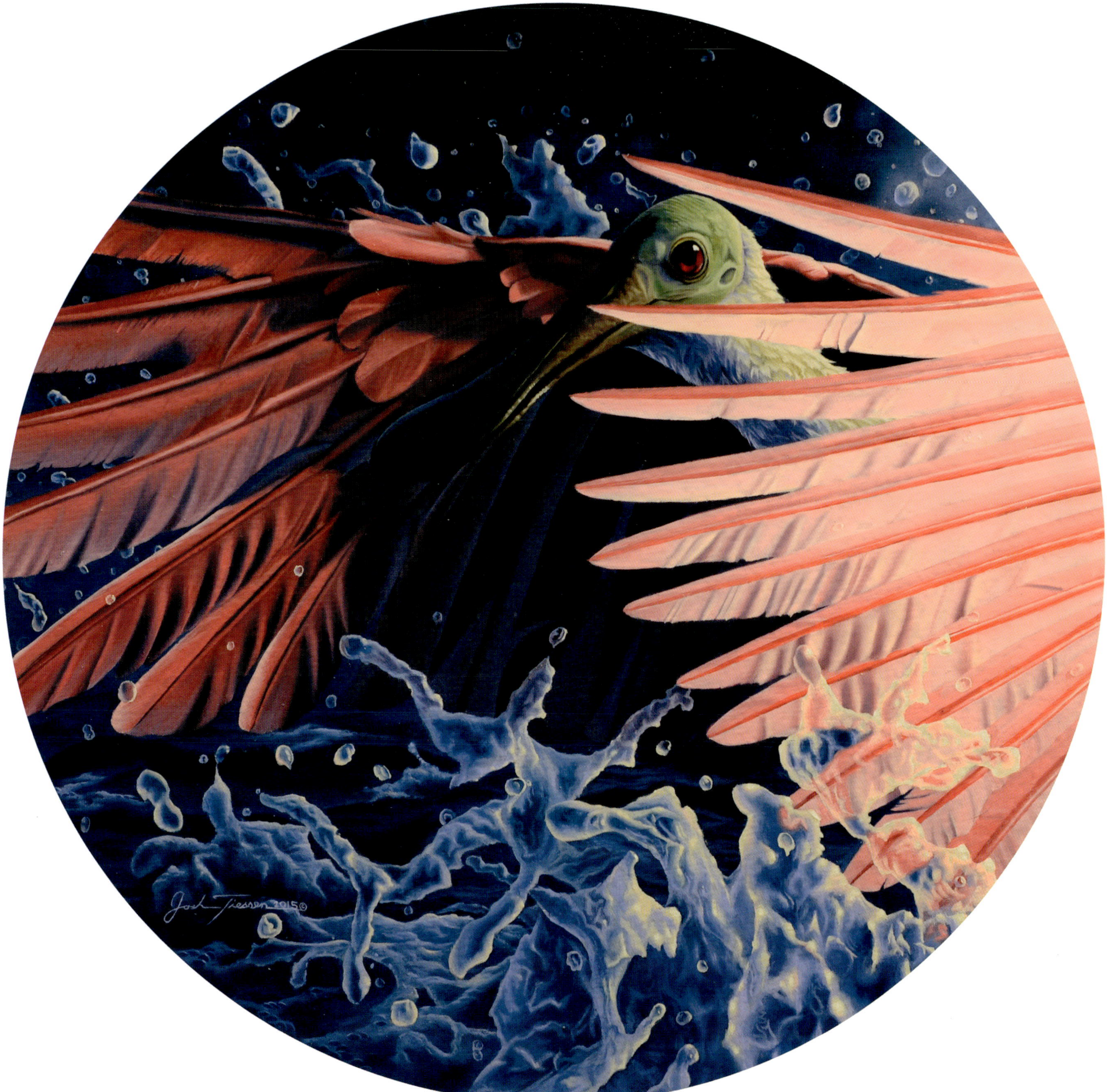
Josh Tiessen 2015©

DEFENDING THE PAINT

At age nine, a few years after my family moved from Russia back to Canada, my brother and I fell in love with basketball. Our school friends had been at the ice rink since they were two and were skating circles around us, so we quickly realized hockey wasn't going to be our sport. Then we found basketball, a relief for our parents who were happy to watch our games from the comfort of a heated gym with a Tim Horton's coffee in hand. To everyone's surprise we were quite good at it, quickly moving up the ranks in city leagues and leading our teams to championship wins. As short white kids from Canada, over time we realized our hopes of making the NBA were next to impossible, so basketball gradually gave way to art. But I still enjoy shooting hoops for recreation on the half-court we made in our backyard. For the last few years I have had this idea of painting an old basketball net with a bird perched on the rim, a sight I often see from my studio windows. I chose an American Goldfinch, as I thought his striking yellow colour would complement the navy backboard square. I positioned him metaphorically guarding his key on a forgotten basketball half-court. While it's not too Canadian of me to have basketball as my favourite sport instead of hockey, I find it interesting that the game was actually invented by a Canadian, Dr. James Naismith, in Springfield, Massachusetts well over a century ago.

Oil on Braced Baltic Birch 20" x 32" x 1" 2014 (Age 19)

International Guild of Realism 11th Annual Juried Exhibition "Best Wildlife Award"
Gallery 1261, Denver, Colorado

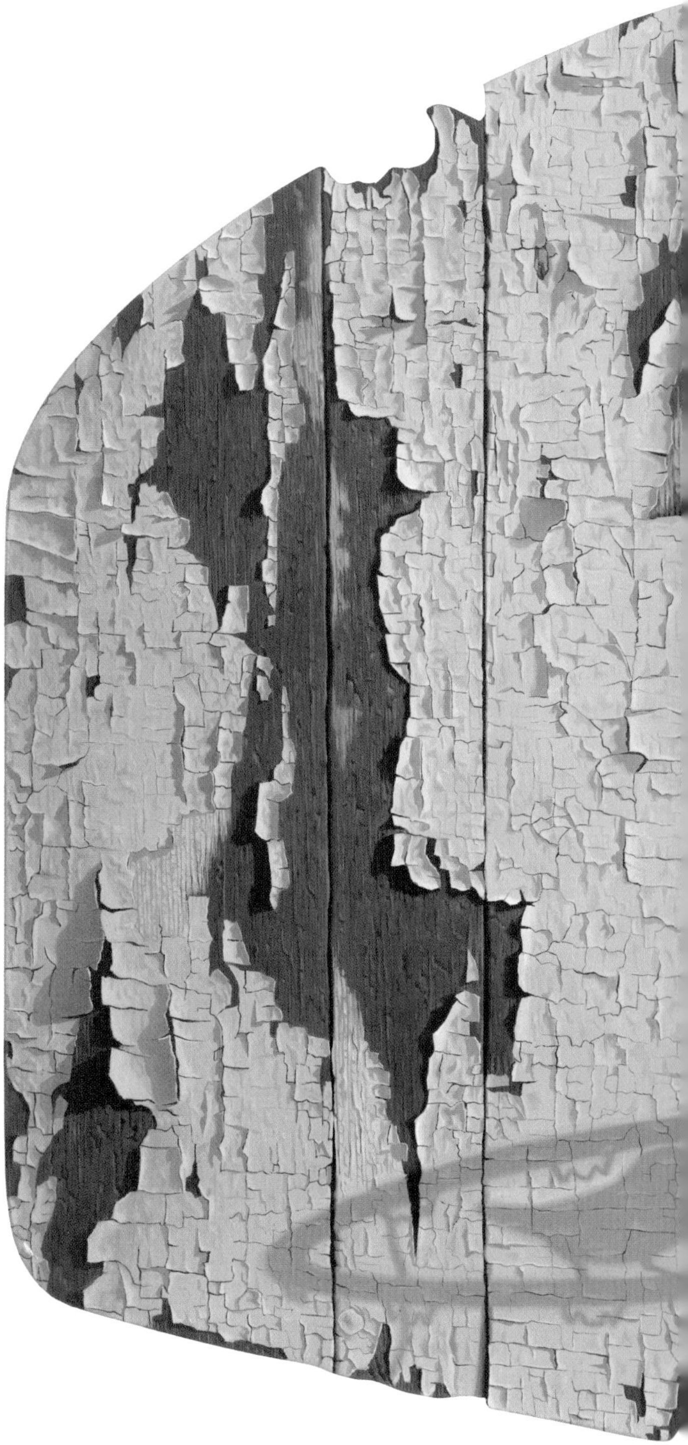

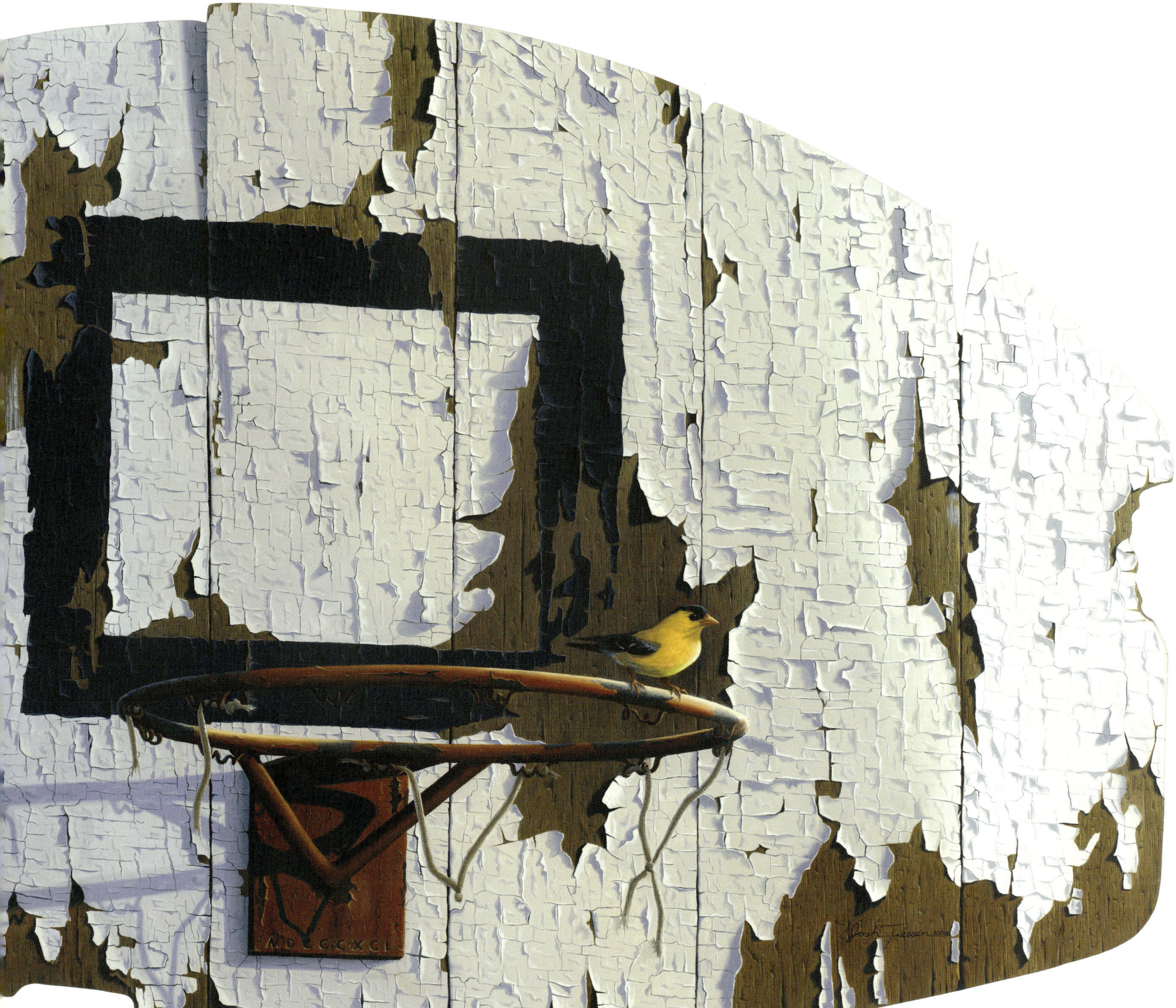
MDCCCXCI

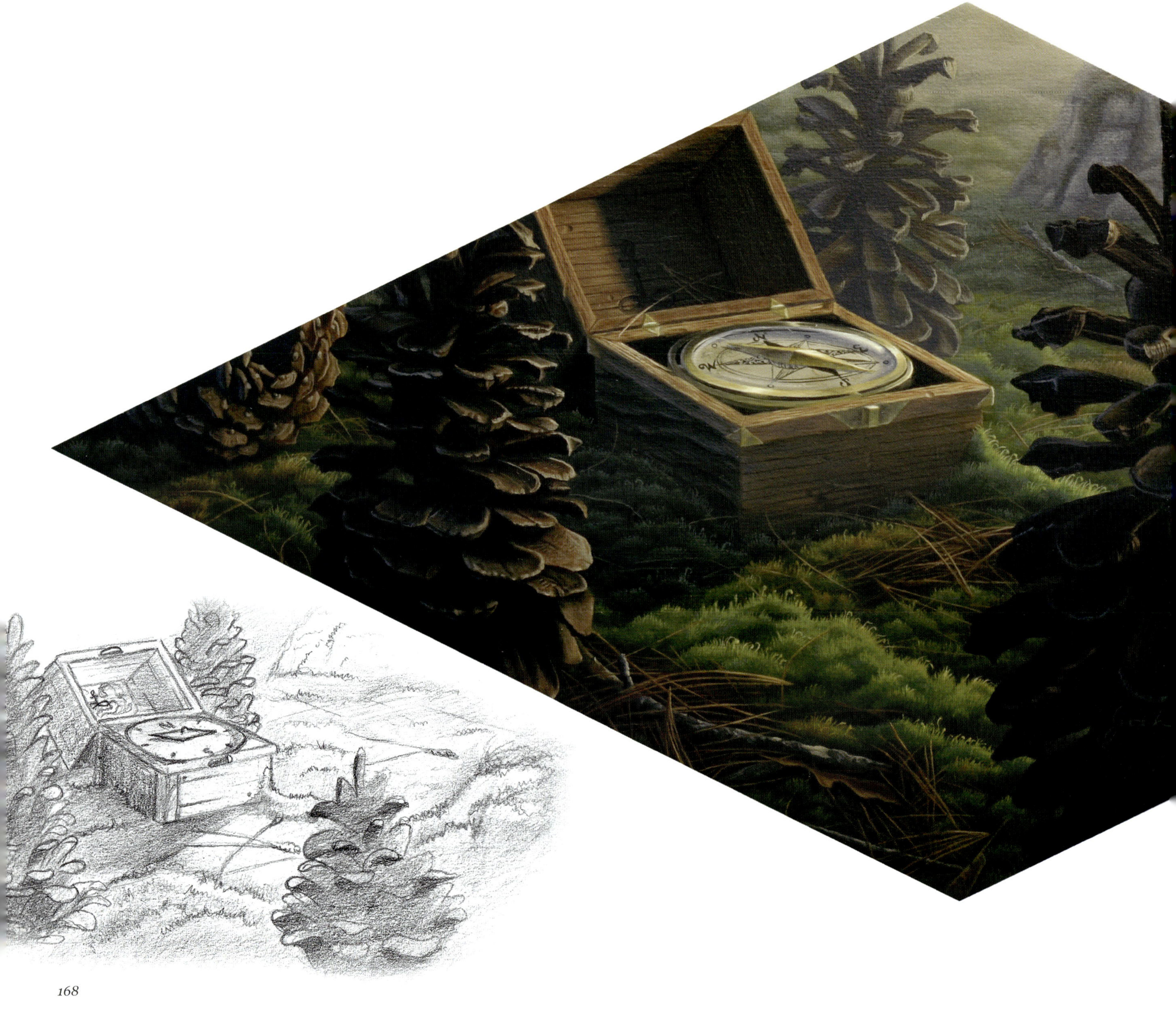

THE WOOD BETWEEN THE WORLDS

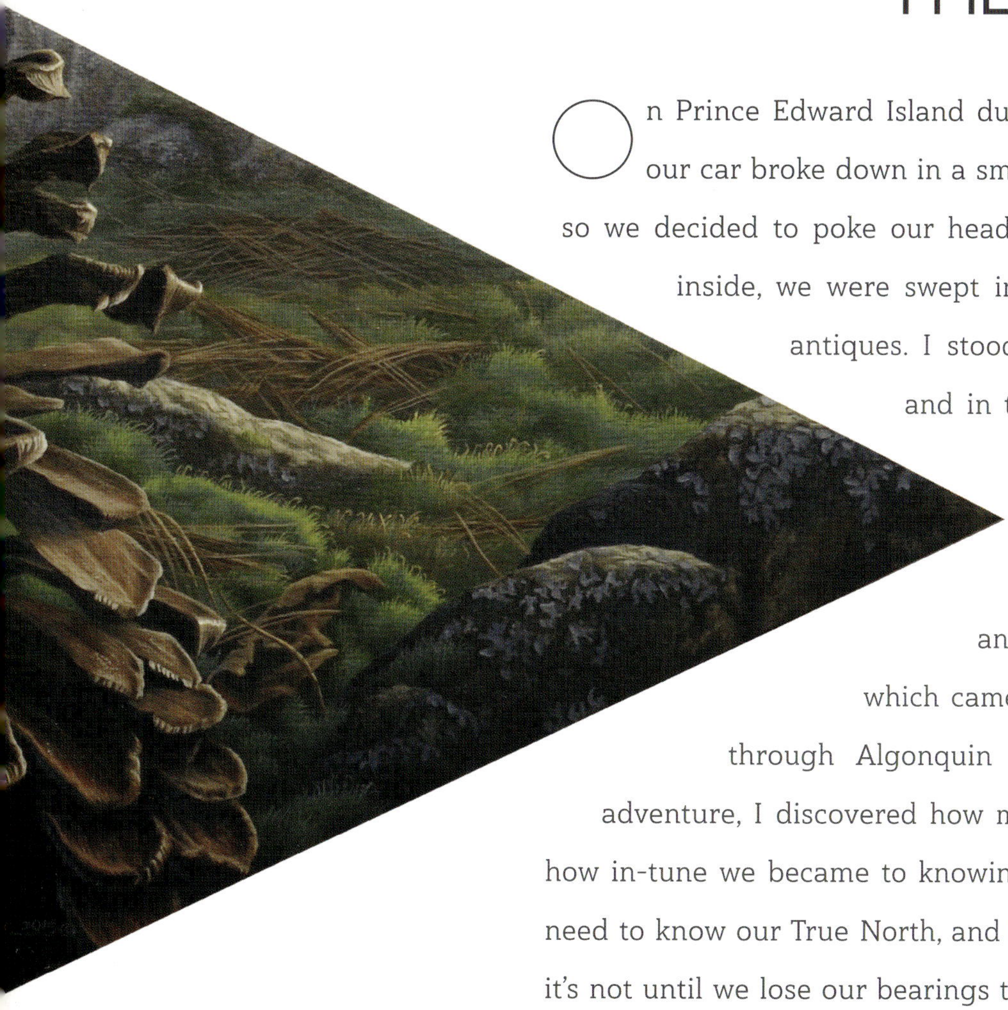

On Prince Edward Island during a road trip to Eastern Canada with my family, our car broke down in a small town. While it was being fixed we were stranded, so we decided to poke our heads into a quaint little chapel-turned-museum. Once inside, we were swept into a nautical dream world of the most charming antiques. I stood transfixed in front of the wooden box compass, and in that moment I knew this inspiring relic would find its way into one of my paintings. I thanked the curator for allowing me to freely take photos. For the environment, I envisioned an ethereal and enchanted mossy forest in the deep wood, an idea which came to me last summer while canoeing and portaging through Algonquin Park in Northern Ontario. During this off-grid adventure, I discovered how much we relied on our compass for navigation and how in-tune we became to knowing true north. It's like that with our lives too, as we need to know our True North, and having a compass to navigate is crucial. Sometimes it's not until we lose our bearings that we realize how important this is. While working on the painting, I enjoyed listening to *The Magician's Nephew* by C.S. Lewis, which inspired the title for the work and described the mystical feeling I wished to convey.

Oil on Baltic Birch, 12" x 20" 2015 (Age 19)

CLOUD OF SUSPICION

Smallest of the big cats, the Clouded Leopard resides elusively in the Himalayan foothills throughout mainland Southeast Asia. Due to deforestation and illegal poaching, this leopard, often called the 'modern saber-tooth' has been classified as vulnerable by IUCN and endangered by the U.S. Fish and Wildlife Service, with fewer than 10,000 mature animals in the wild. Therefore, part of the proceeds from the sale of this painting was donated to conservation efforts. When studying a species in desperate need, it does not feel like I am doing it a favour. Rather, the Clouded Leopard did me the favour of enjoyment seeing two at the Lowry Park Zoo in Tampa, Florida. Compositionally, I employed an inverted triangle to echo the shape of the face, on which I set a triangular sliver of warm dawning sunlight, contrasting the cool mist rising from beneath, adding mystique and drama to the scene.

Oil on Birch 10" x 15" 2016 (Age 20)

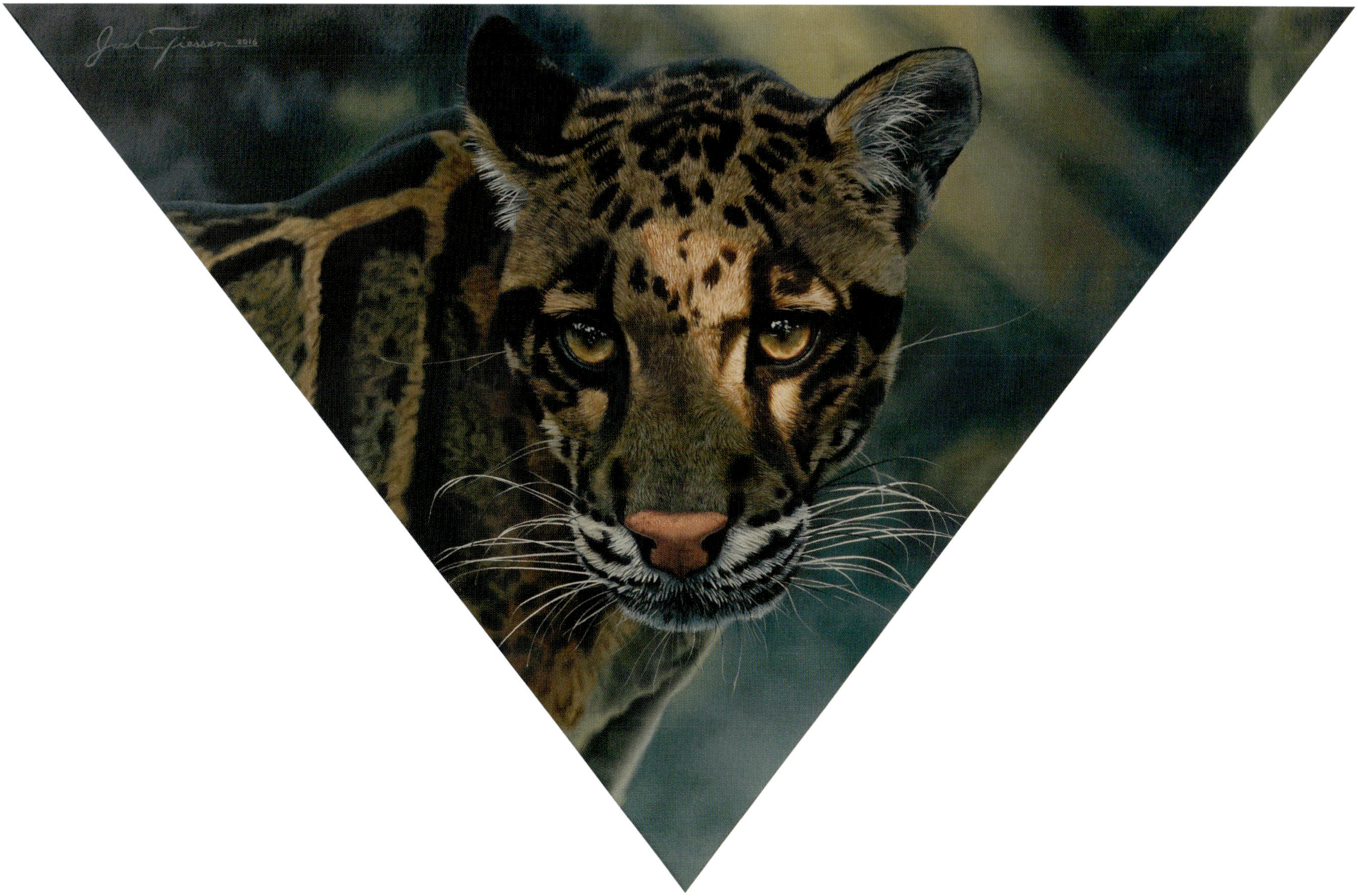

HITCHIN' A RIDE

Thanks to a collector of mine who let me borrow his father's moose mount, I hauled it home and was able to take reference photos in my studio of the large rack of antlers. I studied the texture, pattern and form as I developed sketches. As an artist, I am always intrigued by the recurring elements of design found in the natural world. Having seen a Belted Kingfisher in Algonquin Park, I noted how its crest mimicked the points of the moose's antlers. The background sky and tree line for this painting were inspired by a magnificent sunset view from our island campsite in Algonquin Park. The shape of the painting compliments the distinct profile of the kingfisher, who is tagging along for an evening stroll with the gentle giant.

Oil on Baltic Birch, 16" x 8" 2016 (Age 20)

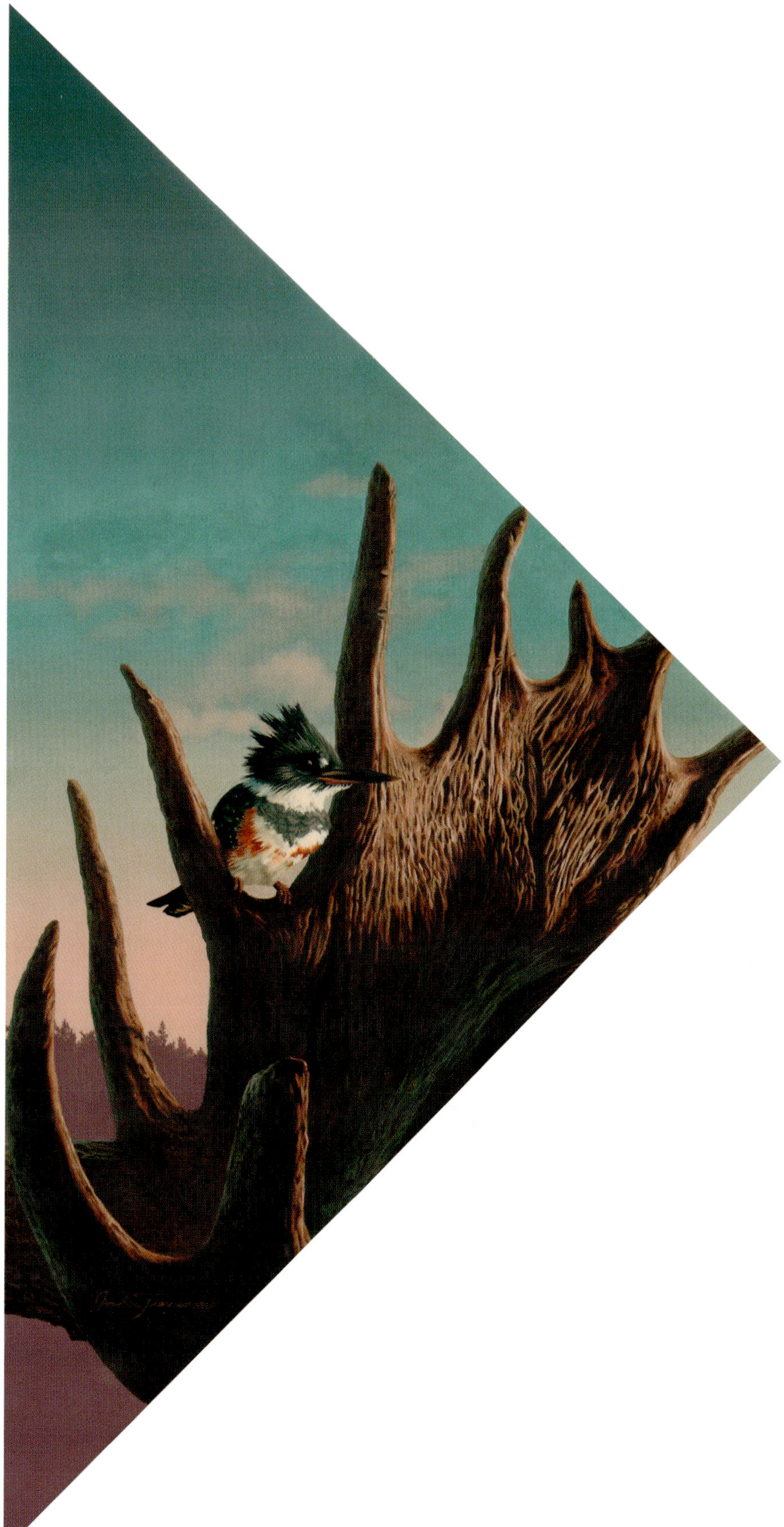

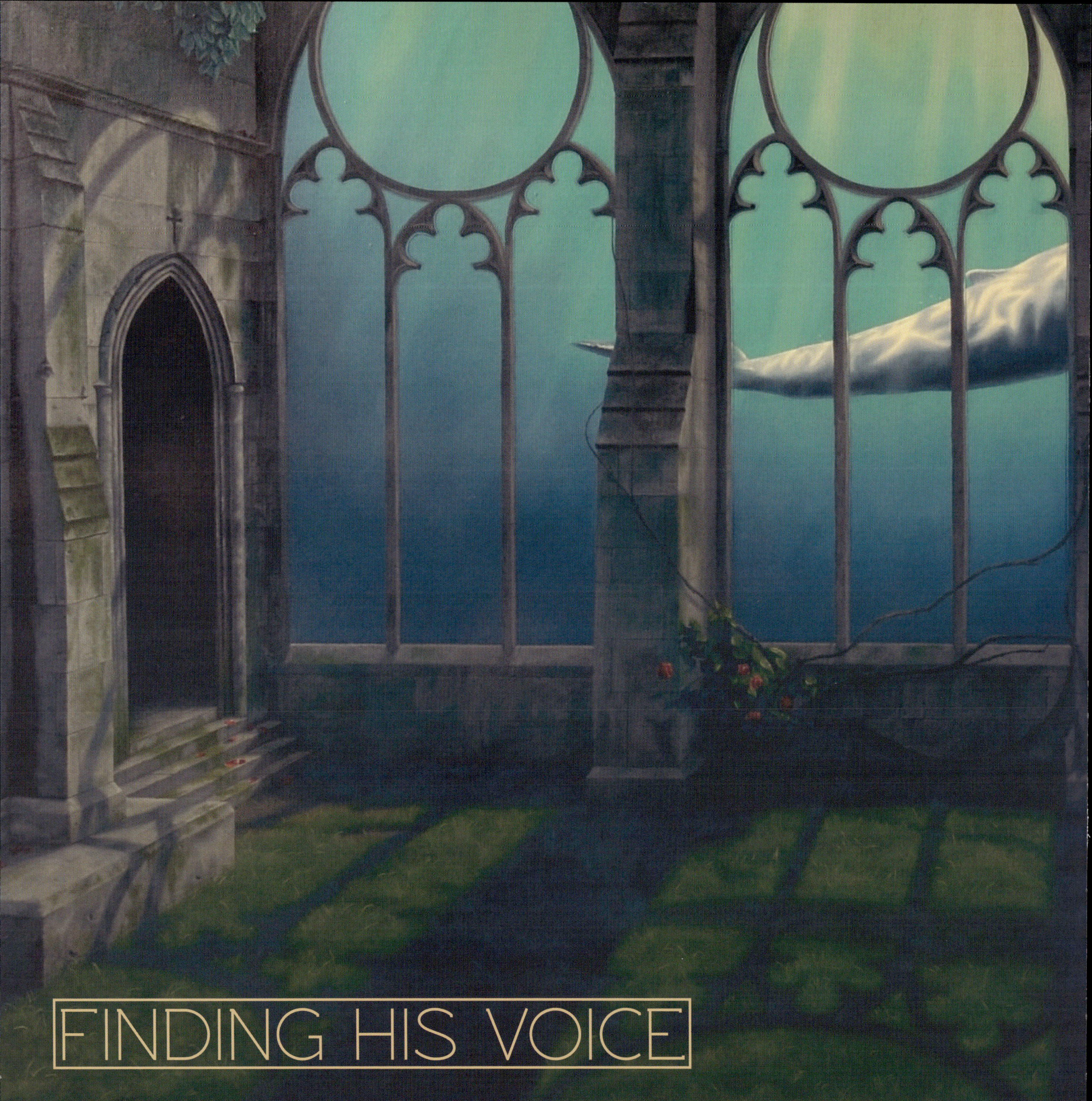
FINDING HIS VOICE

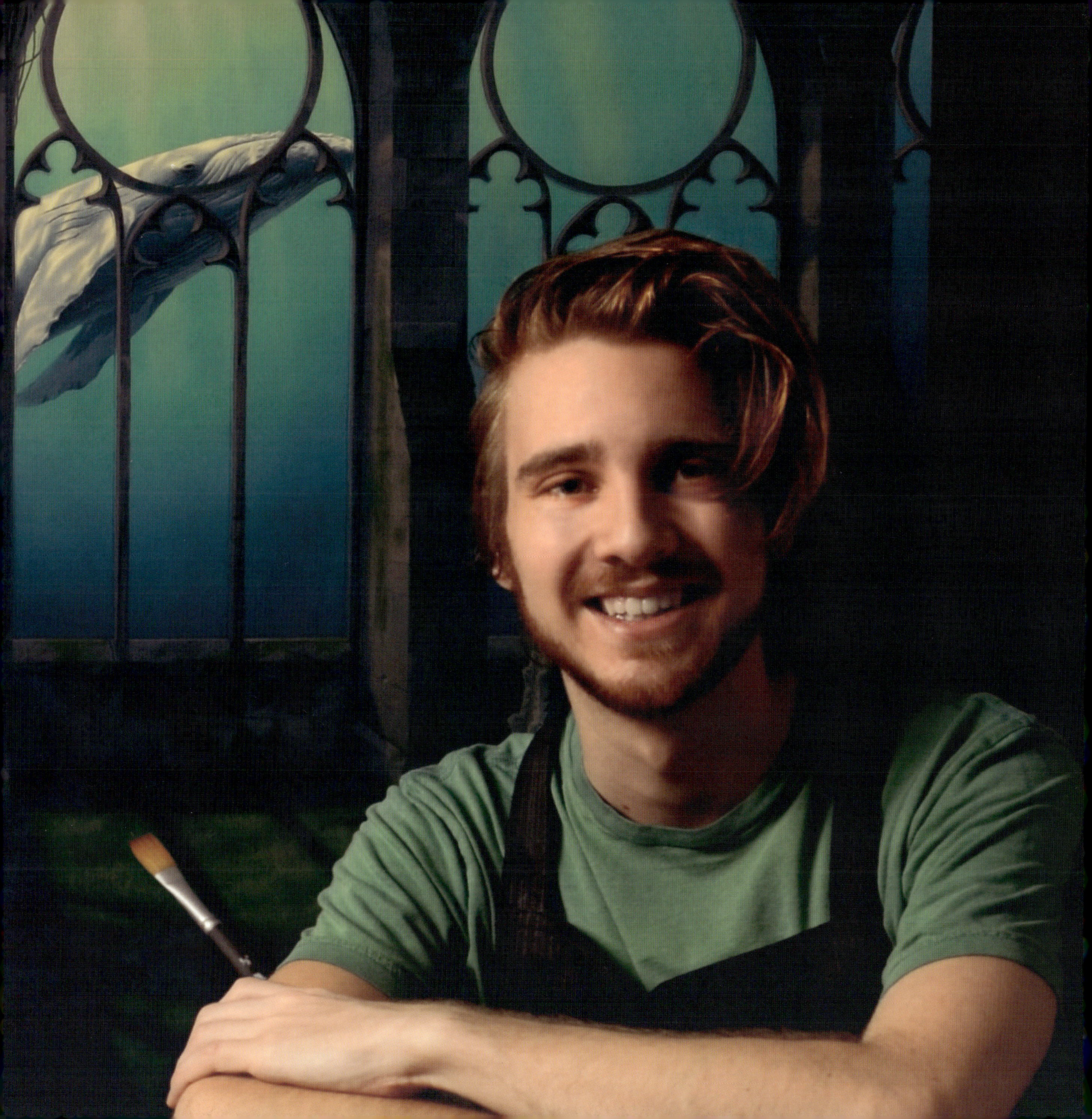

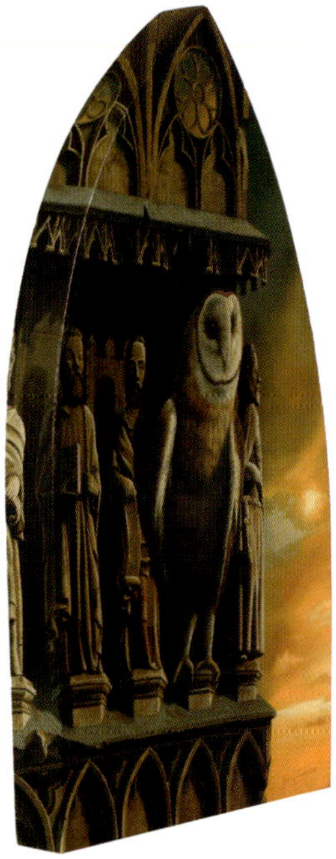

Streams in the Wasteland

HARBINGER

On my night side table I keep a sketchbook for ideas that come to me as I read and sleep. Reading in the book of Isaiah about the destruction of Babylon [i], the description of wild animals inhabiting abandoned cities became an inspiration. Suddenly a flurry of ideas came for a new series, depicting animals in deserted spaces, bringing honour to their Creator [ii] and figuratively calling for redemption in the wake of moral decline. I have been interested in gothic architecture and owls, so both of these came together for the first painting in this series. I designed a shaped braced panel, which has a 2" depth on the top and ½" on the bottom, giving the appearance that the top of the painting is leaning forward. The tall, narrow shape of Gothic cathedrals was intended to cause the viewer to look upward. The symbolic features in this style of architecture captivatied me. The three-leaf design, called a "trefoil" symbolized the trinity, and the four-leaf "quatrefoil" symbolized the four apostles. As I was painting, I thought about the meaning I wanted to infuse in the three statues through added symbols. These are meant to be read chronologically from left to right, symbolizing archetypes of Israelite history, including the book inscribed "Zion," the scroll, and dagger with cross. Ultimately, the crumbling cathedral forms a backdrop of the past, and the living owl reflects the glory of the light, standing as a harbinger of the one who would make a way in the wilderness for the coming Redeemer [iii].

[i] Isaiah 13:19 [ii] Isaiah 43: 20 [iii] Isaiah 40:3, John 1:23

Oil on Braced Baltic Birch 24" x 15" x 2" 2015 (Age 19)

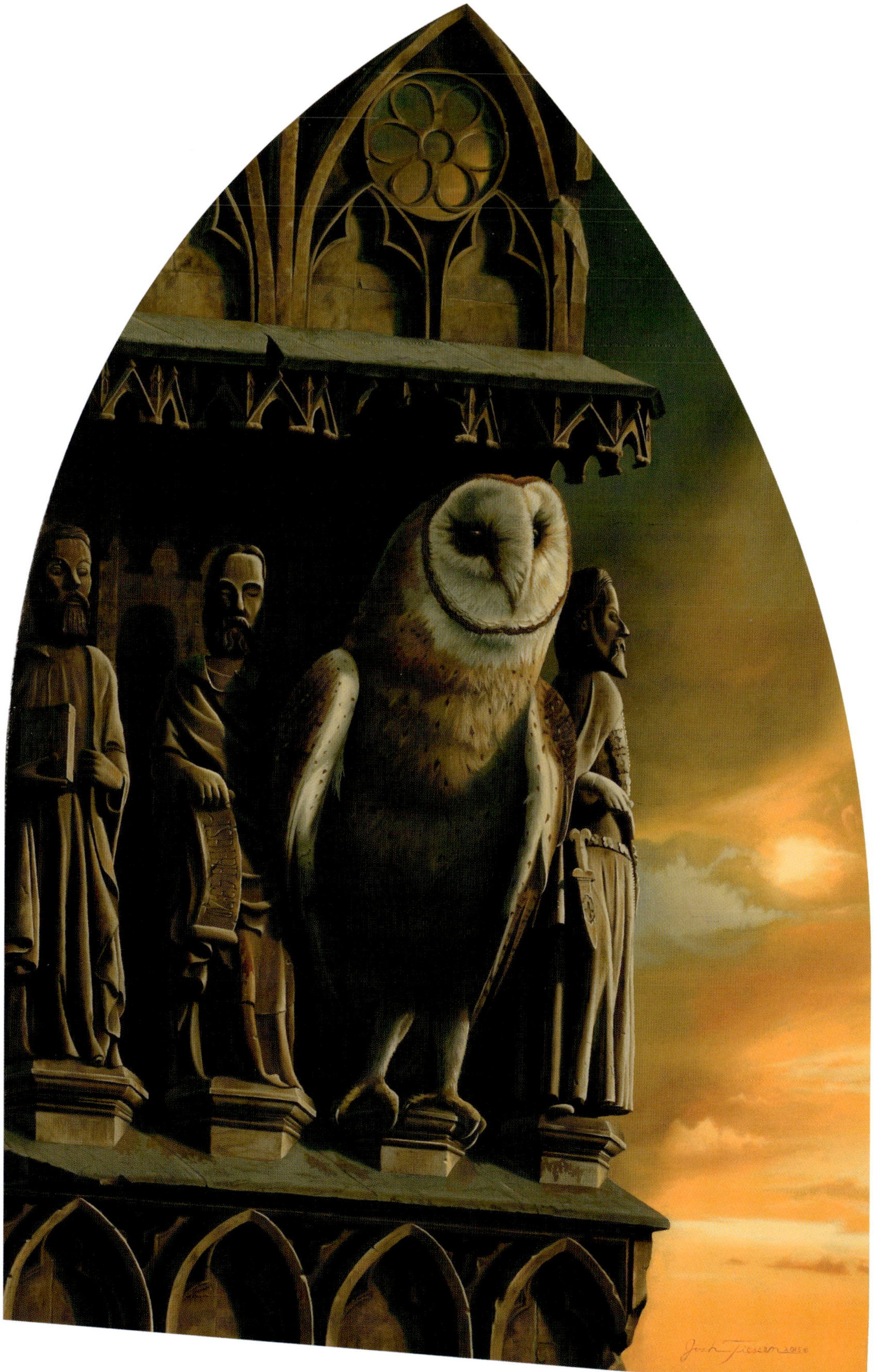

Streams in the Wasteland

WHALE HYMN

When working on a large painting like this one, the long process allows me ample time to conceptually formulate my thoughts on the piece. Continuing my Streams in the Wasteland series, this painting fits the theme of wild animals in abandoned spaces. Gothic architecture fascinates me for its intentional diversity, which also reflects the variety and lack of rigidity in the natural world. The history of Gothic reveals a gradual discovery of the beauty found in natural forms, which could be transferred into stone edifices [i]. I imagined the concept for this painting over a year earlier, then later found architectural reference from the ruins of a 12th century cathedral in London, England. It had been transformed into a peaceful garden intertwined with ivy, red roses and fallen petals, historically symbolic of the Passion of Christ in European art. This would provide an intriguing exterior for an ocean scene emanating through stained glass. I became interested in Humpback Whales watching the BBC series *Ocean Giants*, which recorded epic sights and sounds of the largest mammals to ever live on the planet. The behaviour of whales, specifically their vocalization, remains somewhat of a mystery to scientists. Many believe their 'songs' may be more than mating calls, for the non-utilitarian act of expressing emotions. In contemplating this I looked back to the gothic cathedral, a space for praise where parishioners sang hymns to their Creator. So also metaphorically the haunting chants from the giants of the deep bring honour to their Maker.

---

[i] According to 19th Century Art Critic John Ruskin

Oil on Braced Baltic Birch 36" x 48" x 2" 2015 (Age 19-20)

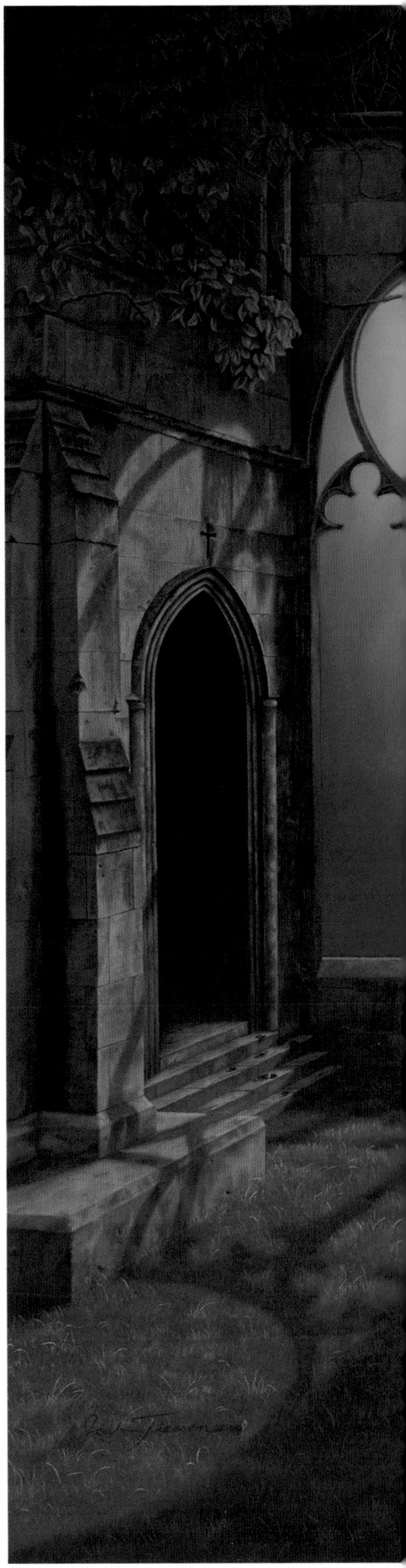

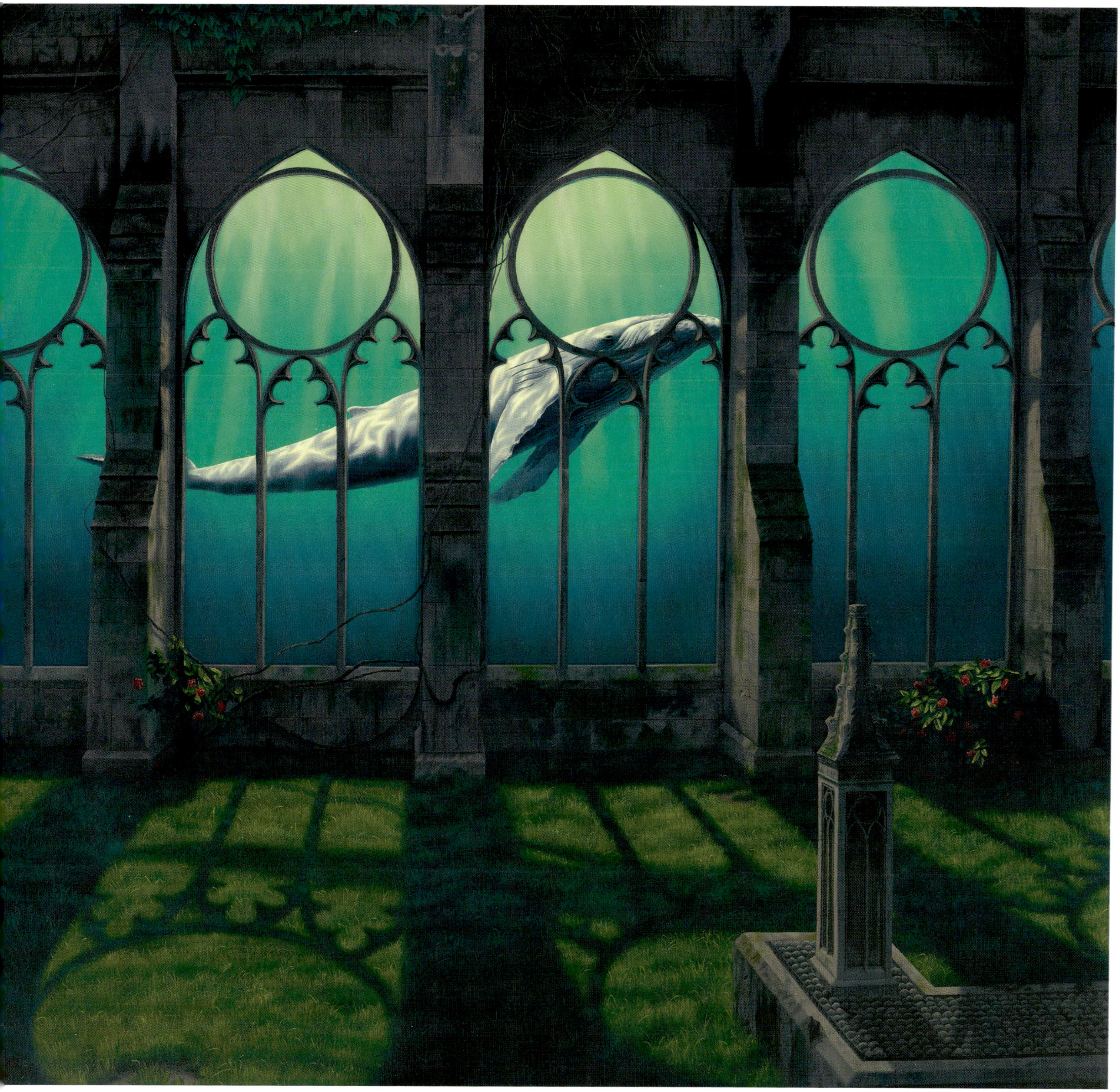

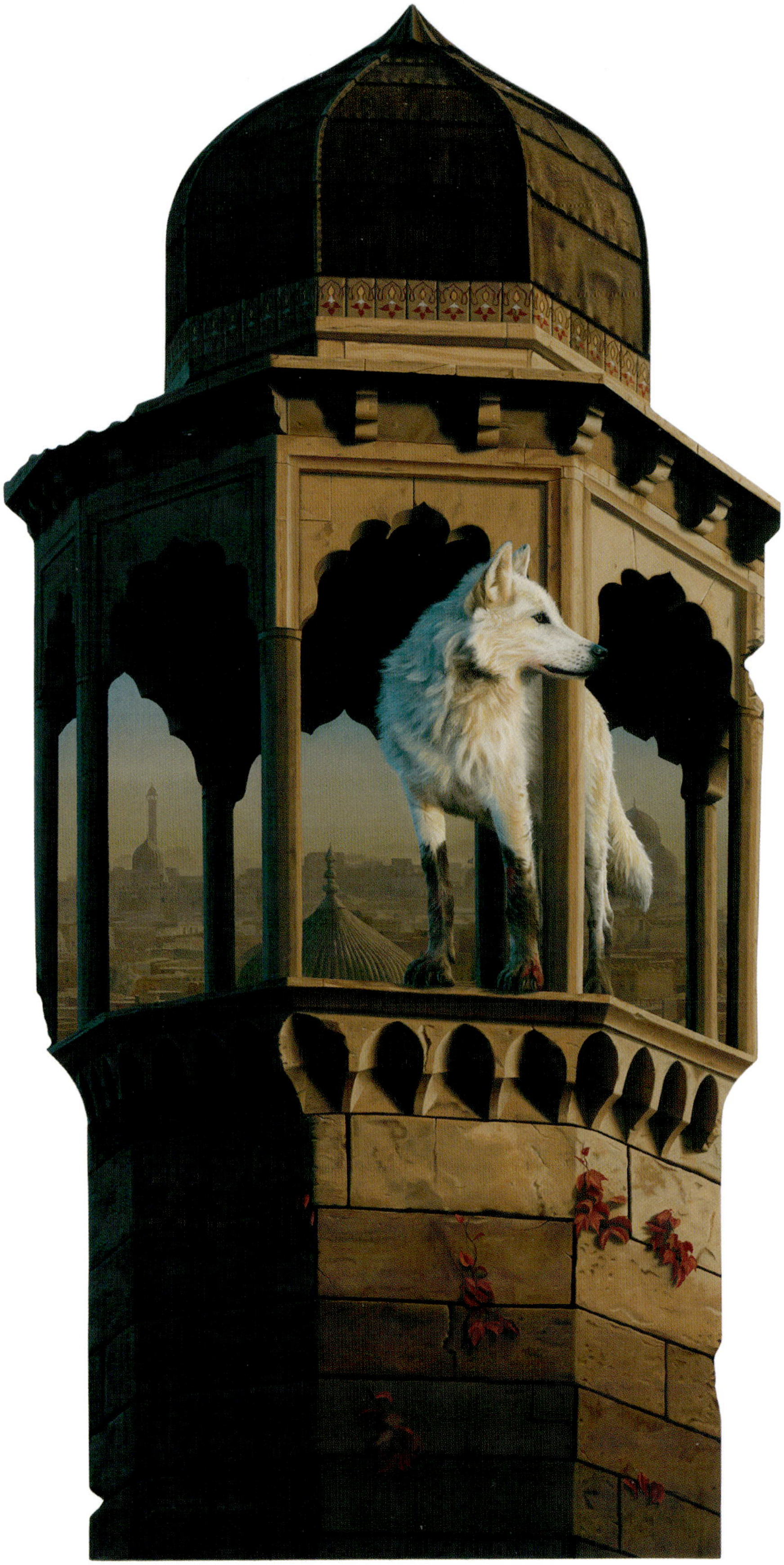

Streams in the Wasteland

BROTHER WOLF

I have become increasingly drawn to Eastern environments, and envisioned juxtaposing an arctic wolf in a Mughal-styled minaret. The architectural elements and geometric patterns in this prayer tower delineate expert design and craftsmanship. I first encountered the Arctic Wolf at Omega Park in Quebec, and was struck by its nobility and force, although for many cultures and religions the wolf has been symbolic of deception and terror. I interpreted this Arctic Wolf's snowy pure coat as a sheep-like façade for its actual ferocious demeanour. The blood around its mouth and on its paws subtly indicates a darker nature, both literally and symbolically. I happened to be studying St. Francis of Assisi while working on this painting, and came across the story of his encounter with the Wolf of Gubbio. As an ascetic mystic who had a thaumaturgic relationship with the natural world, Francis was summoned by the city to stop the infamous wolf from relentlessly devouring animals and people. As the wolf charged, Francis made the sign of the cross and commanded "Brother Wolf" to do no harm. The crowd stood in wonder as the wolf immediately shut its mouth and came peaceful as a lamb to lay at Francis' feet, never to harm the people again. Whether true or apocryphal, this story brings to mind those causing terror in our present world, those who courageously stand against them, and the need for peace in troubling times (John 14:27).

Oil on Braced Baltic Birch 48" x 24" x 2" 2015 (Age 20)

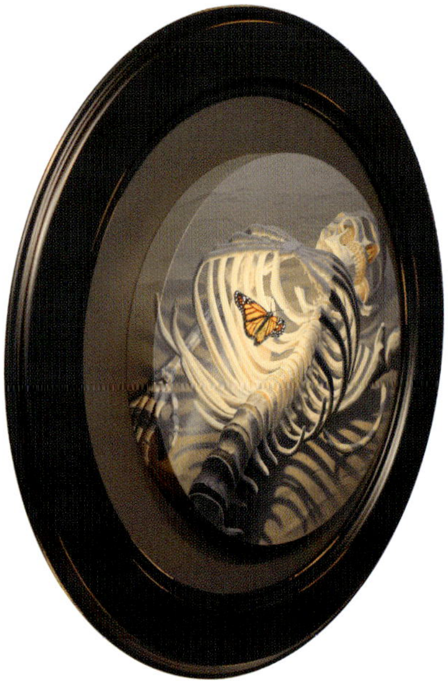

Streams in the Wasteland

CAN THESE BONES LIVE?

The Science Department at my old high school was kind enough to let me borrow their full skeleton model one weekend. I laid out "Charlie," as we called him, on our dining room table and photographed him with my studio lighting. I had previously sketched an imaginary scene of a single butterfly flitting through a cavernous rib cage, emanating light and casting radial shadows. The reference photos helped greatly for anatomical accuracy, and to see where the light and shadows would fall on the three dimensional form. The Old Testament, known as the Tanakh to Jewish people, relays an unusual episode of the prophet Ezekiel's vision, called The Valley of Dry Bones [i]. I approached my painting as a modern interpretation, seeing the Monarch Butterfly as symbolic of breathing new life into these bones. This painting is a precursor to a larger work I have planned, which will bring clarity to this initial macabre piece and further develop the theme of resurrection.

---

[i] Ezekiel 37:1-14

Oil on Braced Baltic Birch 18" x 2" 2016 (Age 20)

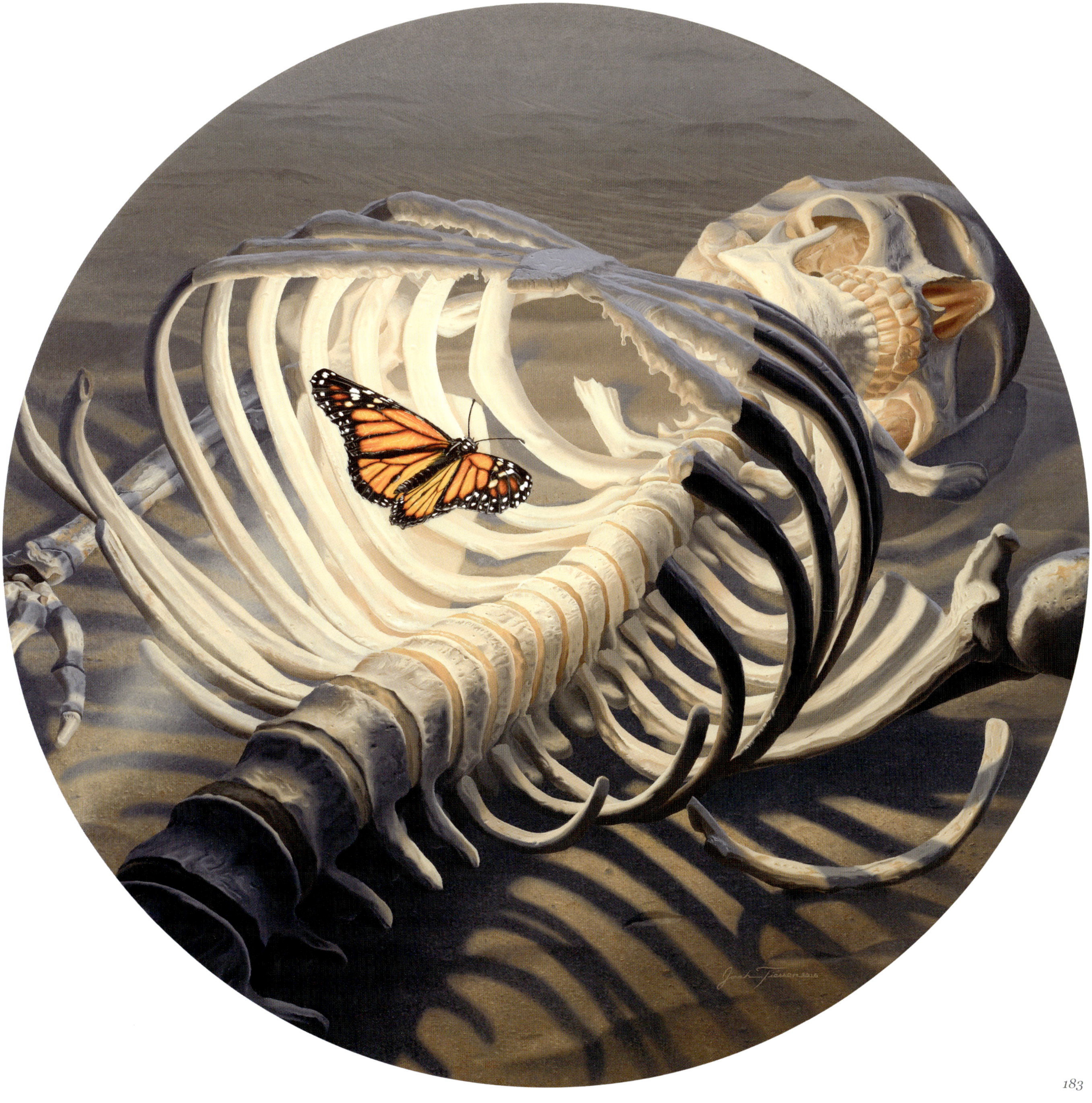

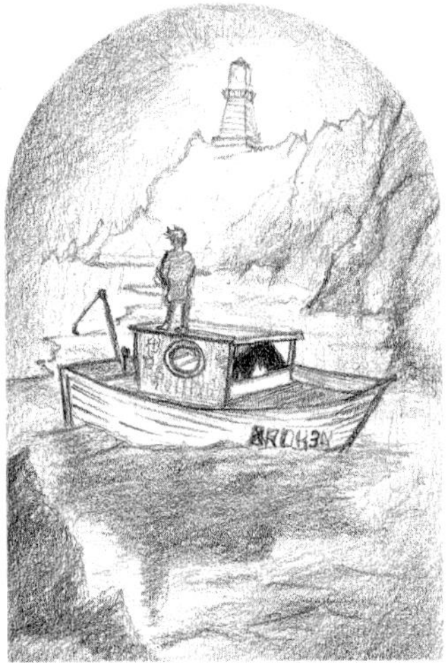

DARK NIGHT OF THE SOUL

I am a contemplative type, who has an innate desire to better understand the meaning of life, yet the constancy of this pursuit is at times wearisome. As Nietzsche described it, when we are philosophizing we sometimes feel like we have cut our moorings and are drifting into the cold abyss. The soul becomes like an unanchored wanderer out on a dark night and, while cognizant of the light, looks to the depths in temporal absence. Weathered by the environment, the soul's vessel is reflected in the empty abandoned boat. In this realm reality is comprehended only in part, like searching for the horizon in a veil of fog or seeing "through a glass, darkly" [i]. This painting is a modern response to the epic masterpiece *Wanderer Above the Sea of Fog*, completed by Caspar David Friedrich in 1818. Darker in compositional tone and metaphysic, my desire is to show how the emptying process of the archetypal figure experiencing a 'dark night of the soul' [ii] allows the Divine to perform a transformational work that moves the wanderer from the darkness of self-introspection into the light.

---

[i] 1 Corinthians 13:12 *KJV* [ii] Attributed to St. John of the Cross

Oil on Baltic Birch 36" x 24" 2016 (Age 20)

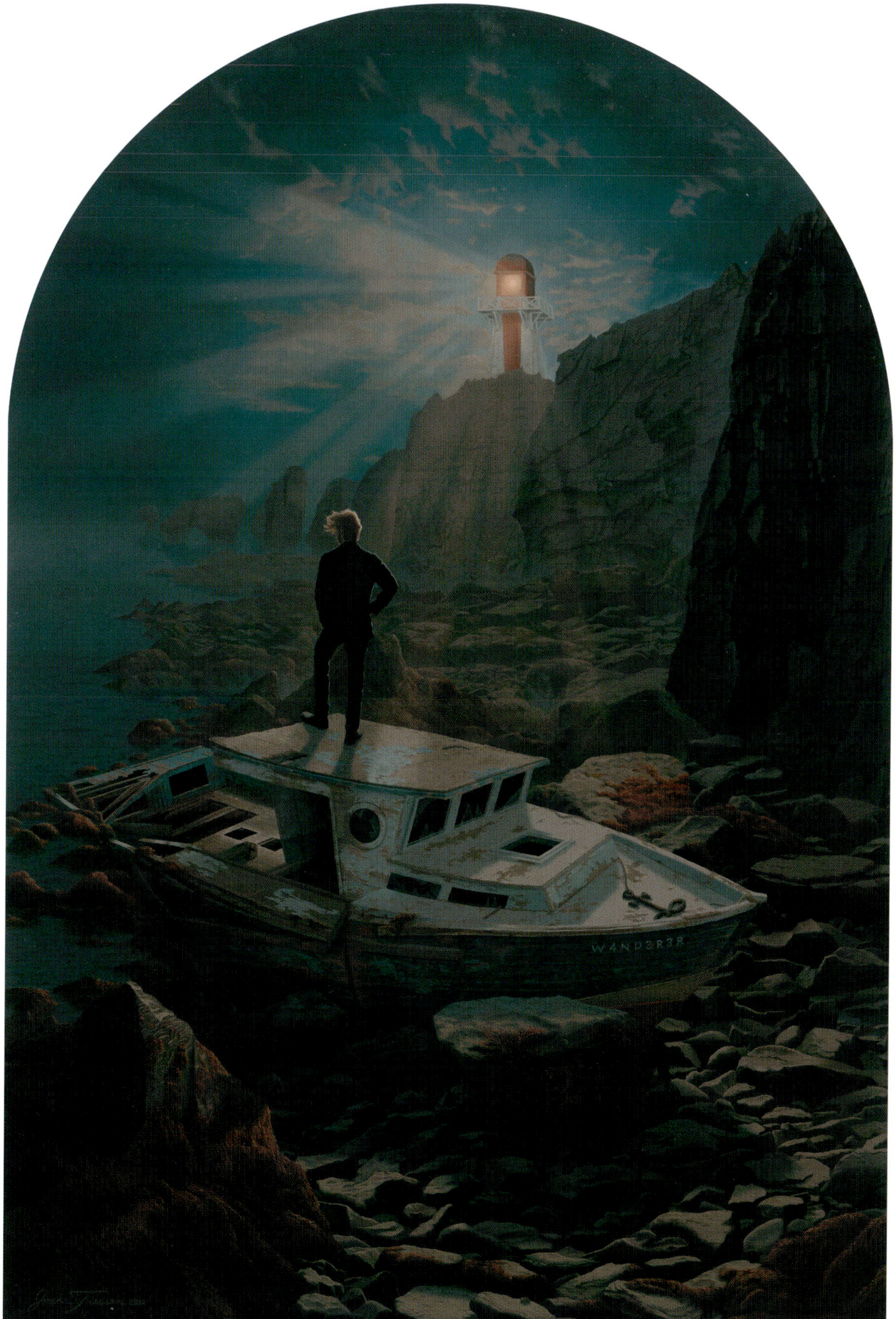
W4ND3R3R

ACKNOWLEDGMENTS

Over the years I have had many collectors and admirers of my art request a coffee table book. The book you have just perused has been several years in the making. Upon turning twenty-one this past summer, having publicly exhibited my art for ten years, the timing now seemed right. Since I am still quite young and have the rest of my life ahead of me as a professional artist, I wanted my first book to be like a time capsule documenting my story and the first decade of my work. This book would not have been published if it weren't for the contribution of several individuals who persevered with me on this project to see it through to completion. I want to express my deepest gratitude to the following people: To Dr. Joanne Ruthsatz for writing the foreward. It has been truly life-changing since she reached out to my family and drove up to Canada that wintery day in February 2013. To my mom, Dr. Julie A. Tiessen, for the countless hours spent compiling and editing material from my speaking presentations, the history of my development written for Dr. Ruthsatz, and from the press and media that have told my story over the years. She is also the proofreader for all of the story descriptions I write for my paintings. To my dad, Dr. Douglas P. Tiessen, for researching the info for the copyright page, managing my art collector database and painting inventory, and compiling the index. To my grandma Marjorie Cairns and friend Tricia Maughan, who provided helpful copyediting and moral support, along with my brother Zac. Lastly, thank you to the many accomplished individuals who wrote quotes for this book. I am incredibly honoured to have your commendations.

ARTS *for a* CHANGE

FOUNDATION

I believe all that we have comes from God, who created the world and is the ultimate Source of everything in it. I give out of sincere gratitude for all the material blessings I enjoy, and seek to responsibly steward that which God has entrusted to me: my gift for art and the financial resources which result from it. These beliefs form the basis for my philanthropic lifestyle. By seventeen I had donated funds and art to over forty charities. My donations were multiplied through charity auctions, with a framed print raising upwards to $1,000. To date, through these fundraisers my art has generated over $50,000 for seventy-five charities. I decided to start my own foundation to better coordinate my charitable giving and art donations. I chose not to use my name, as I wanted to actualize my philosophy of doing 'art with a purpose' to make a difference in the world in partnership with others. So I created the name Arts for a Change Foundation, to benefit individuals and organizations making a difference through humanitarian and conservation efforts. I entrusted Abundance Canada, which has a similar faith base and stewardship philosophy, to manage and disperse funds under my direction. I am thankful to my collectors who have participated with me by purchasing my art and supporting Arts for a Change Foundation.

Part of the proceeds from the sale of this book will be donated to the foundation, which in turn supports numerous charitable organizations

SELECTED EXHIBITIONS

2007 Solo: *Beginnings, Art by Josh Tiessen*, Artway on Two, Joseph Brant Hospital, Burlington, Ontario

2008 Five Person: *Fiesta*, The Wine Village, Stoney Creek, Ontario

2009 Group: Anastasia Gallery, Hamilton, Ontario

Two Person: *Celebration of the Arts*, Paramount Drive Alliance Church, Stoney Creek, Ontario

2010 Solo: *Josh Tiessen, Launching into Fine Art*, Community Wall, Art Gallery of Burlington, Burlington, Ontario

Solo: (Annual, 2010-) *Josh Tiessen Studio Gallery Open House*, Stoney Creek, Ontario

2011 Solo: *Josh Tiessen, Friend of The Eramosa Karst*, Michelangelo Events and Conference Centre, Hamilton, Ontario

Solo: *Graduation Exhibition by Josh Tiessen*, Carmen's Banquet Centre, Hamilton, Ontario

Group: (Annual, 2011-) *Grimsby Festival of Art*, Grimsby, Ontario

2012 Group: (2012 & 2015) *Art Auction Preview*, Lee-Chin Family Gallery, Art Gallery of Burlington, Burlington, Ontario

Solo: *Peter and the Wolf, Artist Josh Tiessen*, Brott Music Festival, Hamilton Place, Hamilton, Ontario

Solo: *Playlist, Josh Tiessen*, Bethany Community Church, St. Catharines, Ontario

Nine Person: *Verge, New Generation Mentor Group*, Lee-Chin Family Gallery, Art Gallery of Burlington, Burlington, Ontario

Solo: *Art Crawl, Josh on James St. N.*, The Studios at Hotel Hamilton, Hamilton, Ontario

Group: (Annual, 2012-) *Pelham Art Festival*, Pelham, Ontario

Group: (Annual, 2012-2013) *Stoney Creek Studio Stroll*, Josh Tiessen Studio Gallery, Stoney Creek, Ontario

Group: (Annual, 2012-) *enKindle Arts Festival*, Bethany Community Church, St. Catharines, Ontario

Twelve Person: *So you want to be an artist?* National Gallery of Canada, Ottawa, Ontario

Group: *Art on Water*, Welland Recreational Canal Corporation, Welland, Ontario

Group: (Annual, 2012-) *Ball's Falls Thanksgiving Festival*, Jordan, Ontario

2013 Group: (Annual, 2013-2015) *The Artist Project*, Exhibition Place, Toronto, Ontario

Three Person: *I Go To Nature*, James North Gallery, Hamilton Artists Inc., Hamilton, Ontario

Group: *SWARM 2013*, Cannon Gallery, Hamilton Artists Inc., Hamilton, Ontario

Solo: *Scheherazade, Artist Josh Tiessen*, Brott Music Festival, McIntyre Performing Arts Centre, Mohawk College, Hamilton, Ontario

Group: (Annual, 2013-2014) *Buckhorn Fine Art Festival*, Buckhorn, Ontario

Solo: *Supercrawl, Josh Tiessen*, The Green Smoothie Bar, Hamilton, Ontario

Group: *International Guild of Realism 8th Annual International Juried Exhibition*, Tempe Center for the Arts, Tempe, Arizona

2014 Solo: *Josh Tiessen, Fine Artist*, Dundas Valley Trail Centre, Dundas, Ontario

Solo: *The Visceral, Exhibition of New Original Works*, Josh Tiessen Studio Gallery, Stoney Creek, Ontario

Group: *Algonquin by Night*, Algonquin Art Centre, Algonquin Park, Ontario

Group: (Annual, 2014-2015) *Art in Action, Burlington Studio Tour*, Guest Artist, Burlington, Ontario

Group: *International Guild of Realism 9th Annual International Juried Exhibition*, Robert Lange Studios, Charleston, South Carolina

2015 Group: (Year-long Travelling Exhibition) *Masterworks from the International Guild of Realism*, R. W. Norton Art Gallery, Shreveport, Louisiana; Appleton Museum of Art, Ocala, Florida; Albany Museum of Art, Albany, Georgia

Solo: *Josh Tiessen, A Decade of Inspiration*, The Bethany Gallery, St. Catharines, Ontario

Group: *Wetlands: An Artist's Perspective*, Algonquin Art Centre, Algonquin Park, Ontario

Group: *International Guild of Realism 10th Annual International Juried Exhibition*, Principle Gallery, Alexandria, Virginia

2016 Group: *Remnants*, Robert Lange Studios, Charleston, South Carolina

Three Person: *Verge Young Adults Exhibition*, The Bethany Gallery, St. Catharines, Ontario

Group: *Metamorphosis*, Algonquin Art Centre, Algonquin Park, Ontario

Group: *International Guild of Realism 11th Annual International Juried Exhibition*, Gallery 1261, Denver, Colorado

SELECTED HONOURS & AWARDS

2009 *Honourable Mention (4th Place)* for *Snow White*, Breakaway Magazine Art Competition (Boys 13-19)

2010 *Outstanding Artistic Execution in Painting (Best in Show)* for *Snow Leopards*, Associated Christian Schools International Fine Arts Festival

Hollyhock Scholarship, awarded to attend Robert Bateman Master Artist Seminar

2011 *Exceptional 2-Dimensional Piece of Show (Best in Show)* for *Behold The Door*, Associated Christian Schools International Fine Arts Festival

St. Thomas Aquinas Foundation Arts Award, Hamilton Wentworth Catholic District School Board

First Place for Teens (13-19) for *Guardian of the Karst*, Buckhorn Fine Art Festival

Future Promise Award for *Guardian of the Karst*, Buckhorn Fine Art Festival

2012 *So you want to be an artist? National Gallery Competition*, 2nd highest votes across Canada for *Overshadowed*, participation in one-month group exhibition at National Gallery of Canada

Queen Elizabeth II Diamond Jubilee Medal, The Government of Canada

Second Place for *Cliffhanger*, Whitehern Historical Museum Teen Art Competition

2013 *Young Entrepreneur of the Year*, The Stoney Creek Chamber of Commerce

Canada's Top 20 Under 20 Award, Youth in Motion

2014 *International Salon Competition Finalist* for *Shipwrecked Treasure* and *Pond's Edge*, Art Renewal Center

Creative Achievement Award for *Ahoy Sleeper*, International Guild of Realism 9th Annual Juried Exhibition, Robert Lange Studios

2015 *#1 Best Local Artist, Diamond Award*, Hamilton Community News Readers' Choice Awards

#1 Best Art Gallery, Diamond Award, Hamilton Community News Readers' Choice Awards

2016 *#1 Best Local Artist, Diamond Award*, Hamilton Community News Readers' Choice

#1 Best Art Gallery, Diamond Award, Hamilton Community News Readers' Choice

Award of Excellence for Best 2 Dimensional Art (Best in Show), Grimsby Festival of Art

Best Wildlife Award for *Defending The Paint*, International Guild of Realism 11th Annual Juried Exhibition, Gallery 1261

International Salon Competition Finalist, Art Renewal Center (Winners TBA)

SELECTED TV & MEDIA

2008 *Urban Cut: Joshua Paul Tiessen*, Urban Cut, Cable 14, Hamilton, Ontario, September.

2010 *Capturing God's Creation*, Alliance Alive Stories for Life, Documentary, Toronto, Ontario, Fall.

2011 *Josh Tiessen: Showcasing God's Creation*, Full Circle, CTS, Burlington, Ontario, January 28.

Hamilton Life: Josh Tiessen, Hamilton Life, Cable 14, Hamilton, Ontario, October 25.

2012 *Stoney Creek's rising art star*, CHCH News, Hamilton, Ontario, June 1.

Josh Tiessen Gives Tour of His Studio, CBC TV, Toronto, Ontario, June 1.

Post Childhood Prodigies, HuffPost Live, Huffington Post, Los Angeles, California, September 13.

2013 *17-year-old Prodigy Artist*, Our City, Cable 14, Hamilton, Ontario, January 14.

Tiessen Brothers Discovered as Art Prodigies, CBC Radio, Toronto, Ontario, March 11.

Stoney Creek Art Prodigies, CBC TV, Toronto, Ontario, March 11.

Young Entrepreneur Josh Tiessen, Documentary, Moetion Picture Productions, Hamilton, Ontario, May 9.

Morning File: Josh Tiessen, CFMU 93.3, Hamilton, Ontario, July 3.

Glorifying God with Your Talents and Gifts, 100 Huntley Street, CTS, Burlington, Ontario, July 31.

Josh Tiessen, Teenage Wildlife Artist, Arts Connection, Faith FM 94.3, Kitchener/Waterloo, Ontario, September 2.

2014 *Josh Tiessen Artist,* TERRA at Home, CHCH TV, Hamilton, Ontario, February 22.

Creating Art for a Purpose, 100 Huntley Street, CTS, Burlington, Ontario, October 8.

2015 *Born An Artist: Two generations with painting in their bones,* CTV Canada AM, Febrary 18.

Painting a Path, Documentary, Ryerson University Journalism Department, Toronto, Ontario, April 9.

Josh Tiessen Fine Artist, Documentary, Stone Forest Media, Kitchener, Ontario, November 26.

2016 *Prodigy*, Trailer for *The Prodigy's Cousin: The Family Link Between Autism and Extraordinary Talent*, Camoriano Productions, Columbus, Ohio, January 18.

Prodigy Brothers Josh and Zac Tiessen, CHCH Morning Live, February 15.

SELECTED PUBLICATIONS

2007 *Young artist's works inspired by his travels around the world*, Burlington Post, April 13, p. 37.

2009 *Local artist gives painting to MP*, Stoney Creek News, March 20, p. 3.

2010 *Reflecting God's Creation*, CMAlliance Magazine, Fall, pp. 30-32.

These Teens Are Our Next Big Successes! Hamilton Men's Magazine, Winter, pp. 42-43.

Josh Tiessen Studio Gallery, Snap'd Hamilton, December, pp. 13-14.

2011 *Young Artist Garnering Admirers Throughout Art World*, Stoney Creek News, September 1, p. 3.

Inspired by Bateman: Young wildlife artist, Niagara This Week, September 8, p. 5.

Prodigy Artist Shoots for the Stars, Hamilton OpenFile.ca, November 3.

Josh Tiessen Wins Prestigious Canadian Art Awards, Balance, Fall/Winter, p. 10.

2012 *Tiessen gains international recognition, Hamilton Community News*, February 15.

Heading to National Gallery? Stoney Creek teen aims high with his entry in So You Want To Be An Artist, Hamilton Spectator, Saturday, April 7, G1.

Stoney Creek teen's art hangs with Van Gogh at National Gallery, CBC News, June 5.

10 Art Prodigies You Should Know, Huffington Post, New York, July 27.

Difference makers garner Diamond Jubilee medals, Stoney Creek News, September 27, pp. 3, 17.

2013 *Identified as arts prodigies, Ontario brothers now contributing to science*, CBC News, Mar. 8.

Teen artist wins Stoney Creek Chamber of Commerce Young Entrepreneur of the Year, Stoney Creek News, April 25, p.16.

An art prodigy, The Voice of Pelham, May 1, p.1.

'Top 20 Under 20' recognizes young Canadians making a difference, Globe and Mail, June 5.

Stoney Creek painter Josh Tiessen one of Canada's Top 20 Under 20, CBC News, June 6.

Sit back and watch the music come to life, The Hamilton Spectator, July 4, p. G4.

Canada's got talent, inventiveness: Child prodigies to take part in innovation conference, The Hamilton Spectator, July 4, p. A4.

Artists for Conservation 2013 International Exhibit of Nature in Art, AFC, Sept. pp. 191-192.

2014 *Juxtaposing Elements*, International Artist Magazine, February/March, pp. 108-115.

Wonderful Wildlife, Southwest Art Magazine, March, p. 76.

Josh Tiessen: No ordinary teenager, Mennonite Foundation of Canada Annual Report, May, p. 5.

Josh Tiessen: An Art Prodigy in Algonquin, Algonquin Art Centre Season Program, June, pp. 12-13.

Student Leadership: Josh Tiessen, The gift of art can make the world a better place, LeadersInSchool.com.au, Fall.

Artists for Conservation 2014 International Exhibit of Nature in Art, AFC, October, pp. 196-197.

Beauty in Realism, American Art Collector Magazine, November, pp. 158-163.

2015 *Josh Tiessen Studio Gallery Open House*, Snapd Hamilton, January 2015, p. 16.

Ten Artists To Look For at The Artist Project Toronto, CityByHeart.com, February 20.

Meet the Artist – Josh Tiessen, Princeton Artist Brush Company, WillowWolfe.ca, May 27.

Realistic Representations, American Art Collector, September, pp.177-188.

Artists for Conservation 2015 International Exhibit of Nature in Art, AFC, October, p. 192.

Off-Season Artists: Josh Tiessen, Interview for blog on AlgonquinArtCentre.com, December 17.

2016 *Psychology: Making Connections*, 2nd Can. ed., Chapter 9 Prodigies, McGraw-Hill Ryerson.

Presenting Generation Z: Josh Tiessen, Hamilton Business, The Hamilton Spectator, February 10.

The Prodigy's Cousin: The Family Link Between Autism and Extraordinary Talent, Chapter 8 Another Path to Prodigy, Penguin Random House.

What is the source of genius? These sibling prodigies may offer clues, Toronto Star, March 5.

8 Teen Geniuses From Canada That Will Make You Question Your Entire Life, Narcity.com, March 8.

Remnants, American Art Collector, May, pp. 116-117.

Artist Spotlight: Josh Tiessen in the Studio, Featured Artist on PrincetonBrush.com, August 3.

From Classical to Contemporary, American Art Collector, September, pp. 76-83.

Artists for Conservation 2016 International Exhibit of Nature in Art, AFC, October, pp. 190-191.

INDEX OF WORKS

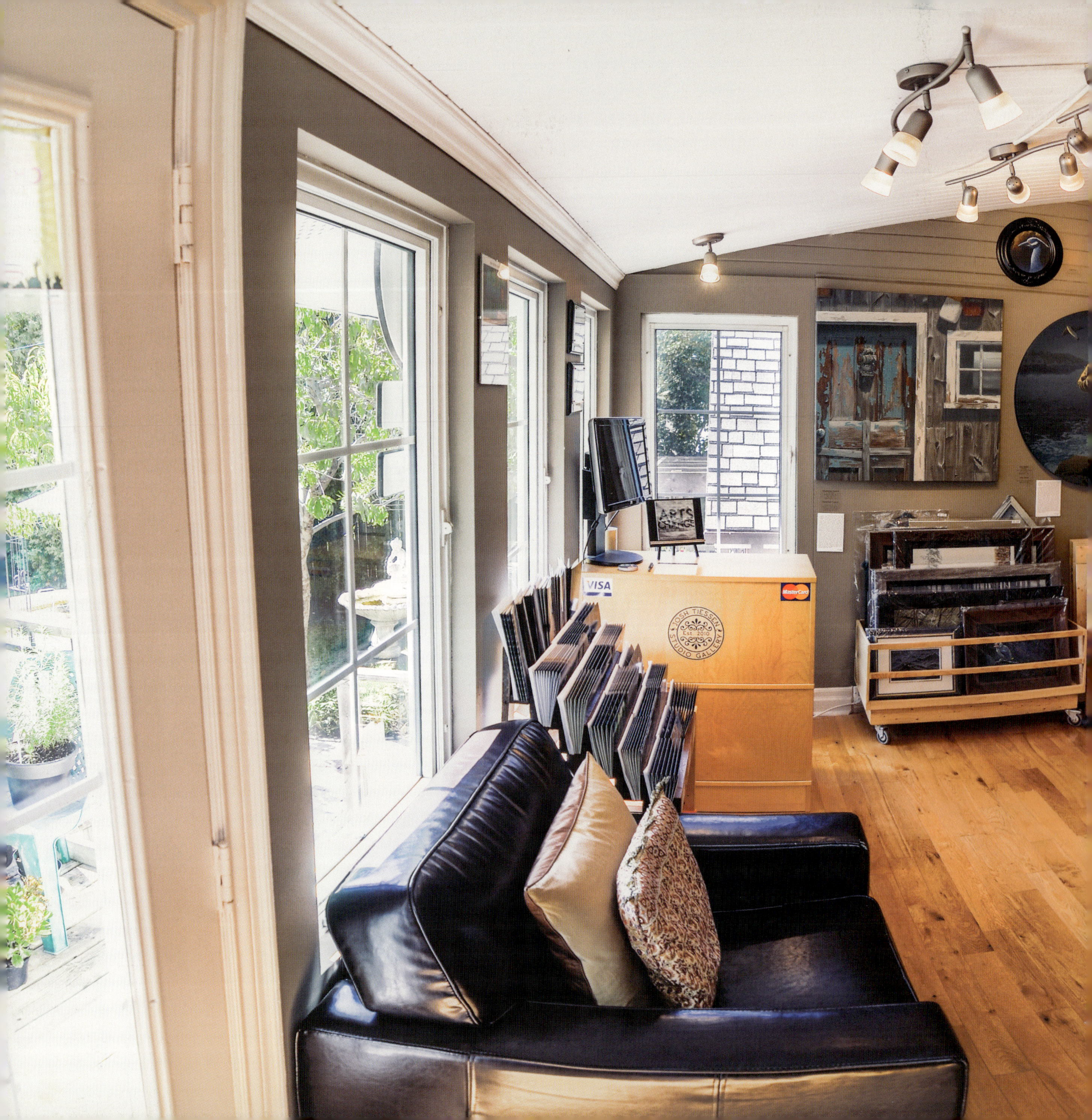
VISA
MasterCard
JOSH TIESSEN
Est. 2010
STUDIO GALLERY

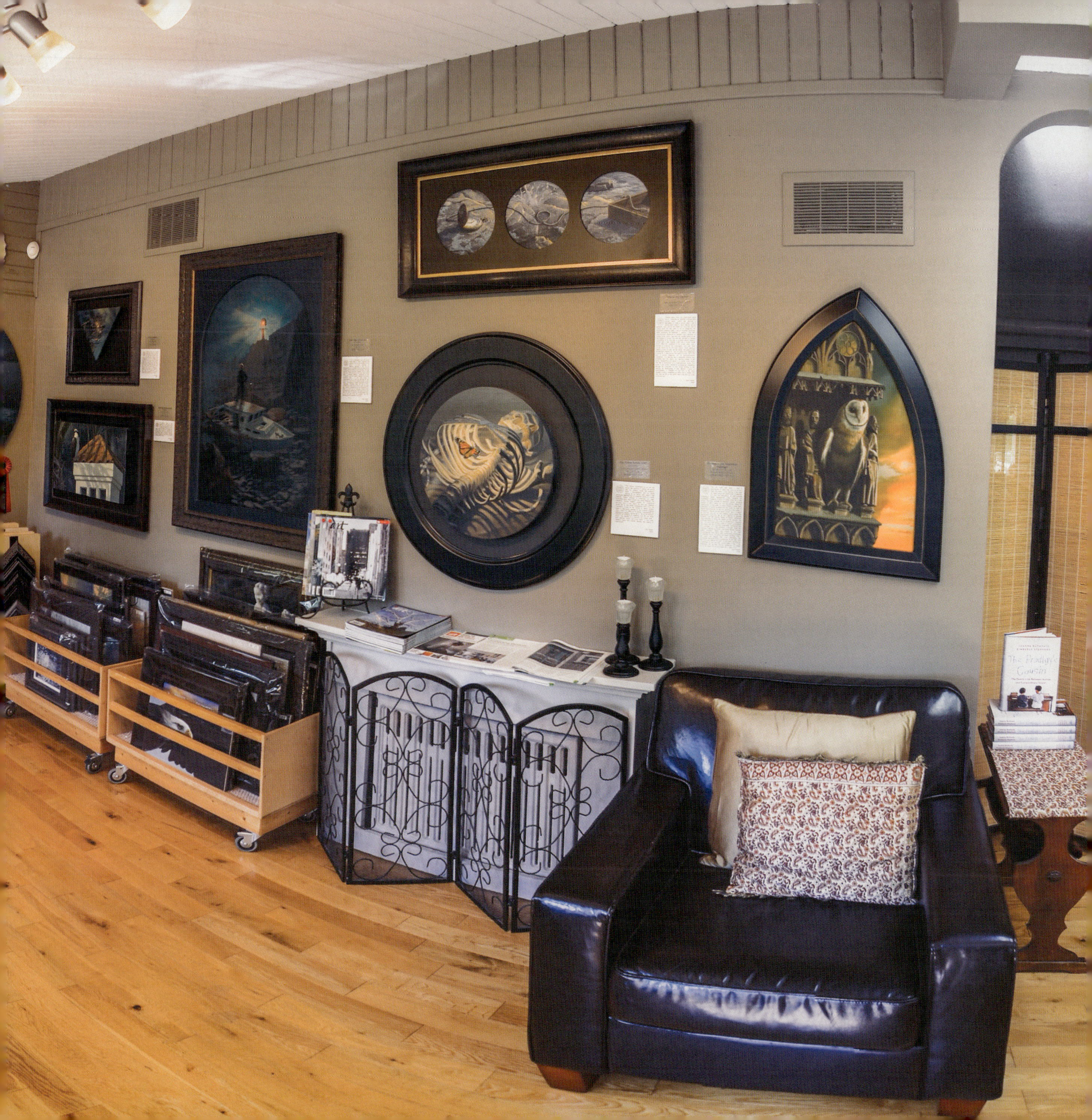

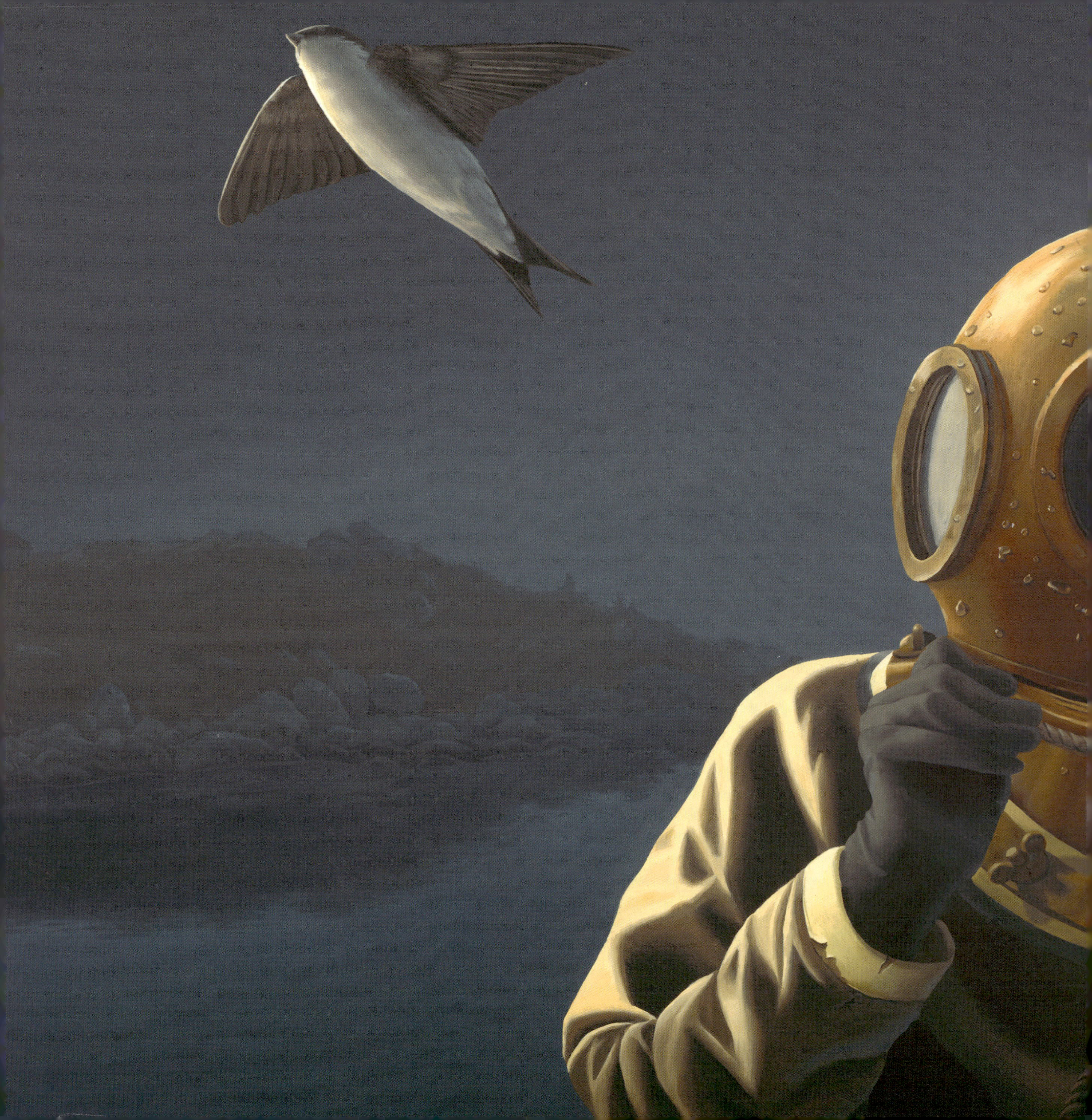

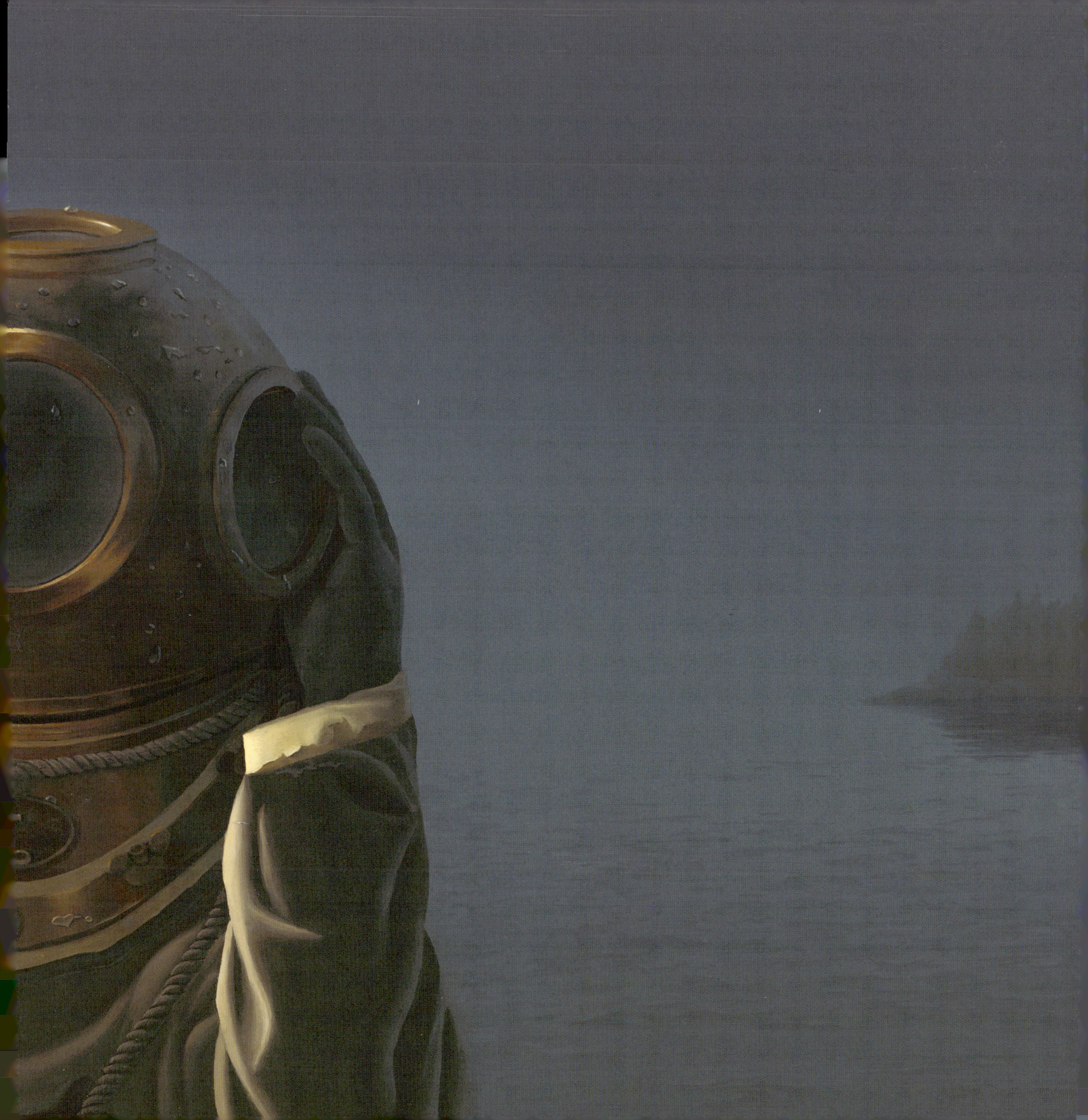

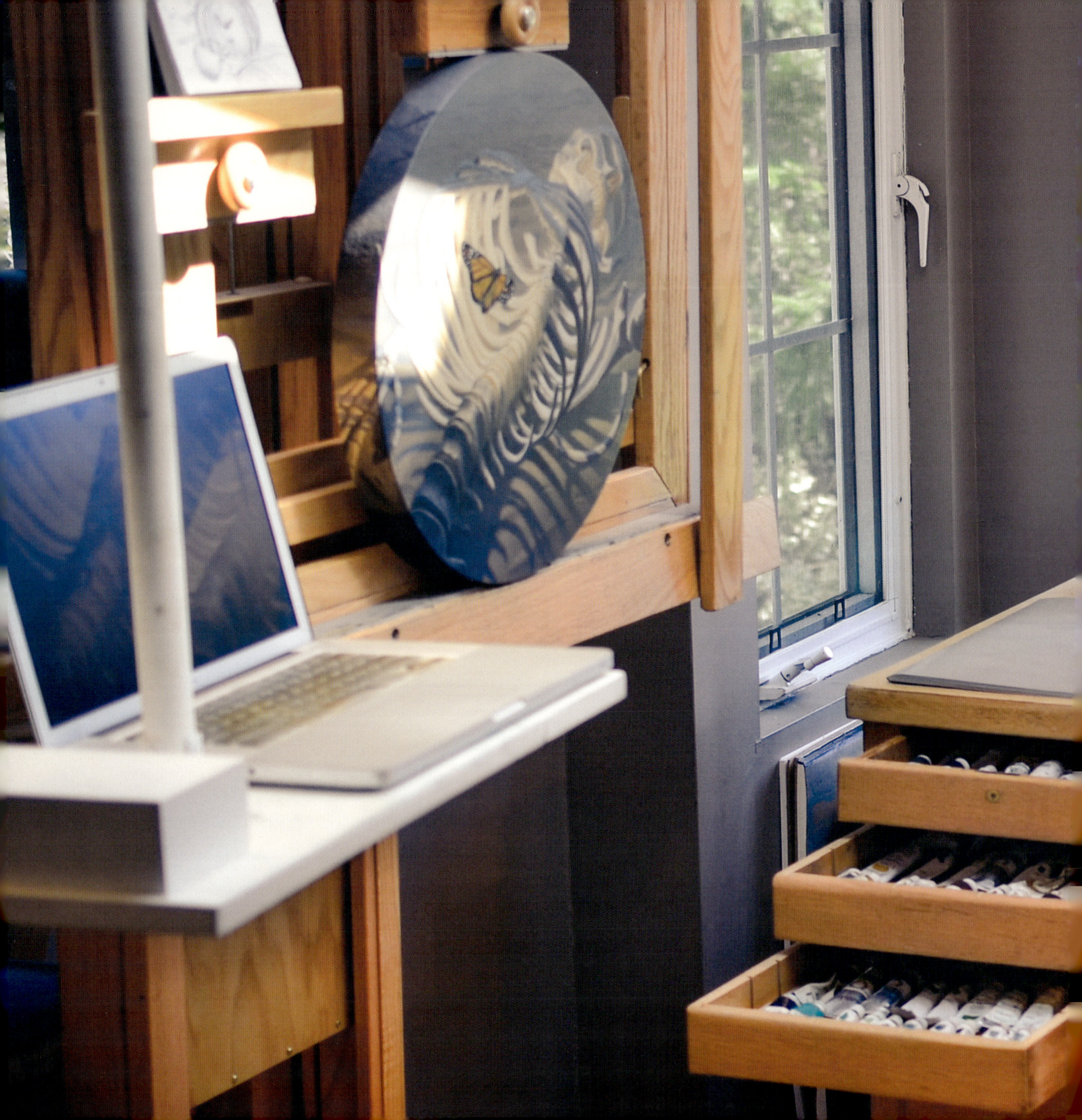

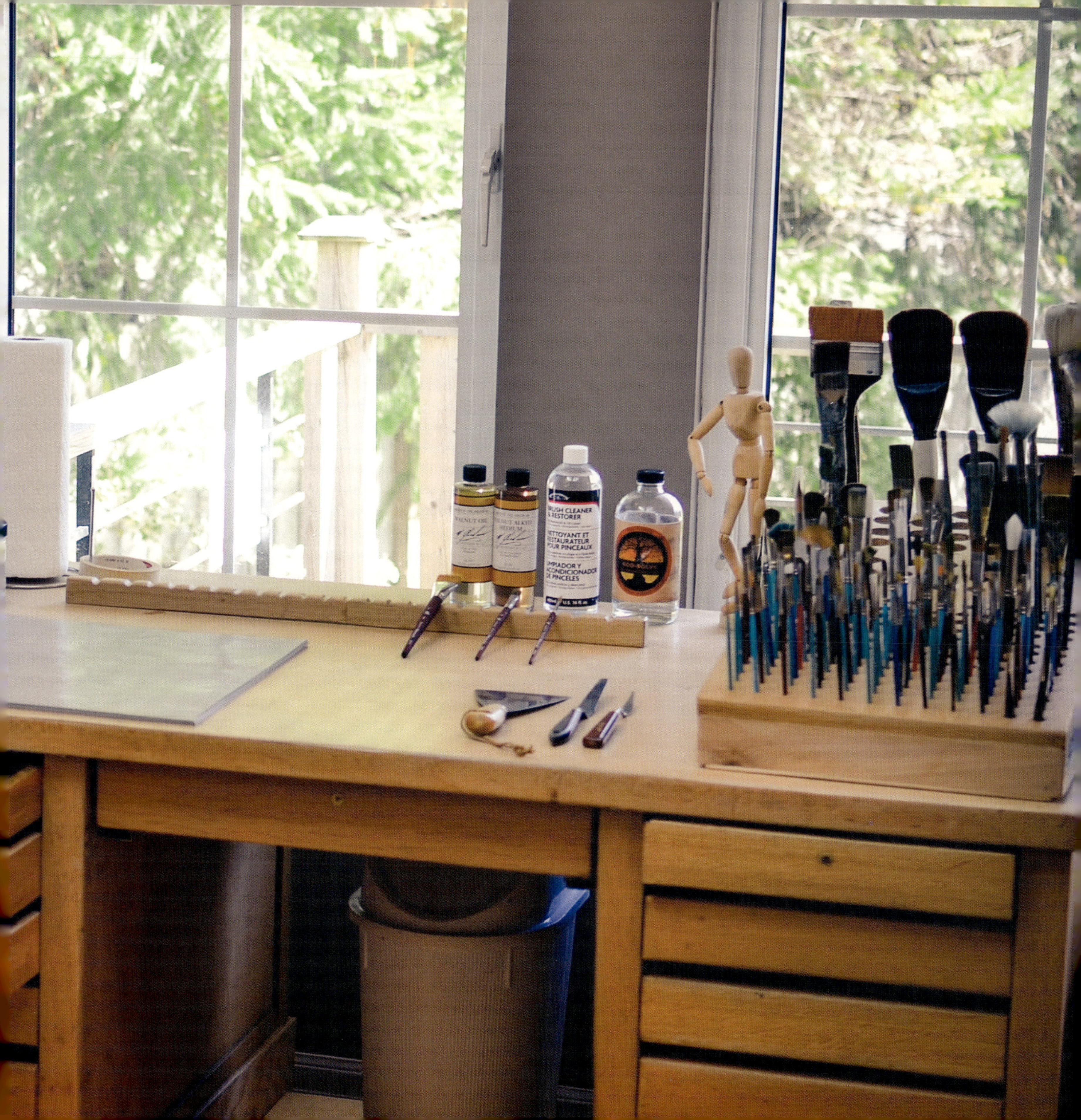

WALNUT OIL
WALNUT ALKYD MEDIUM
BRUSH CLEANER & RESTORER
NETTOYANT ET RESTAURATEUR POUR PINCEAUX
LIMPIADOR Y ACONDICIONADOR DE PINCELES

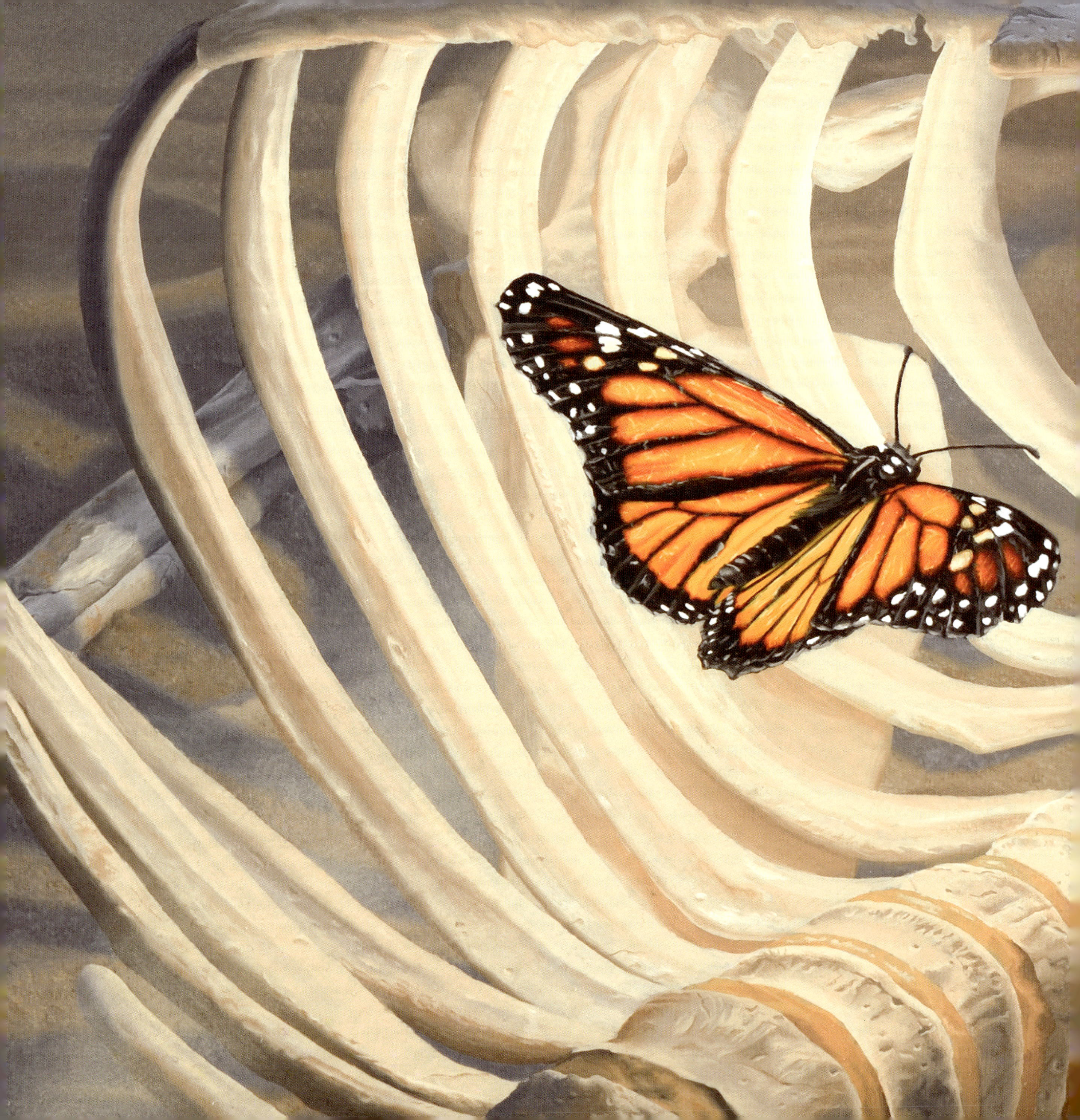

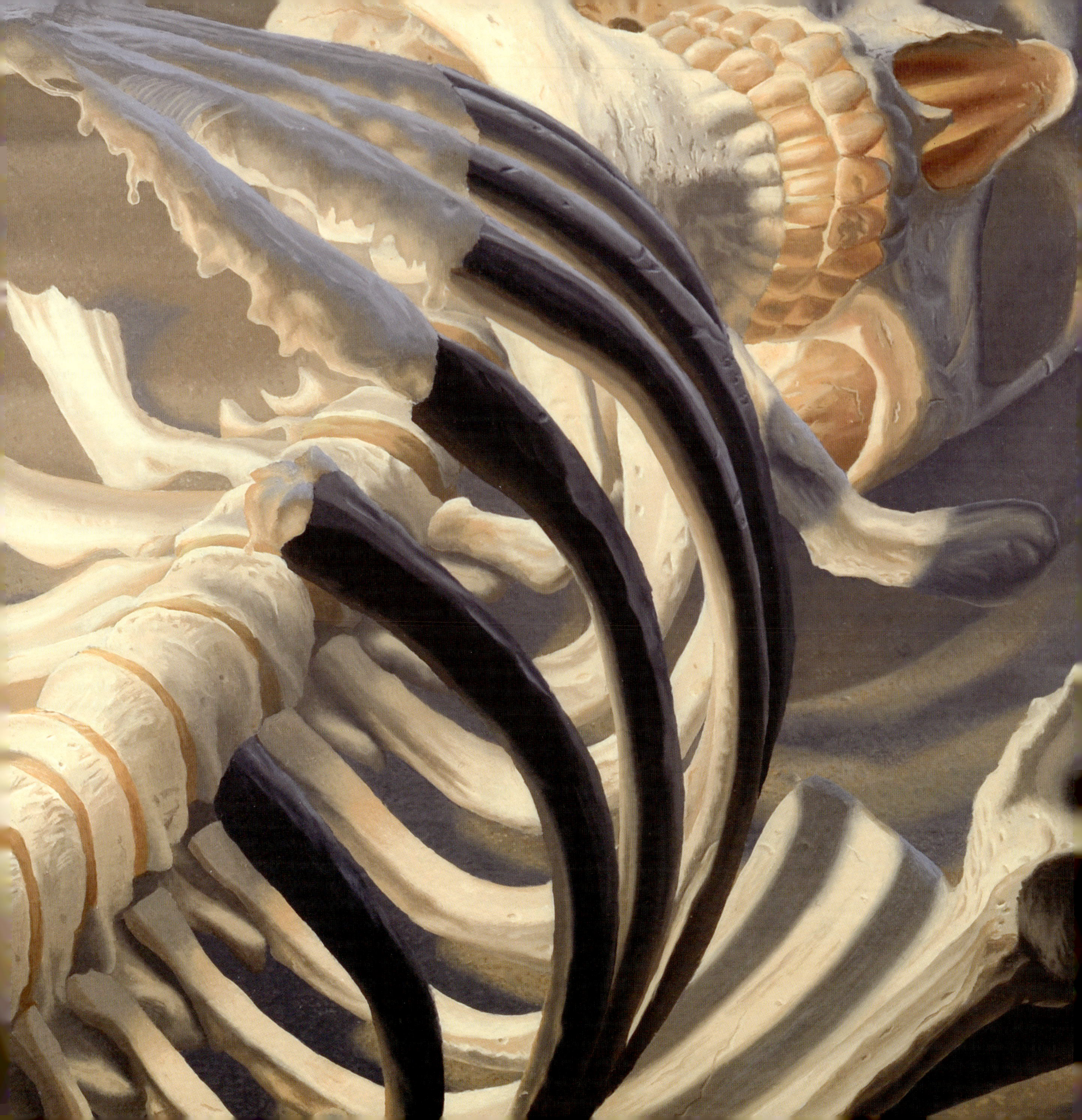

MORE INFORMATION

For more information on Josh Tiessen's

CV, portfolio, events, web store and more, please visit

www.joshtiessen.com

To see works in progress, time-lapse videos, latest news, etc.

follow Josh on social media

/joshtiessen

Visit Josh at his studio gallery

JOSH TIESSEN STUDIO GALLERY Est. 2010

148 King St. E. Stoney Creek, Ontario · L8G 1L5

info@joshtiessen.com | 905-664-5049

See website for business hours, event openings and closures